Security Risk Management
Body of Knowledge

Security Risk Management
Body of Knowledge

JULIAN TALBOT

and

MILES JAKEMAN

WILEY

John Wiley & Sons, Inc., Publication

Published by John Wiley & Sons, Inc., Hoboken, New Jersey
Published simultaneously in Canada

For general information on our other products and services or for technical support, please contact our Customer Care Department within the United States at (800) 762-2974, outside the United States at (317) 572-3993, or fax (317) 572-4002.

Wiley also publishes its books in a variety of electronic formats. Some content that appears in print may not be available in electronic formats. For more information about Wiley products, visit our web site at www.wiley.com.

Library of Congress Cataloging-in-Publication Data is Available

ISBN: 978-0-470-45462-6

Printed in the United States of America

10 9 8 7 6 5 4 3 2 1

Contents

14 ABOUT THE LEAD AUTHORS   417

BIBLIOGRAPHY AND OTHER REFERENCES   419

INDEX   427

Preface

Originally, we set out to write a short reference manual on enterprise security risk management as part of our contribution to increasing the professionalization of the industry, and to improving the body of knowledge in this area. It quickly became evident that the field of security, despite an ancient pedigree and growing knowledge among practitioners, did not have an agreed body of knowledge to reference.

This, of course, will come as no surprise to our fellow practitioners. They are well aware of the limitations in our profession and that we still struggle to achieve consistency on even such basics as definitions for threat, risk, and vulnerability, much less across security practices, approaches, or training requirements. It is not for lack of trying—many texts, standards, and guidelines exist in the field. What is missing, however, is a unified framework that links elements of physical, information, and personnel security with each other and indeed with the latest research in areas such as management, financial theory, behavioral psychology, and technology.

After we had repeated numerous times, "someone should really write something along these lines," we eventually decided that it may as well be us who started the process. In conjunction with RMIA, we then approached the broader network of security professionals to seek their contributions, peer review, as well as frank and honest feedback on how to proceed.

The enormity of the subject is daunting as security touches on the most profound elements of society and the human psyche. The literature is also overwhelming, and each day new material is published. Consequently, we have had to be selective. We have done our best, however, to ensure that omissions are the result of a decision rather than an oversight.

For this project, we have been dependent on the generosity and contributions of others. Old friends and new from a wide variety of disciplines have provided invaluable assistance, criticism, and encouragement. To these people who have volunteered their time, effort, and intellectual property with no reward other than our gratitude, we are forever indebted. To this group goes much of the credit; the errors and omissions are ours.

For our part, we have poured the best of our intellectual capital into this document in the interests that it may add to the profession and prove useful to you, the reader. We also encourage you to join us in contributing to future editions so that SRMBOK can continue to reflect the growing body of knowledge for this field.

One day, we will finish that short reference manual on security. In the meantime, we hope this contribution proves to be a valuable starting point.

JULIAN TALBOT AND MILES JAKEMAN

Acknowledgments

RMIA gratefully acknowledges the assistance provided by members of the SRMBOK Working Group who contributed to, wrote components of, edited, or peer reviewed this material before publication. Unlike other books and standards, SRMBOK was developed by practitioners who donated their time and knowledge for the advancement of the profession, rather than their own personal gain. A very special thanks must go to Jakeman Business Solutions Pty Ltd (JBS), which not only provided the lead authors and project managers to compile the numerous articles and comments received but also financially underwrote SRMBOK.

A few people also rendered assistance far beyond the call of duty, and we owe a special debt to Bob Ross, Jason Brown, Konrad Buczynski, Spanky Kirsch, Lee Hutchison, and Don Williams for their countless comments, suggestions, and honest feedback. We would also like to acknowledge the generous assistance and contributions of the following persons:

- Adam Fitzpatrick
- Allan Halsey
- Allen Fleckner
- Anthony Moorehouse
- Anthony Northover
- Athol Yates
- Bernard Poerschke
- Bob Ross
- Brendan Rasmussen
- Brian Kelly
- Brian Roylett
- Broughton Steele
- Charles Bishop
- Clive Williams
- Dai Hockaday
- Damian Hine
- David Schofield
- David Van Lambaart
- Deborah Watkins
- Don McLean
- Don Williams
- Donna O'Brien
- Frazer Holmes
- Garry Young
- Geoff Harris
- Gerold Knight
- Glen Gardiner
- Glen Morgan
- Grant Whitehorn
- Ian Gordon
- Jason Brown
- Jeff Corkill
- Jim Allen
- John-Martin Collett
- John Greaves
- John Green
- Julian Claxton
- Julian Gaillard
- Katherine Krilov

- Konrad Buczynski
- Leigh Dixon
- Keith Mills
- Le-Anne Jakeman
- Lee Hutchison
- Lennon Hopkins
- Lloyd Masters
- Mark Edmonds
- Mark Dinnison
- Mark Golsby
- Mark Jarratt
- Mark Patch
- Mark Wylie
- Michael MacLean
- Michael Roach

- Mike Rothery
- Neil Connell
- Neil Porter
- Noel Mungovan
- Pam McGilvray
- Paul Curwell
- Paul Longley
- Phil Taleulei
- Phillip Carr
- Rex Stevenson, AO
- Richard Turner
- Rob Krauss
- Rob Smart
- Robert Sadleir
- Roger Fitzgerald

- Ross Babbage
- Ry Crozier
- Scott Petrie
- Shane Cassidy
- Spanky Kirsch
- Steven Hancock
- Steve Rohan-Jones
- Stewart Hayes
- Susan Trappett
- Tonya Graham
- Tim Green
- Tony Pierce
- Tony Solomon
- Wayne Olsen

As RMIA is a not-for-profit organization, proceeds from the sales of SRMBOK will go toward further professionalizing the Security Risk Management community and in funding the ongoing maintenance and development of future editions.

Sponsors

Finally, RMIA and the members of the SRMBOK working group would sincerely like to thank the sponsors who supported the initial development of SRMBOK through the provision of considerable financial resources. Key sponsors included JBS, ATMAAC International, and the Australian Government Department of the Prime Minister and Cabinet. Other sponsors included ADI Thales and Siemens Australia.

BRIAN ROYLETT, National President, RMIA

About (SRMBOK) Security Risk Management Body of Knowledge

SRMBOK was developed as an initiative of the Risk Management Institution of Australasia Limited (RMIA) to contribute to the identification and documentation of agreed better practice in Security Risk Management.

It is designed to provide the reader with a framework for formalizing risk management thinking in today's complex environment and details the Security Risk Management process in a format that can be applied by executive managers and security risk management practitioners.

SRMBOK provides both a graphical and written framework for bringing better practice to bear when addressing and treating security risks. The objective of SRMBOK is to support Security Risk Management practitioners with both technical and business guidance.

Status of this document

This document is the second release of SRMBOK. It endeavors to remain consistent with the overall body of better practice guidance in the discipline of security risk management while also introducing new material from other disciplines, such as occupational health and safety, financial risk management, engineering, and business continuity.

In particular, SRMBOK has been developed to align with the ISO 31000 Risk Management Standard and the Australian and New Zealand Standard for Risk Management (AS/NZS 4360:2004).

> *The intention of SRMBOK is that it should be a living document. Thus, this document will be updated, replaced, or made obsolete by other documents over time. Interested parties and subject matter experts are invited to contribute to the ongoing development and refinement of this body of knowledge.*

It is hoped that there will be feedback and suggestions for improvement from subject matter experts about this relatively young document. Comments on SRMBOK should be submitted via the online discussion forum at www.srmbok .com or sent to srmbok@rmia.org.au. Subject matter experts who are interested in contributing to subsequent editions in a closed "wiki" environment should in the first instance contact the administrator at www.srmbok.com or www. rmia.org.au. Alternatively, please feel free to contact the lead authors at julian. talbot@jakeman.com.au and miles@jakeman.com.au.

WHAT IS SRMBOK?

SRMBOK is a repository of knowledge in the form of a book that provides an overview of those areas of Security Risk Management that are generally recognized as better practice.[a] The identification of better practice has been a key element in developing SRMBOK. It is built on several hundred years of experience among the authors and coauthors, two years of research and development, and peer review workshops in four major cities before finally being subjected to peer review by independent subject matter experts prior to publication.

It is not the intent of SRMBOK to establish compliance proscriptions, proprietary solutions, or technology-based solutions. The concepts outlined here were selected on the basis they embody principles that are timeless, or at least enduring. As Security Risk Management is a dynamic and evolving field, what we offer here is a snapshot of better practice, and subsequent editions will be refined through industry participation supported by continuing research as the discipline and environmental context continue to evolve.

> The Security Risk Management Body of Knowledge (SRMBOK) is as follows: *An all-encompassing term that describes the sum of knowledge regarding readily accepted better practices, innovations and research within the evolving field of Security Risk Management.*

Some key objectives of the material covered in SRMBOK include:

- A common platform and terminology to establish Security Risk Management frameworks for government, Nongovernmental organization (NGO), and private sector organizations

---

[a]Better practice is defined for our purposes as those practices that will work well in *most situations, most of the time*. It does not mean that the techniques described should always be applied uniformly in all situations. The decision as to what is appropriate at that time is best made by the responsible managers for any given area or activity. SRMBOK uses the term "better practice" rather than "best practice" to recognize that what is best practice today may be out of date tomorrow and that no single best practice can be universally applied to every situation.

- A vulnerability analysis, Security Risk Management, and resilience framework for protection of assets in a robust, reliable, and repeatable fashion that is consistent with and can be aligned to industry standards, current practice, and government security doctrine
- Detailed guidance for customizing and implementing organizational security specifications and vulnerability assessment tools consistent with better practice across industries
- Support for the development of consistent vocational training and higher education
- Collate a toolkit for security risk professionals and allied disciplines
- Compile a library of appropriate tactics and strategies
- Detailed, specific, tangible advice and case studies to assist consistent implementation.

HOW CAN SRMBOK HELP?

The aim of SRMBOK is to improve the effectiveness of organizational and individual Security Risk Management practices. In particular, the goal is to improve the resilience of organizations, communities, and individuals by documenting and integrating best-practice concepts from a range of complementary disciplines in a way that assists practitioners, leaders, managers, and politicians to assess, demonstrate, and deliver the fullest potential value of Security Risk Management.

SRMBOK aims to assist readers improve their skills, knowledge, and awareness of the range of factors that affect security and safety.

Terminology

Although most Security Risk Management systems follow consistent themes, some of the subtle differences in terminology and process can often make it challenging for one system to be compared or applied with another.

Confusion surrounding frequently interchanged terms such as threat and risk, likelihood, and probability is unlikely to go away, particularly as most of these terms not only are translated differently between languages but also reflect different cultural nuances. Languages themselves are of course dynamic, and the use of terms such as risk and threat vary over time even within the same language. Nonetheless, it has been possible in most disciplines to provide technical definitions and relationships of terms for commonly used words and such is the intent of the subsequent chapters.

A key focus of SRMBOK, therefore, has been the provision of a common lexicon to assist practitioners integrate, compare, and apply Security Risk Management more effectively.

SRMBOK is of course more than a translator between differing platforms—it is also designed to capture and integrate existing better practice, including the following:

- Standard descriptions of Security Risk Management processes
- Guidance to relationships among the standard processes
- Standard metrics to measure process performance across industries and organizations
- Management practices that produce best-in-class performance

The ultimate goal is to enhance our abilities to protect assets, capabilities, and the community in general by documenting systems and cultures as follows that can be:

- Implemented purposefully to achieve competitive advantage
- Described without ambiguity and readily communicated
- Measured, managed, and controlled in a manner that demonstrates both duty of care and return on investment
- Tuned and retuned to a specific purpose

WHAT DOES SRMBOK COVER?

SRMBOK is written with modern Security Risk Management in mind, but the material it contains is designed to be principles based and broadly applicable to all elements and types of protective security. It addresses Security Risk Management from a holistic approach as a subset of general management but with a focus on protection of assets, functionality, and capability.

As illustrated in Figure 1, SRMBOK divides security into the following categories to analyze, illustrate, and integrate the principles and processes of Security Risk Management, which are required to provide security-in-depth:

- **Practice areas:** the activity groups that embody distinct areas of expertise within Security Risk Management
- **Assets:** items, functions, or processes that an individual, community, or organization values and needs to protect to provide and support capabilities
- **Knowledge areas:** the foundation set of concepts, principles, experience, and skills that a security risk practitioner requires to manage security risk effectively and efficiently
- **Competency areas:** a group of closely related skill sets that a practitioner is well qualified to perform to implement security measures
- **Activity areas:** principle security risk countermeasure areas through the life cycle of SRM from preincident prevention (intelligence and protective security) to post-event response (emergency management and business continuity)

ORGANIZATIONAL/ENVIRONMENTAL SECURITY CONTEXT

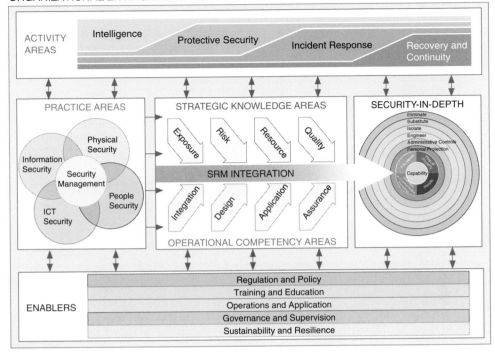

FIGURE 1 Overview of SRM resilience model.

- **Enablers:** elements required to ensure the application of Security Risk Management processes and activities in a sustained fashion

These concepts are explained in detail in the respective section on each, and their relationship to the others is described in Chapter 11 (SRM Integration). Many separate guides to SRMBOK discusses and illustrate principles in specific areas, e.g., transport security, travel safety, explosives incidents, building a business case for security, and so on.

WHAT SRMBOK DOES NOT INCLUDE

As a single document, SRMBOK cannot include detailed examination of all aspects of Security Risk Management, nor can it cover all the other disciplines that affect SRM, many of which are worthy of, or already have, their own body of knowledge.

It is also not intended to be a primer on the topic of Security Risk Management. Several excellent texts meet this purpose for the casual or inexperienced reader, many of which are listed in the bibliography section. Although it is suitable for readers with little or no SRM experience, it contains many advanced concepts and, as such, requires a degree of commitment from readers if they are to gain full value from it.

Although much of the way in which information is presented here may be new to some readers, SRMBOK itself introduces little that is truly new to Security Risk Management. Rather, it integrates existing knowledge with better practices, methodologies, and tools from complementary disciplines.

Where possible, we have provided additional (but by no means exhaustive) reference material and bibliography.

WORKING THROUGH THE CHAPTERS

Time is precious, and most of us have deadlines and responsibilities that provide us little opportunity for reflection or unguided research.

Although the earnest student of Security Risk Management is encouraged to read SRMBOK from start to finish, it is written so that it can be approached in sections as and when needed, and it has been structured in two main parts. The target audience is different for each part and for the elements within them.

> It is recommended that all readers familiarize themselves with the core concepts of SRMBOK as outlined in Chapter 4 (SRMBOK Framework). This chapter highlights the central SRMBOK framework and the relationship of the various SRM elements to each other. It will also assist readers to identify which chapter(s) and supporting guides to SRMBOK they might refer to first. This section is also discussed in greater detail in the section on SRM Integration (Chapter 11) after the key concepts have been introduced in more detail.

Applications and Case Studies

SRMBOK is also supported by many Guides to SRMBOK that provide detailed guidance and examples of how the SRMBOK framework has been applied across areas such as follows:

- Access management
- Business continuity and resilience
- Command, control, and communications
- Consequence management and business continuity management
- Counterterrorism
- Crime prevention through environmental design
- Crisis management
- Environmental security
- Events and mass gatherings
- Executive protection
- Explosives and bomb threats

- Home-based work
- Human rights and security
- Implementing Security Risk Management
- Intellectual property protection
- Intelligence approach to SRM
- Investigations and root cause analysis
- Maritime security and piracy
- Mass transport security
- Organizational structure
- Pandemic
- Personal protective practices
- Psychology of security
- Red teaming and scenario modeling
- Resilience and critical infrastructure protection
- Security risk assessment—asset, function, or project based
- Security risk assessment—enterprise based [enterprise secutiry risk assessment (ESRA)]
- Security specifications and postures
- Security training
- SRM management systems (SRM-MS)
- Supply chain security
- The security manager
- Transnational security
- Travel security

This list of guides will vary and expand over time because of the ever-changing threat and risk context as additional guides to SRMBOK are created and revised.

AUDIENCE FOR SRMBOK

SRMBOK has been designed as a reference guide with the following main audiences in mind:

- Executive managers and senior officials
- Line managers with a Security Risk Management responsibility
- Consultants, advisers, and other Security Risk Management professionals
- Educators and trainers developing Security Risk Management courses
- Students of Security Risk Management

Each chapter contains cross-references to relevant information in other chapters, and a bibliography is included to make it easier to find supporting information from other sources. There is also a lexicon designed for all audiences.

The sections on Security Risk Management context and security governance are designed to set the scene and, although applicable to everyone, are intended primarily for Chief Executive Officers, directors, and other senior executives.

For Chief Security Officers (CSOs), consultants, or management personnel with SRM responsibilities, the strategic knowledge areas, operational competency areas, practice areas, activity areas, SRM enablers, asset areas, and SRM integration provide an overview of SRM. With a sound understanding of these topics, a line manager, consultant, or practitioner should be able to provide leadership in managing organizational security risks.

The Guides to SRMBOK provide the user with a greater understanding of the theory and application of SRMBOK concepts and practical implementation of organizational resilience. These guides are designed to assist managers understand areas that they might have responsibility for, as well as security risk practitioners who might be either seeking greater insight into an area that they are already familiar with, or where they need to conduct research for activities outside their existing knowledge.

Security Risk Management
Body of Knowledge

Introduction and Overview 1

1.1 WHY SRMBOK?

We live in a world of uncertainty; the world is changing at an ever accelerating pace. Life, society, economics, weather patterns, international relations, and risks are becoming more and more complex. The nature of work, travel, recreation, and communication is radically altering. We live in a world where, seemingly with each passing year, the past is less and less a guide to the future.

Security is involved in one way or another in virtually every decision we make and every activity we undertake. The contributions that Security Risk Management (SRM) make to society, personal safety, and national stability are easy to underestimate but hard to overlook. We have been concerned about safety, security, and protection since the dawn of our species and yet will still struggle to consistently define or reliably manage our security risks.

This is to a large extent understandable—although the fundamentals remain consistent, advances in security and related disciplines continue unabated. The global environment has never been more volatile, and societal expectations for security are increasing if anything.

The complexities of globalization, public expectation, regulatory requirements, transnational issues, multijurisdictional risks, crime, terrorism, advances in information technology, cyber attacks, and pandemics have created a security risk environment that has never been more challenging.

Despite the continuing development of security as a discipline, no single framework pulls together all the excellent but disparate work that practitioners and researchers are continually developing. Overall, there is little dispute that risk is a factor that must be considered by decision makers when deciding what, if anything, should be done about a risk that falls within their responsibility. Security is one such area where there has been less than total agreement as to what this means in practical terms.

> *The body of knowledge (BOK) surrounding Security Risk Management continues to evolve, but even the most dynamic of fields needs a point of common agreement, or at least agreed debate. It is unreasonable to expect SRMBOK to be all things to all people, but we the society, and the profession, need a place to collectively discuss and shape our thinking surrounding core concepts in SRM.*

Much of the existing body of knowledge on risk management was developed for issues that do not possess the same degree of complexity, uncertainty, and ambiguity as those associated with modern security-related decision making. For example, managing financial or operational risk can be quantified more easily than some of the abstract concepts that security practitioners must manage. These areas offer us insights into the tools and techniques that have been pioneered in other disciplines. Areas such as safety management systems, financial formulas, project methodologies, engineering science, hazard identification, and human factors analysis, to name just a few, also have much to offer security practitioners.

1.1.1 Key Challenges

The abundance of valuable but disparate material from Security Risk Management and other disciplines presents a significant challenge for developing a common framework to assess and consider risk when making security and related policy decisions. In addition to risk assessment methodological questions, other questions plague organizational risk deliberations. Among them are the following:

- Who is responsible for the risk assessment?
- Who is responsible for managing risk?
- How should alternative courses of action be developed, and how should they be evaluated?
- How does one perform cost/benefit analysis on an abstract problem where potential consequences are astronomical but probability is unknown and may be close to zero?

- How should terrorist and criminal adaptive responses to security measures be taken into account as potential security measures are being considered?

Security professionals everywhere are making some progress in answering these questions, and more significantly, the profession is developing a more mature understanding of the complexities involved. Increasingly, academic and practical research is also refining our understanding of the issues and giving us a basis for more risk-informed decision making.

Much of the past practices in security have revolved around the three Gs (guns, guards, gates), national security, intelligence and defense, firewalls, and cryptography. As important as these are, moving from a focus on threat mitigation to benefit realization is a growing imperative for many security professionals and for most organizations.

1.2 WHERE DO WE GO FROM HERE?

> "The empires of the future are the empires of the mind."
>
> SIR WINSTON CHURCHILL

We are facing an increasingly complex and interdependent future in which information and intangible assets are likely to become increasingly valuable, and tangible assets are likely to diminish in value by comparison.

Risk-management activities in the 21st century are likely to continue to move away from the early focus on compliance and loss minimization toward opportunity realization. Although Security Risk Management will continue to require sound management of threats and minimization of losses, already we are starting to see threat mitigation as just part of standard management practice, rather than a standalone discipline.

The organizations and societies of today are seeking a greater understanding of the true nature of risks. This is not an altruistic or inherent desire for risk management per se, but it is an endeavor to better exploit opportunities and minimize harm.[1] As illustrated in Figure 1.1, organizations typically start out as risk controllers with a focus on compliance and loss minimization. Over time, they realize that quality SRM adds value to operational performance, and if integrated across the enterprise, SRM can become a significant contributor to both organizational resilience and opportunity realization.

It is likely that some organizations will always view security as a cost center rather than as profit center. Those that have sound Security Risk Management systems in place, however, will have competitive advantages in many areas:

- Personnel screening can help to select the best candidates and also increase marketability to clients who may be concerned about protecting their intellectual property or funds.
- Information security management helps to introduce products to market without advance knowledge by competitors.

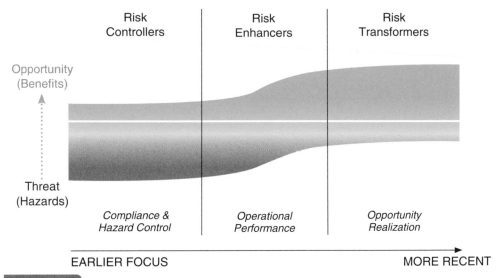

Risk Controllers	Risk Enhancers	Risk Transformers

Opportunity (Benefits)

Threat (Hazards)

Compliance & Hazard Control | *Operational Performance* | *Opportunity Realization*

EARLIER FOCUS   MORE RECENT

FIGURE 1.1 The security risk management journey

- Appropriate physical security is likely to increase profitability at a venue when customers know they will be safe and their cars will not be vandalized while they are inside.
- Organizations that have prepared by developing a sound Security Risk Management system can quickly and safely deploy to higher risk locations to take advantage of opportunities ahead of their competitors.
- Appropriate security will mean that managers can focus on opportunity realization rather than on filling out incident reports or chasing down missing equipment.

Just as threat mitigation seeks to avoid threats turning into losses, so does opportunity realization seek to manage the conversion of opportunities into benefits. Although most of us realize intuitively that Security Risk Management is integral to opportunity realization, the framework and tools to demonstrate this transition from risk controllers to risk transformers is comparatively in its infancy. The process of moving from being perceived as a cost center to being recognized as a profit center is integral to achieving effective organizational Security Risk Management.

SRMBOK aims to provide a framework that security professionals can use to integrate Security Risk Management along with lessons from other disciplines, such as engineering, occupational health and safety, behavioral psychology, and finance.

1.3 WHAT IS SECURITY RISK MANAGEMENT?

It is appropriate from the outset to define the scope of SRMBOK by defining the term "Security Risk Management." SRMBOK starts with the fundamental premise that Security Risk Management is an essential part of any individual's, organization's or community's wider risk-management activities.

SRMBOK takes the position that there is no such thing as perfect security and that all security involves making trade-offs. For example, most of us willingly accept the risk of being involved in a car accident or assaulted in exchange for the benefits of living in a modern society. If we wanted to avoid completely the risk of being assaulted, we would live on a deserted island. This deserted island choice, however, is likely to increase other personal risks and reduce our longevity as a result of the lack of health-care services. We also accept the additional cost of fitting a lock to our front doors and the inconvenience of having to lock the door on the way out in exchange for reducing the risk of burglary. Similarly, we accept a little inconvenience when undergoing security checks before flying as well as a small additional cost for that security with good grace because it reduces our real or perceived risk.

1.3.1 Security

> *Security is the condition of being protected against danger or loss. It is achieved through the mitigation of adverse consequences associated with the intentional or unwarranted actions of others.*
>
> *In general usage, security is a concept similar to safety, but as a technical term, security means that something is not only secure but also that it has been secured. In this context, security refers to the measures used to protect sensitive organizational assets that collectively create, enable, and sustain organizational capability. Such assets will differ depending on the nature of the organization's activities but typically include classified or sensitive information, physical assets of value, people, unique processes, alliances/partnerships, and intellectual capital.*
>
> *Individuals or actions that encroach on the condition of protection cause a breach of security.*

As suggested from the word "unwarranted" in this definition, the intentional actions of others that are legal and acceptable, at least in the eyes of the defender, are excluded from the scope of security. For example, the actions of others in derivatives trading or commercial enterprise may have adverse consequences, but preventing those lawful and normal consequences is the domain of areas such as financial risk management. They would not normally be security issues unless fraud or similar was involved.

The use of the word "intentional" similarly clarifies the distinction between security and areas such as safety. Security involves protection from deliberate acts, whereas safety risk management includes the management of risks from unintended events such as motor vehicle accidents and falls.

There is a strong overlap between safety and security (as there is between security and finance, engineering, psychology, etc.); in fact, many languages have only one word for both concepts. Many activities will involve a wide range of threats from different sources (e.g., a journey to a high-risk country involves risks from crime, foreign currency fluctuations, and road safety, to name but a few).

It can be tempting to include security as a subset of safety, and in some cases, this would be correct. For example, even the protection of national security classified information could be indirectly related to protecting the lives of the nation's citizens or the identity of agents in the field. However, security as a subset of safety is inappropriate when we consider financial and property threats such as fraud, embezzlement, commercial espionage, and website hacking, where the impact on personnel safety is tenuous, if it exists at all.

1.3.2 Perceived versus Actual Risk

Like many other areas of risk management, security involves making trade-offs. Security decisions often include a range of costs as well as compromises to convenience, privacy, and so on, and in many cases, we will have to trade one or more of these elements.

Within this, we will often be called on to make decisions and trade-offs regarding perceived versus actual risks. Sometimes, managing the actual risk will also mitigate the perceived risks and vice versa. Sometimes not.

Often, it might appear that the actual risks are more important than the perceived risk, and in some cases, this is appropriate. There are many reasons, however, why we might choose to focus more on managing perceived risks. Removing nail clippers from airline passengers may have little to do with managing the actual risk of hijack, but it is part of the process that visibly demonstrates that something is being done. In fact, the risk of hijack may well be perceived by the traveling public to be much higher than it actually is. The greater risk associated with airline hijackings is probably not one of hijack but the economic losses to the community and the increased incidence of road fatalities if people lose confidence in aviation safety.[2,a]

Similarly, it will often be appropriate to put in place measures such as tamper-proof packaging on food and drugs, even though it is still entirely possible to contaminate the goods inside. Such measures in practice will only deter the lazy or ignorant would-be poisoner, but they do reassure the consumer to continue purchasing the product.

---

[a]In December 2001, David Myers, who is a Professor of Psychology at Hope College, postulated that if Americans "now fly 20 percent less and instead drive half those unflown miles, we will spend 2 percent more time in motor vehicles. This translates into 800 more people dying as passengers and pedestrians. So, in just the next year the terrorists may indirectly kill three times more people on our highways than died on those four fated planes." As it transpired, domestic air travel in the United States following the terrorist attacks of September 11 dropped more than 30% relative to the same period the previous year, and U.S. motor vehicle fatalities were 1,085 higher in 2002 than in 2001.

Of course, these issues of perceived versus actual risk are largely subjective and will vary depending on individual risk appetite and understanding. The greater driver in this decision-making process is likely to be personal or organizational agendas, which will involve greater or lesser good to various parties.

Although most people as individuals are concerned about the safety of the traveling public, for example, the various stakeholders all have different agendas. The airlines are not as interested in treating the real risk of hijacking as they are in treating the perceived risk. An actual hijack is a dramatic but rare event. The perceived risk of hijack can result in a dramatic impact on every quarterly revenue statement. Airlines, like any business, have an agenda to spend the bare minimum of their own money but recognize the return on investment by managing security perceptions. Meanwhile, politicians are facing the next election cycle—or next coup if not in a democratic society, and have their own agenda to consider. Being seen to be doing something and acting quickly will generally be more important in the first instance than actually understanding and addressing the real security risk.

The key word here of course is "risk." Each stakeholder's agenda is driven by their own perception of risk, and it might not be the same as the actual risks. For example, mobile phone technology has sufficient encryption on most digital systems to allow them to ensure that it can be marketed as encrypted but not enough to ensure that an average personal computer (PC) with some basic equipment cannot break the encryption. The cost of research and the bandwidth implications for significantly enhanced encryption are not commercially rewarded in the current threat environment, so the security is a compromise.

These are just a few of the examples of how various security agendas interact with the perceived and real security threats to make trade-offs that affect us all. This is a theme that is reflected throughout SRMBOK and one to which there is no easy or immediate answer.

1.3.3 Security Risks

> *A security risk is any event that could result in the compromise of organizational assets. The unauthorized use, loss, damage, disclosure, or modification of organizational assets for the profit, personal interest, or political interests of individuals, groups, or other entities constitutes a compromise of the asset, and it also includes the risk of harm to people. Compromise of organizational assets may adversely affect the enterprise, its business units, and their clients. As such, consideration of security risk is a vital component of risk management.*

Several methods can be used to identify security risks. One method of identifying threats with the potential to affect the organization adversely is to group them according to their source, motivation, and method of operation, as shown in Table 1.1.

Table 1.1 Threat groupings by source, motive and method

Source	Motive	Method of Operation
Criminal	Profit	Theft, robbery, assault, fraud, disclosure
Terrorist	Political manipulation	Bombing, hijacking, kidnapping, assassination
Foreign intelligence services	Strategic, military, political, or economic advantage	Espionage, sabotage, subversion, disclosure
Commercial or industrial competitors	Profit, competitive edge	Industrial or economic espionage
Malicious people	Revenge, fame, discredit	Disclosure, destruction, vandalism

Table 1.2 Grouping assets by risk and threat

Organization Assets	Risks	Threats
Buildings, facilities	Destruction, damage, or unavailability of the building or facility	Fire, explosion, hoaxes, power failure, contamination, unauthorized access
Information system	Loss or compromise of security classified material, loss of confidentiality, availability or integrity of information	Unauthorized users, forensic disc examination, careless handling of printout, careless transmission
Management's confidence in the business unit or program	Loss of management or public confidence in the business unit or program, or its processes	Mishandling of sensitive data, inconsistent policy or service delivery, adverse media coverage
Organizational reputation	Loss of organizational reputation	Poor service, mishandling of sensitive data, inconsistent policy or service delivery, adverse media coverage

Another method to identify threat sources that can become security risks is to focus on the assets (functions, resources, and values) that are essential for the organization to perform its role and to group them according to the threat and consequent risk posed, as shown in Table 1.2.

A third method is to examine at the organizational exposures or vulnerabilities and to then use these to review the suitability of existing security controls (Table 1.3).

Table 1.3 Asset group and organizational exposures

Asset Group	Possible Exposures or Vulnerabilities Identified
People Assets	Abduction
	Assassination
	Attack, assault, or harassment
	Bombing
	Civil disorder
	Co-location with high risk tenants
	Conferences/exhibitions
	Crime
	Cultural or religious differences
	Discrimination/prejudice
	Disgruntled employee
	Domestic violence
	Drive by shooting
	Family influence
	Financial stress or gain/influence
	Impersonation of staff member
	Inadequate procedures
	Inadequate training
	Inadequate vetting
	Isolation
	Kidnap
	Language
	Loyalty/coercion/corruption/collusion
	Mail handling and receipt
	Mismanagement
	Organizational structure and responsibilities
	Physical assault
	Poisoning
	Reluctance to adopt security policy
	Robbery
	Sexual assault
	Sexual preference or discrimination
	Stress related behavioral issues
	Travel
	Verbal assault or harassment
	Workplace violence
	Public perception
	Staff attraction
	Staff retention

Asset Group	Possible Exposures or Vulnerabilities Identified
Information Assets	Destruction or corruption
	Disruption of service
	Commercial espionage
	Fire/arson
	Fraud
	Inadvertent disclosure
	Leakage
	Loss of data or sensitive trade material
	Manipulation of data/information
	Sabotage
	Staff loyalty
Physical Assets/Information and Communications Technology (ICT)	Break-in
	Co-location with high-risk tenants
	Commercial espionage—electronic surveillance/listening Device
	Fire/arson
	Inadequate emergency management procedures
	Inadequate threat details
	Failure of equipment (e.g., maintenance and reliability)
	Hacking
	Funding
	Mail handling
	Maintenance
	Procurement methodology
	Unauthorized or forced access
	Vandalism
	Vehicle bombing
	Sabotage
	Theft

Identified threats will represent sources of security risks (i.e., how and why a particular security risk event might happen). Information obtained from a formal threat assessment will then assist in determining the likelihood of particular risks occurring.

1.3.4 Security Risk Management

The focus of SRMBOK is toward the direct and unwarranted actions of people. The term "security" can of course be a much broader term. For example, if we consider security as a "state of being protected from hazards, danger, harm, loss or injury," it also includes elements of protection from natural disasters and concepts of organizational resilience. SRMBOK accordingly, although focused on intentional acts, takes an all-hazards approach that considers the broader interplay of environment and other factors that can impact an organization or individual. In terms of natural hazards, for example, organizational resilience takes into account both the direct impact of natural disasters (e.g., power outages and infrastructure) and the indirect impacts, such as fire, looting, civil unrest, and so on.

> *Security Risk Management is the culture, processes, and structures that are directed toward maximizing benefits and minimizing adverse effects associated with the intentional and unwarranted actions of others against organizational assets.[3]*

The definition used above complements and supports an all-hazards approach to organizational resilience that, in practice, is achieved by supporting the preparedness, protection, and preservation of people, property, information, and organizational capability.[4]

Although some terminology used in Security Risk Management is common to other forms of risk management, most threat assessment processes and risk treatments used are unique to the Security Risk Management profession and play a definitive role in the progression of an organization's objectives.

Like most security professionals, SRMBOK considers threat and risk as different concepts. Threat is a hazard or source of risk (criminals, terrorists, etc.)— usually measured in terms of intent and capability. Meanwhile, risk considers the likelihood of an attack with the most credible impact(s) or consequence on assets. Security Risk Management, therefore, involves understanding the threat as part of the objective of determining and applying countermeasures to manage (treat) the risks.

> *Threat determines risk, which in turn determines countermeasures.*
>
> *In practice, this is a cycle where each countermeasure changes the context and either introduces new risks or at the very least will modify the threat actors' methods of attack. This in turn modifies the risk and so on.*

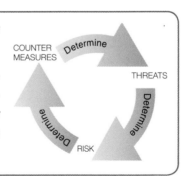

1.4 HOW DOES SRM RELATE TO RISK MANAGEMENT?

Security Risk Management is a subset and essential part of a broader risk management system. As illustrated in Figure 1.2, SRM is simply another management discipline fitting predominantly within the sphere of risk management.

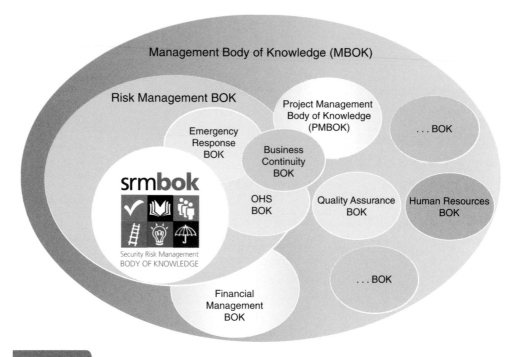

FIGURE 1.2 Relationship of SRMBOK within the Risk Management Body of Knowledge

> *Risk management is "the culture, processes and structures that are directed towards realizing potential opportunities whilst managing adverse effects."[3]*
>
> *This definition implies that risk management is a coordinated activity to direct and control an organization with regard to risk.[5]*

In a fully integrated risk-management system, Security Risk Management is interlinked at each stage with all other risk-management activities being undertaken (e.g., financial, safety, marketing, reputation, regulatory, etc.). Although the application of Security Risk Management requires discipline-specific knowledge, the overall risk-management process remains the same.

As noted in ISO 31000 Risk Management, the elements of a framework for managing risks are shown in Figure 1.3.

> *SRMBOK addresses this in more detail in section 5 on Governance Frameworks (page 65), and section 13 on Implementing an Integrated ERM Program (page 331).*

A typical risk-management process as described in both ISO 31000 Risk Management and the AS/NZS4360:2004 Risk Management Standard is illustrated in Figure 1.4.

FIGURE 1.3 Risk-Management Framework (ISO 31000:2008)

FIGURE 1.4 Risk-Management Process (AS/NZS4360:2004)

SRMBOK generally adopts the ISO 31000 Risk Management Standard or the AS/NZS4360:2004 model of risk management, and it is consistent with the HB167 Security Risk Management Handbook (companion guide to AS/NZS4360:2004) and AS/NZS ISO/IEC 27001:2006 Information Security Standard. Of course, many more international standards are of relevance, and SRMBOK is inclusive of the broader body of knowledge rather than of any single methodology or system.

1.5 CONCLUSION

SRMBOK has been prepared as a framework in which our current and evolving understanding of the answers to many issues discussed in this chapter can be integrated. The focus is not on a specific assessment methodology but rather on a flexible and customizable overview of the organizational and managerial aspects of risk management, including:

- The integration of security into enterprise risk management
- The focus on opportunity realization
- Efforts to increase standardization and comparability across various methodologies
- The futility of searching for a one-size-fits-all risk-assessment methodology
- The necessity of retaining more narrowly focused risk assessments.

Security Risk Management Context 2

2.1 THE CHANGING SECURITY ENVIRONMENT

Managing risk in an evolving global environment has never been more challenging. The geopolitical map of the world has changed dramatically in recent years with little indication that the pace of change is likely to decrease. Business and financial risk is something that anyone involved in commerce or management has to assess on a daily basis. For organizations with operations outside the legal frameworks of their home country, regional and global geopolitical issues can add complexities that are easily underestimated or misunderstood.

Most individuals and organizations in the western world are either already operating across national boundaries or are exposed to risks associated with globalization and transnationalism. For many commercial organizations, the pursuit of growth and new opportunities may lead to the establishment of overseas interests, whereas organizations such as aid groups and nongovernmental organizations often run overseas projects as part of their core mission. The range of risks will vary depending on context of location, individual, organization, community, or industry sector, but the management of risks associated with these factors requires a suitable risk-management framework.

2.2 CHANGING CONCEPTS IN SECURITY RISK MANAGEMENT

The traditional view of security has moved from "guns, guards, and gates" through "ciphers, safety and society" toward the evolving and dynamic concept of "providing resilience." It is fair to say that modern society demands much more than just safety or technical prowess of advanced systems and data encryption.

Although traditional security was associated with worthy concerns of physiological needs and safety, we are increasingly meeting those needs. Further up Maslow's hierarchy (Figure 2.1) are the needs of love, esteem, and self-actualization that cannot be met by simply providing a safe and secure environment.

Collectively, society expects our basic needs to be brought to our door in an uninterrupted and seamless stream such that we can focus on our higher requirements.

As technologies evolve and our standard of living increases, we face more complex threats, such as bioterrorism and global warming, and greater demands from society to sustain, protect, and improve our existence in all areas. Increasingly, the notion of security is expanding to include the notions of resilience, sustainability, and critical services assurance. Collectively, this notion of resilience revolves around maintaining capability rather than protecting any particular assets.

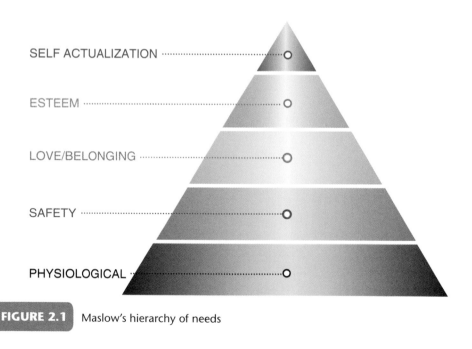

FIGURE 2.1 Maslow's hierarchy of needs

We expect our governments, organizations, and corporations to continue to meet our needs for food, water, safety, lifestyle, and self-actualization. This has much less to do with the traditional concepts of protection of assets (people, information, and property) than it has to do with the functions and capabilities that such assets provide.

This ability to sustain the capabilities that meet the needs and expectations of stakeholders is not dependent on any given facility, individual, or design—rather, it is the capability to continue delivery of services or product that is actually the core asset. For example, it is less important to protect a gas plant than to continue providing gas to homes and businesses. Whether this is achieved by protecting the gas plant, running several geographically dispersed gas plants, or having arrangements in place with other gas plants to supply the customer in time of crisis is less relevant—other than so far as we should choose the most reliable and cost-effective solution(s).

This concept of resilience and sustaining capabilities rather than just protecting assets is equally applicable at the individual level as at the organizational or national security level (Figure 2.2). Ultimately, the capability to provide for your family is more important than any particular job, house, or possessions. The ability to access bank accounts 24 hours per day from anywhere in the world has much greater value than cash under the bed.

Similarly, as manufacturing costs continue to fall, it is far more effective to replace most nonprecious items at short notice than to expend undue resources, locking them up like a fortress.

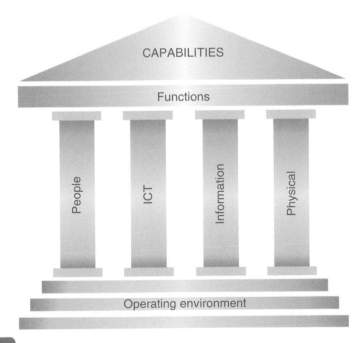

FIGURE 2.2 Organizational resilience—capabilities, functions, and assets

2.3 ORIGINS OF SECURITY AND RISK MANAGEMENT

Arguably, security and risk management are the world's third oldest professions. As Roper points out, "Og," who is a caveman of the late Pleistocene era, probably considered the protection of his key assets (his food supplies, spearheads, flints, and animal skins) as core to the achievement of his organizational objectives (in this case, protecting and caring for his clan).[6]

Og hid his food and tools, placed barriers at his cave entrance, ensured that only a few other trusted clan members were aware of their location, and ensured that his family group were aware of the importance of these control measures. Addressing the pertinent operational safety concerns of the time, Og even provided his trusted group with personal protective equipment like leather shoes, furs, weapons, and fire to mitigate against the identified risks of the day.

Casting forward several thousand years, much has changed, although some things remain the same. Even in the most favorable circumstances, no organization operates in a risk-free environment. As Peter Bernstein so eloquently points out, "the reason why there is risk in the first place: without that qualification, everything would be predictable, and in a world where every event is identical to a previous event no change would ever occur."[7] It is intrinsic, therefore, to the nature of life and business that we take risks. Equally, governments and not-for-profit organizations face funding, reputation, and service-delivery risks as a matter of course.

Although the current focus on organizational security may lead to the perception that the core concepts behind Security Risk Management are a response to new threats, the opposite is true: The human need for security features second on Maslow's hierarchy of needs (Figure 2.1) behind only functional necessities like water, food, and sleep.

The history of risk management in general is also marked by the ongoing debate between quantitative risk management and qualitative risk management. The debate over whether numbers, statistics, and calculated probabilities is a better indicator of future events than subjective analysis is likely to come to an uneasy truce in the near future. Both approaches have their value and are generally complementary rather than conflicting.

2.4 TRENDS AND FUTURE DIRECTIONS

The story of Security Risk Management is marked by technological advances, procedural improvements, and an ongoing battle of brinkmanship with those who seek to benefit from our harm. No sooner do we improve the quality of our security controls than the attackers will find another chink in the armor. A truism from the security industry is that "we know every trick in the book—except the one they are using right now...."

This battle of wits is likely to continue into the future, and advances in areas such as genetics, nanotechnology, and robotics are only likely to increase this complexity. Some experts predict that we are likely to see exponential increases in this area and that computers with artificial intelligence (AI) equivalent to human beings and the ability to pass the Turing test (simulating a living person well enough to fool an interrogator) will be available by 2027.[8]

However long it takes to pass the Turing test, it is likely that in the near future, we will expect artificial intelligence systems to have an increasing impact on society. The use of AI systems in support of such basic elements of traffic control, power generation, and manufacturing will introduce a new level of paradigm shift in the way we think about security. Although we currently use a variety of systems such as firewalls and employee screening to control access to key systems, we will have to reevaluate the term "employee screening" when the computing system is the employee.

In the near future, we will face new and uncertain risks; for example, we are starting to witness criminal elements hacking Bluetooth® systems.[b] Security Risk Management will need to keep up with incredible advances in information technology in the near future, and there is little doubt that the discipline will increasingly become a standard component of organizational management systems, whereas the timeless nature of Security Risk Management will be a feature in the successful businesses of tomorrow. As the concept of goods and services becomes more virtual and technological advances highlight the importance of intellectual property, the development of information security techniques and the employment of more sophisticated physical security barriers will punctuate Security Risk Management.

Education and training will become increasingly significant as the complexity of security risks and solutions increases. Professionalism of the sector is another trend that is likely to gather momentum. Some things, however, will remain the same. People are likely to remain a key element in the equation, and security measures will continue to deter or delay attackers.

2.5 GLOBALIZATION, OPPORTUNITY, AND VOLATILITY

Even in the safest of countries, extrajurisdictional responsibilities, foreign exchange risk, and cultural barriers will add to the complexity of daily operations. All too often, organizations operating overseas have been known to focus on risks they are familiar with, such as occupational health and safety (OHS), project management, and financial risks to the detriment of unique regional or cultural threats.

Even organizations that operate exclusively within the confines of their home, legal frameworks are not immune to geopolitical issues, and many mistakenly assume that geopolitical risk does not apply to them. The war in Iraq has shown the impact that oil prices can have on global transport and travel costs. Even the

---

[b]Bluetooth is a registered trademark of Bluetooth SIG Incorporated (www.Bluetooth.org).

property sector is not immune. In many areas of the world, booming economies are linked with international impacts of unprecedented levels of investment in the mining and resource sector.

As organizations grow to have greater international interaction and presence, they experience increased exposure to conflict and geopolitical risks. As the world shrinks, many organizations have become increasingly vulnerable as, until relatively recently, strategies were often based on previously stable geopolitical relations. In this context, to remain a global player today, an organization must be able to survive not only economic downturns but also geopolitical developments.

The steady march of globalization involves risk for a range of reasons not least of all because global definitions and quality of governance differ vastly. Traditional political risks such as corruption and mismanagement still apply, but an increasing spectrum of political and economic activity occurring outside government control or oversight means that vulnerabilities have increased throughout the networks of globalization.

2.6 TRANSNATIONAL AND EXTRAJURISDICTIONAL RISKS

For organizations with international operations, transnational issues add an extra dimension to risk management, which they all too often fail to fully appreciate. Even in the safest of countries, extrajurisdictional responsibilities, foreign exchange risk, and cultural barriers will add to the complexity of daily operations. Frequently, organizations that operate overseas have been known to focus on risks they are familiar with, such as OHS, project management, financial, and so on, to the detriment of unique regional risks such as human trafficking and cultural sensitivities, smuggling, civil unrest, and deforestation.

Developments in the evolving security environment will continue to influence directly the course and pattern of multinational business, but this is only one of the many risk exposures that is faced by global business. The world is increasingly less safe leading to an increased cost of doing business, which demands a higher risk premium and greater focus on transnational security issues.

So who will be the winners in the global village? Lowest cost producers, countries with the infrastructure to meet a sudden surge in business, and multinationals with established bases in the region. In the new paradigm, there are strategic and competitive advantages for organizations that manage risk well. The clear message is that organizations that excel at managing geopolitical risk will be the ones to survive and thrive in the networked 21st century.

Organizations must understand their specific relationship to globalization and geopolitics, identify the sites of risk for their activities, and adopt forecasting tools to enhance resilience with respect to emerging threats. Geopolitical risk analysis and management are intricately intertwined with organizational success.

2.7 LAW, REGULATORY FRAMEWORK, AND RAMIFICATIONS FOR MANAGEMENT

In an increasingly interactive world with relatively unfettered movements of trade, investment, and people across borders, defining and managing geopolitical risk is no easy task. A broad definition might include the analysis of political, social, security, and business practice issues that impact on an organization's ability to reach its goals. These include the unforeseen actions (or inaction) of a foreign government or entity, an organization's home government, or a third party.

It may even come as a surprise to many organizations that national laws can apply to entities outside national borders. Increasingly, any organization that operates overseas is becoming potentially answerable concurrently to the laws of each country in which it has a presence. Significant risks such as these can be easily overlooked in a new environment by even the most experienced risk practitioners because of a lack of familiarity. It is very tempting for specialists to apply standards they used in a previous location, but sound risk-based decision making is critical, and a blanket approach may often be inadequate or excessive. The consequences of inadequate risk management are obvious. Overly protective advice, however, may only involve unnecessary expense, but staff are likely to ignore instructions that they do not recognize a need for, which leads to a loss of credibility and compliance.

In one Middle East oil field, security staff almost had a revolt on their hands when they tried to put a blanket ban on weekend trips away on grounds of security. Ever ready to question authority figures, the Australians in particular asked to see the threat assessments that had led to the ban. Eventually, the revolt was diffused when a thorough risk analysis established that it was relatively safe to do some sightseeing. Security backed down on their previous position but not without a loss of face and credibility among expatriate staff.

Apart from the traditional security-related issues of petty crime, theft, and kidnapping, there are also increasing geopolitical risk factors. Terrorism attacks receive almost daily mention, and whether it is Madrid, Istanbul, or Breslan, the world is witnessing a steady deterioration in the security environment. The global security environment has also changed, and now we are directly targeted by a new kind of transnational terrorism that threatens peace, security, and prosperity.

The tragic events of September 11, 2001, Bali in October 2002, and Jakarta in 2004 have emphasized the importance of monitoring and managing the risk of terrorism. Globally, security risk is a serious impediment to business operations, and it result in considerable cost increases for insurance and protective measures. Increases in security, insurance, and general operating costs put more strain on tight budgets, potentially introducing other operating risks. Unexpected costs can increase dramatically. For example, in Dubai, where multinational and local organizations compete for space in the most secure buildings, an already booming real estate market is becoming conditioned to expect 20% or more annual rent increases as the norm.

At the same time, however, forward-thinking global organizations that can manage their security and operational risks can operate successfully in a range of higher risk environments.

2.8 DIVERSIFICATION OR CONCENTRATION?

Like currency markets, technology can serve to increase risk as well as to control it. The technologies that facilitate global cooperation also enable illicit interactions and terrorist groups. Global dependence on communications and transportation systems is growing steadily, building up an increasing array of complex, economically important, and time-sensitive subsystems.

Geopolitical risk, however, is not limited to globally networked systems and industries. On the surface, it may seem that domestic developments and supply chain disruptions affect mostly large multinationals, but rising insurance costs and heightened security measures apply to organizations of all sizes. The world has entered the realm of greater international interaction and increasing geopolitical complexity. In tandem comes heightened exposure to conflict and a new vulnerability because strategies were often based on the assumption of fundamentally stable geopolitical relations.

A basic rule of risk management is to "avoid concentration, try diversification." But diversify across what? With the increasingly competitive business environment, many organizations are seeking geographic diversification as a way to achieve organic growth, reduce volatility of income streams, and provide a degree of protection from market cycles. Perhaps the most common form of risk transfer in this environment is to obtain political risk insurance. This insurance is available in the public and private sectors and is widely held by international investors and businesses.

Larger organizations often have mature systems and are very experienced when planning expansion into new countries with good attention to the new risks of those locations. However, it can be the little things like travel safety awareness or road safety that can be forgotten unless there is a well-maintained risk-management framework to back it up. Many organizations look to consultants with expertise in international risk assessments, enterprise security management, crisis management planning, and other specialist areas for advice. Many organizations find that developing and maintaining a coherent and systematic risk-management and decision-making framework is the key to protecting their operations. Appropriately benchmarked standards and programs that will protect personnel, assets, and reputation can be a very cost-effective way to mitigate any potential legal liabilities.

In some circumstances, a risk can be managed by direct action. In the case of kidnapping, for example, it is possible to hire bodyguards or take protective measures to reduce the likelihood of such an occurrence. Often, risk management in a foreign country will require some lateral thinking. One approach to managing political risk is to negotiate a better deal with the host country government in an area such as taxation relief. This can only be done, however, if the organization knows the cultural context of the issue and its implications for business operations. Through this process, Security Risk Management can be turned directly into an asset.

2.9 POLITICAL AWARENESS

Alliances within the host country and even within the government can elevate an organization's position and help avoid or manage risk. This may be risky in itself if the faction or government they have aligned themselves with falls into disfavor. But it does constitute one method of active management of risk. Building long-term relationships, for example, with key decision makers in key areas can help organizations to overcome challenges and remain at the forefront of emerging opportunities.

Managing community relations is another core activity for experienced organizations that operate in developing nations. Often one of the most volatile risk parameters is the civil unrest that can escalate virtually unchecked if community expectations for sharing in the wealth of a project are not managed and met. A consistent process of engagement and communication with community leaders, as well as investment in services such as schools and medical clinics, has paid ongoing dividends for many organizations. In many cases, these relatively simple arrangements provide the goodwill that has made the difference between being able to operate or having to close shop.

Getting a sense of where in the world is the best place to expand requires significant analysis and is no easy task; however, a many organizations can assist in this area. Insurers, bankers, and international risk-management consulting houses regularly publish reviews of the political and economic risks that face corporations doing business globally. This information is often available for free online or can be purchased as part of a subscription service, which can provide an update on issues such as regional government interference, legal and regulatory issues, terrorism and war, currency, and credit risk.

Assessing current levels of risk is one thing, however. Currency devaluations, failed economic plans, regulatory changes, coups, and other national financial shocks are notoriously difficult to predict and may have disastrous consequences for global operators.

In 2001, the U.S. Department of Defense allocated funding for the development of an information futures market. Based on geopolitical data for eight countries in the Middle East, these futures were designed to aggregate better quality information for the government's war against terrorism. Known as the Policy Analysis Market (PAM), the electronic forum would have allowed people inside and outside government to express opinions about events unfolding in the Middle East that relate to military activity, political stability, economic activity, or U.S. policies. Essentially a plan for a web-based futures trading forum to gather expert opinions about possible future terrorist activity, the fledgling research project was canceled 2 days after its public release when a firestorm of criticism charged that traders could profit on others' misfortune.

In lieu of PAM or something like it, managing geopolitical risk requires a multidisciplinary team to identify risks accurately and comprehensively with a risk-informed approach to decision making. Identifying and understanding the organization's most volatile risk parameter and then monitoring it constantly is crucial. For a bank, it might be reputation; for a mine site, the most volatile risk might be an environmental incident. It will be different for each circumstance, but it is essential to know in advance what it is and have a management plan with elements such as contingency plans, media plans and evacuation plans, and so on tested and ready to go.

2.10 RISK VERSUS REWARD

Developments in the evolving security environment will continue to influence directly the course and pattern of multinational business, but it is only one of the many risk exposures that global business faces. The world is increasingly less safe leading to an increased cost of doing business, which demands a higher risk premium.

It is axiomatic that investments in developed countries are less risky than in developing countries. But that should not obscure the fact that business in the developed world has its failures. Many of these failures are large and cause serious dislocations with Pan Am, Barings Bank, and Enron, just to name a few. Generally, domestic organizations are assumed (often wrongly) to have better knowledge and capacity to cope with risks in their own countries than foreign organizations. The latter are often covered or protected through various types of insurance, and invariably these organizations have more resources and recourse options to deal with emerging issues than domestic investors.

In its semiannual *Global Financial Stability Report* on September 15, 2004, the International Monetary Fund (IMF) stated that robust global growth and risk diversification have helped world markets to gain significant resilience. In an increasingly globalized market, however, the potential for global equity market collapses, the increasing role of a few powerful nations in global trade, and market imbalances can have a significantly greater impact on emerging markets.

2.11 SUMMARY OF KEY POINTS

In the past few decades, the security risk environment has become more complex, in terms of both the number of near-term, tangible threats and the mid-to-long-term, less tangible threats likely to emerge from the conjunction of many driving forces in the natural environment. This security environment will continue to evolve and challenge all of us to understand and manage existing, expected, and other yet unknown risks.

SRMBOK has been designed as a flexible platform to assist security practitioners, managers, politicians, and society in general to continue to meet risks from a variety of sources, including:

- Traditional threats such as terrorism and crime
- Globalization and interdependence

Table 2.1 Changing paradigms that affect security risk management

Criteria	Old Paradigm	New Paradigm	21st Century Paradigm
	Industrial Age	Information Age	Networked Age
Threat source/ actor intent	State versus state	State versus state + state versus violent nonstate actors	Asymmetric
Threat source/ actor capabilities	Mobilized national capabilities	Standing national capabilities	Diffused and uncontrolled multidimensional capabilities
Level of social and technological change	Stability	Change	Constant flux
Exercise of power	Control	Empowerment	Governed
Market	Competition	Collaboration	"Co-opetition"
Focus of organization	Things	People and relationships	Adaptive
Social and organizational characteristics	Uniformity	Diversity	Fit for purpose
Organizational assets of value	Physical products (such as equipment or stores)	People, physical products, and information	People, physical products, and intellectual capital
Security governance arrangements	Conformance	Passive and centered on compliance	Active board involvement centered on assurance
Security planning arrangements	Best-case scenario	Worst-case scenario	Most credible worst-case scenario
Security response arrangements	Replace	Recover	Resilient
Communication arrangements	One-way dialog (communicating to stakeholders)	Two-way dialog (communicating with stakeholders)	Multifaceted and interconnected

- Increasing reliance on information and related technologies
- Regulation and compliance issues
- Transnational and extrajurisdictional risks

The fundamental paradigm shift from asset protection to organizational resilience with capabilities as the key driver will shape the security environment significantly over coming decades (Table 2.1). Organizations that wish to enhance their performance will need to understand and successfully integrate Security Risk Management within routine planning and operations to become a fundamental part of managers' and community leaders' tool bag, as much as budget management, communication, or decision-making skills.

Security
Governance | 3

3.1 INTRODUCTION

Boards or their equivalent structures at the head of an organization need to ensure that they have sufficient oversight and knowledge of the respective elements of the organization's Security Risk Management framework to ensure that duty-of-care obligations are met.

Providing strategic direction for an organization requires senior managers and leaders to understand what drives the creation of value and what destroys it. This in turn means that the pursuit of opportunities must entail comprehension of the risks to take and the risks to avoid. Risk exposures are becoming greater and more complex, diverse, and dynamic. Changes in technology, communications, transportation, global financial networks, and the rate of change mean that most organizations now operate in an entirely different environment from just 10 years ago.[9]

Security Risk Management is an integral part of sound risk-management practice, and the fallout from unseen events can have wide-ranging effects on organizations and communities. The ability to understand

and manage security risks as part of a holistic management system provides not just sound protective systems but can be the foundation for critical competitive advantage for many organizations and agencies.

Security governance deals with the processes and management systems within which an organization operates. The people, policies, and processes that provide this framework need to offer managers sufficient guidance to ensure that the responsible persons are both held to account and can make decisions and take actions to optimize outcomes within their respective areas of responsibility.

3.2 WHAT IS SECURITY GOVERNANCE?

Security Risk Management and security governance, although interdependent, are not the same thing. Security governance requires the design and application of a collective of management systems and frameworks that can assist organizations to ensure that all security functions are designed, implemented, and operating effectively.

Security governance starts from the top down and sets the scene for a culture of accountability that shapes and empowers responsible and appropriate SRM practices. Security management systems establish policies, processes, and related controls within and subservient to the security governance framework. The implementation and maintenance of those security controls becomes the responsibility of security operations executives and line managers.

3.3 DUTY OF CARE

Security governance principles are based on the concept that we have a duty of care to those around us, those under our care, and to various stakeholders. Whether this is to protect those persons from harm, to protect their assets, or simply to show good stewardship, governance frameworks should be developed in such a way as to reflect this fundamental principle.

Most executives are bound by legislation and organizational policies to provide a safe and healthy work environment. Directors and officeholders of corporations, nongovernment organizations, and government agencies face liability to meet duty-of-care obligations for the safety and security of their personnel. This duty of care to stakeholders is reflected in corporations' law, compliance regulations such as Sarbanes–Oxley, transnational legislations such as the U.S. Foreign Corrupt Practices Act, and occupational heath and safety legislation across most jurisdictions.

Regulators are becoming increasingly comfortable with applying legislation more broadly, whereas shareholders are also demanding greater accountability from private organizations. Society's views are also reflected in many areas, not least of all in the actions of legislators and the judiciary.

> *The degree of emphasis society places on duty-of-care obligations can be inferred from an Australian NSW Supreme Court of Appeal judgment in which the court awarded $571,362 in damages to a sales assistant who was assaulted by a thief when visiting a client in Port Moresby. The court found that the employer had been negligent in its duty of care when it provided inadequate security awareness training regarding conditions in Papua New Guinea and how to deal with them.*
>
> *(Pacific Access Pty Limited v Davies, 2001).*

Additionally, the fact that the incident occurred in Papua New Guinea yet the legal action was in Australia highlights the multijurisdictional nature of duty-of-care obligations, as well as the societal expectations regarding the protection of our people and assets.

Duty of care is, of course, not limited to statutory obligations. All organizations are accountable ultimately to one or more stakeholders, whether they be shareholders, taxpayers, or individuals. The duty of care is often outlined, albeit indirectly, in organizational objectives and internal policies. Supporting these objectives in a business resilience framework is a key objective of Security Risk Management.

Duty-of-care obligations also extend to a responsibility to protect and enhance shareholder value. Part of this duty includes providing security management systems and governance that enhance the capability of the organization and contribute to certainty of desired outcomes. This area is often difficult to quantify or assess, although it is self-evident that a major security breach will have an adverse impact on shareholder value. What is less obvious is how to assess the value of a catastrophic impact. Research by Knight and Pretty examined 15 man-made disasters that had happened to public companies since 1980, with total financial losses of around USD$19 billion.[10] The study found that the share price of any corporation suffering a disaster falls by around 5% to 8% within the first few days following the disaster. Typically, the recovery of the share price then depends on how well the recovery is effected. Knight and Pretty found that firms suffering catastrophes fall into two relatively distinct groups—recoverers and nonrecoverers:

- The recoverers regain the confidence of investors by rapidly taking control and reestablishing their operational capability. Their share price not only recovers the initial loss but also may increase within around 100 days by 10–15% compared with the preincident share price.
- The nonrecoverers drift at the lower share price before settling at a price around 15% below the preincident price.

Interestingly, whether the losses were fully covered by insurance does not seem to have much influence.

Although it may be tempting to believe that influencing the downstream consequences of major incidents is beyond the abilities of most organizations, the study suggests otherwise. If a company communicates well with shareholders, and investors view the event as well managed, then the impact on organizational value seems to be generally positive. For example, Knight and Pretty observed that when the first Tylenol tampering incident occurred in 1982, Johnson & Johnson were unprepared and had no plan in place.[c] It subsequently suffered a 10% decline in market capitalization by 50 days after the event, and market capitalization declined 18% after 180 days. By contrast, a second Tylenol tampering incident that affected the same company in 1986 occurred at a time when Johnson & Johnson had a plan in place that it implemented effectively. The key to the plan was the participation of senior management as public spokespersons to manage perceptions and win back the trust of the public. As a result, 50 days after the event, the market value of the company was 8% higher than before the incident, and after 180 days, it had risen by 11%.

> The learning point from this is that managing intangibles, such as reputation, perceived risk, and actual risk, requires a plan and the involvement of all levels of an organization. Knight and Pretty noted in their report that, "Although all catastrophes have an initial negative impact on value, paradoxically they offer an opportunity for management to demonstrate their talent in dealing with difficult circumstances."[10]

3.4 RESILIENCE

> A resilient organization is one that can achieve its core objectives, even in the face of adversity. It enables organizations to adapt and grow regardless of the exigencies, events, and risks within their operating environment.
>
> The capacity for resilience lies in the culture, attitude, and values of an organization. In the modern world, resilience is less about assets, organizational functions, or even delivery of product or services than it is about sustaining a desired capability. The concept of resilience is focused on securing organizational vision and objectives rather than loss prevention or rebuilding to pre-event conditions.

---

[c]An employee or former employee of Johnson & Johnson injected cyanide into Tylenol (paracetamol) pain-relieving capsules. Seven people died, and 31 million bottles of capsules were recalled.

3.4.1 What is Resilience?

"…it is not the strongest of the species that survives, nor the most intelligent that survives. It is the one that is the most adaptable to change."[d]

Resilience is the ability of an organization, individual, or community to minimize the harmful or deleterious consequences of disruptive events and to use the event as a trigger to strengthen and develop. The key here is the ability of the organization to do more than return to the previous level of productivity but to learn, recover, and exceed the pre-event level.

The event may have caused the loss of life and irreparably damaged or destroyed critical infrastructure, property, equipment, heirlooms, and artifacts. Examples of such events include the World Trade Center attack of September 11, 2001 (commonly referred to as 9/11), Hurricane Katrina in 2005, or the recent subprime economic crisis. Importantly, disruptive events may be of any scale or magnitude to require resilience, such as structural review, organizational downsizing, business merger, and car accidents. Each of these examples requires an individual, organization, or community to adopt or use a resilient outlook to restore stability and progress.

Resilience, then, is less about creating hardened structures and rigid processes or relying on standard procedures and more about developing a flexible, responsive, and adaptable way of thinking, behaving, and dealing with the impact of change within both the external and the internal environment.

3.4.2 Individuals, Organizations, and Communities

Individuals

The first noted work on individual resilience derives from Manfred Blueler's investigations into schizophrenia, poverty, physical illness, and trauma.[11] In his ground-breaking study, Blueler observed that almost 75% of the children of the mentally ill patients remained mentally sound or invulnerable despite their inherent disadvantages. The developmental psychopathologic studies of Garmezy also revealed that resilience derived from an incongruity or paradox; many children who experience considerable extreme stressors overcome hardship and also "exhibit behavioral adaptation and manifest competence."[12] Essentially, these children had developed the capacity to think, feel, and behave in ways that enabled them to offset, overcome, and grow despite their environmental hardships. Other examples of individual resilience may include Nelson Mandela, Helen Keller, and Michael Milton; all demonstrated the capacity to overcome significant challenges to redefine themselves constantly and achieve their potential.

Organizations

Building resilience in organizations or developing organizational resilience requires the consideration of areas such as enterprise risk management, business

---

[d]Attributed to Charles Darwin.

continuity management, security, occupational health and safety, and human resources. An integrated response to emerging or sudden events requires these business units to prepare their people, processes, and platforms for unexpected eventualities. Gary Hamel and Liisa Valikangas[13] conducted some of the initial research into resilience within organizations. They outlined that resilience was about "having the capacity to change before the case for change becomes desperately obvious."[14] Achieving this capacity requires the organization to respond to four key challenges:

- Cognitive challenge—the ability to be aware of the environment and to think freely
- Strategic challenge—the development of alternatives
- Political challenge—the flexibility to respond and divert resources to new experiments
- Ideological challenge—a capacity to embrace renewal, a cultural mindset

Regardless of the general strategy, organizational culture is a major determinant of resilience. Research from high-reliability organizations (HROs) suggests that a commitment to resilience is one of a handful of key determinants of an organization's ability to contain or survive unexpected events.[e] As such, it is worth considering that we should treat investments in culture as an investment in resilience.[15]

Examples of resilient organizations include:

- Wal-Mart with its data management systems that, post Hurricane Katrina, was able to bring 66% of its stores in the affected region back into operation with 48 hours, and 93% within 7 days. The company used its proprietary systems to start planning alternative routes and emergency staging areas—even while Katrina was still a tropical depression in the Atlantic Ocean. An automated inventory management system created visibility into the location of needed resources. And, because every truck is equipped with on-board computer technologies, shipments could be redirected at any time.
- Sandler O'Neill, is a New York City-based relationships banking firm that was devastated by 9/11, including the loss of 67 of their 180 employees. Within 1 year, Sandler had recovered and rebuilt with record profits and new lines of business, all while managing the grief of families and surviving staff.

---

[e]HROs constitute a group of closely studied organizations that include among others power grid despatching centers, air traffic control systems, nuclear aircraft carriers, nuclear power plants, hospital emergency departments, and hostage negotiation teams. These organizations rarely fail despite working in abundantly complex and demanding high-pressure environments in which failure could be catastrophic.

Communities

Weaving the Net; Promoting Mental Health and Wellness Through Resilient Communities[16] considers how resilience develops in a range of communities.[f] The report outlined several factors that contributed to the development of wellness and resilience within these communities, which included the ability to build on trust, engagement, civic leadership, and diversity. Community resilience also implies the capacity to "disaster proof" or future proof geographically based communities. The focus on resilience in communities is sustainability and survivability from natural or ecological threats, demographic shifts, and political interference.

3.4.3 The Concept of Resilience

The concept of resilience model[17] enables each unit (individual, organization, and community) to address relevant needs and to develop their level of resilience. Each unit should consider the cognitive, emotional, and physical aspects of resilience (Figure 3.1).

Cognitive resilience is the ability to use the "head" to create a staunch acceptance of reality. Our cognitive dialog plays an important role in our creation of reality. As Buddha said, "with our thoughts we create the world."

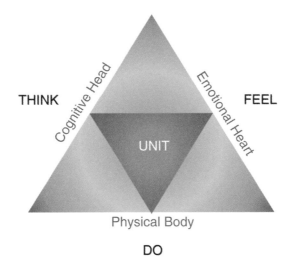

FIGURE 3.1 Components of resilience

---

[f]A community, in this instance, is a group of people who live in a similar geographical place. A broader definition identifies that a community may also be people with shared interests, ideas, and perhaps ideals, such as the "international community," the scientific community. Essentially, a community provides a forum for the development of interdependence and the fulfillment of individual need.

Individuals may often create thoughts that increase fears and worries that erode their ability to cope in stressful situations. Conversely, individuals also have the ability to create thoughts that increase our ability to cope with stressful events. On an organizational or community level, groups of people can shy away from facing the realities of problems, such as mental illness, and often succumb to "group think" in which a problem is ignored until it becomes critical and compromises the unit's ability to cope. For all units, understanding the power of perceptions and minimizing the gap between our view of the behavior of others and their intention generates a fuller picture of reality.

Emotional resilience is the ability to use the "heart" to create a belief that life is meaningful. Our emotions give us the passion and the desire to progress. Indeed, to paraphrase Plato, emotion is one of the main drivers for human behavior.

On an individual level, the ability to recognize, comprehend, and demonstrate an understanding of your own and others' emotions enables people to derive a better perception of the environment. On an organizational and community level, being able to identify the feeling, vibe, mode, or climate within the workplace or society enables people to perform to their potential.

Physical resilience is the ability to use the "body" to improvise, adapt, and move forward to a better future. Virgil said that "the greatest wealth is health," which is true for both body and mind. Physical resilience is about uniting positive energy and thoughts with physical persistence.

On an individual level, the motivation and commitment to improving your own physical health contributes to building personal resilience. On an organizational and community level, a commitment to health and well-being provides all people with the opportunity to flourish and fulfill their potential.

3.4.4 Building Resilience

Building resilience in communities and organizations requires:

- Commitment to excellence
- Situational awareness
- Management of keystone vulnerabilities
- Adaptive capacity within a complex, dynamic, and interdependent environment
- Desire to focus on potential instead of on process

Resilient organizations do not fear failure but embrace the opportunity provided to learn and transform. As Confucius points out, "Our greatest glory is not in never falling, but in rising every time we fall." Resilient organizations adapt readily to disruptions, threats, and challenges because their responses are automatic, spontaneous, and flexible just like the body's autonomic systems, which efficiently and effectively adjust to change such as increasing your heart rate to run. See Figure 3.2.[20]

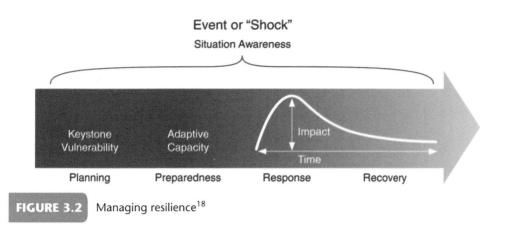

FIGURE 3.2 Managing resilience[18]

An instructive example of resilience in action is that of HROs such as nuclear power plants, aircraft carriers, and air traffic control. According to Rochlin, these institutions are notable because "these organizations have not just failed to fail; they have actively managed to avoid failures in an environment rich with the potential for error."[19] That ability to reduce actively and reliably the chances of mistakes occurring, rather than to avoid the hazards, has been the distinguishing hallmark of most HROs. These experiences offer lessons for the application of Security Risk Management at the enterprise level. Work by Karl Weick and Kathleen Sutcliffe[22] suggests that five key elements embedded in the culture of HROs contribute to a state of mindfulness:

- Preoccupation with failure
- Reluctance to simplify interpretations
- Sensitivity to operations
- Commitment to resilience
- Deference to expertise

Each of these is discussed in more detail below.

Preoccupation with Failure

HROs celebrate their successes, but Weick also notes that "a chronic worry in HROs is that analytic error is embedded in ongoing activities and that unexpected failure modes and limitations of foresight may amplify those analytic errors."[15] As a result, HROs regularly check and recheck processes and systems with a view to identify weak points and celebrate those occasions when weak points are found.

Reluctance to Simplify Interpretations.

Most organizations are happy to handle complex issues by simplifying them and categorizing them, thus ignoring certain aspects. HROs, however, take nothing for granted and support cultures that attempt to suppress simplification because it limits their ability to envision all possible undesirable effects as well as the precautions necessary to avoid these effects. HROs pay attention to detail and actively seek to know what they do not know. They endeavor to uncover those issues that might disconfirm their intuitions, despite being unpleasant, uncertain, or disputed. Skepticism is also deemed necessary to counteract the complacency that many typical organizational management systems foster.

Sensitivity to Operations

Weick describes sensitivity to operations as pointing to "an ongoing concern with the unexpected. Unexpected events usually originate in latent failures which are loopholes in the system's defenses, barriers and safeguards whose potential existed for some time prior to the onset of the accident sequence, though usually without any obvious bad effect."[15] Management focus at all levels to managing normal operations offers opportunities to learn about deficiencies that could signal the development of undesirable or unexpected events before they become an incident. HROs recognize each potential near-miss or out-of-course event as offering a window on the health of the system.

Commitment to Resilience

HROs develop capabilities to detect, contain, and return from those inevitable errors that are a part of an indeterminate world. The hallmark of an HRO is that incidents do not disable it. Resilience involves a process of improvising workarounds that keep the system functioning and of keeping errors small in the first place.

Deference to Expertise

HROs put a premium on personnel with deep experience, skills of recombination, and training. They cultivate diversity, not just because it helps them notice more in complex environments, but also because rigid hierarchies have their own special vulnerability to error. As highlighted by the work of James Reason and HFACs, errors at higher levels tend to pick up and combine with errors at lower levels, exposing an organization to further escalation.

HROs consciously evoke a fundamental principle of Security Risk Management—risk should be managed at the point at which it occurs. This is where the expertise and experience should reside to make the required decisions quickly and correctly, regardless of position or title.

3.4.4.2 Other Lessons from HROs. Other lessons from HROs include the strong support and reward for reporting of errors based on recognition that the value of remaining fully informed and aware far outweighs whatever satisfaction that might be gained from identifying and punishing an individual.

3.4.4.3 Success Breeds its Own Failure—The Icarus Paradox. On the occasions when Security Risk Management systems fail, it is often not because of a lack of tools, will, or imagination to mitigate risk. Rather, it is often because our perceptions of the threat have failed us. Many experiments have shown that people who succeed in tasks are less able to change their approaches even after circumstances change.

Starbuck and Milliken[20] in their analysis of the Challenger shuttle disaster noted: "Success breeds confidence and fantasy. When an organization succeeds, its managers usually attribute success to themselves or at least to their organization, rather than to luck. The organization's members grow more confident of their own abilities, of their manager's skills, and of their organization's existing programs and procedures. They trust the procedures to keep them appraised of developing problems, in the belief that these procedures focus on the most important events and ignore the least significant ones." This level of complacency is a breeding ground for inadequate or ineffective organizational Security Risk Management.

In other words, these organizations run organically, automatically, and autonomically, like the human body. Internally, they are committed to resilience and have resilience champions at every level. They anticipate change and challenge and actively work to learn from these opportunities. Such organizations have a strong sense of purpose, understand the expectations and needs of their stakeholders, engage diverse teams, devolve leadership, and unify all relevant groups and individuals as a team in times of adversity.

For individuals, organizations, and communities to become resilient, it is useful to paraphrase Aristotle and remember we are what we repeatedly do: Resilience then is not an act but a habit.[21]

> *Resilience trumps protection: Security is often perceived as a protective, even defensive, posture. But Maginot lines are inherently flawed: Fences and firewalls can always be breached. Rather, the focus should be on security risk management and resilience, not on security and protection. Resilience—the capability to anticipate risk, limit impact, and bounce back rapidly—is the ultimate objective of both economic security and organizational competitiveness.*

3.5 SECURITY CULTURE

> *"Security culture is the logical result of a well-driven security awareness program. Once people become aware of threats it is in their nature to react to it. Motivated people want to solve a problem if they feel concerned about it."*[22]

Security culture is not of course an objective in itself but rather state of mind and "the way things are done around here" which supports the achievement of broader objectives. Implementing or even defining a security culture that will do this is no simple task and relies on many elements to shape bahaviors, attitudes, and trust.

One insight to what makes a high-performing security culture might come from Human Factors researcher James Reason, who has over many years developed a detailed and persuasive argument that a safety culture is an informed culture.[23] Given the similarities between safety and security, we should consider the idea that a high-performing security culture is also equally an informed culture. Adapting Reason's work in this area leads us to suggest that an informed security culture constitutes one in which those who manage, operate, and apply the security system have current knowledge about the human, technical, organizational, and environmental factors that determine the effectiveness of that system as a whole.

Reason also argues that it takes four main subcultures to assure an informed culture:[24]

> *"Assumptions, values and artifacts must line up consistently around the issues of:*
>
> *(1) what gets reported when people make errors or experience near misses (reporting culture);*
>
> *(2) how many people apportion blame when something goes wrong (just culture);*
>
> *(3) how readily people can adapt to sudden and radical increments in pressure, pacing, and intensity (flexible culture); and*
>
> *(4) how adequately people can convert the lessons that they have learned into reconfiguration of assumptions, frameworks and action (learning culture).*
>
> *All four are necessary for people to be informed and safe."*

3.6 GOVERNANCE FRAMEWORKS

Effective risk management, including security risks, is a cornerstone of sound governance. A key area of SRMBOK focus is the development of agreed models and governance arrangements that can provide core guidance to practitioners and responsible executives alike.

Corporate management and boards have historically viewed governance, risk management, and compliance (GRC) as discretely managed and separate activities. More often than not these activities are coordinated from many separate operational areas across the organization with no single point of ownership, control, or accountability. This approach can result in reporting and communication gaps as well as redundancies and confusion. As stakeholder demands for increased integrity climb, these gaps can sharply and negatively impact corporate value. New definitions, requirements, and standards are emerging from internal and external sources, which forces boards and managers to rethink the roles, responsibilities, and relationships of discrete GRC activities.[25]

Essentially, corporate governance is a guidance system composed of standard management practices that operate within a governance framework designed to suit the organization. These practices are essentially common management tools drawn together into a logical, interrelated system focused on achieving results. They can be universally applied to any organization irrespective of their size or statutory and regulatory environments.

Although much has been written about governance and several excellent general compliance frameworks already exist, such as the GRC framework shown in Figure 3.3, the unique elements of Security Risk Management require some specific guidance to assist boards and executive teams with self-assessment and strategic applications of SRM-related governance frameworks.

At the core of governance is the requirement for executive management to ensure that they have:

- Sufficient expertise among their ranks to understand and manage adequately the organization's security exposures

- An understanding of the relationship among corporate governance, risk management, controls, strategies, and continuous improvement

- A desire to obtain value and improved performance from governance, risk, and compliance.

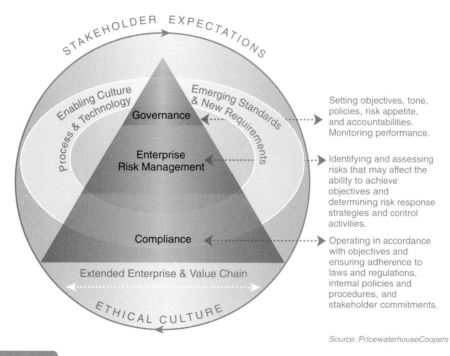

Source: PricewaterhouseCoopers

FIGURE 3.3 Integrating governance, risk, and compliance

This requires executive management to ensure that the following attributes are in place (see Figure 3.4):

- Organizational values, ethics, and behavioral **expectations are known,** clearly communicated, and alive in the organization
- Business strategy and **objectives are understood** and the organization's people, processes, and technology are aligned to support the achievement of strategic objectives
- **Risk appetites** and tolerances within the business units **are appropriate** and aligned with the expectation of corporate leadership and stakeholders.
- **Key threats and risks have been identified,** assessed, and are being actively treated
- Adequate culture, process, and technology controls are in place to ensure **performance and reporting expectations are met**
- **Information reported** to management, the board, and stakeholders **is accurate reliable, timely, and complete**
- **Compliance and assurance expectations are identified** and effectively communicated, and actions are taken in a timely manner

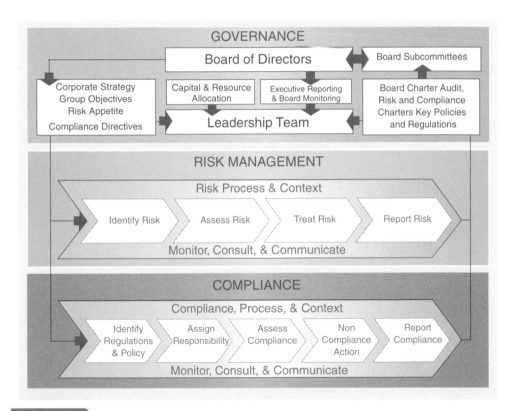

FIGURE 3.4 A sample governance, risk, and compliance operating model

- **The right operating model** is in place to drive sustainable performance and realize stakeholder value

The challenges for all senior management teams in achieving truly effective governance are to:

- Effectively communicate the policies, strategies, and principles of operation not only to the executive but also to every operational layer of the corporation
- Effectively monitor operational performance and allocate resources accordingly
- Be able to measure and monitor compliance with internal and external policies and regulation
- Achieve and to be observed to have achieved genuine transparency of operation in the marketplace
- Establish that the information presented in all corporate disclosure is based on fact
- Establish reasonable comfort in the minds of the shareholders and public that compliance obligations are being met

> *SRMBOK addresses this in more detail in the Guide to SRMBOK on Governance, although there is a range of operational-level templates provided in Section 15 to assist organizations in managing day-to-day arrangements.*

3.7 INCIDENT MANAGEMENT AND REPORTING

Reporting, analysis, and data management associated with security incidents are addressed in some detail in the Guide to SRMBOK on Incident Management and Reporting, with a particular focus on the actionability of information both within the actual report and from trends, identified through analysis of incidents. Categorization and analysis of incident reports in a manner consistent with other organizational standards is essential to maximize the value of information received as well as the fundamentals of ensuring quality and timely reports.

Organizational culture plays a key role in incident reporting. Security cultures are highly dependent on the knowledge gained from rare incidents, mistakes, and near-misses. Near-misses in particular are free lessons or windows into the health of the system. The key element here is that the organizational culture has to support a no-blame environment where people feel safe to report near-misses or minor events that might otherwise go unnoticed.

Incident reporting frameworks can be lead indicators for proactive security measures rather than simply lag indicators of past problems. Near-miss and hazard reporting can be the key drivers of ongoing system improvement rather than the traditional approach, which requires major periodic investments of time and resources immediately following an event. Near-miss and hazard reporting also provides an opportunity to gain insights in the system when it fails, not in the presence of attackers but more typically when it fails benignly in the presence of the system users, e.g., staff, customers, and so on.

Investigation and follow-up of security reports are slightly different from other environments. The key challenges for the security investigation are:

- Whether robust criteria exist in that organization to assess potentially abstract or unknown attack vectors and consequential failures
- The requirement to do so while maintaining need-to-know principles at all levels from safe combinations all the way up to international strategy

3.8 SUMMARY OF KEY POINTS

Security governance deals with the processes and management systems within which an organization operates. The people, policies, and processes that provide this framework need to provide managers with sufficient guidance to ensure that the accountable persons are:

- Held to account
- Able to make decisions and take actions to optimize outcomes within their respective areas of responsibility

Boards or their equivalent structures at the head of an organization need to ensure that they have sufficient oversight and knowledge of the respective elements of the organization's Security Risk Management framework to ensure that duty-of-care obligations are met.

SRMBOK Framework 4

This chapter provides a high-level overview of some concepts that are discussed in more detail in the following chapters. It illustrates the relationship of various elements to each other and some high-level distinctions in terminology, such as the differences among assets, practice areas, and activity areas.

No single item in any given framework is a cure-all for security risks. This is true for any methodology or group of methodologies. Successful Security Risk Management is dependent on the following:

- Coordinated and effective application of security governance, knowledge areas, competency areas, practice areas, enablers, and assets
- Dedication, experience, aptitude, and capability of the security practitioner or manager who is accountable

The framework outlined in SRMBOK is intended not as a definitive treatise but as a record of an ongoing discussion as to what constitutes the better elements of accepted and evolving practice. The framework and elements outlined above are also intended to offer a common ground for a variety of methodologies to be compared, aligned, and used in concert.

In particular it is intended that these elements should support benchmarking and comparison regarding security assessments, security plans, and organizational SRM capability gaps.

Figure 4.1 shows the relationship between SRM knowledge areas (exposure, risk, resources, and quality) and SRM competency areas (business integration, functional design, application, assurance), and SRM integration.

FIGURE 4.1 Relationship of knowledge and competency to SRM

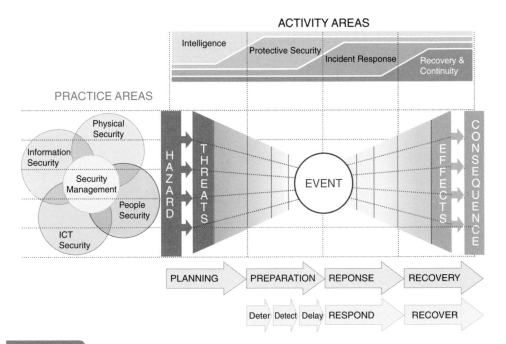

FIGURE 4.2 Integration of practice areas with activity areas and bow-tie

These concepts are explored in each of the respective chapters in more detail; however, they form key concepts of the SRMBOK integration process. Knowledge areas are those four areas in which all security practitioners must have sound knowledge of if they are to be effective. By contrast, practitioners need only be competent in any one of the four categories of competencies (from an organizational perspective).

Figure 4.2 illustrates some of the five core practice areas that security practitioners operate in and the relationship of activity areas (intelligence, protective security, emergency response, and business continuity) that security practitioners will be active in.

The combined interaction of elements illustrated in Figure 4.3 is one view of how organizations and communities implement security-in-depth to achieve resilience. Similarly, the model illustrates a type of Security Risk Management that incorporates the best elements of a range of risk and vulnerability management systems. It is sufficiently comprehensive that it can be applied (by advanced practitioners) to complex security environments; however, each of these models is intended to be fully scalable from back-of-envelope up to multinational exercises.

ORGANIZATIONAL/ENVIRONMENTAL SECURITY CONTEXT

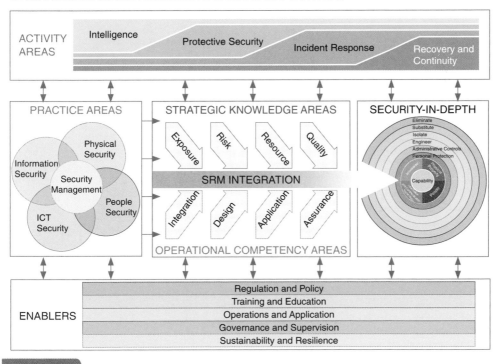

FIGURE 4.3 SRMBOK organizational resilience model

4.1 SRMBOK GUIDING PRINCIPLES

The principles outlined in the following table propose a baseline (minimum) standard at the broad operational, technical, and user levels. Organizations should assess security risks based on the nature of their business and on the information in their care, and the principles should be applied as required to protect their assets and ensure organizational resilience.

4.1.1 Principle 1—Commitment

The primary principle is management leadership and commitment. It is critical to have the leadership and commitment of management because they drive the process of integrating safe security and risk cultures into core business.

In providing leadership, senior management must commit to Security Risk Management and ensure that adequate human and financial resources are allocated. This will enable implementation and integration of Security Risk Management with other management systems. Senior management must also be willing to participate in an initial review of the organization's current position, as well as be involved in subsequent reviews. This will provide a clear picture of performance over time, including:

- Hot spots or business units that have higher numbers of security-related incidents
- Security and safety trends
- The effectiveness of methods used for risk assessment/control
- The identification of gaps in the system
- Overall compliance with legislative, regulatory, and operational requirements

4.1.2 Principle 2—Organization-wide Security and Risk Policies

Senior management should provide clear directions regarding the importance of security and risk management within their organization in the form of a commitment statement and security policy.

As part of this process, organizations should define and publish a set of clear guidelines for the classification of sensitive assets held, handled, created, or received according to sensitivity, confidentiality, and business importance based on their legislative, regulatory, and contractual obligations. To maintain a suitable level of protection for assets, organizations should identify and document major assets and processes, and they should assign responsibilities for the maintenance of their security.

Policies should be reviewed and evaluated in line with changes to environmental context, business processes, or security risks. These should then be communicated as appropriate to all staff, contractors, suppliers, and customers.

Policies should consist of a hierarchy of documents that express how the Security Risk Management system links with legislative and corporate objectives, assigned responsibilities, methodologies and guidelines/standards, as well as the organization's commitment to continuous improvement. This hierarchy of documentation is shown graphically as part of the wider contextual and regulatory framework (Figure 4.4):

4.1.3 Principle 3—Link Strategy, Planning, and Delivery

Organizations should outline how the policies and commitments are going to be met.

For example:

- Communicating the agency's requirements
- Undertaking security and SRM system training
- Completing annual security risk assessments to determine budget requirements

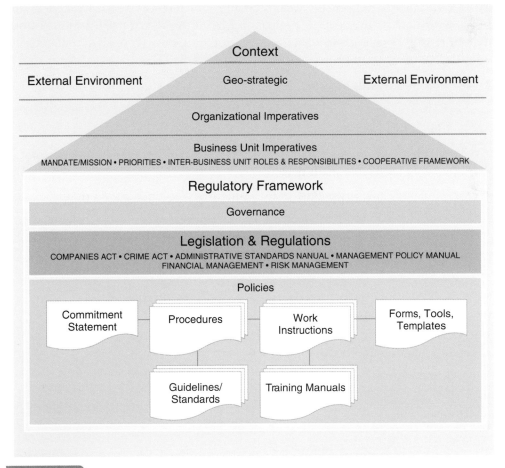

FIGURE 4.4 Security governance framework

- Monitoring and using threat assessments and intelligence received to define and update risk profiles
- Undertaking security incident reporting and analysis
- Allocating resources and providing requisite physical assets to mitigate risk to the as low as reasonably practical (ALARP) level
- Undertaking subsequent security risk reviews based on risk profiles
- Benchmarking our findings to measure effectiveness
- Reporting back to management on findings and the need to make adjustments

Ultimately, strategy in this context provides the nexus between what senior management requires to be done and how the different operational business units intend to carry it out.

All levels of staff will need to be made aware of security and safety risks. It is of paramount importance, therefore, that information about security risk is readily available so that management and staff can take responsibility for managing security risks. This means that training, education, and security awareness briefings should form a central part of all planning. Additionally, business unit managers will need to integrate their SRM activities with related elements of other corporate governance arrangements, including:

- Business continuity planning
- Emergency and crisis management
- Broader risk management systems

As part of planning for implementations, business managers will be required to map out and formally document:

- Details of their priorities, objectives, targets, and performance indicators
- Financial and human resources allocated to assist in achieving these objectives, including the allocation of responsibilities
- Communication mechanisms for informing staff of the implementation of, or improvements to, the management system
- Particulars of security or safety audit procedures currently in place, or to be implemented, in core business activities
- Activities necessary to bring the business unit to full compliance with all relevant legislation and policies
- The procedures that will allow for the regular monitoring and evaluation of the system

4.1.4 Principle 4—Establish and Manage to an Agreed Risk Threshold

Regardless of the business unit's functions or security concerns, the central messages surrounding Security Risk Management remain the same:

- **Do not accept unnecessary risk.** Unnecessary risk comes without a commensurate return in benefits or opportunities. The most logical options for accomplishing tasks are those that meet all business requirements with the least risk. Notwithstanding the acceptable risk threshold that may be appropriate for a task, risks should be treated wherever possible so that the residual risks are judged to be ALARP. The basis for the ALARP judgment is that the risk should be treated to the point where the cost of further treatment is excessive compared with the resulting reduction in risk, no further treatment is possible, or the risk is negligible. Options to mitigate the consequence of a risk are to be adopted wherever this can be reasonably achieved with the resources available.
- **Accept risk only when the benefits outweigh the cost.** Risk is judged to be tolerable if the importance and benefits of the task for the organization are of such magnitude that acceptance of the risks associated with the task is justified. Risks are therefore tolerated in the conduct of the activity, with the intent to reduce the risk to a negligible level if and when this becomes practicable.
- **Make risk decisions at the appropriate level.** A fundamental principle of the management system is that those accountable for the success or failure of the task must be included in the risk evaluation and decision process. However, they are required to elevate decisions to the next level in the chain of command where it is determined that available risk treatment options, in the immediate operational context, will not reduce the residual risk to an acceptable level.

4.1.5 Principle 5—People Security

People are the strongest and weakest links in Security Risk Management.

Organizations should minimize the risk of loss or misuse of assets by ensuring that security controls are incorporated into recruitment, supervision, and separation processes for all staff, contractors, suppliers, customers, and other individuals that may be able to access organizational assets.

Ongoing security awareness should be incorporated into organizational training programs to communicate responsibilities and disciplinary processes regarding the appropriate use of corporate information and systems.

4.1.6 Principle 6—Physical and Environmental Security

Security controls should be in place to protect the physical security of all assets.

The level of control implemented should minimize the risk of equipment or physical assets being rendered inoperable or inaccessible, or accessed or removed without appropriate authorization.

4.1.7 Principle 7—Operational Security Management

Security controls should be in place to safeguard all operations and systems.

Operational security controls should ensure that risks to information integrity, availability, and confidentiality are minimized in the operational environment, in online service delivery, or in exchanging information by any means in the internal or external information environment.

4.1.8 Principle 8—Business Continuity and Resilience

A managed process that includes documented plans should be in place to enable the operational environment to be restored or recovered in the event of a disaster or security failure.

Plans should include methods for reducing known risks to business continuity and identifying actions for the continuation of business activities in the event of unforeseen failures or disasters.

4.1.9 Principle 9—Test

Once the proposed system is in place, test, measure, and evaluate performance to enable the organization to monitor the effectiveness of the system and, where necessary, make adjustments to ensure a process of continuous improvement.

The types of testing and tools to be used are likely to vary based on what is being evaluated. For example, evaluating the usefulness of a security awareness training session may be done with a participant's "smile sheet," which obtains feedback on perceptions, including "Did they like it? Was the material relevant to their work? How could the session be improved?" Alternatively, when conducting a risk review in a location that had recently suffered a serious security incident, more detailed discovery and analysis will need to be undertaken by competent risk assessors.

Timings for scheduled test activities should be incorporated into the documentation developed by business unit managers as part of the planning component. Ultimately, though, all testing should be developed in an effort to determine whether:

- Listed objectives and scope have been met

- Agreed budgets—resources, capital, equipment—have not been exceeded

- Any specified added-value or quality requirements have been achieved

4.1.10 Principle 10—Measure and Review

During the planning component, procedures for measurement and review of the system should be developed.

These procedures should provide information on:

- Persons responsible for the monitoring and evaluation processes
- Systems developed for the measurement of performance, for example, a security management information system that records:
  - Number of reviews, incidents (by type and number), severity/consequences, and so on.

- Reasons why performance may be below the organization's targets and objectives (possibly through deficiencies in the system)
- Any instances of noncompliance with legislative/regulatory requirements
- Opportunities to improve performance through adjustment of the system
- Required changes and the effectiveness of any changes previously made
- The audit procedures and tools to be used, which will independently confirm gaps between the effectiveness of the current system and what would be considered the best practice system

For these reasons, it is also necessary to have a system that allows for both preventive and corrective action to be taken where required. Much progress in SRM has come as a result of reactive measures after an incident. Generally, these incidents are investigated to find out what happened and what can be done to control any risk of future exposure to the hazard. During any investigation, it is vital that corrective action be identified so that the incident does not recur, or if it does, then as a minimum, the appropriate measures will have been put in place to minimize any risk to the health or safety of staff involved.

4.1.11 Principle 11—Document Control

Organizations should establish, implement, and maintain procedures for controlling all relevant documents and data required by the Security Risk Management system.

This is required to ensure that:

- They can be readily located.
- They are periodically reviewed, revised as necessary, and approved for adequacy by competent and responsible personnel.
- Current versions of relevant documents and data are available at all locations where operations essential to the effective functioning of the management system are performed.
- Obsolete documents and data are promptly removed from all points of issue and points of use or otherwise assured against unintended use.
- Archival documents and data retained for legal or knowledge preservation purposes, or both, are suitably identified.

Documentation and data should be legible, dated (with dates of revision), readily identifiable, and maintained in an orderly manner for a specified period. Procedures and responsibilities should also be established and maintained concerning the creation, organization, and modification of the various types of documents and data and the agency will need to define a means for precluding the use of obsolete documents.

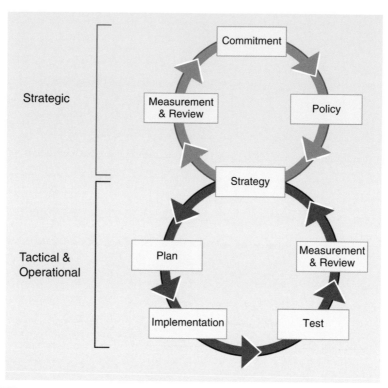

FIGURE 4.5 Inter-relationship of SRMBOK better practice principles

4.1.12 Principle 12—Assurance

Organizational security controls for all assets, processes, systems, and infrastructure should adhere to any legislative or regulatory obligations under which the organization operates.

The inter-relationship between these components is shown in Figure 4.5.

Practice Areas 5

5.1 INTRODUCTION

SRMBOK takes a practitioner-based approach to categorizing security areas based on practice areas (see Figure 5.1). This approach was developed following extensive consultation with industry and government and reflects the five key categories by which security professionals tend to categorize their involvement in the profession. The SRMBOK practice areas are as follows:

- Security management
- Physical security
- People security
- Information security
- Information and Community Technology (ICT) security

As illustrated in Figure 5.2, each of the practice areas shares areas of overlap with each other and with security management in particular.

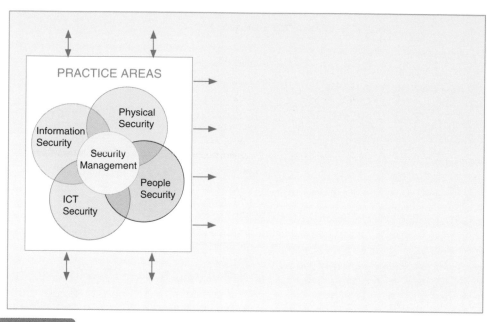

FIGURE 5.1 SRMBOK practice areas

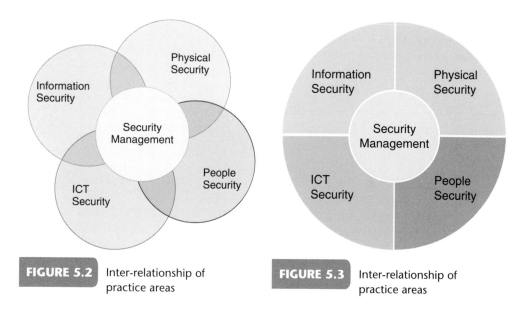

FIGURE 5.2 Inter-relationship of practice areas

FIGURE 5.3 Inter-relationship of practice areas

For greater clarity of illustration, SRMBOK also uses the graphic in Figure 5.3 to illustrate the relationship of each of the practice areas as inseparable elements of a Security Risk Management system.

Table 5.1 describes some of the key differentiators of the areas and the respective activities involved in each.

These practice areas were selected because most security professionals begin their careers in one of these areas. Some practitioners start their careers as protective

Table 5.1 Overview of security practice areas

Area	Description	Activities	Practitioners
Management	Conceptual, administrative management, and virtual SRM arrangements	Management and leadership Threat assessments Security management systems and frameworks Education and training Security objectives Policies, procedures, and standards Compliance/regulatory frameworks	Chief Security Officer (CSO) Security managers, advisers, and consultants Persons involved in: • Investigations • Fraud • Intelligence • Counterintelligence • Defense
Physical	Protection of physical assets as well as physical security measures designed to protect intangible assets or capabilities	Crime prevention through environmental design (CPTED) Design and implementation of procedures and physical controls for protection of facilities, property, capabilities, and physical aspects of ICT systems	Physical security advisers and consultants Guards, locksmiths, alarm and Closed Circuit Television (CCTV) installers, and so on
Information	Protection of information and IP from loss or compromise by human actors	Development and application of classification frameworks Protection of intellectual capital, organizational knowledge, classified or sensitive information, customer/supplier relations, financial relations, licensing, franchising and distribution channels, and reputation/brand	Information security advisers and consultants Chief Information Officers (CIO)

Area	Description	Activities	Practitioners
ICT	Protection of ICT systems and information stored in ICT systems from loss or compromise	Application of technology that is designed to secure information during collection, storage, retrieval, processing, analysis, and transmission	IT security advisers, cryptographers, ICT security architects, firewall specialists and related programmers
People	Controls for protection from security risks associated with people	Employment screening Security clearances Identity management Privacy Personal protective practices	Human resources professionals Security vetting officers Biometric security system installers

security specialists; however, most practitioners are promoted into management areas or pursue a broader consulting/advisory role after first establishing themselves in one of the other practice areas.

> *The hierarchy of controls concept, as outlined in the section on Strategic Knowledge Areas, provides guidance on how practice areas may be applied using the security-in-depth framework.*

5.2 SECURITY MANAGEMENT

5.2.1 What is Security Management?

Security management is the term used to apply to the development and application of conceptual practices that provide the framework for all areas of SRM to work both individually and more particularly as part of a greater whole.

It also provides a framework for the specialist SRM practice area but most importantly helps decision makers to match resources and risk treatments with identified threats.

Protective security also assists managers to promote an SRM culture within organizations.

This chapter examines protective security principles and provides practitioners with an operational appreciation for the implementation of protective security and SRM practices in organizations. Security management practices and protective security concepts provide the framework for asset protection and risk management processes applied under the other practice areas. It also outlines a skill set for practitioners who may pursue a career in SRM but who may not have commenced their careers in one of the specialist practice areas.

The purpose of protective security is to provide a conceptual framework and decision-making environment to integrate the physical, people, ICT, and information security (information security) practice areas. This integrative function enables organizations to develop a complete SRM strategy.

Security management is the broad mixture of application principles and concepts that are sometimes also known as protective security. This area comprises all elements of conceptual, virtual, or procedural asset protection, including:

- Risk management
- Threat assessments
- Intelligence
- Investigations
- Root cause analysis
- Administrative controls
- Governance arrangements

Security management is positioned centrally in Figure 5.3 because it influences each of the other practice areas. Each practice area is interdependent and overlaps; no single area is more important than any other.

The main focus of all areas of SRMBOK is predominantly on this application of protective security as a conceptual framework for security management. It should be noted that the term "security management" in this context does not refer only to the management of security or the activities of managers. It is focused on the management activities of all levels of an organization or on the management-related activities of an individual.

> *Management is defined as follows:* "The guidance and control of action required to execute a program"[26]
>
> (U.S. BUREAU OF JUSTICE ASSISTANCE)

5.2.2 Elements

Security management provides a framework for better practice in asset protection. Any organization, regardless of size, complexity, or industry, can implement SRM practices to secure key assets and to manage security-related risks. Typical activities and responsibilities that are part of security management include:

- Security Risk Management frameworks (SRMFs)
- Performance management and benchmarking
- Policy, procedures, and standards

- Threat identification and the use of intelligence
- Threat assessments
- Investigations
- Root cause analysis
- Design basis threat
- Asset and business impact identification
- Identification and protection of significant organizational infrastructure
- Security training
- Supply chain protection
- Business resilience
- Incident reporting
- Law enforcement presence and effectiveness
- Criminal trends
- Client base, including means and level of access as well as type and frequency of interaction
- Management support

5.2.3 Applying Security Management Practices

Any of the practice areas can operate independently; however, they can only realize their full benefits when integrated appropriately. ICT security technologies, such as firewalls, encryption devices, and controlled information access points, for example, although important, need to be integrated with a range of other information control technologies. Security measures such as secure containers, classified document registers, building or room specific access passes, and identification cards also contribute to the security of information. Personnel security processes, which include the vetting of those who access secure information, are similarly integral to an overall SRM plan.

5.2.4 Summary of Key Points

Security management is the term used to apply to the development and application of conceptual practices that provide the framework for all areas of SRM to work both individually and more particularly as part of a greater whole.

It also provides a framework for the specialist SRM practice area but most importantly helps decision makers to match resources and risk treatments with identified threats.

Protective security also assists managers to promote a SRM culture within organizations.

A number of templates are in provided in chapter 13 that have been designed to allow individuals to capture information pertinent to their own organizational context, including:

- Security risk registers
- Risk treatment forms
- An outline security plan
- A property selection and security planning checklist
- An example commitment statement to security and risk management
- A bomb threat checklist

5.3 PHYSICAL SECURITY

Scope

Although the traditional 3Gs (guns, guards, and gates) remain useful in physical security, they represent only a small proportion of physical security protective measures.

Physical security involves the physical protection of personnel, hardware, property, networks, and data from deliberate acts and events. These acts and events can include burglary, theft, vandalism, and terrorism and could cause loss or damage to an organization or individual.

Purpose

The purpose of a physical security system is to prevent altogether or reduce the likelihood of sabotage, theft, trespass, espionage, vandalism, or terrorism. A security system must provide the capability to detect, assess, communicate, delay, and respond to a suspected physical breach of security.

5.3.1 Physical Security and SRM

Treatments that relate to other SRM practice areas are often relevant to physical security issues, and comprehensive protective security plans should include a consideration of physical security.

Security safeguards should include:

- Access control systems[g]
- Executive protection and background investigations
- Security staff
- Integration with other physical safety issues that could potentially pose a threat to staff or others
- Building safety standards as well as construction and maintenance frameworks relevant to CPTED principles
- The installation of emergency response systems, including fire prevention and other incident response mechanisms and procedures

---

[g]Card systems, passes, and permits are considered to be part of people security.

5.3.2 Asset Identification in Physical Security Risk Management

The establishment of a physical security context is a useful first step in identifying assets that require protection. This context should include an analysis of the internal and external environment and the way in which this environment affects the security and operation of an organization. This analysis should include consideration of:

- Terrain (including natural barriers and natural security impediments)
- Physical attributes of assets, including lighting and proximity to other structures, parking, access, and thoroughfares
- Existing physical security measures
- Accessibility
- Population and demographics

5.3.3 Controls and Protective Barriers

The Oxford English Dictionary defines the term barrier as "an obstacle that prevents movement or access."

Physical barriers are one of the more visual and versatile elements of physical security. Fences, bollards, doors, and screens protect assets from a range of threats.

They can be used to:

- Define the perimeter of an asset
- Control and deny access
- Detect and deter unauthorized entry
- Delay intrusion

Barriers can be both natural and structural. Natural barriers should be identified in an initial asset appraisal and used if appropriate. Structural barriers should be placed not only to enhance physical security but also to act as a psychological deterrent to people that may contemplate an attack on the asset.

Barriers should enhance security and at the same time reduce the need for more costly human or technological security measures. Barriers should also increase the effectiveness of other measures, such as lighting, CCTV, and security guards.

The nature and appearance of a barrier should also complement the needs of an organization. Barbed-wire fencing may be an effective barrier in some situations, but it would be inappropriate for use in a shopping center. Barriers should be made from materials that can act as a deterrent against likely threats. Ballistic glass, fences covered by hedges, and security bollards to limit vehicular access are all commonly used by organizations concerned about the aesthetics of the asset being protected.

5.3.4 Design of Physical Security Measures—Access

Controlling access to an asset could be classed as the first component of a physical SRM plan. It should be noted that the emphasis is on controlling and managing access rather than on simply restricting or preventing access.

Physical access control can also refer to the ability of a ballistic projectile or blast wave to breach barriers. It is not possible to protect against blast waves of all magnitudes. It is, however, possible to modify the effect of a blast by deciding which areas will be harder or weaker, which can influence the impact and direction of a blast wave. For example, the walls of a car park may be designed to provide relatively little resistance to a blast. These walls may fail more quickly than the hardened windows of office areas, which means the shape and direction of a blast wave may be modified to reduce the likely impact on an asset.

5.3.5 Visibility and Sustainability

Unobstructed visibility of perimeter fencing and other barriers may enable potential intrusions or attacks against an asset to be detected. Lighting and light amplification technologies should:

- Enable security guards to observe activities in a given area without disclosing their presence to those who are being observed
- Be used in conjunction with other protective measures, such as fixed guard posts, foot patrols, fences, as well as other barriers and alarm systems
- Be directed outward to ensure that vision from within the asset is not impaired (this can include guards and other means such as CCTV)
- Silhouette intruders against a contrasting background
- Eliminate shadows

Security posts should be tactically placed to maximize both the field of vision of security guards and their deterrence factor. Although foliage can be used as a barrier, it should not provide a potential sanctuary to an intruder or impair the vision of guards or CCTV cameras.

All physical security assets require maintenance and sustenance. Guards and guard dogs require ongoing training, food, water, shelter, and protection. Cameras, lighting, and other electronic systems require power, and barriers require maintenance.

A lack of adequate maintenance or sustenance can reduce the effectiveness of security measures. Reserve power supplies or caches of spare protective equipment can help to maintain security in adverse conditions.

5.3.6 Protecting Mixed Access Areas

Mixed access areas are defined as areas within an organization or facility that may be accessed by members of the public and by personnel working with or for the organization. Organizations with mixed access areas include hospitals, defense establishments, casinos, prisons, and entertainment venues. At these organizations, members of the public may require access to administrative, client service, or entertainment areas, but stringent controls may apply to other areas, such as drug cabinets, cash stores, and dressing rooms. Mixed access areas necessitate sound planning to optimize personnel movement flows. Control of mixed access areas can be achieved through the use of CPTED, need-to-go, biometrics, and aids such as the red, amber, and green security planning/design methodology.

5.3.7 Restricted Access Group (RAG) Modeling

In most organizations three categories of access are appropriate:

- Restricted access areas for managers and members of staff (trusted individuals)
- Accompanied access areas where visitors and trusted individuals are permitted under controlled circumstances, such as under escort
- Group access areas where access is relatively uncontrolled, such as parks and other public areas

An example of this would be a hospital where:

- Group access areas include hospital grounds and public waiting areas
- Accompanied access areas include emergency treatment rooms

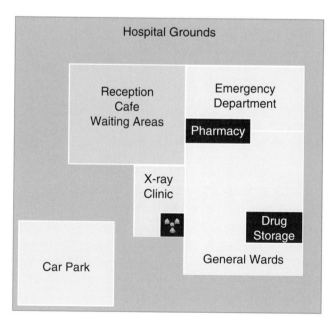

FIGURE 5.4 Example of RAG modeling

- Restricted access areas include the hospital pharmacy, where controlled substances are located

This model should be adapted to the needs of an organization. Hospital wards are normally group access areas during visiting hours, but they become accompanied access areas at other times.

A notional RAG model for a hospital is shown in Figure 5.4 with red, amber, and green shading for restricted, accompanied and group access areas respectively.

Simplicity and clarity are important features of the RAG system. This enables security managers to induct quickly or brief security and other staff, as well as security service providers, contractors, and management.

It is not important which colors are actually used, but rather that there is a shared understanding of how, where, and why access control measures have been applied.

5.4 PEOPLE SECURITY

People security has two main components. The first involves the protection of people, e.g., staff, family, society, and visitors, from harm. The second involves the protection of an organization or other people from threats to security that are most appropriately controlled by the interaction of people, i.e., vetting and personal protective practices. This embodies the concept of duty of care toward staff and visitors but recognizes that these groups can also pose a threat to security.

1. *Those elements of security associated with protection of humans (usually in groups).*

2. *Those elements of security where people are the key element in applying or breaching security.*

Legislative provisions regarding duty-of-care legislation stipulate that organizations actively contribute to the safety and security of the public, whereas the safety of employees and contractors is a key part of maintaining a productive workplace and retaining quality staff. Although elements of personal safety, such as travel safety and residential security practices, as distinct from physical security measures, engagement of contractors and security training are considered here, it should be emphasized that these are also relevant to other SRM practice areas.

The concept of people security derives from the understanding that people are central to an organization's internal and external operational security environments and to business continuity.

People security is an umbrella term that considers security issues such as socio-political issues, human security, recruitment, vetting, fraud control, coercion, and corruption, which are inherent in managing people as part of a comprehensive security program. The focus of this practice area is to apply measures at an organizational level, which can protect against security risks associated with staff, contractors, visitors, and the general population.

SRM principles apply to people security in a similar way to the other SRM practice areas. Often information and physical security treatments will apply to people security issues and comprehensive protective security plans often include a component of people security. Important subgroups within people security include:

- **Human security** refers to the protection of individuals.
- **Personnel security** involves the security-related management of employees and contractors, such as security clearances (vetting), employment screening, and ongoing assessment.
- **Identity security** (although closely linked to personnel security) is a distinct subset of people security because of the unique characteristics associated with this area. It addresses issues such as identity fraud, biometrics, privacy, and protection of individual financial, medical, and other sensitive information.
- **Personal protective practices** include those elements of physical, procedural, and conceptual activities, which an individual can address or be responsible for in the interests of their own personal security. Examples include close personal protection, travel, and residential security practices (as distinct from physical security measures).
- **Human factors** and behaviors will be the principle determinant of security outcomes in most situations. Effective SRM relies on the exercise of sound judgment on the part of management and staff (and to some extent, on visitors as well). Human factors have the potential to reinforce or undermine the SRM in organizations.

Each of these is discussed in detail in the following sections.

5.4.1 Human Security

Human security is defined as follows: "A relatively new concept, but one that is now widely used to describe the complex of interrelated threats associated with civil war, genocide and the displacement of populations. The distinction between human security and national security is an important one. While national security focuses on the defense of the state from external attack, human security is about protecting individuals and communities from any form of political violence."[27]

HUMAN SECURITY REPORT, 2005

In the SRMBOK, human security is considered as an outcome or a measure of the success of collective national, regional, and local SRM efforts.

5.4.2 Personnel Security

As a component of people security, personnel security is commonly defined as a process whereby only suitable people obtain and retain access to sensitive or security classified resources. Effective personnel security management imposes a series of responsibilities on all organizational staff, including the clearance subject, management, recruitment areas, and work colleagues. The granting of a security clearance is not the end of the personnel security management strategy. Security awareness and sound security management standards should be an integral part of an organization's everyday operations and management philosophy. Agencies should ensure that people who have access to security classified resources, and their managers, understand and accept their day-to-day responsibilities for managing the protection of the resources under their control.

When a person is appointed to a position of trust, an organization should determine whether the initial appointment checks provide enough assurance that the employee can be entrusted with sensitive information.

Screening does not, on its own, provide a guarantee of integrity and trustworthiness. Because individuals and their circumstances change, screening is only as good as the investigations done at the time, and an ongoing review or aftercare program should also be undertaken to ensure the screening process remains valid. Any new information or concerns that may affect an employee's reliability must be advised promptly to the appropriate authority.

Organizations need to be mindful of some sensitivities that may surround personnel security, which include screening and vetting. Organizations that seek to employ creative, open-minded, and inquisitive employees may not be able to do so if their screening process excludes people with the psychological makeup that is intrinsic to people that exhibit these qualities, such as big picture focus or dislike of rigid or hierarchical managerial frameworks. This may compromise an organization's ability to recruit people into important positions, potentially posing a greater risk to organizational effectiveness than the risk of employing what may seem to be an unsuitable employee.

Additionally, because of the costs associated with the screening process, it is better practice for organizations to define their positions of trust and conduct screening against personnel in accordance with these security requirements.

5.4.2.1 Employment Checking. When a person applies for a permanent staff position, the type of checks required would be determined by the sensitivity of the assets that they can access but as a minimum should include checking:

- Character referees
- The completeness and accuracy of the curriculum vitae, including qualifications

When a candidate is selected but not yet appointed, additional checks should be conducted, including:

- Confirmation of both identity and character through referees
- Criminal history checks with either local authorities and/or relevant national or international organizations

Temporary staff should be similarly checked. When temporary staff come through an agency, the agency contracts should clearly specify responsibilities for screening and for the notification procedures to be followed if screening is not complete or reveals cause for concern.

5.4.2.2 Ongoing Evaluation and Peer Support. Periodic psychological evaluations of people in high stress roles, particularly where public safety or national security is at risk, should be mandatory. Astronauts, intelligence analysts, soldiers, airline pilots, medical doctors, and train drivers are often subject to intense training and ongoing responsibilities, which can take a heavy toll on them and their families. As noted, people's circumstances and behaviors change over time and ongoing assessments may detect signs that they may be dealing with issues such as divorce, bereavement, or depression that could affect their psychological well-being or performance at work.

Periodic psychological assessment and counseling can often detect and resolve problems before they lead to a security breach. Training can also be provided to staff members in basic peer support and mental health first aid. These may be a highly desirable and cost-effective way of providing unobtrusive workplace monitoring and support and may help to prevent emotional or home-life issues from becoming a workplace or security problem.

5.4.2.3 Personnel Security Control. Maintaining, control of access, records, and administrative measures associated with staff, volunteers, visitors, and contractors requires a robust framework of controls. Maintenance of records and documentation can include:

- The issue and retrieval of security-related items such as keys, codes, combinations, badges, and system passwords
- The custody and use of all information system assets, such as loan or issue of computer hardware, e.g., laptops, computer software, and specialized equipment

New duties or tasks that require modification of an individual's security and access level should trigger the following steps:

- If the individual requires access to different or more sensitive data, then organizations should make administrative arrangements to ensure access to that data occurs only after an appropriate screening process is successfully completed.
- If an individual requires a lower level of access, organizations should inform the individual of their new level of access and enter these changes in the employee's position description.

On termination or transfer of employment, when the employee's duties change, or when an individual no longer requires access to an organization's data, for example following termination or transfer, then organizations should:

- Revoke access privileges, e.g., user-ID and passwords, to system and data resources and secure areas
- Retrieve sensitive material including access control items, e.g., keys and badges
- Retrieve all hardware, software and documentation issued or loaned to the employee

Organizations should have corrective and disciplinary procedures in place to address any breach of security or privacy.

Staff performance reviews should also assess performance related to security and the manner in which the staff member handles an organization's sensitive information.

In the case of contracted personnel and services, contracts should stipulate that such personnel are bound by the organization's policies and procedures regarding the security and privacy of information. These personnel should also be asked to complete and sign a confidentiality and privacy agreement form. Example wording for such an agreement is shown as follows:

Maintaining Confidential Information

Organization XYZ agrees and shall ensure that its staff:

- To hold in strictest confidence, and not to use except for the benefit of JBS, or to disclose to any person, firm, or corporation without written authorization of JBS, any confidential information
- Do not disclose to JBS or induce JBS to use any confidential information of other persons or companies, including former employees (if any)
- To execute any further document regarding the protection of any confidential information as JBS may request from time to time
- Only disclose confidential information to the organization XYZ's staff who have a need to know such confidential information
- Shall not make any public statement (which includes advertising, promotion, media releases, print material, and other specified communications) in relation to the existence or nature of this agreement without the prior written permission of JBS.

Organization XYZ shall notify JBS in writing immediately after becoming aware of any breach of this clause.

Post Contract Completion or Termination

Immediately after termination, determination, abandonment, completion, or performance of this agreement, whether pursuant to the provisions of this agreement or otherwise:

- Organization XYZ will lose all right to hold, keep, or use the confidential information and will immediately return to JBS the confidential information and all copies or records of the whole or part of it.

- All data including technical data, JBS furnished material, completed services and services in progress, confidential information, and such other information and materials as may have been accumulated by organization XYZ in performing the services (including all technical data and intellectual property provided to JBS by organization XYZ) shall be immediately delivered to JBS by organization XYZ.

Volunteers, students, staff, and professional staff should all be bound by policies and procedures relating to the security and privacy of an organization's information.

5.4.3 Personal Protective Practices

5.4.3.1 Security Awareness and Training. Organizations should provide orientation and training to all employees, professional staff, contract staff, and volunteers regarding policies and procedures for ensuring the privacy and security of an organization's data. Orientation and training programs should include:

- Security and privacy policy
- Security procedures
- Employee responsibilities
- Reporting of security and privacy violations

A certificate of attendance at a security awareness or training program should be placed on the employee's personnel file. Security awareness and training programs should be provided on a periodic basis, e.g., annually and biannually, to help maintain an awareness of security responsibility and to provide information about new policies or procedures. Where appropriate, training should involve competency-based assessment.

5.4.3.2 Travel Safety. Uncertain or unstable geopolitical environments may lead to an elevated risk for travelers associated with particular industry sectors, such as defense-related industries, reconstruction, aid provision, as well as resource access and security. Other sectors, which include international transport, freight, or government organizations routinely comprise regional instability as a risk to travel safety. In all cases, protecting the organization's personnel that travel overseas is an important part of a comprehensive SRM process.

The duty of care that an organization shows toward staff that travel overseas may also extend to the safety of staff while traveling to and from work. The duty of care may even extend families of staff, contractors, visitors, delegation members and indeed anyone over whom the organization has a prevailing influence regarding their decision to travel or their activities while travelling.

Risks to people overseas are as varied as the countries through which people may travel and include:

- Commercial espionage
- Terrorism
- Local and transnational crime
- War
- Health issues
- Weather
- Psychologically disturbed people

Predeparture training in self-awareness and protection is readily available for people intending to travel to a country where identified risks pose a significant threat to the safety of travelers.

Better practice in travel security involves:

- Endorsement of the travel safety program by the senior executive
- Identification of a manager that is given responsibility for travel safety
- Development, communication and regular updates of the travel safety policy
- Implementation of a formal strategic sourcing and supplier contract management program

Many organizations rely on consular assistance or diplomatic relationships to help ensure the safety of their employees overseas. These agencies, however willing and able to assist, already have a full workload and cannot offer the level of assistance that may be required in an emergency. Individuals and organizations should therefore use these as a guide but ensure they consider and provide for the safety of employees overseas.

SRMBOK recommends organizations with employees travelling overseas should consider the following steps to ensure the safety and security of their personnel:

- Step 1: define a threat-risk profile for travel destinations and monitor this regularly
- Step 2: develop predefined contingency/response arrangements
- Step 3: implement a compulsory notification to travel policy, which includes registering with the relevant embassy or consulate
- Step 4: capture all travel details centrally
- Step 5: consider IP/classified material exposure
- Step 6: provide overseas awareness briefings on their places of travel
- Step 7: make medical checkups, inoculations and travel/medical insurance compulsory
- Step 8: implement a traveller tracking system

- Step 9: provide ongoing updates throughout the person's travel period
- Step 10: conduct post-travel debriefings to identify enhancements to the program

5.4.4 Identity Security

In larger organizations in which it is difficult to vouch for everyone's identity, individuals, employed either directly by an organization or under contract, should be issued with authorized identification and computer access codes. These should provide the holder with the level of access that is appropriate to their duties and level of responsibility. The cards or badges should be tamper resistant and at a minimum contain:

- Name
- Facial-view photograph
- Signature of card holder
- Signature of issuing authority
- Validity period or expiry date
- Badge or card control serial number
- Information on how lost cards can be returned to the issuing authority, e.g., through a police station or to a listed post office box

The card or badge should:

- Be visually and uniquely associated with a given secure area
- Visually indicate the type of access privileges granted to the card holder, e.g., escort required, unrestricted access

Whether or not the identity badge should bear the identification or address of the organization or facility in which it is used is a risk-based decision that different organizations need to make within the context of their environment. Standard operating procedures should be established for the regular review and update of identification cards or access badges. These procedures should cover:

- The method of ongoing verification
- Framework for withdrawal if necessary
- Replacement when supported by a threat and risk assessment
- Replacement due to damage
- Reporting and replacement due to loss or theft
- Recovery of expired cards
- Recovery of cards when employment is terminated or when an employee is transferred and requires a change in access privileges
- Significant facial changes

As a general principle, only one identification card or access badge should be issued to each person and records should be kept of the issue of all cards to a level that will support internal audit of verification as appropriate.

Organizations should control and secure blank identification cards and access badge stock by documenting their issue and retrieval, storing them in a secure container or safe, and undertaking regular stocktakes/audit checks.

5.4.5 Identity Management

Identity management is a broad administrative area that deals with identifying individuals in a system, such as a country, a network, or an enterprise, and controlling their access to resources within that system by associating user rights and restrictions with the established identity.

Identity verification is core to this activity as any failure to identify an individual correctly in the first instance will only result in the perpetuation of identity fraud by issuing additional and subsequent identity.

5.4.6 Human Factors in Security Risk Management

Many organizations rely on physical and technology solutions to protect their assets. All too often, they believe that installing firewalls, alarms, access control, or blast mitigation systems will address their security risks and make them impervious to security breaches. Although these are an integral part of any security plan, it is important to manage the often undervalued human factor and its impact on security (both positively and negatively).

People are the foundation of any organization, network, or system, and the success or failure of a Security Risk Management program is largely dependent on the people who design, implement, manage, use, and work with the processes and technologies.[28] The way in which humans interact with these solutions can be the key determinant of their success or failure. The attitude of staff and stakeholders toward security is likely to influence whether they comply with security policies, apply existing controls, and fund security investments on a daily basis. Human factors takes a systems-based approach to understanding and managing the interaction of humans with their environment. It looks to the underlying causes, rather than simply apportioning blame to the individual or ascribe misfortunes, including incidents and mishaps to the human factor.

> *Human factors can be described as the study of interfaces among humans, their environment, and technology. In particular, it describes how humans interact physically and psychologically in relation to particular environments, activities, or systems, including reactions and preferences with respect to sensory stimuli.*

Postincident investigations regularly identify a range of causal factors that enabled a perpetrator to carry out an attack, whether successful or otherwise. In the past, investigators have often ignored or underreported human factors as a cause of security events. This practice has sometimes produced analyses that overlooked key elements of underlying security failures. It is tempting to consider offenders as just another threat that operates independently of human motivations, but this is rarely the case. Although most organizations have limited ability to influence offender behaviors, it would be naive to believe there is no element of human interaction that the organizations can influence. CPTED is just one example of a multidisciplinary approach predicated on deterring criminal behavior by influencing the environment and, therefore, offender decisions that precede criminal acts.

Of even more importance to an organization is the understanding that the interaction of staff with security systems is predominantly within an organization's control. All too often, security breaches occur as a result of vulnerabilities created by the actions of staff, visitors, or other insiders whether deliberate or in error. As described by Reason,[34] active failures are actions or inactions of human beings that are the immediate cause of a mishap—or in this case, a security incident. Traditionally referred to as errors, they are the last acts committed by individuals prior to an incident. Reason describes error as potentially meaning several things:

- Error as the failure itself, e.g., the decision was an error (decision, perceptual, or skill-based errors)

- Error as the cause of failure, e.g., this event was caused by human error (failure to provide guidance)

- Error as a process or, more specifically, as a departure from some kind of standard (exceptional, routine, intentional, or unintentional).[29]

In the security context, errors include a wide range of acts that can lead to a security breach. Actions such as allowing tailgating into secure areas, leaving passwords written next to a computer or chocking open a fire door are all examples of errors. Similarly, errors can include latent failures, such as failing to update a security policy and under-resourcing a critical security function. All of these constitute elements of people security that have direct and indirect impacts on all areas of the total security management system.

Several human error classification schemes are available, and the most appropriate application is likely to depend on what systems are already in place within the organization as well as the context in which they are used. Some of these tools include probabilistic risk assessment, human reliability assessment, and task profile analyses. Another useful application is the characterizing of errors into two broad categories of discrete action and information processing.[30] Discrete action classification is based on the premise that a specific action or set of actions produces an undesired outcome. This categorization considers the following types of errors:

- Errors of omission occur when a person fails to undertake a particular action in an element of task performance.

- Errors of commission occur when someone includes an unnecessary or prohibitive action within a task performance that results in incorrect performance.
- Sequence errors are a subclass of commission errors that occur when a person conducts a task out of sequence.
- Timing errors are also considered a subclass of errors of commission. They take place when a person does not perform the prescribed task within the necessary time frame, i.e., too slowly or too quickly.

These classifications are very compatible with the limited work performed in the classification of human error in security. In an article designed to address this issue in the information security area, Wood and Bank[36] classify the types of human error as:

- Navigation errors as a user navigates through a computer system using commands that may result in ambiguity
- Data input errors as basic omission or commission errors
- Motor action errors whereby a situation requires precise muscular motor coordination which the user is unable to successfully perform[31]

The U.S. Department of Defense research in the naval aviation area has adapted Reason's work to produce the Human Factors Analysis and Classification System (HFACS).[32] HFACS asserts that human error is a causal factor in 80–90% of incidents and present in another 50–60%. Although limited empirical data and research exists regarding human factors analysis in the SRM field, anecdotal evidence and results of incident investigations suggest that human factors are the root cause of many security incidents.[28] The HFACS taxonomy categorizes human errors at four levels:

- Acts
- Preconditions
- Supervision
- Organizational influences

These four tiers and the next level of human factors categories are illustrated in Figure 5.5.[h]

This model offers many strengths for the analysis of security vulnerabilities and is complementary to the concepts of security-in-depth explored in the section on hierarchy of controls and Swiss-cheese theory.

Although the Swiss-cheese model conveys the impression that the slices of cheese and the location of their respective holes are independent, this may be misleading. The work of Reason and frameworks such as HFACS among others offer an insight into the interdependent nature of incident causation and, thus, the types of security strategies that might be considered to mitigate vulnerabilities and root causes of incidents. These concepts are mutually supporting, and the

---

[h]Adapted from Human Factors Analysis Classification System (U.S. DoD).

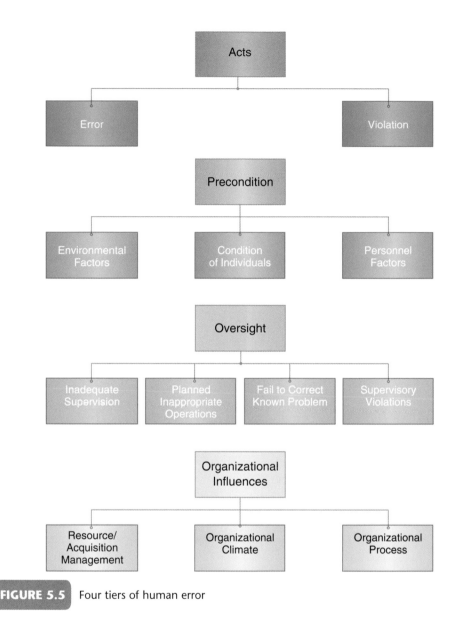

FIGURE 5.5 Four tiers of human error

linking of Swiss-cheese theory with human factors are illustrated in Figure 5.6 below.

In adapting HFACS taxonomy in the Security Risk Management environment, we have assumed that the error does not lie with the offender but rather with human elements in the protective controls in place. For example, if the rear door of a building is left open and a thief or arsonist takes advantage of this to enter a facility and cause harm, the causal chain may have commenced with the act or decision to open the rear doors to increase airflow in hot weather. But the actual root cause in this scenario might be traced back to

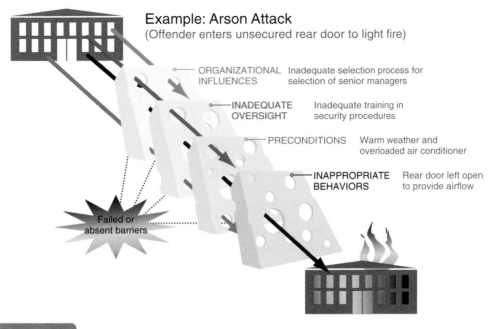

Example: Arson Attack
(Offender enters unsecured rear door to light fire)

ORGANIZATIONAL INFLUENCES — Inadequate selection process for selection of senior managers

INADEQUATE OVERSIGHT — Inadequate training in security procedures

PRECONDITIONS — Warm weather and overloaded air conditioner

INAPPROPRIATE BEHAVIORS — Rear door left open to provide airflow

Failed or absent barriers

FIGURE 5.6 Example of human factors as Swiss-cheese barriers

inadequate recruitment and selection procedures (Figure 5.6). The actions of the offender, from the offenders perspective at least, do not constitute human error because the offender succeeded in a deliberate action. There may be a significant range of human factors predisposing that action, e.g., poverty, lack of education, and unemployment; however, these root causes are more related to societal activities and would generally fall outside the scope of the security professionals scope.

> This concept is explored in depth, and a taxonomy of security-related human factors is provided in the Guide to SRMBOK on root cause analysis.

On the surface, dealing with the human factor may seem trivial, but it is one of the most complex undertakings within security that directly affects the success or failure of any given security management system. Although we have known about the human factor for a long time, numerous studies and years of experience have demonstrated that technology still receives the funding but, alone, has not actually provided more secure infrastructures or decreased the exposure to our businesses and services.[28] Ultimately, people directly engineer, procure, implement, and control security (or the lack thereof). We need to plan our security programs accordingly and instill in our organizations a security culture that begins and ends with each person.

5.4.7 Human Resource Management and Security Procedures

The security-in-depth management of personnel security issues provides an organization with a solid base for attracting and retaining low-risk/high-suitability staff. Regardless of the size or complexity of an organization, any business or government enterprise can benefit from implementing the following processes:

- Staff job descriptions should indicate the appropriate level of access to an organization's information and information systems. This level should be determined on a need-to-know basis and enable the staff member to perform their duties.

- Prospective employees should be screened for knowledge of an organization's information principles and demonstration of appropriate practice relating to an organization's information issues, confidentiality, and security. Reference checks and security clearances should be undertaken as appropriate to the position.

- Organizations should confirm that personnel are aware of, and bound by, a code of ethics or conduct.

- As a condition of employment, each employee should sign a witnessed and dated confidentiality and privacy agreement indicating that they have been made aware of the organization's security and privacy policy and the consequences of breaching that policy.

Prior to an employee's start date, organizations should formally advise employees of:

- Their authorized level of security access
- Their responsibilities with respect to the security and privacy of the organization's data
- What to do in circumstances where they receive, or see others receiving, inappropriate levels of security material

5.4.8 Summary of Key Points

- Human factors analysis indicates that most SRM incidents result from human error. The implementation of people SRM protocols in an organization provides a level of protection against risk and enhances an organization's ability to attract, identify, and retain valued staff.

- Identity security processes provide security risk managers with an access control mechanism to protect human, physical and information assets. ID management programs should be coordinated with other information security and physical security treatments to ensure the compartmentalization of sensitive information and the use of appropriately cleared and vetted staff.

- A thorough examination of risks faced by employees traveling or stationed overseas should be part of any organization's people security. Travel security methodologies provide an organization with greater assurance that their duty-of-care obligations to their staff are being met.

5.5 ICT SECURITY

The security of information systems, and the information those systems manage, becomes more critical as we move into a knowledge-based economy. Information systems that manage and distribute information, such as e-mail, data warehousing systems, search engines, or servers are all vulnerable to infiltration, malfunction, or human error.[i] These threats require sound SRM as ICT systems continue to grow in importance, both for individual organizations and for countries as a whole.

SRM methodologies are continually challenged by advances in technology. As ICT systems play an increasingly important and diverse role in every day life and business, threats to ICT security will become potentially more serious. Hackers, online vandals, disgruntled employees, and human error all present challenges for security risk managers.

Scope
The term "ICT security" refers to the confluence of information, physical technologies, and security management. An example of this is the digital encryption of mobile telephony, whereby physical integrated circuit design is led by conceptual development of encryption algorithms based on a risk assessment.

5.5.1 ICT Identification

Most integrated ICT systems are made up of a range of assets that require protection. These include procedures, data and information, software, hardware, and networking resources. The key outputs are capabilities—in this case, the ICT capability required by an organization to maintain business continuity.

5.5.2 Protecting ICT Systems

Protection of ICT systems has grown into a massive industry. The technical measures necessary to protect ICT systems are covered elsewhere and are beyond the scope of SRMBOK. However, despite the speed with which technology, threats, and security solutions evolve, the fundamental elements of providing security in depth and sound SRM are relevant and have enduring value.

---

[i]Strictly speaking a malfunction of a system would not normally be caused by a security threat; however, it is included here for comprehensiveness as the malfunction could 1) lead to a vulnerability that modifies the security risk or 2) could be the result of a security breach such as inadequate access control.

Sound technical measures and security solutions are necessary to protect an organization's ICT systems, but they are not sufficient. All practice areas lean extensively on each other to provide security in depth. Poor SRM may result in infiltration of an ICT network by an external actor or, more likely, by a trusted insider. Sound SRM can help to reduce the likelihood of this happening or prevent it altogether.

5.5.3 ICT and Other Practice Areas

Protective SRM principles apply to the protection of information technology and communications systems in a similar way to other types of assets.

All practice areas are interdependent, and ICT security is no exception. For example, encryption and other methods of ensuring confidentiality are important components of ICT security. But the physical security of computer servers and other computing equipment is no less important (many ICT security standards provide guidelines on how to secure equipment, including the thickness of walls and different kinds of door locks for different applications).

5.5.4 Interdependency of Systems

Most ICT systems will rely on or be accessible to internal and external systems. An ICT security assessment that treats internal systems only may result in security solutions that leave an ICT system vulnerable to infiltration or exploitation. Internet gateways are an obvious example of the interdependence of internal and external systems. Other, less obvious examples of external systems that may affect an organizations ICT security include the ICT systems of:

- Clients
- Resource providers
- Internet service providers
- Telecommunications companies
- Supply chains
- Accounting firms

This list indicates that an internal focus on ICT security is not sufficient. Legal frameworks and industry standards that require a company to meet specific technological or organizational requirements for ICT systems should also be examined and assessed to determine whether they are relevant to SRM.

Figure 5.7 illustrates an example of an organization's ICT systems and the ways in which these are interdependent. In this example, both internal and external systems are shown, and each system has both internal and external stakeholders.

From an ICT security perspective, both individual components and complete systems are assets. Even though an organization may not own or even be able to influence a particular component of a system, connectivity to that component may be considered an asset.

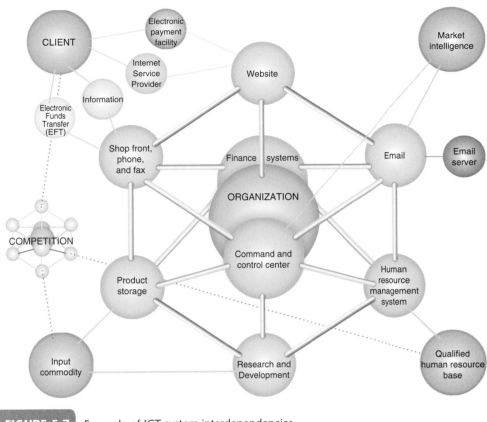

FIGURE 5.7 Example of ICT system interdependencies

5.5.5 Physical Elements of ICT Security

The confidentiality, integrity, and availability of an ICT system may all be compromised if an attacker can gain access to a critical ICT infrastructure that is inadequately protected. Security solutions designed to protect ICT systems, such as firewalls and antivirus programs, may not prevent a security breach if, for example, the room housing servers and other infrastructure is not properly secured. SRM practitioners and managers can decide whether the physical security of ICT infrastructure is addressed under the physical security or ICT practice areas.

Standards bodies provide guidance on physical security specifications for ICT systems for different environments. These bodies include:

- International Telecommunications Union (ITU)
- International Standards Organization (ISO)
- Electronic Industries Alliance (EIA)
- Standards Australia/Standards New Zealand

In addition, the Australian Government has developed several documents relevant to the physical security of ICT systems, including the Protective Security Manual and ACSI 33 Australian Government Information and Communications Technology Security Manual.

5.5.6 Threats to ICT Assets

ICT systems can be susceptible to a range of threats and problems, including:

- Automated or user-initiated network-aware attacks
- Malicious system misuse
- Installation of rogue software
- Unavailability of ICT staff

5.5.6.1 Automated or User-Initiated Network-Aware Attacks. These attacks, such as viruses, worms, and trojan horses, can result in:

- Destruction of valuable files
- Exposure of critical files to corruption or theft
- Loss of productivity
- Possibly machine control

The recovery and reconstruction phase following an attack can distract experienced ICT staff from other important maintenance and development issues. These problems may lead to more disruption to the organization at a later date.

5.5.6.2 Malicious System Misuse. Misuse by staff or other stakeholders can cause considerable damage to ICT systems and to intangible assets like a company's reputation. Asset protection against this kind of threat should include people and physical security risk treatments for ICT systems owned and used by the organization.

5.5.6.3 Installation of Rogue Software. Uncontrolled software installation can have a destabilizing effect on wider system integrity and expose critical files to corruption or disruption. An organization should include doctrine and procedures for the installation of software in their ICT management plan. Only software that is appropriately tested and vetted by ICT staff should be installed on an organization's ICT systems.

5.5.6.4 Unavailability of ICT staff. An organization may be more susceptible to threats to ICT security if suitably qualified and experienced ICT staff are not available to resolve problems because of illness or reduced staffing. The retention and leadership of quality ICT service providers that are employed directly by the organization and the sound management of outsourced staff is a critical factor when treating ICT-related risks.

5.5.6.5 Obsolescence. Obsolescence of equipment is not of itself a threat; however, it is noted here in the context of a potential vulnerability that (like inadequate maintenance systems) could increase the risk of a threat materializing. Planned expenditure on software upgrades and the acquisition of interoperable equipment is an important consideration in the assessment and management of ICT security risks.

5.5.7 Summary of Key Points

- ICT security involves the protection of all information systems; however, the key objective remains the preservation of capability rather than merely the preservation of ICT infrastructure.
- The principles involved in the protection of ICT systems involves the application of fundamental SRM principles.
- ICT security methodologies provide an organization's executive with greater assurance that their stakeholder, statutory, and duty-of-care obligations are being met.

5.6 INFORMATION SECURITY

Information can be defined in a variety of ways, and for the purposes of this section, we will consider it as knowledge communicated or received concerning some fact or circumstance that is of value, whether codified or intangible.

The protection of information is an increasing challenge for all organizations regardless of size. Patent laws provide some level of protection to organizations that wish to secure proprietary information.[j] However, operating in a global market requires more astute of information security and a greater understanding of risk-management techniques.

The minds of employees, volunteers, and contractors alike often hold much of the knowledge and value considered crucial to any organization's success. As a result, this information can be the most difficult to protect. People are valuable, mobile, fragile, and hard to control or isolate.

The old maxim that knowledge is power may hold true, but for many organizations, it is the use of that knowledge that generates profit or other desired outcomes. Whenever information is used or made available for operational purposes, it becomes more vulnerable to security threats.

---

[j]Intellectual property rights are not respected in all countries; by filing a patent, an organization may provide enough detail about a new product or process to enable a competitor to produce a similar product or process. Organizations may choose to not file a patent, preferring to keep their invention as a trade secret (which can involve a different set of risks).

Scope

> *Information security refers to the adoption of measures to prevent the unau-*
> *thorized use, misuse, modification, or denial of use of information, knowledge,*
> *facts, data, or capabilities.*

Information security does not apply solely to soft copy or electronically stored information. Hard copy documents also require information management and protection and, in some cases, are more susceptible to loss or misuse.

This practice area addresses all forms of information. It applies to anyone who creates, distributes, manages, or otherwise handles information. It focuses on the application of human factors, information classification, and the need-to-know principle to identify and protect valuable information, which includes intellectual property.

Purpose

The purpose of information security protection is to assist organizations and individuals with arrangements for the following:

- Identifying information according to type and format
- Classifying information according to its sensitivity
- Applying appropriate security markings to information
- Correctly handling information according to security markings

5.6.1 Principles of Information Security

SRM principles apply to information in a similar way to other assets. Protective, physical, ICT, and people security treatments are often relevant to information security. Comprehensive protective security plans should include a component of information security. As shown below, information security involves a range of elements, which include the following (see Figure 5.8):

- Confidentiality
- Integrity
- Availability
- Utility or usefulness
- Authenticity or nonrepudiation
- Control or possession

Each of these elements must be present if information is to be secured adequately. Table 5.2 provides an outline of each of these elements.

FIGURE 5.8 Principles of information security

Table 5.2 Principles of information security—definition of terms

Principle	Is met by assurance that...
Confidentiality	The information is maintained in a secure manner with appropriately controlled access.
Integrity	The information is not altered.
Availability	The information will be available in a timely fashion when required.
Utility or usefulness	The information will still be accessible and in a format that can be used by persons authorized to access the data.
Authenticity or nonrepudiation	The sender of data is provided with proof of delivery. The recipient is provided with proof of the sender's identity.
Control or possession	No one other than authorized custodians or recipients can access all information or parts thereof.

5.6.2 The Information Security Life Cycle

The term "information life cycle" is used to convey the manner in which information is subject to various processes at different times, from the time of creation or acquisition through to destruction and acquittal. It must be noted that, although many types and formats of information do not always fit neatly into every stage of the life cycle, security measures applicable to those stages should be applied (see Figure 5.9).

The life cycle is characterized by the following stages:

- **Creation/acquisition.** This stage involves the initial creation of information or its acquisition from another source. The developer (information owner) must classify and mark information at this important stage.

- **Distribution.** Transfer rules and controls ensure that only authorized people are afforded access. Discussions, presentations, e-mails, traditional post, and the simple observation of an activity or routine are typical methods of transfer. Distribution places information at risk of unauthorized access through incorrect addressing, interception, or inadvertent acquisition.

- **Use.** This stage covers the general use of information and includes copying. Personnel must remain particularly vigilant to the risk of compromise as exposure of information increases where multiple copies exist.

- **Storage.** Between periods of use or when information becomes redundant or outdated, information is stored using several methods and controls. These include archiving of paper-based records and electronic storage of information through the use of local network drives, backup and storage devices, as well as removable media, such as memory sticks, external hard disk drives, and CD/DVDs. Significant consideration must also be given to privacy, security, and practical issues associated with information retained by individuals in the form of files, knowledge, and experience.

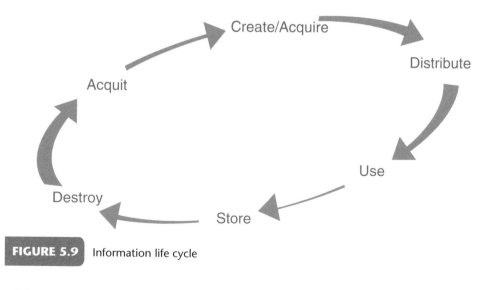

FIGURE 5.9 Information life cycle

- **Destruction.** Destruction applies to information that needs to be removed permanently from storage media.[k] Security procedures for destruction are particularly relevant where information is received from or held on behalf of other parties, e.g., national security material, contracts, etc., as a failure to meet requirements of the next step (acquittal) may result in liability.
- **Acquittal.** When information is destroyed, it is common that records of destruction or permanent transfer to another entity are recorded; this is especially the case where third-party information is involved. Acquittal records form the basis for assuring information owners and management that correct destruction or transfer has occurred and that authorized methods and processes have been used.

Each step in the information life cycle exhibits a different set of vulnerabilities and, therefore, each step requires different security solutions.

5.6.3 Vulnerability of Information

Information is vulnerable to a variety of threats. Organizations and even individuals can collect information by exploiting security vulnerabilities in information systems. The most important part of an information system is the people that use and operate the system. People and the information they have access to are also vulnerable to security threats and exploitation. In addition, human error and equipment malfunction may threaten the security of valued information.

Figure 5.10 provides a model of information flow that is typical for many organizations. It shows how information that is created in an organization can be rapidly disseminated globally, whether this is appropriate or not. Each step exhibits its own vulnerabilities and risk of compromise or loss of information. These may be exploited if the relevant security strategies are not in place.

Threats to an organization's information are numerous but can be broadly categorized in three ways: threats from "inside the system," "against the system," and "despite the system," as shown in Figure 5.11.

Threats generated from inside the system include the following:

- The compromise of trade secrets by trusted insiders
- Human or systemic error that may occur during the filing or maintenance of a patent or trademark
- Contradictory laws across national or state borders
- Predatory patenting, where a company seeks patent rights over another company's technology

Risk treatments could include the following:

- The use of aggressive employment contracts, which may prevent former staff from working with competing companies for a defined period
- Paying former employees a "bonus" to help encourage discretion and integrity

---

[k]This stage is not applicable to all forms of information, such as knowledge, which cannot clearly be purged.

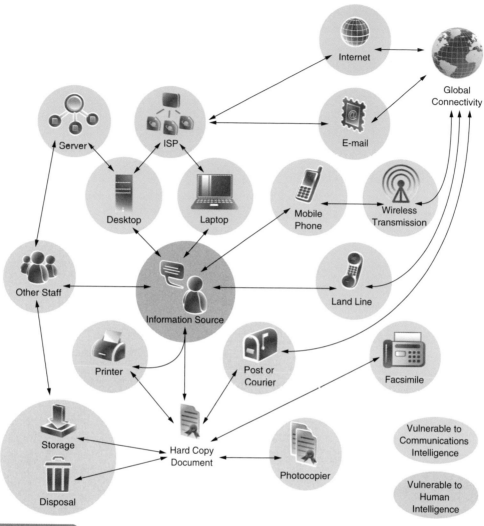

FIGURE 5.10 Example of information flows and vulnerabilities

- The use of failsafe or quality assurance systems to minimize the likelihood that human or systemic error will compromise IP rights
- The investment in expert IP advice and management techniques

Threats against the system include actions by parties operating outside existing legal frameworks, reverse engineering, product piracy, and theft of a company's IP.

The treatment prescribed for an external threat depends on environmental factors specific to both the organization and the identified threat. If the identified threat involves, for example, the illegal manufacture of goods outside an existing legal arrangement (overrun manufacture) in a country or state where laws or authorities fail to protect registered Intellectual property (IP), a company

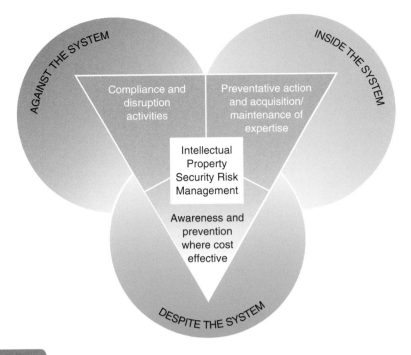

FIGURE 5.11 Threats to intellectual property

could consider a risk treatment option that involved the partial assembly of a product in several locations. This treatment would prevent one assembly plant having access to all the components of a product and may prevent overrun manufacture.

Threats presenting a challenge to an organization's IP can exist despite the system and despite comprehensive risk management. No matter how careful or thorough an organization is in managing risk inside or against IP legal frameworks, residual threat from opportunistic actors may still exist.

5.6.4 Compartmentalization of Information

The compartmentalization of information refers to a process where access to information is granted to a limited number of persons who directly need to know certain elements of a larger store of information to perform specific tasks.

This information management technique limits risk by controlling access to information and by limiting the number of users who can access the whole information picture. This structure limits the risk to the entire store of information and to the people that access it and is particularly useful in managing access to sensitive material.[1] The methods used to collect sensitive material are often more valuable than the individual items of sensitive material themselves. Restricting

---

[1]People that can access sensitive information, or that can access an organization's entire data holdings, may be more attractive targets for intelligence collectors.

access to this material helps protect the source of the information and helps to ensure that information can be collected from that source in the future.

5.6.5 Classifying Information

5.6.5.1 Procedures. The process of security classification should occur immediately after creation or acquisition of information. Better practice indicates that a preliminary assessment of classification should be made prior to creation or acquisition of information, so that appropriate security measures can be taken from inception.

A security classification is based on the type, sensitivity, longevity, commercial value, and requirements for access of the information to be classified. The process of classification must ensure not only that information is protected but also that information is accessible to enough recipients to enable the achievement of business objectives.

Organizations should establish their own procedures for classifying information; it is recommended that the following steps be considered:

- Determine the type of information and compliance obligations
- Assess sensitivity of information and worst-case damage if the information was passed to an unauthorized person or organization
- Determine appropriate security marking to be used
- Determine if a limited distribution marking (LDM) is required to restrict access even more
- Apply marking(s) as required and control information in accordance with handling requirements of the organization or relevant third parties

5.6.5.2 Security Classification Markings. Security markings are an essential information security management tool and support the practical implementation of the six principles of information security (see Figure 5.12). Use of caveats and other restrictions are common within government and defense. LDM may also be used in support of security markings and stipulate more limits on how information should be distributed (Figure 5.13). Examples of typical markings might include Tender Bid Team Only or XYZ Group of Companies Only.

Organizational standards should clearly describe the application of classifications, caveats, and LDM, including text attributes, positioning, and elements that must appear in document headers and footers.

LDM should be developed by the information owner to reflect a quantifiable group of personnel; where it is not possible to describe a specific group in the definition, a named list of recipients should be applied. In this instance, the LDM is to read Limited Distribution—Named Recipients Only.

A range of security marking stickers, rubber stamps, barcodes, and radio frequency identity tags (RFID) is also commercially available for the purpose of applying security markings to items that may otherwise be difficult to mark (Table 5.3).

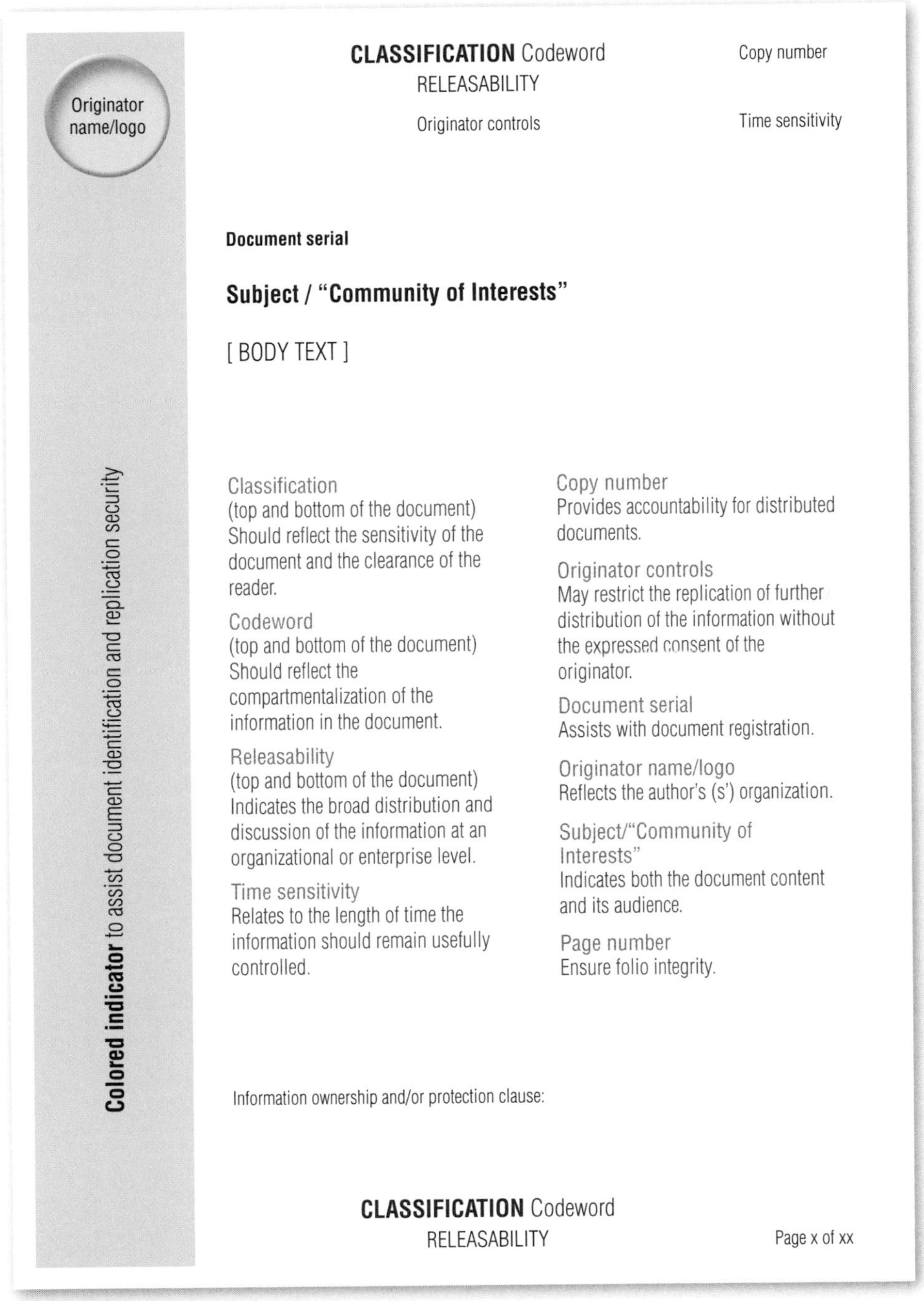

CLASSIFICATION Codeword   Copy number
RELEASABILITY

Originator controls   Time sensitivity

Document serial

Subject / "Community of Interests"

[BODY TEXT]

Classification
(top and bottom of the document)
Should reflect the sensitivity of the
document and the clearance of the
reader.

Codeword
(top and bottom of the document)
Should reflect the
compartmentalization of the
information in the document.

Releasability
(top and bottom of the document)
Indicates the broad distribution and
discussion of the information at an
organizational or enterprise level.

Time sensitivity
Relates to the length of time the
information should remain usefully
controlled.

Copy number
Provides accountability for distributed
documents.

Originator controls
May restrict the replication of further
distribution of the information without
the expressed consent of the
originator.

Document serial
Assists with document registration.

Originator name/logo
Reflects the author's (s') organization.

Subject/"Community of
Interests"
Indicates both the document content
and its audience.

Page number
Ensure folio integrity.

Information ownership and/or protection clause:

CLASSIFICATION Codeword
RELEASABILITY   Page x of xx

Colored indicator to assist document identification and replication security

FIGURE 5.12 Example of security classification markings

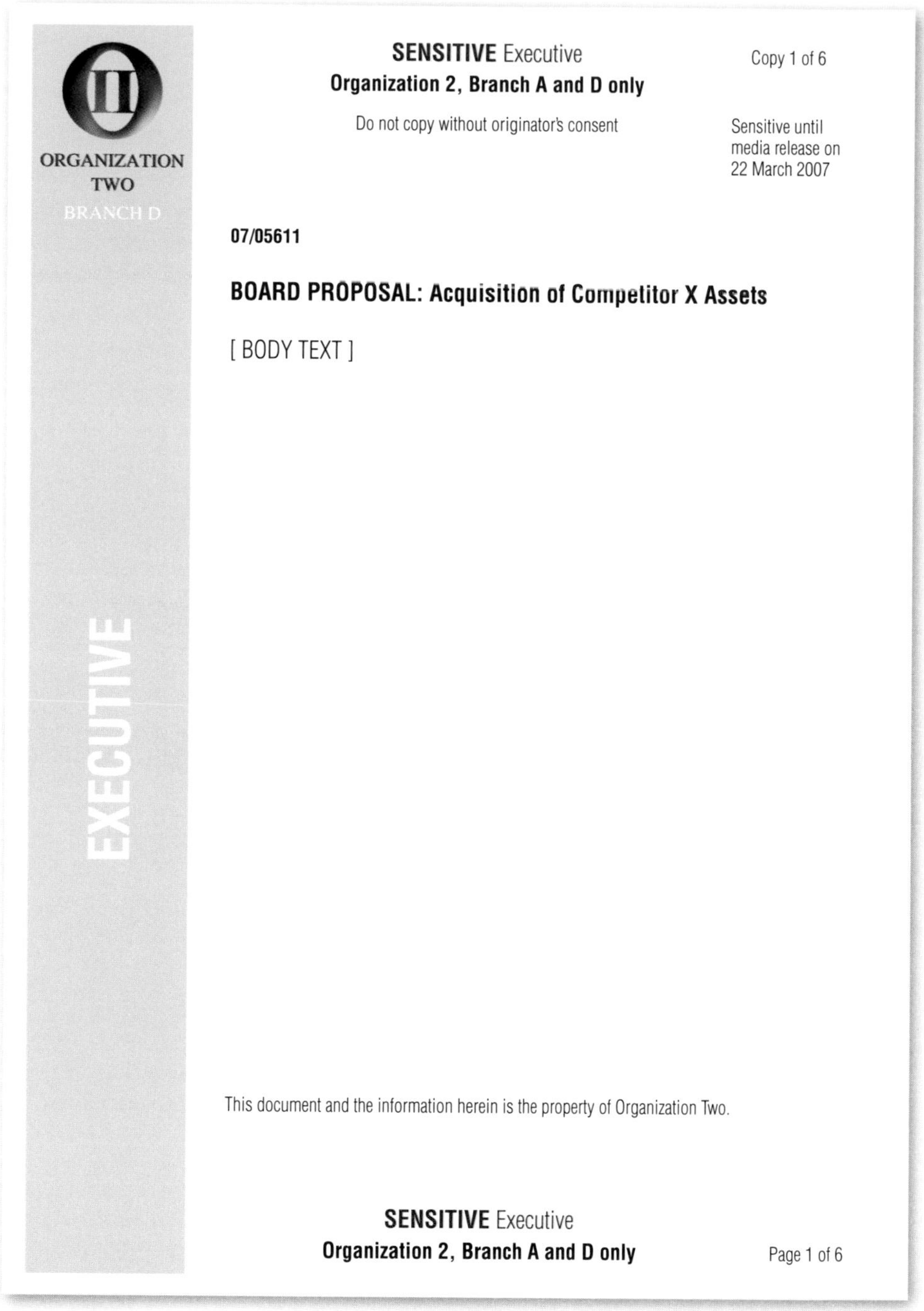

ORGANIZATION TWO

BRANCH D

SENSITIVE Executive
Organization 2, Branch A and D only

Do not copy without originator's consent

Copy 1 of 6

Sensitive until
media release on
22 March 2007

07/05611

BOARD PROPOSAL: Acquisition of Competitor X Assets

[BODY TEXT]

EXECUTIVE

This document and the information herein is the property of Organization Two.

SENSITIVE Executive
Organization 2, Branch A and D only

Page 1 of 6

FIGURE 5.13 Example of commercial security classification markings

Security Marking	Definition
	Organization XYZ
Not marked, or marked: Unclassified—noncontrolled	Day-to-day information prepared in the knowledge that it may be circulated widely to external parties and no harm could come to organization XYZ as a result. If the information were released to the media or competitors, organization XYZ could expect no harm or damage to business or corporate interests and no financial loss. Examples include: • Academic papers for industry • Media releases • Routine administrative correspondence • Organization XYZ news stories
Personnel-in-confidence Security-in-confidence, or commercial-in-confidence	Private, security, or commercial information prepared with an expectation it may be shared with external parties with a legitimate need to know, subject to relevant restrictions. If the information were released to the media or competitors, organization XYZ could expect minimal damage to corporate interests, including reputation; minor potential for financial loss; minor embarrassment to the company or its business partners; and minor detriment to employees or customers. Examples include the following: • Insurance arrangements • Nonsensitive tender or contract pricing • Nonsensitive internal project reports • Nonsensitive reorganization proposals • Minutes of nonsensitive meetings • Site maps/plans with generic planning details • Personnel/employee records
Organization XYZ sensitive	Proprietary information requiring a degree of protection above that of a "clear desk policy" or of a sensitive nature and prepared primarily for circulation within a functional group of the company and/or external parties with a legitimate need to know. If the information were released to the media or competitors, organization XYZ could expect some damage to corporate interests, including reputation; some financial loss; embarrassment to the company or its business partners; and detriment to employees or customers. Examples include the following: • Security surveys/assessments • Sensitive tender or contract details • Sensitive internal project reports • Minutes of sensitive meetings • Sensitive environmental impact statements/reports • Sensitive reorganization proposals • Site maps/plans with sensitive details marked

Security Marking	Definition
Organization XYZ highly sensitive	Proprietary information requiring a substantial degree of protection and prepared for circulation within a controlled group and shared with external parties that have an explicit and legitimate need to know. If the information were released to the media or competitors organization XYZ could expect serious damage to business or corporate interests, significant financial loss to the company, or gain to a competitor or significant detriment to employees or customers. Examples include the following: • Highly sensitive tender or contract detail • Highly sensitive company legal advice • Intellectual property of significant monetary value • Technology conferring a competitive advantage • High-level committee/board papers • Strategic alliance information
Organization XYZ extremely sensitive	Proprietary information that requires the highest degree of protection and prepared for circulation within a named group of employees only. Only in exceptional circumstances and by the authority of senior business group/division or company management may such information be shared outside this group. If the information were released to the media or competitors organization XYZ could expect very serious damage to business or corporate interests, very substantial financial loss to the company, or gain to a competitor. Commercial security arrangements at this level are at the highest possible and the marking should be used sparingly. Examples include the following: • Critical business plans, mergers, or strategies • Critical investigation reports • Intellectual property of a highly significant monetary value • Leading edge commercial technologies conferring a significant competitive advantage
	Government And Military
XX-in-confidence Protected Highly protected Restricted Confidential Secret Top secret	Government and military readers should refer to relevant protective security manuals (PSMs) and defense security manuals (DSMs), available through your Facility Security Officer.

Security Marking	Handling Requirements	
	Organization XYZ	
Not marked, or Unclassified-noncontrolled	All stages of the information life cycle (ILC)	No specific controls required. However, personnel are to remain vigilant to poorly classified information and notify the information owner immediately where identified.
Personnel-in-confidence Security-in-confidence, or Commercial-in-confidence	Create/acquire	Security markings mandatory. Copy numbering, LDMs, and listing in document register optional.
	Use/copy	May be copied without Information owner's permission; copies are to be kept to a minimum. Access by unauthorized parties must be prevented.
	Transfer	Unless LDMs indicate otherwise, transfer to external parties with a legitimate need to know is authorized without the permission of the information owner. External parties must be informed of handling requirements. Single envelope, normal post, and nonencrypted e-mail/fax permitted.
	Store/archive	Must be stored in a manner that prevents unauthorized access.
	Destroy	Must be destroyed using secure destruction method, e.g., shredding, secure disposal/ recycling supplier, degaussed, or permanently erased.
	Acquit	No requirement to acquit formally unless listed in document register.
Organization XYZ sensitive	Create/acquire	Security markings mandatory. Copy numbering, LDMs, and listing in document register optional.
	Use/copy	May be copied without information owner's permission; copies are to be kept to a minimum. Unauthorized access must be prevented at all times.
	Transfer	Unless LDMs indicate otherwise, transfer to internal/external parties with a legitimate need to know is authorized without the permission of the information owner. A confidentiality agreement must be signed. Single opaque envelope, normal post, and nonencrypted e-mail/fax permitted.
	Store/archive	Must be stored in a manner that prevents unauthorized access.
	Destroy	Must be destroyed using secure destruction method, e.g., shredding, secure disposal/ recycling supplier, degaussed, or permanently erased.
	Acquit	No requirement to acquit formally unless listed in document register.

Security Marking	Handling Requirements	
Organization XYZ highly sensitive	Create/acquire	Security markings mandatory, limited LDMs optional. Copy numbering and listing in document register optional.
	Use/copy	May be copied only after information owner's permission has been obtained; copies are to be kept to a minimum. Unauthorized access must be prevented at all times.
	Transfer	Unless LDMs indicate otherwise, transfer to external parties with a legitimate need to know is authorized, after the permission of the information owner has been obtained. A confidentiality agreement must be signed prior to transfer to external parties. External parties must provide an assurance of their capacity to protect information to Organization XYZ's standards. Double opaque envelope, registered post, and approved grade of encrypted e-mail/fax transmission mandatory (e-mail within organization XYZ WAN is acceptable)
	Store/archive	Must be stored in a manner that prevents unauthorized access. Not to be stored on open-access environments.
	Destroy	Must be destroyed using secure destruction method, e.g., shredding, secure disposal/ recycling supplier, degaussed, or permanently erased.
	Acquit	No requirement to formally acquit unless listed in document register.
Organization XYZ extremely sensitive	Create/acquire	Security and LDMs mandatory. Copy numbering and listing in document register mandatory.
	Use/copy	Information is not to be viewed where this is a possibility of casual access by unauthorized personnel. Information is not to be copied.
	Transfer	Distribution is restricted to named individuals only. Only in extreme or critical circumstances can this type of document be transferred to an external party—where this is the case, they must demonstrate a capacity to protect the information to Organization XYZ's strict standards. A confidentiality agreement must be signed. Receipt must be formally acknowledged and document register updated. Double envelope with wafer/tamper evident seals on inner envelope and approved courier mandatory. Not to be transferred electronically.

Security Marking	Handling Requirements	
	Store/archive	Must be stored in a manner that prevents unauthorized access. Not to be stored on BPMS or similar open-access environments.
	Destroy	Must be destroyed using secure destruction method, e.g., shredding, secure disposal/recycling supplier, degaussed, or permanently erased.
	Acquit	Must be formally acquitted from document register when destroyed or advice of destruction has been received from recipient(s).
Government And Military		
Xx-in-confidence	Where information is marked "XX-IN-CONFIDENCE" by, or on behalf of Australian Government or Defense, it must to be handled according to the requirements of the Protective Security Manual (as per RESTRICTED).	
Restricted Protected/ confidential Highly protected/secret	Government and military readers should refer to relevant PSMs and DSMs, which are available through your facility security officer.	

5.6.6 Intellectual Property

Intellectual property is a unique component of information that can be defined as a product of the intellect that has commercial value, which includes copyrighted property such as literary or artistic works, and ideational property, such as patents, appellations of origin, business methods, and industrial processes.

The act of creating IP[33] does not necessarily confer rights to the ownership of that IP. Inventors and organizations may use various instruments to register their IP and to obtain the legal rights of ownership, thus providing a degree of risk treatment, including:

- Patents
- Trademarks
- Designs
- Plant breeders' rights[33]

Ironically, patents and other instruments designed to protect IP may actually increase the risk that IP rights may be infringed. For example, to file a patent, an individual or organization must provide some detail on the invention, which can include diagrams. IP law is less well developed, and IP rights are not well respected in some countries compared with to others. Third parties may misuse an inventor's or organization's IP, and it may be difficult for the injured party to enforce their rights through the legal system, especially in some overseas jurisdictions.

The success of an IP product can also exacerbate the associated security risks because the more successful the product, the more attractive it is to copy. Some inventors and organizations choose not to file patents or to use other instruments designed to protect IP, instead choosing to keep their invention a trade secret. This presents its own risks; the likelihood that a trade secret may be compromised could rest on the confidentiality and the level of integrity of staff that become privy to the trade secret.

5.6.7 Summary of Key Points

- Information security is the process of protecting data from unauthorized access, use, disclosure, destruction, modification, or disruption. Information management techniques—such as document access controls, hard and soft copy security mechanisms, and the use of available legal frameworks to protect an organization's sensitive or proprietary information—should be used in concert to protect an organization's information.
- Establishing and applying organizational standards for classification and handling of information from inception to destruction is fundamental to the achievement of organizational goals.

A range of strategies can be employed to protect information; like all Security Risk Management systems, a combination of strategies will help to ensure the protection of information and help to support the goals of an organization through providing security in depth.

Strategic Knowledge Areas 6

6.1 INTRODUCTION

At its core, Security Risk Management (SRM) involves protecting assets by identifying, understanding, and mitigating threats, while trading-off competing or even potentially conflicting priorities. Although SRM resources are focused generally toward asset protection, the fundamental objective of Security Risk Management is better described as "supporting organizational resilience to assist the achievement of objectives." In practice, this usually means the protection and operational continuity of assets that support the maintenance of organizational function and capabilities.

Resource limitations, organizational culture, risk appetites, and changing threat environments mean that the balance between risk and reward is continually in flux and will often vary between as well as within organizations (Figure 6.1).

In many respects, SRM involves analyzing and understanding the threat contexts of organizational exposures, the application of resources, and the monitoring of systems quality to achieve a level of risk that is cost effective and as low as reasonably practicable (ALARP) (Figure 6.2).

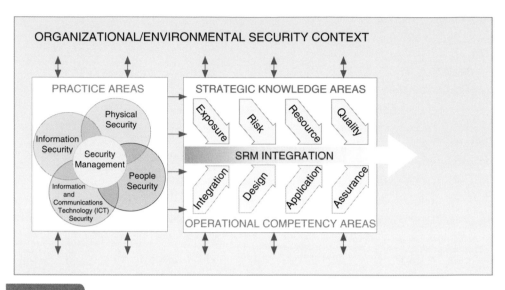

FIGURE 6.1 SRMBOK strategic knowledge areas

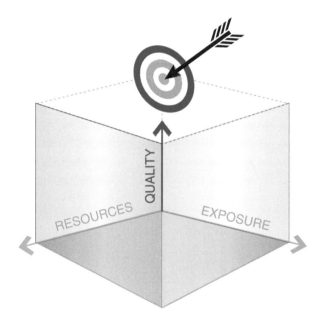

FIGURE 6.2 Risk, exposure, resources, and quality

6.1.1 The Four Pillars of Security Risk Management

The principle knowledge areas that a security practitioner or manager must understand if they are to adequately understand and mitigate security risks are as follows:

• **Exposure**—timeframe (in terms of duration and frequency) in which an asset is exposed to potential threats or opportunities

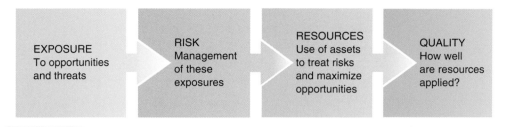

Elements of the SRM knowledge areas

- **Risk**—degree of uncertainty associated with positive or negative outcomes
- **Resources**—security personnel, funds, capabilities, and so on, which can be brought to bear
- **Quality**—totality of properties that result in acceptability or suitability for purpose

For simplicity, it can be useful to think of these four elements as sequential steps, as illustrated in Figure 6.3. It is necessary first to understand exposure in terms of the duration or frequency of interaction with the prevailing environment, then to apply risk analysis techniques to evaluate them before applying resources to treat them, and finally to monitor, review, and assess the quality of our security system.[m]

From a practitioner's viewpoint, this concept is better illustrated as a cycle whereby after evaluating and adjusting the quality of SRM measures, the process commences at the beginning again through reviewing the new exposures.

Of course many cycles exist within each step here. For instance, exposure is often informed by an intelligence cycle, the risk process is well documented in publications such as AS/NZS 4360:2004 Risk Management Standard, resource application is addressed in project methodologies such as PRINCE2, and quality is well documented in ISO 9000. Each of these elements have many cyclical processes within them.

6.1.2 The Quadruple Constraints of Security Risk Management

> *The quadruple constraints of SRM define the elements that a security risk practitioner must trade off and balance to achieve an optimal outcome for their circumstances. Any change in one will result in a corresponding increase or decrease in one or more of the other elements. The key question here is to find the appropriate balance between certain harm and potential harm.*

---

[m]Recognizing that much of what is likely to occur may well be unknown and unknowable[34] (from Reference 34, page 9).

In a theoretical, perfect model, each of these elements would be changing dynamically in response to environmental changes (Figure 6.4). In practice, it is not possible to do so and a perfect balance point in trading off these elements does not exist. Rather, the goal is to optimize all four in coordination for each particular asset, organization, and its circumstances.

Reducing risk, for example, could be achieved by increasing resources. Reducing risk to zero, however, would be likely to require virtually infinite resources or a reduction of overall exposure to the point where a project or activity is effectively abandoned—thereby leaving little opportunity to achieve the project goals. Similarly, realizing opportunities (positive risk) requires increased exposure, which may also result in increase downside risk. Achieving total protection for an international resources project, for example, might require more security resources than the net value of resources at that location.

It is important to note that in this context positive is not necessarily good or bad, only that it is a positive correlation, i.e., if one element increases so will the other (Table 6.1). Similarly, a negative or inverse correlation simply means that if you increase one element, the other is likely to decrease. This is illustrated in Figure 6.5 where, for example, risk increases (on the X-axis) as resources decrease (on the Y-axis). This relationship is of course much more complex—inappropriately applied resources may have no effect at all or may even increase the risk. For the purposes of illustration, we have assumed that we are living in an ideal world where security resources are always applied appropriately after due analysis, which is often not the case as we will illustrate later. Similarly, increased resources would usually result in a lowered risk—indicating a negative

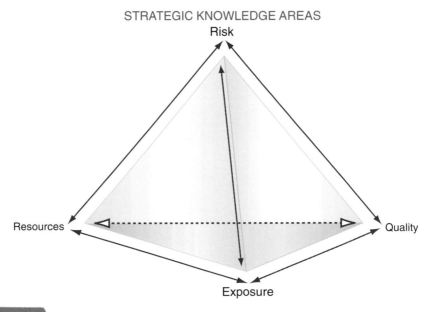

FIGURE 6.4 SRM quadruple constraints

Table 6.1	Correlations among SRM constraints
	Risk
Exposure	POSITIVE
Resources	NEGATIVE
Quality	NEGATIVE

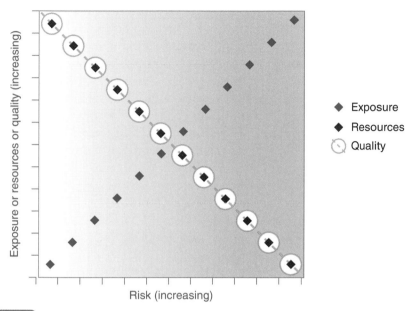

FIGURE 6.5 Correlation of exposure, resources, and quality against risk

correlation. Another view of the relationship of risk and resources is also illustrated in Figure 6.44: ALARP Cost/Benefit Trade-off.

Similarly, Figure 6.5 illustrates the negative correlation between risk and quality, whereby increases in quality should normally result in a reduction in risk, assuming resources and exposure are unchanged. This might be something as simple, for example, as randomizing the rosters in a maximum security prison so that prisoners cannot time an escape attempt for shift change. If no change is required in resourcing and the exposure is unchanged, then prisoners will still attempt to escape, but the net risk is reduced because prisoners cannot collude among themselves or others to schedule an escape attempt at what might otherwise be an optimal time.

Similarly, increased exposure because of longer opening hours for a service station is likely to lead to increased risk indicating a positive correlation.

6.1.2.1 As Low As Reasonably Practicable. Most organizations and individuals choose to manage risk to a point where the benefits do not outweigh the costs of risk reduction. This concept is enshrined in most of the occupational health and safety legislation as the risk level that employers should target. It is also a useful concept for security professionals to base mitigation strategies on.

This concept is illustrated in Figure 6.6 whereby ideally we would reduce all risks to the point where they are so low as to be negligible or at least to the point where they can be managed by routine procedures. In fact, most risks we face are already at this level and we accept them relatively unconsciously. For most of us in affluent societies, for example, the risk of being pickpocketed is so low that we do not feel the need to carry cash in separate pockets or hidden money pouches. We similarly manage slightly higher risks such as crossing the road by routine procedures that were taught to us when we were schoolchildren.

Another view of this ALARP principle can be observed in Figure 6.7 where the balance point or trade-off between resources and quality acting against exposure produces a point of equilibrium. This is the point where appropriate, not necessarily equal, application of resources (e.g., people, money, and barriers) as well as quality and fitness for purposes reduces exposures to the point where overall risk is ALARP.

This principle is possibly best illustrated if resources and quality are inadequate to meet the actual exposure (see Figure 6.8) as a result of which the risk moves out of the ALARP region. Gradations from 2 to 10 have also been added to this graphic to align with risk rating based on likelihood and consequence as calculated using a risk matrix (see Figure 6.9).

Similarly, a high level of resource application still equates to a higher risk if exposures are high and SRM quality is poor, as illustrated in Figure 6.10.

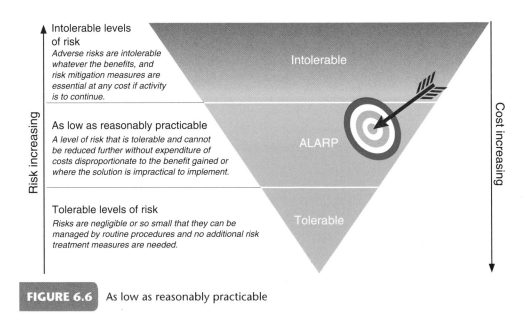

FIGURE 6.6 As low as reasonably practicable

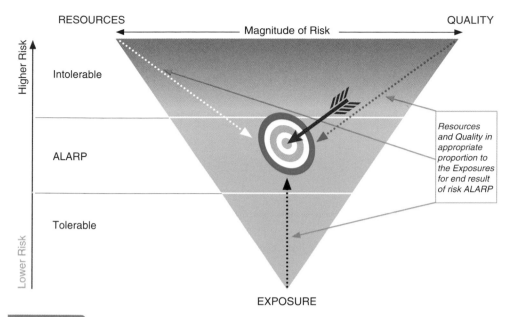

FIGURE 6.7 Risk equilibrium (optimal trade-off)

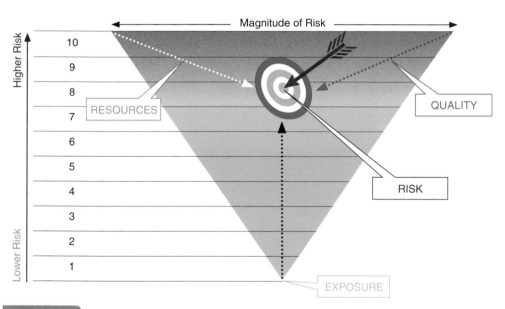

FIGURE 6.8 Inadequate resources and quality results in higher risk

Alternatively, for those organizations that practice opportunity realization, a similar matrix can be developed to ensure that all opportunities can be identified, assessed and prioritized in order of importance. An example of an opportunity realization matrix is shown at Figure 6.11.

srmbok

Security Risk Management
BODY OF KNOWLEDGE

Example Risk Rating Matrix

	Consequence →				
People	Minor skills impact.	Minor impact to capability.	Unavailability of core skills affecting services.	Unavailability of critical skills or personnel.	Protracted unavailability of critical skills/people.
	Protracted unavailability of critical skills/people.	Injury requiring treatment by medical practitioner.	Major injury / hospitalization.	Single death and/ or multiple major injuries.	Multiple deaths.
Information	Compromise of information otherwise available in the public domain.	Minor compromise of information sensitive to internal or subunit interests.	Compromise of information sensitive to this organization's operations.	Compromise of information sensitive to organizational interests.	Compromise of information with significant ongoing impact.
Property & Equipment	Minor damage or vandalism to asset.	Minor damage or loss of <5% of total assets.	Damage or loss of <20% of total assets.	Extensive damage or loss <50% of total assets.	Destruction or complete loss of >50% of assets including intellectual property.
Reputation	Local mention only. Quickly forgotten. Freedom to operate unaffected. Self improvement review required.	Scrutiny by Executive, internal committees or internal audit to prevent escalation. Short term local media concern. Some impact on local level activities.	Persistent national concern. Scrutiny required by external agencies. Long term "brand" impact.	Persistent intense national public, political, and media scrutiny. Long-term "brand" impact. Major operations severely restricted.	International concern, Governmenal Inquiry or sustained adverse national/ international media. "Brand" significantly affects organizational abilities.
Financial	1% of Project or Organizational annual budget.	2–5% of Project or Organizational annual budget.	5–10 % of Project or Organizational annual budget.	> 10% Project or Organizational annual budget.	> 30% of Project or Organizational annual budget.
Capability	Minimal impact on noncore business operations. The impact can be dealt with by routine operations.	Some impact on business areas in terms of delays, systems quality but able to be dealt with at operational level.	Impact on the organization resulting in reduced performance such that targets are not met. Organizations existence is not threatened, but could be subject to significant review or changed ways of operations.	Breakdown of key activities leading to reduction in performance (e.g., service delays, revenue loss, client dissatisfaction, legislative breaches). Survival of the project/activity/ organization is threatened.	Critical failure(s) preventing core activities from being performed. The impact threatens the survival of the project or the organization itself.

Qualitative Likelihood	Quantitative Likelihood		Insignificant	Negligible	Moderate	Major	Extensive
Is expected to occur in most circumstances.	Has occurred on an annual basis in this organization in the past or circumstances are in train that will cause it to happen.	**Almost Certain**	6	7	8	9	10
Will probably occur in most circumstances.	Has occurred in the last few years in this organization or has occurred recently in other similar organizations or circumstances have occurred that will cause it to happen in the next few years.	**Likely**	5	6	7	8	9
Might occur at some time.	Has occurred at least once in the history of this organization or is considered to have a 5% chance of occuring in the next few years.	**Possible**	4	5	6	7	8
Could occur at some time.	Has never occurred in this organization but has occurred infrequently in other similar organizations or is considered to have a 1% chance of occurring in the next few years.	**Unlikely**	3	4	5	6	7
May occur only in exceptional circumstances.	Is possible but has not occurred to date in any similar organization and is considered to have very much less than a 1% chance of occurring in the short term.	**Rare**	2	3	4	5	6

Likelihood (vertical axis label)

Very High (VH)	Immediate action required by the Executive with detailed planning, allocation of resources, and regular monitoring
High (H)	High risk, senior management attention needed
Medium (M)	Management responsibility must be specified
Low (L)	Monitor and manage by routine procedures
Very Low (VL)	Managed by routine procedures

FIGURE 6.9 Example of risk rating matrix

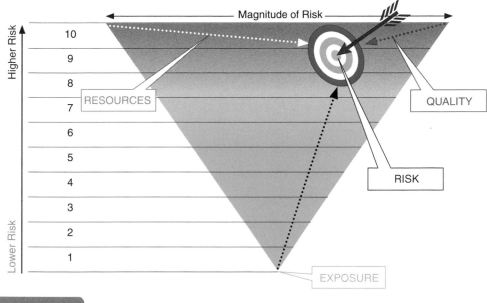

FIGURE 6.10 Lower quality equates to higher risk

6.2 EXPOSURE

Before any risk judgments can be made or effective treatments applied, it is necessary to make a thorough assessment of all identifiable or credible risk exposures. Exposure analysis, although critical to all areas of risk management, lies at the heart of security risk management. In other types of risk management, it is important to acknowledge and consider vulnerabilities, however, the unique difference in Security Risk Management is that other human beings (rather than circumstances, mechanical failure or natural disaster) are likely to seek actively to attack or exploit an organization's vulnerabilities. Indeed, the traditional approach to Security Risk Management has been based on either rectifying vulnerabilities post incident or seeking to reduce vulnerabilities identified through a red-team approach.

> *The main objective of exposure assessment is to identify the assets at risk, and the duration and frequency in which they are at risk.*

Although exposure is normally established as part of context setting in the risk management process, it has been separately identified here as one of the quadruple constraints because of its inherently dynamic nature. Establishing context as part of the risk management process—see section 6.3.6.3—differs from exposure analysis for many reasons, not least that exposure is a subset of context. Risk ratings will vary dynamically depending on (a) the duration of exposure and (b) the nature of assets that are subject to potential risks.

srmbok

Security Risk Management
BODY OF KNOWLEDGE

Example Opportunity Rating Matrix

	Opportunity →				
People	Minimal skills improvement.	Minor improvement to capability.	Moderate enhancement in core skills affecting services.	Major enhancement to critical skills or personnel.	Extensive improvement to critical skills/people.
Information	Acquire information not readily available in the public domain.	Acquire or improve safeguards to information sensitive to internal or subunit interests.	Acquire or improve safeguards to information sensitive to enterprise-wide operations.	Acquire or improve safeguards information sensitive to national interests or registered intellectual property.	Allows the organization to acquire or improve safeguards to information of the highest value.
Property & Equipment	Minimal improvement to asset (<2%).	Minor improvement of asset or increase in its value (2–5%).	Moderate improvement of Asset or increase in its value (>5%).	Major improvement to Asset or its value (>10%).	Extensive improvement to asset or its value (>25%).
Reputation	Minimal self-improvement or increase in brand value (<2%).	Increases brand value by 2–5% or removes requirement for scrutiny by executive, internal committees, or internal audit.	Increases brand value by >5% or removes requirement for scrutiny by external organizations.	Increases brand value by >10% or prevents intense public, political or media scrutiny.	Increases brand value by >25% or prevents a Royal Commission, Parliamentary inquiry, or sustained adverse national/international media campaign.
Business Process & Systems	Minimal improvement on noncore business operations.	Minor improvement on business areas, such as in terms of delays or systems quality.	Moderate improvement in business resulting in enhanced performance. These improvements may need to be subject to significant review or changed ways of operations.	Enhancement in key activities resulting in major improvements in business performance (e.g., reduced service delays, client dissatisfaction, increased revenue, cost reductions, and process improvement).	Enhancement in key activities resulting in extensive improvements in business performance (e.g., reduced service delays, client dissatisfaction, increased revenue, cost reductions, and process improvement).
Financial	<2% improvement in Project or Organizational annual budget.	2–5% improvement in Project or Organizational annual budget.	> 5% improvement in Project or Organizational annual budget.	> 10% improvement in Project or Organizational annual budget.	> 25% improvement in Project or Organizational annual budget.
Capability	Minimal improvement in noncore business operations.	Minor improvement in noncore business operations, such as a reduction in delays.	Moderate improvement in non core or core business operations. May adversely impact competitors.	Major improvement in noncore or core business operations. Will have a major impact on competitor organizational capabilities if implemented.	Extensive improvement in core business operations. Will have a critical impact on competitor organizational capabilities if implemented.

Qualitative Likelihood	Quantitative Likelihood		Insignificant	Minor	Moderate	Major	Extensive
Is expected to occur in most circumstances.	Has occurred on an annual basis in this organization in the past or circumstances are in train that will cause it to happen.	**Almost Certain**	6	7	8	9	10
Will probably occur in most circumstances.	Has occurred in the last few years in this organization or has occurred recently in other similar organizations or circumstances have occurred that will cause it to happen in the next few years.	**Likely**	5	6	7	8	9
Might occur at some time.	Has occurred at least once in the history of this organization or is considered to have a 5% chance of occurring in the next few years.	**Possible**	4	5	6	7	8
Could occur at some time.	Has never occurred in this organization but has occurred infrequently in other similar organizations or is considered to have a 1% chance of occurring in the next few years.	**Unlikely**	3	4	5	6	7
May occur only in exceptional circumstances.	Is possible but has not occurred to date in any similar organization and is considered to have very much less than 1% chance of occurring in the short term.	**Rare**	2	3	4	5	6

Likelihood (vertical axis label)

Very High (VH)	Amazing opportunity requiring immediate action by the Executive
High (H)	Strong or valuable opportunity that requires senior management attention
Medium (M)	Management responsibility must be specified
Low (L)	Managed by routine procedures

FIGURE 6.11 Opportunity realization matrix

For example, a 10-day Heads of Government meeting will have a different risk rating from a 10-day carnival. Equally, a 10-day trade exhibition will have a different risk profile and rating from a 365-day "World Fair". Finally, a convenience store that is only open during daylight hours could have a different exposure from a convenience store that is open 24/7 in the same area.

Other factors such as changes in organizational culture, risk management practices, programs, or activities will invariably modify and form part of the organizational context but may or may not vary exposure. Similarly, context may remain unchanged, but a variation in travel routines may increase or decrease exposure. To retain the existing level of risk after an increase in travel frequency may require additional resources or improved quality may need to be implemented into existing risk management practices.

6.2.1 Assessing Exposure

"While simple to state in principle, applying risk management is difficult in practice, in part because assessing threats is an uncertain process due to limited historical data on which to assess the probability of various types of risk."
WILLIAM O. JENKINS JR., DIRECTOR, HOMELAND SECURITY AND JUSTICE ISSUES, GAO.[35]

When considering your own exposure, you should always examine the wider context for collateral exposure. Collateral exposure is the presence of other third-party high-vulnerability entities or high-threat targets. This could include your organization being in close proximity to attractive targets, such as embassies, places of worship, military installations, utility plants, or transport hubs, depending on the nature of the threat; or to other hazards subject to malicious or incidental threats, such as chemical storage facilities (accidental spill, explosion threats), commercial, industrial, or global icons, e.g., international food Chains, mining conglomerates, on companies associated with third-world child labor. Because of collateral exposure, it is important to determine the nature of the relationship between your entity and the third party, which includes the controls developed by the third party itself. For example, living on the same street as several foreign ambassadors may actually reduce your overall exposure as they are likely to have funded security services provided by the host country.

Broder describes three factors that need to be identified and evaluated as part of exposure analysis:

- The types of loss or nature of hazards that can affect the assets involved
- The likelihood of those hazards materializing in a loss event
- The credible consequences as a result of such event/s.[36]

Although an estimation of likelihood and consequence will reflect on and inform exposure assessment, these are dealt with in more detail in the following section (risk). Exposure in the Security Risk Management context is similar to the concept of gross risk or greenfield risk, and a multitude of assessment systems have been developed to assist in this regard. The principle objective of exposure assessment is to provide an informed basis for decision making by understanding what the organization is exposed to. The key building blocks involved in creating and therefore assessing exposures are the interactions of three elements:

- The threat(s)
- The asset(s)
- The significance of any interaction between the above two elements, which shows vulnerability.[37]

These three elements are discussed below in greater detail and can be variously assessed using the following existing methodologies:

- Threat assessment
- Vulnerability assessment
- Criticality assessment

6.2.2 What is Threat?

Threat is usually assessed and described using a combination of intent and capability of a threat actor, whether individual or organization, to attack or adversely impact an item of value such an asset, function, or capability. As such, threat develops predominantly as an extant force to the organization or community of the individual. It is important to note that definition includes both extant and insider threat.

The HB167 Security Risk Management Handbook extends this to include "anything that has the potential to prevent or hinder the achievement of objectives or disrupt the processes that support them."

6.2.2.1 The Threat Assessment. Security risks can be differentiated from other risk functions by several criteria, not least of all that security threats spring primarily from deliberate intention rather than from accidental, natural, or systemic causes.

People—not acts of god, mechanical failures, or management systems—create security threats. People not only can execute deliberate actions to release hazards or cause loss, but also can apply creative intellect to their misdeeds. This ability to apply intelligence enables human beings to identify and evaluate any existing security barriers and to devise and test ways of bypassing them.

Consequently, the first necessary activity in any security risk process is to understand the threat. Does a threat exist? Do any criminally, subversive, politically motivated or issue-motivated threat actors pose a risk to the organization, and if so, what are the likely attack vectors? Once a threat assessment has been made, the typical processes and methodologies of general risk management commence, and the subsequent steps after the threat assessment are common to both security and general risk management functions.

Formal threat assessments are usually conducted by intelligence professionals; however, it is reasonable to suggest that as individuals, we conduct ongoing threat assessments in our daily life as a relatively unconscious process, which includes, for example, decisions such as where to park our car or whether to take a holiday in a particular country.

The most common form of formal threat assessments is usually conducted either as an output of intelligence processes or as part of an organizational security risk assessment. These latter threat assessments are often conducted by security risk professionals informed by generic threat assessment information, consultation with subject matter experts, review of incidents, analysis of open source information, and so on. Such an approach almost invariably involves some element of subjective estimation. Data and information commonly do not exist to determine, with a degree of precision, the likely probability of variables within the model because

- The data or information may not have been collected before
- The data or information are too expensive to obtain
- The problem being modeled are new
- Past data or information are no longer relevant because of changes in the environmental context
- Data or information are scarce

In such situations, one way of determining the likelihood of threat occurrence is to rely on the knowledge and experiences of subject matter experts and attempt to fill in the information holes based on their considered opinions. This strategy obviously has some limitations but may be the best tool available as any quantifiable or statistical tool is likely to be equally flawed through incomplete data inputs.

A commonly used technique to overcome limitations associated with opinions or imprecise information is the admiralty scale. This scale provides a means of rating the reliability and accuracy, and hence usefulness, of information through a graduated alphanumeric scale. The reliability of the information source is assessed on criteria such as the previous quality of information supplied by the source as well as the situation, location, and likely access of the source at that time of the information collected. The accuracy of the information provided is assessed as an actual or perceived relative measurement in relation to each item of information received. For example, this accuracy can be based on a comparison of the supplied information with other confirmed facts or other previously but not necessarily confirmed information, or with trends or patterns of other events or threats.

Reliability of Source		Accuracy of Information	
A	Completely reliable	1	Confirmed by other sources
B	Usually reliable	2	Probably true and accurate
C	Fairly reliable	3	Possibly true and accurate
D	Not usually reliable	4	Doubtful
E	Unreliable	5	Improbable
F	Cannot be judged or assessed	6	Cannot be judged or assessed

Another approach is to adopt a green team and a red team. Under this arrangement, the green team would develop the threat assessment, and a second team, the red team, would then independently review the logic of the first group. In so doing, bias can be removed, and the logic flow of deductions can be confirmed. Such an approach is also a useful tool in reviewing a range of documents, which includes procurement evaluations or risk treatment plans.

6.2.2.2 Assessing Threat. The twin drivers often used to determine threat are intent and likelihood, which are themselves functions of the motivation and attributes of the threat actor. For example, motivation is a long-term driver that may be expressed as a "desire to overthrow the government to provide equality for the underprivileged." A more immediate intent, however, is possibly to be something like "use violence to destabilize the government and raise our international profile." Depending on the threat actor's desires and their confidence in their ability to achieve those desires, they may consider a variety of ways to achieve this intent. Similarly, if the threat actor has the resources and capability to use explosives, for example, they may choose to attack against members of the public with bomb attacks to materialize that capability (Figure 6.12).

Understanding the difference between motivation (strategic objectives) and general or specific intent is a key challenge but one that offers insights into early countermeasures. In the above example, the gap between motivation and intent may be very small if abundant weapons are available, and recruits may be more available if there is a cultural acceptance of the use of violence among the community.

Similarly, a drug addict may be motivated by the need to get money to buy drugs, but the manifested intent will vary depending on their desire, e.g., how urgent is the need and confidence, and what opportunities present. The resources and knowledge available to them will also influence their actions. If they have a well-paid job or a private inheritance, they probably have no criminal intent beyond the purchase and use of drugs. If their resources are limited, the options may come down to prostitution, washing car windows at traffic lights, or resorting to robbery. The ability to interrupt this motivation to intent gap, at least to some degree, may be as simple as introducing permits that allow people to wash car windows at traffic lights.

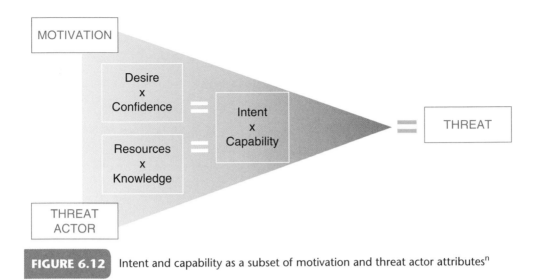

Intent and capability as a subset of motivation and threat actor attributes[n]

Another element, not shown in the above graphics, is risk aversion. This element pervades all steps of the equation and is best considered when analyzing either the final threat or each element. Depending on the level of risk aversion, many potential offenders may be swayed in their course by the potential penalties, e.g., being dismissed from their job or going to jail. Similarly, the risk tolerance will also determine what level of resources the offender may have. If they do not care about being caught they may be more prepared to take risks to gather information, acquire explosives, and so on.

These concepts are extended in Figure 6.13 to illustrate the relationship between terms in more detail shows.

Attractiveness of the target or asset is included here as it reflects the potential influence that a highly attractive target could make to threat actor intent. This attractiveness could include elements, such as:

- Recognizability/visibility to the attacker, e.g., World Trade Center, national leaders, Sydney Opera House
- Desirability in terms of achieving the attackers aims or motivations, e.g., media worthiness, shock value
- Vulnerability, e.g., public transport or a gas plant

These qualities will influence the intent of an attacker. For instance, the intent of an attack on a gas plant might be to disable it, whereas the intent of a

---

[n]It should be noted that this graphic is illustrative only. The relationship between intent and capability, desire, and confidence, or resources and knowledge is usually much more complex than a simple mathematical formula. It may, for example, in some cases be binary in nature in so much as it either exists or it does not; i.e., both resources and knowledge are required—one without the other means that there is no capability.

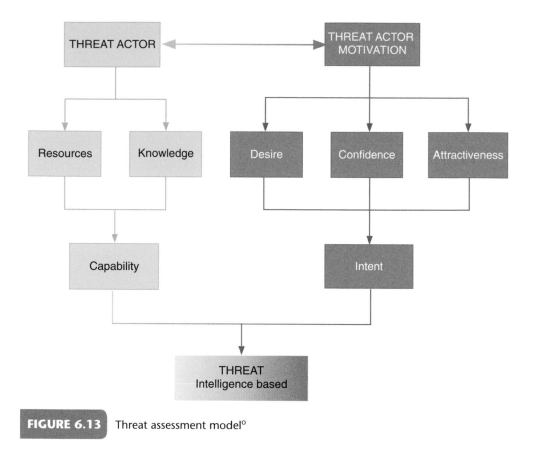

FIGURE 6.13 Threat assessment model[o]

shopping center attack might be for mass casualties. In both these cases, these specific intents are subsets of the general intent that might, for example, include media coverage as part of the broader motivation (money, regime change, political leverage, etc.).

The process outlined in Figure 6.13 can be applied at all levels from individuals to a nation state. For example, it could be done as a back-of-envelope high-level discussion for a relatively minor event, such as a half-day workshop with work colleagues or for a school fair. Equally, for a multinational corporation or government agency, it could run in to dozens of pages with a chapter covering each of the elements.

> *Application of this methodology is discussed in depth in the separate Guide to SRMBOK on Security Risk Assessments and Management.*

---

[o]Note: This is a high-level representation of the respective elements that build to an understanding of threat. For example, threat actor attributes and threat actor motivation are often interrelated. For the purposes of analysis; however, they will usually bear separate examination.

6.2.2.3 Warning Signs and Indicators. Threat assessments are often linked to warning signs or indicators, so that changes in the threat environment or the likelihood of occurrence can be monitored over time. Experts who evaluate possible indicators that an individual is at risk of harming himself or others know to seek out many sources for clues or certain red flags that merit attention. A single warning sign by itself usually does not warrant overt action by a threat assessment specialist. It should, however, attract the attention of an assessor who has been sensitized to look for other possible warning signs. If additional warning signs are present, then more fact finding is warranted to determine whether there is a likelihood of danger.

Some warning signs carry more weight than others. For instance, a fascination with, and possession of, firearms is more significant than being a loner, because possession of firearms gives one the capacity to carry out an attack. But if a person simply possesses firearms and has no other warning signs, it is unlikely that he represents a significant risk of danger.

When a cluster of indicators is present, then the risk becomes more serious. Thus, a person who possesses firearms, is a loner, shows an interest in past shooting situations, writes stories about homicide and suicide, exhibits aberrant behavior, has talked about retribution against others, and has a history of mental illness and refuses counseling would obviously be considered a significant risk of becoming dangerous to himself or others. A school threat assessment team on learning about such a list of warning signs would be in a position to take immediate action, including the following:

- Talking to the student and developing a treatment plan with conditions for remaining in school
- Calling the parents or other guardians
- Requesting permission to receive medical and educational records
- Checking with law enforcement to ascertain whether there have been any interactions with police
- Talking with roommates and faculty
- Suspending the student until the student has been treated and doctors indicate the student is not a safety risk

6.2.2.4 Threat Perspectives. Another useful approach to establishing threat levels is to identify the relationship between the threat actor, and the as the threat actor is likely to have a different perspective and motivation than the target's protector. There are many perspectives to this, however, a useful discussion tool for promoting common understanding is to consider the following:

- The protector's view of the threat actor
- The threat actor's view of the potential or actual target

Intelligence is nearly always incomplete so, at best, it will form a general view in either direction; however, the better the threat actors and their motivation are understood, the greater the likelihood of effectively protecting against them.

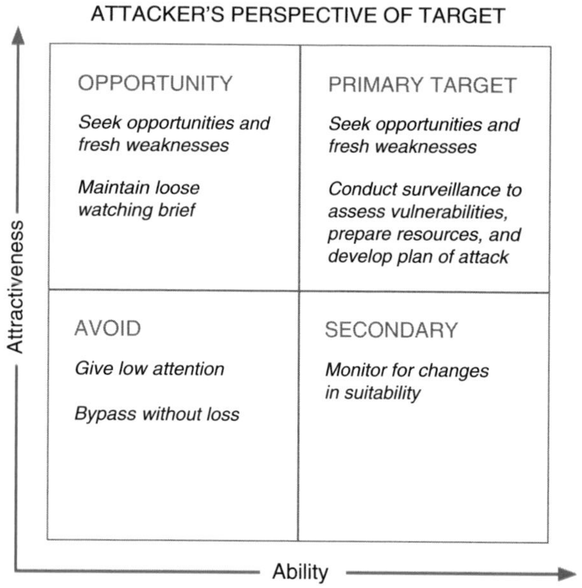

ATTACKER'S PERSPECTIVE OF TARGET

OPPORTUNITY	**PRIMARY TARGET**
Seek opportunities and fresh weaknesses	*Seek opportunities and fresh weaknesses*
Maintain loose watching brief	*Conduct surveillance to assess vulnerabilities, prepare resources, and develop plan of attack*
AVOID	**SECONDARY**
Give low attention	*Monitor for changes in suitability*
Bypass without loss	

Attractiveness (vertical axis) — Ability → (horizontal axis)

FIGURE 6.14 Attacker's perspective of the target

The concept of attractiveness (Y-axis) is more complex than illustrated in Figure 6.14, but in practice, this shorthand provides an insight into the desirability of a particular asset, activity, project, community, or organization, and so on.

Using the concept of threat perspectives (Figure 6.15) assists with prioritizing treatment strategies. It can also be a convenient briefing tool for providing executive staff with an overview of the various organizational threats as illustrated in Figure 6.16.

In Figure 6.16, threat actor 1 is described under the irritant category, whereas threat actor 2 constitutes a critical threat.

This concept assumes that the protectors have a reasonable level of information about the attacker. Although not always the case, more high profile and well-known threat actors, such as the Irish Republican Army (IRA) during the 1980s, can have their intent and capability clearly determined. Similarly, home burglaries are a threat with which we are well experienced and can apply the Law of Large Numbers toward an informed assessment.[p]

---

[p]The Law of Large Numbers is also known as Bernoulli's Theorem (not to be confused with the law in physics that bears the same name) after Jacob Bernoulli who developed the mathematical proof in 1713. In essence, it suggests that the greater the statistical population sampled, the closer the observed result will be to the statistical averages. For example, we do not know the intent or capability of any given burglar against any particular house, but in most cities, there will be many burglaries each year. We can therefore make a reasonable assessment of the intent and capability of the typical representatives of this group (burglars).

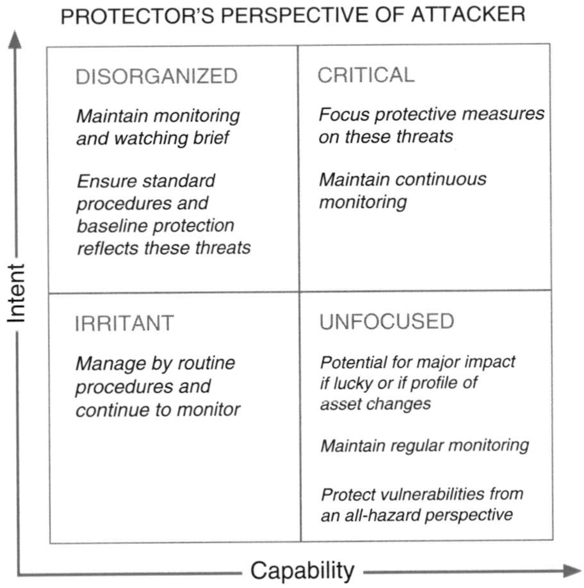

PROTECTOR'S PERSPECTIVE OF ATTACKER
DISORGANIZED
Maintain monitoring and watching brief
Ensure standard procedures and baseline protection reflects these threats
CRITICAL
Focus protective measures on these threats
Maintain continuous monitoring
IRRITANT
Manage by routine procedures and continue to monitor
UNFOCUSED
Potential for major impact if lucky or if profile of asset changes
Maintain regular monitoring
Protect vulnerabilities from an all-hazard perspective
Intent
Capability

FIGURE 6.15 Protector's perspective of the threat actor

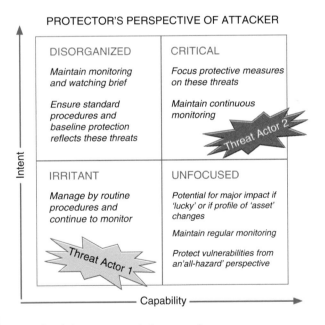

PROTECTOR'S PERSPECTIVE OF ATTACKER
DISORGANIZED
Maintain monitoring and watching brief
Ensure standard procedures and baseline protection reflects these threats
CRITICAL
Focus protective measures on these threats
Maintain continuous monitoring
Threat Actor 2
IRRITANT
Manage by routine procedures and continue to monitor
Threat Actor 1
UNFOCUSED
Potential for major impact if 'lucky' or if profile of 'asset' changes
Maintain regular monitoring
Protect vulnerabilities from an'all-hazard' perspective
Intent
Capability

FIGURE 6.16 Example of threat actor relative groupings

In Figure 6.17, my organization has been assessed as a secondary target for threat actor 2, which indicates that they might seek to exploit an evolving weakness if identified. Of more concern is that, in this example, the assessment indicates that the factory next door to my organization is considered a primary

ATTACKER'S PERSPECTIVE OF TARGET

OPPORTUNITY	PRIMARY TARGET
Seek opportunities and fresh weaknesses	Seek opportunities and fresh weaknes...
Maintain loose watching brief	Conduct s... assess vu... prepare res... develop plan o...
AVOID	SECONDARY
Give low attention	Monitor for changes in suitability
Bypass without loss	

Factory next door to my organization

My organization

Attractiveness (vertical axis)

Ability (horizontal axis)

FIGURE 6.17 Example of threat actor 2 perspectives

target by threat actor 2. Treatments and ongoing monitoring strategies should reflect this understanding.

6.2.3 Vulnerability Assessment

A vulnerability assessment involves a process (verb) or outputs (noun) associated with reviewing assets and/or security systems to identify weaknesses. Usually, it is conducted from a greenfield perspective (baseline) to identify how they could fail or could be successfully attacked.

Vulnerability can be considered a function of accessibility, deterrence ability and the degree of hardness, or the ability to withstand an attack. Generally speaking, the criticality of an element is not influenced by its vulnerability nor by any extant threat.[38]

A variety of tools and frameworks has been developed for vulnerability assessment, and their relative strengths and weaknesses often reflect their respective development pathways. A vulnerability assessment is typically conducted by a security risk professional, albeit informed by intelligence and threat information, and with the assistance of subject matter experts and stakeholders.[q]

---

[q]The other main party involved in a vulnerability assessment will usually be the adversarial party – ie. the threat actor seeking to identify vulnerabilities in order to exploit them. These threat actors will usually conduct a less comprehensive vulnerability analysis however it is important to consider that many are well resourced. International organized crime groups are one such group, however some of the relatively sophisticated vulnerability assessment methodologies such as CARVER were developed by military organizations in order to better attack an adversary.

6.2.3.1 Types of Vulnerability Assessment. In 2003, the U.S. Department of Homeland Security published The Vulnerability Assessment Methodologies Report, which describes and evaluates 44 such methodologies.[39] The report drew the following four key recommendations:

- The most robust methodologies do not solely focus on one sector of the economy.
- The quality of the assessor in all cases is very important. In other words, a mediocre methodology, which is well applied by a knowledgeable assessor, will yield an acceptable and useful result, whereas a good methodology in the hands of an unskilled assessor will not produce very useful results.
- Although all methodologies determined some measure of risk, few actually calculated a numerical value for that risk. Numerical values assigned were in nearly every case ordinal rather (rather than absolute) but were useful to provide a level of comparison and granularity.
- Training required to use the methodologies accurately varied greatly in time and cost. The quality and diligence of the assessor is as important or more important than the specific methodology used. A well-qualified and knowledgeable assessor minimizes the need for additional expensive training, can conduct the assessment more quickly, and will provide a more accurate, useful assessment.

Typically, most vulnerability assessment tools can be categorized as follows:

- Asset based
- Functionality/capability based

> *Although the terms "risk assessment" and "vulnerability assessment" are sometimes used interchangeably, it is important to note that a vulnerability assessment is only one part of the overall risk assessment and management process.*

6.2.3.2 Techniques. The assessment of security vulnerabilities can take many forms from the qualitative/subjective to quantitative/objective assessment. An overview of the U.S. Department of Justice CARVER and OCTAVE methodologies are provided below as examples of commonly used vulnerability and risk assessment frameworks.

US Department of Justice Framework

The US Department of Justice approach to determining vulnerability and target attractiveness uses a numeric (semiquantitative) scale to rate seven factors, each of which are scored from 0 (low) to 5 (high):

- Level of visibility
- Asset value of target
- Target value to potential threat actor
- Threat actors access to the target asset

- Target threat of (susceptibility to) hazard
- Site population
- Potential for collateral damage or mass casualties

There is also a checklist assessment for public health, which is integrated to determine a risk profile.[40]

CARVER

CARVER is derived from a US Department of Defense acronym for prioritizing the relative attractiveness or vulnerability of targets. It involves identifying the most attractive targets for attack, that is, the most vulnerable. The mnemonic stands for the following:[41]

1. **Criticality**—measure of public health and economic impacts of an attack
2. **Accessibility**—ability to physically access and egress from a target
3. **Recuperability**—ability of system to recover from an attack
4. **Vulnerability**—ease of accomplishing an attack
5. **Effect**—amount of direct loss from an attack as measured by loss in production
6. **Recognizability**—ease of identifying a target

In addition, the modified CARVER tool evaluates a seventh attribute, which is the combined health, economic, and psychological impacts of an attack, or the shock attributes of a target.

Each element is rated on a 1 to 10 scale using descriptive indicators and numeric quantities to provide an overall semiquantitative score, which provides a level of granularity when comparing the vulnerability of one target with another. Although developed primarily for military targets, it is suitable for almost any type of asset or project.

OCTAVE

OCTAVE has been developed by CERT (part of the Software Engineering Institute operated by Carnegie Mellon University) as a structured approach for evaluating operational information security risk. Less of a pure vulnerability assessment tool and more of a risk tool, OCTAVE, which is a mnemonic for Operationally Critical Threat, Asset, and Vulnerability Evaluation, can still be useful in determining vulnerability.

6.2.3.3 Overview of Vulnerability Assessment. A review of several vulnerability assessment models highlights several common features; however, if one separates the elements of threat assessment and criticality assessment, the following areas remain:

- The opportunities that are or may be presented to attack the target
- The susceptibility to attack or effectiveness of any given hazard against the target

Opportunity can be considered a function of asset targetability that can be evaluated in terms of:

- Recognizability as a target
- Exposure (in terms of duration, etc.)
- Accessibility of the target[r]

Effectiveness is a function of the hazard attributes of:

- Suitability
- Availability
- Deployability of the hazard

In general terms, opportunity will affect likelihood, whereas the effectiveness of the hazard will affect consequence. Collectively the interrelation of these attributes might be displayed as illustrated in Figure 6.18.

6.2.4 Criticality Assessment

Criticality assessment attempts to prioritize organizational infrastructure, assets, or elements by relative importance or dependence on that element. In practice, this is often related to (but not synonymous with) the magnitude of the

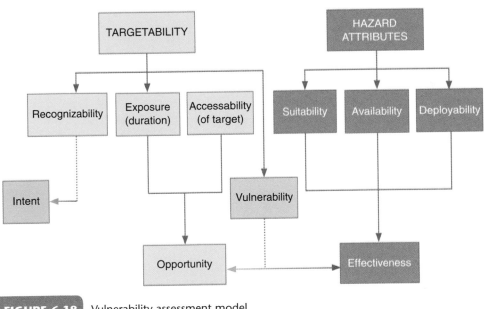

FIGURE 6.18   Vulnerability assessment model

---

[r]In practice, recognizability is likely to modify intent but is included here as it is a function of asset targetability.

downstream impacts created by the element's destruction or disablement.[38] It is also known as "business impact assessment" in corporate environments or "asset assessment" in some methodologies.

Criticality assessment may be based on the magnitude of potential casualties, long-term effects on organizational objectives, and economic or sociopolitical impacts. It is important to note that impact in this context is independent of the attack vector. Criticality analysis attempts to identify those elements that by their very nature magnify the effect of attack. An example of this might include power stations or gas plants, which are critical to the community and economy independent of the direct cost of any attack—and independent of whether the damage is caused by mishap or deliberate attack.

Criticality assessment is a vital step in the identification of risk as it assists prioritization threats as well as the understanding of an organization's, community's, or individual's vulnerability to those threats. It also assists with risk identification as well as analysis and treatments to focus on priority assets that are of most importance to an organization, community, or individual.[41]

Fundamentally, criticality is driven by the organizational or asset attributes and can be considered to be a function of the asset's environmental context, recuperability (recoverability), temporal qualities (e.g., time taken to replace or repair), and the relative dependence/reliance on that asset/function/capability. This is illustrated in Figure 6.19.

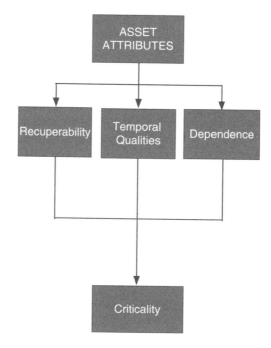

FIGURE 6.19 Criticality assessment model

6.2.5 The External Environment

Assessment of exposure may also be varied dynamically by elements that are generally outside the control of an organization or individual, such as the following:

- **Political**—change of government, policy changes, machinery of government changes
- **Economic**—labor market, exchange rates, global economy
- **Socio cultural**—demographic shifts, stakeholder expectation changes
- **Technological**—obsolescence, cost of procuring current technology, opportunities that develop from technology
- **Environmental**—obligations and expectations for environmental protections
- **Legal**—regulatory changes, corporations law, compliance environment

This grouping is based on what is commonly referred to as the PESTEL model.[42]

6.2.5.1 Security Risks in the Supply Chain. As supply chains become increasingly transformed into lean, complex, and globally dispersed arrangements, organizations are becoming correspondingly more vulnerable to supply chain disruptions. Although most organizations can readily observe a supply chain value proposition in terms of improving efficiencies and reducing costs, many executives are having a hard time determining the economic consequences of supply chain disruptions.

A report by Hendricks and Singhal[43] shows that supply chain disruptions can have a significant negative effect on profitability with potential for a 107% drop on operating income, 7% lower sales growth, and 11% growth in cost, and that firms continue to operate for at least 2 years at a lower performance level after experiencing disruptions. The report also recommended that, although the focus on making supply chains more efficient and lean makes economic sense, organizations should recognize that lean and efficient supply chains face a higher risk of disruptions. In many instances, supply chain investments and initiatives should be undertaken not to reduce costs but because they increase reliability of the supply chains.

> *Supply chain management* is the process of planning, implementing, and controlling the operations of the supply chain to satisfy customer requirements as efficiently as possible. Supply chain management spans all movement and storage of raw materials, work-in-process inventory, and finished goods from the point of origin to the point of consumption.
>
> *Supply chain Security Risk Management* is the process of assessing, mitigating, and managing security risks at all stages of the organization's supply chain. It provides security quality assurance from suppliers via a structured approach for measuring, managing, and monitoring threats and vulnerability levels to the supply chain.

As well as PESTEL-related concepts, organizations need to ensure they do not take an introspective view when determining their exposure to threats and risks, as many risks they face in an increasingly globalized and outsourced world are in fact outside of their organization and direct ownership, yet they still reside in the organization's supply chain. For example:

- Parts or raw material suppliers
- Outsourced manufacturers
- Internet service providers (ISPs) that carry much of an organization's e-mail traffic and often host websites, applications, and e-commerce offerings
- Utility suppliers, including electricity, water, telecommunications, and gas
- Other critical infrastructure owners, such as maritime points of entry, oil refineries, and aviation terminals
- Subcontractors that access an organization's premises and sensitive assets/information
- Couriers that transport commercially sensitive materials, such as tender responses or business contracts
- Distributors stocking completed products ready for sale

Tylenol Poisoning—1982

In 1982, McNeil Consumer Products, a subsidiary of Johnson & Johnson, was confronted with a crisis when seven people on Chicago's West Side died mysteriously. Authorities determined that each of the people that died had ingested an Extra-strength Tylenol capsule laced with cyanide, which had been placed into the capsules following distribution to retail outlets. The news of this incident traveled quickly and was the cause of a massive, nationwide panic.

After the poisonings, which caused Tylenol's share of the painkiller market to plunge from 35% to 7%, Johnson & Johnson was required to spend an estimated $125 million to recall 31 million old packages of Tylenol capsules; develop new, triple-sealed, tamper-resistant packaging; and promote the new safer product.[44]

Mars Blackmail—May 2006

Extortionist threats to Mars subsidiary MasterFoods (in which the extortionist claimed to have poisoned seven bars) forced it to withdraw two chocolate brands from sale in New South Wales, which cost the company more than $10 million in lost sales and in destroying potentially contaminated products.

The head of MasterFoods' operations in Australia, Andy Weston-Webb, said the company received about 100 calls a day from worried consumers during the scare.[45]

It is interesting to note in the above examples that the responses to the supply chain risk revolved around three key elements—recall of existing stock, introduction of tamper-resistant packaging, and public relations. Although the introduction, or threatened introduction, of poison to the food was a significant issue for the organizations concerned, the three main treatments all revolved around restoring consumer confidence. Statistically, the actual threat to consumers was insignificant in terms of likelihood, but the potential costs to reputation, sales, and potential lawsuits constituted a major impact to the affected organizations.

Similarly, the tamper-resistant packaging subsequently introduced to many pharmaceuticals and foodstuffs is actually not that tamper resistant. For example, although it is more difficult to interfere with sealed foodstuffs, it is not impossible for the determined extortionist to pierce a container with a hypodermic needle and then cover the hole with a price tag.

This highlights the differing agendas of stakeholders, such as the public, government agencies, retailers, and manufacturers, and the importance of balancing perceived risk versus actual risk. An example follows:

- The public and government expect that products that will be safe for consumption.
- Manufacturers and retailers expect to make a profit.

The cost to implement tamper-resistant packaging that is actually tamper proof is likely to be prohibitive and may even reduce sales when groups such as the elderly choose to purchase products in containers that are easier to open.

The balance for the security risk professional, therefore, is to provide advice regarding appropriate cost-effective solutions that treat not only the actual risk (poisoning), but also the equally important perceived risk (that the product may be unsafe). Tamper-resistant packaging achieves both of these aims. It makes the product harder for a would-be poisoner to interfere with the product without leaving signs that they have done so, which contributes to the following:

- Reducing the likelihood that they will choose that product
- Reducing the likelihood that someone will purchase or consume a product with a broken seal
- Increasing the potential for detecting contaminated product in the supply chain

6.2.5.2 Supply Chain Arrangements Checklist. Does your organization know the risks that supply chain actors pose? For example:

- What if a courier was providing copies of your tender responses or business contracts to a competitor?
- Could your organization survive if telecommunication services became unavailable for days or weeks?
- Do you have arrangements with more than one parts or raw materials supplier in the event that they become insolvent and can no longer provide you with the necessary materials?

- Does your organization store backups of sensitive information off-site and have these service providers been appropriately cleared?
- What are your media management and product packaging strategies should your organization suffer a Tylenol-style crisis?

If these questions cannot be answered, then the security risk analysis component of a risk assessment is deficient.

Several standards are now being produced solely to address supply chain security considerations, which include the following:

- *ISO 28000:2005—Specifications for security management systems in the supply chain*
- *ISO 28004:2006—Security management systems for the supply chain— Guidelines for the implementation of ISO/PAS 28000.*

Some governments are also now legislating the following security measures and requirements:

- *Sarbanes Oxley—For example, Section 401 requires companies to account for risk in their off-balance-sheet transactions, such as their supply chains. Section 404 also requires companies to establish controls that provide reasonable protection against preventable events that could have an impact on a company's value.*
- *Australian Customs Cargo Compliance Program*
- *U.S. Customs Customs-Trade Partnership Against Terrorism (C-TPAT) and Operation Safe Commerce initiatives*
- *World Customs Organization Framework of Standards to Secure and Facilitate Global Trade (SAFE)*
- *International Ship and Port Facility Security (ISPS) Code, 2002.*

Procuring Products and Services across the Supply Chain

In terms of procurement, where an organization engages an external service provider, there is potential for unauthorized access to organizational assets, such as commercially sensitive information.

Although the responsibility to perform certain organizational functions or services can be transferred to an external service provider, accountability should not be transferred because an organization will always remain accountable to its own shareholders and other stakeholders for the effective and secure performance of its mandated functions. Accordingly, in considering procurement options, organizations should address the concomitant risk to the security of its assets and functions in line with the risks and controls covered as part of its organizational security plan, as follows:

- Extent to which its performance is critical to the meeting of government and organization objectives

- Consequences posed by inadequate performance of the function
- Type of risk inherent in the function
- Degree of exposure of the function to threat
- Strategies to address the identified risks and timeframes
- Appropriate security strategies for transitioning security arrangements at the completion or termination of the contract, to ensure that assets and records (both electronic and hard copy) are removed from the control of the service provider with minimal disruption to organizational operations

Once these issues have been covered and it is agreed that the organization will approach the market to secure or outsource products and services, the procurement documentation should include a draft contract that contains any security provisions relevant to the property or services being procured and should indicate clauses that are mandatory to meet the minimum organizational standards as well as those that are optional or desirable. These provisions should also be reflected as appropriate in the evaluation plan for the procurement and service provider(s) selection.

Contracts

The contract between an organization and a service provider is the basis for the organization's control and oversight of the functions it has contracted out. The role of the contract is to establish clearly the rules underpinning the relationship between the organization and the service provider. The contract should contain a reference to any security obligations placed on the service provider and provisions to update these obligations.

Where a contract requires the service provider to access commercially sensitive information or other organizational assets, these matters should be addressed in both the documentation and any evaluation criteria by having prospective service providers agree to meet the following requirements:

- A conflict of interest declaration should be completed to disclose any potential conflict of interest that would impact on security in the performance of functions or services on behalf of the organization.
- Service provider staff requiring access to commercially sensitive information or other specified assets should agree to be cleared to the appropriate level.
- Service provider premises and facilities should be suitable for the storage and handling of sensitive assets/information up to and including the nominated level.
- The service provider should have systems that can meet designated security specifications or postures (by threat level) for the processing, storage, transmission and disposal of specified organizational assets.
- Access to sensitive organizational assets/information should occur in an appropriately secure environment.
- Where sensitive organizational assets/information are to be stored on the service provider's premises as a result of an outsourcing arrangement, the draft

contract should include clauses that enable the organization's security or audit staff to conduct security reviews and audits of the service provider's records, contract material, and premises

- If the service provider is likely to subcontract the performance of any part of the contracted function, a clause should be included in the contract to make the service provider fully responsible for ensuring that all the security requirements under the contract are met. (Organizations may also consider inserting a clause requiring the service provider to consult the organization before subcontracting any sensitive asset or function involving access.)

- Service providers understand that intellectual property/capital generated under the contract, on behalf of the organization, is the property of the organization and is not to be disclosed without authorization.

- A deed of confidentiality should be completed so that the service provider's staff and any subcontracted service providers:

    - Adhere to the procedures for handling, processing and storing sensitive organizational information and other assets

    - Understand the contract terms relating to any information used or generated under the contract. (Generally, contracts should specify that such information belongs to the organization and should never be used for any purpose other than that determined by the organization with whom the service provider has contracted.)

Contract Management

Contract management involves monitoring both the performance of contracted functions and the adherence to the protective security standards specified in the contract. Ultimately, the organization maintains responsibility for ensuring that the security standards for processing, storage, transmission, and disposal of specified organizational assets are met by the service provider and/or any subcontracted service providers involved in the provision of the service. This may require the organization providing training and other enablers to the service provider regarding how the organization undertakes Security Risk Management.

Despite having outsourced the activity, the organization should seek to develop a positive working relationship with their service providers, as this will promote open communication and add value to the security environment through the prompt identification and resolution of issues. Organizations should always retain an ability to terminate a contract for security breaches or the inability of a service provider to remedy those breaches under the terms of the contract.

To do this, the organization must monitor the service provider's security procedures on a regular basis. A clause in the contract that provides the organization with access to the service provider's premises, records and/or equipment, will help with managing the contract and providing an avenue for regular monitoring, to ensure that the service provider is complying with its security obligations. The service provider should require a similar undertaking from any subcontracted service provider.

Because a security incident might have wide-ranging and critical consequences for the organization, it should try to keep itself informed of security incidents likely to affect the performance of the contracted or outsourced function. If notified by the service provider, the organization needs to consider and implement procedures necessary to deal with the risk. Incidents also provide valuable information for future risk reviews and assessments and will help evaluate current security plans and procedures.

Other Supply Chain Points to Consider

Yossi Sheffi, *in his 2001 article for the* International Journal of Logistics Management, *identified many conflicts or trade-offs that must be considered when considering Security Risk Management and the supply chain:* [46]

- Repeatability versus unpredictability—*Repeatable processes and procedures reduce costs and ensure quality. Unpredictability in terms of suppliers, transportation routes, and schedules provides a higher impost on security and may increase unit costs.*
- Lowest bidder versus known supplier—*Lowest bidder increases overall unit profit but does not mean best value for money or most secure solution. Dealing with a defined pool of known and cleared suppliers promotes better security, even though it may also bring higher costs associated with stringent security packaging and movement requirements.*
- Centralization versus dispersion—*Many supply chain activities are conducted better and more economically from central locations. The dispersion of assets and personnel mitigates against terror or natural disaster incidents but at higher cost because of the need to deploy security solutions across multiple sites.*
- Managing risk versus delivering value—*What value to the supply chain does increased security bring versus managing the risk of a high-impact, low-probability event? Many security measures should be judged successful if they are never enacted.*
- Collaboration versus secrecy—*Increased collaboration between enterprises brings a higher level of supply chain effectiveness and efficiency. Need-to-know is a principle of information and operational security. What is the risk of sharing enterprise data with other organizations? How much corporate and security data can be exposed before there are ramifications for the organization's resilience or profitability?*
- Redundancy versus efficiency—*Redundancy in the supply chain is a prudent risk management tool to ensure continuity of supply in the event of a contingency arising. Modern supply chains are geared for a just-in-time supply approach for greater efficiency and profit. How much redundancy is enough or too much?*

Figure 6.20 demonstrates the following:

- The trade-off between supply chain efficiencies, including repeatable processes, lowest bidder, centralized processes and facilities, delivering high value to customers, collaborative approach to operations, and high level of supply chain efficiency
- A high level of supply chain security, which includes managing process and procedural unpredictability, dispersed operations, high level of risk acceptance and management, high level of process and procedural secrecy, and high level of supply chain redundancy.

The dilemma for the Security Risk Manager is to balance the competing demands of efficiency and high returns against security and survivability.

6.2.6 Internal Environment

The internal environment refers to those elements that are typically within the control of an organization or individual and might include elements such as the following:[42]

- Delivery—services, products, or projects
- Capacity and capability—resources, relationships, operations, or reputation
- Risk management performance—governance or resilience

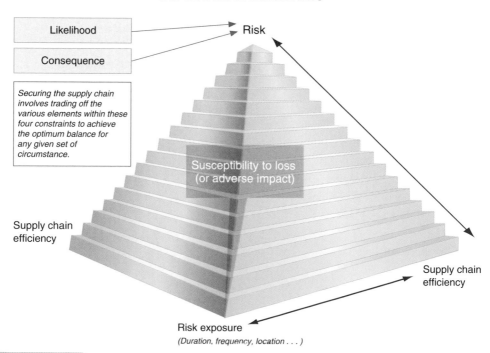

FIGURE 6.20 Impact of SRM quadruple constraints on supply chains

6.2.7 Temporal Qualities

Temporal qualities of exposure can include the following:

- Duration of an event
- Opening hours of a venue
- Time of day
- Day, week, or month of the year
- Time restrictions on travel
- Timelines for project delivery

The length of time an asset is at its most exposed to an identified threat is known as an exposure timeframe. Using a public event as an example, the exposure timeframe for a mass casualty attack by a vehicle-based improvised explosive device (VBIED) at an indoor public event may be the length of time that the greatest proportion of the crowd is outside a venue prior to entry at a choke point like mandatory bag checks. Equally, the exposure timeframe for an airborne toxin at the same event may be when the greatest proportion of a crowd at the same event is inside the building.

6.2.8 Frequency of Activities

An increase in the frequency of activities, for example, international travel, can also lead to an increased exposure of an individual or organization in one of more of the three exposure areas. In the case of travel, it may increase the threat; if threat actors become aware of this travel, then it could increase the vulnerability of an individual to attack, the overall exposure, or criticality if the increased travel is linked to achievement of core objectives, e.g., sales.

> *An increase in frequency does not automatically equate to increased risk. Infrequently conducted activities may introduce a higher risk if a lack of familiarity means that they are poorly executed. For example, employment screening activities may actually be a higher risk if recruitment is an infrequent activity for an organization as the screening staff are likely to be less familiar with procedures that could potentially increase organizational exposure to risk of hiring a dishonest or inappropriate employee.*

6.2.9 Summary of Key Points

Exposure assessment is similar to, but not synonymous with, risk context and risk identification. It is a separate element to these areas and a critical activity that informs all phases of the risk management process.

A range of applicable methodologies exist; however, the three key elements that collectively provide an overall understanding of exposure and in turn inform other risk management activities are as follows:

- Threat assessment
- Vulnerability assessment
- Criticality assessment

When determining threats, vulnerabilities, and criticalities, it is important for organizations to include consideration of their supply chains and ensure that the appropriate security controls extend across these.

6.3 RISK

> *"Risk arises out of uncertainty and is the exposure to the possibility of such things as financial loss or gain, physical damage, injury or delay as a consequence of pursuing or not pursuing a particular course of action."*
> (HB254:2005 GOVERNANCE, RISK MANAGEMENT AND CONTROL ASSURANCE)

6.3.1 History of Security Risk Management

Our modern concept of risk management has its roots in the Hindu-Arabic numbering system that reached the West sometime around the 13th century.[48] It came into its own as a discipline with the development of probability theory in 1654 by Blaise Pascal, and Pierre de Fermat used statistical probability to predict the future. Since then, mathematicians and actuaries have built increasingly complex models that have contributed to much of the advances in modern society.

By 1713, Jacob Bernoulli had proven The Law of Large Numbers, which is also known as Bernoulli's Theorem; it suggests that the greater the statistical population sampled, the closer the observed result will be to the statistical averages.[s] He went on to develop methods of statistical sampling that have contributed to everything from opinion polls to testing of new products and medical research.

The intervening 300 years observed slow but steady mathematical and scientific research that continued to contribute to our understanding of risk management, portfolio diversification, share trading, rocket science, and insurance. By contrast, Security Risk Management remained predominantly with the night watchman, soldier, and intelligence community.

The advent of electronics and related technologies in the 20th century has given us incredible advances in the standard of living. Many of these, such as radar, communications, composite materials, and weapons, have been honed in

---

[s]Not to be confused with the law in physics that bears the same name.

the cauldron of war, but each in their way have contributed to Security Risk Management either through development of new protective technologies or a requirement to protect valuables from offenders who are using advanced technology.

For thousands of years, information security had not changed much past the most rudimentary of ciphers and need-to-know principles. In the 20th century, telephone, radio, and more recently, computer technologies have introduced an entire new element of security. Similarly, advances in management theory have introduced new capabilities with business case modeling, risk assessment, and personnel practices. The introduction of financial techniques such as net present value (NPV), management systems such as ISO 9000, and risk management standards such as AS/NZS 4360:2004 have spearheaded greater consistency in the application of risk management within most disciplines but not least of all the security profession.

This process of ongoing refinement and development has brought us to the early 21st century, where we have an abundance of still developing and sometimes inconsistent Security Risk Management models, concepts, and techniques.

6.3.2 Key Challenges

Our brains are wired for storytelling and for fight-or-flight risk decisions, not statistical uncertainty. We tell ourselves simple stories to explain complex things we do not and, most importantly, cannot know. The truth is that we have no idea whether we will be subject to a major attack tomorrow, and whatever estimation we make is sure to be grossly simplified, if not flat out wrong.

This understanding is, of course, nothing new. Four hundred years ago, Francis Bacon warned that our minds not only struggle to interpret the world around us but also may be programmed to deceive us. "Beware the fallacies into which undisciplined thinkers most easily fall - they are the real distorting prisms of human nature." Indeed, we are programmed toward "assuming more order than exists in chaotic nature."

As Bruce Schneier points out, we can calculate the risk of any number of security threats, which include murder, mugging, identity theft, and so on. Insurance companies do it all the time. The reality, however, is that "security is also a feeling, based not on probabilities and mathematical calculations, but on your psychological reactions to both risks and countermeasures. You might feel terribly afraid of terrorism, or you might feel like it's not something worth worrying about." [47]

We have evolved to manage risk in the emotional center of the brain—an adequate system when we lived in small Neanderthal communities. The complexity of the modern world and the new security trade-offs that come with it mean that we need to apply more rational and scientific approaches to risk management.

Some scary things are not really as risky as they seem, and others are better handled by staying in the scary situation to set up a more advantageous future response. This means that there is an evolutionary advantage to being able to hold off the fight-or-flight response while you work out a more sophisticated analysis of the situation and your options. We humans have a much more sophisticated pathway to deal with analysis that is the neocortex, which is a more advanced part of the brain that developed very recently, evolutionarily speaking, and only appears in mammals.

The neocortex is intelligent and analytic. It can reason. It can make more nuanced trade-offs. It is also much slower. So here is the first fundamental problem: We have two systems for reacting to risk: a primitive intuitive system and a more advanced analytic system, and they are operating in parallel. And it is hard for the neocortex to contradict the amygdala. Essentially, the neocortex, which is the part of our brain that has to make our modern complex security trade-offs, is still a piece of software beta testing.

We often place too much weight on the odds that past events will repeat, diligently trying to follow the path of other successful people or projects when unrepeatable chance may be a better explanation. Many major security events are usually rare and unpredictable.

Black swans, as they are known, is a reference to a 17th century philosophical thought experiment whereby in Europe all anyone had ever observed were white swans; indeed, "all swans are white" had long been used as the standard example of a scientific truth. So what was the chance of seeing a black one? Impossible to calculate—at least until black swans were discovered in Western Australia in the 17th century.

Nassim Taleb argues that most big events in our world are rare and unpredictable, and thus trying to extract generalizations to explain them may be emotionally satisfying, but it is practically useless.[47] The 911 attacks are one such example. Stock market crashes are another. Mark Twain is credited with the statement that "History doesn't repeat, but it rhymes," and Taleb's addition to this assertion is that "History does not crawl, it jumps."

6.3.3 Current Issues in Risk Management

There is little dispute that risk is a factor that must be considered as decision makers decide what, if anything, should be done about a given activity or exposure. There has been far less agreement, however, on what this means in practical terms. Much of the existing body of knowledge on risk assessment and risk management was developed for issues that do not possess the same degree of complexity, uncertainty, and ambiguity as those associated with security decision making.

This fact presents a significant challenge for developing a common framework to assess and consider risk as a factor when making security and related policy decisions.

In addition to the methodological questions, other issues need to be answered. Who is responsible for risk assessment? Who is qualified? Who is responsible? How should alternative courses of action be developed and how should they be evaluated? How does one perform a cost/benefit analysis on a potential problem whose actual probability is unknown, and may be close to zero, but for which the potential consequences are astronomical? How should attackers' adaptive responses to security measures be taken into account as potential security measures are being considered?

We are making some progress in answering these questions and, more significantly, in developing a more mature understanding of the complexities involved and the distribution of risk responsibilities across organizations and communities.

6.3.4 Security Risk Management

Risk is a concept that denotes a potential impact on objectives. In an SRM context, this will usually mean a negative/adverse impact on assets, functions, capabilities, or a combination of these three. Nevertheless, it is also important to remember that another objective of Security Risk Management is to assist organizations and individuals to realize opportunities. Risk is usually measured in terms of the probability of an event occurring and the consequence of that event.

Risk is an evolving concept that not only grows and varies as we gain more understanding but also varies between cultures and communities. Figure 6.21 illustrates by way of example, a timeline of major milestones in the evolution of risk assessment by the U.S. Department of Homeland Security (DHS), in a homeland security context. This timeline in Figure 6.21 is illustrative of some concepts whereby risk within DHS (in the homeland security context) has evolved from being equated with population ($R = P$) to being a function of Threat $\times$ Vulnerability and Consequence ($R = T * C$ and V).

Although Figure 6.21 refers to the specifics of the DHS, this concept of change and evolution remains common to most organizations and risk methodologies. For our purposes, SRMBOK applies the process from the AS/NZS

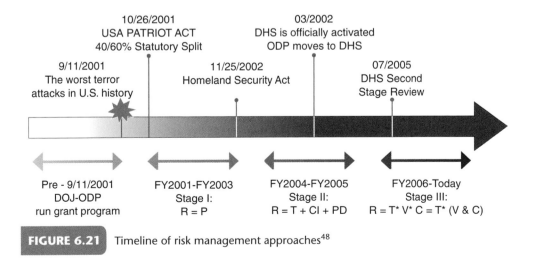

FIGURE 6.21   Timeline of risk management approaches[48]

4360:2004 Risk Management Standard (illustrated in Figure 6.24); however, it is important to understand that no risk management process or methodology is necessarily right or wrong. Rather, some may be more or less appropriate for any particular situation or requirement.

To determine threats and vulnerabilities, an organization, community, or individual must undertake risk assessments. More importantly perhaps, that entity must determine, apply, and monitor risk management practices. This collective activity is known as the risk management process (Figure 6.22).

The term "risk" is often used in ways that imply that it is possible to articulate or measure risk clearly. In many respects, however, this quantification or measurement of risk may be misleading, as such data are usually based on historical figures rather than current circumstances. In SRM, the severity and frequency of security attacks or threats is of little use if an organization has never sustained a particular type of attack.

For example, if an organization has never been the subject of a hacking attack or bomb incident, that fact may or may not reflect the future likelihood of such an event, particularly if security measures have been upgraded recently. It is important to consider then that in many respects, risk in the SRM context involves uncertainty rather than quantitative risk management. Frank Knight[49] in Risk, Uncertainty, and Profit, described the distinction between risk and uncertainty, thus:

> *Uncertainty must be taken in a sense radically distinct from the familiar notion of risk, from which it has never been properly separated. The essential fact is that risk means in some cases a quantity susceptible of measurement, while at other times it is something distinctly not of this character; and there are far-reaching and crucial differences in the bearings of the phenomena depending on which of the two is really present and operating. ... It will appear that a measurable uncertainty, or risk proper, as we shall use the term, is so far different from an unmeasurable one, that it is not in effect an uncertainty at all.[49]*

This element of uncertainty also highlights that risk is not always about negative consequences. Positive risk refers to risk that an organization initiates to make a more significant gain possible. An example of positive risk could be the initiation of a project, such as new oil exploration, that is expected to deliver ongoing financial benefits.

Just as hazards can be a precursor to a threat that may culminate in realization of negative consequences, so can potential be a precursor of opportunity, which can lead to benefits (positive consequences).

Risk-Informed Decision Making

Risk is an inescapable part of business or any endeavor, and the one thing that is certain about the future is its uncertainty. Nearly all operational tasks and

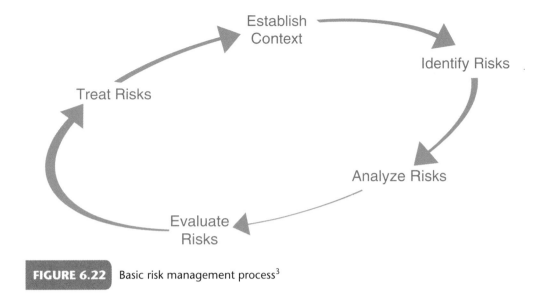

FIGURE 6.22 Basic risk management process[3]

processes are now viewed through the prism of risk,[50] and Security Risk Management is very much in this camp. The prime activity of Security Risk Management may be to protect assets, functions, and capabilities, but one fundamental aspect of this is informed decision making to shape operational activities and optimize the allocation of resources. This process is known as risk-based decision making (RBDM).

6.3.5 Methodologies

At the highest level, a risk-assessment process should include the following components:

- **The establishment of an organizational context**—This establishes the strategic, organizational, and threat/risk context in which the assessment process takes place. Criteria against which threat/risk will be evaluated are established, and the structure of the analysis is defined. This can be achieved through the collection and collation of information regarding an organization's internal and external environments. The analysis of that information and the production of targeted intelligence should provide the basis for an accurate contextual assessment.

- **The identification of risks**—Following the production of a contextual assessment, an organization should be able to develop a threat assessment to identify why, how, and in what form internal and external threats might develop.

- **The analysis and evaluation likelihood and consequence**—Following the identification of credible threats, an organization should perform a stock take to determine the effectiveness of existing barriers and control mechanisms against those threats. A red team exercise is a particular method of identifying the strengths and weaknesses of new or existing systems. An analysis of the consequences and likelihood of an identified risk materializing, and the effectiveness of barriers, are combined to produce an estimated level of risk.

> *The Guide to SRMBOK on Red Team Exercises contains more information on this topic.*

- **The development of a treatment plan**—An effective treatment plan must include a combination of information, people, and physical Security Risk Management measures. It must be based on an appreciation of the root cause of identified risks and provide a solution that includes change management principles. A treatment plan should also include contingency protocols and business continuity strategies if an identified treatment should fail.

- **The establishment of a new context**—The identification and preventative treatment of identified risks will, in most cases, alter the initial assessment of an organization's internal and external environment. The implementation of change management processes may also provide some contextual changes that should be taken into account. Security Risk Management is an ongoing process, and new threat assessments should continually emerge.

6.3.5.1 Other Considerations. The U.S. Department of Homeland Security issued a 10-step risk-assessment methodology criterion, Vulnerability Assessment Report, 2003, which used the following criteria to evaluate the quality of risk and vulnerability analysis models. The evaluation criteria developed by a panel of subject matter experts suggested that risk methodologies should:

- Clearly identify the infrastructure sector being assessed
- Specify the type of security discipline addressed, e.g., physical, information and operations
- Collect specific data pertaining to each asset
- Identify critical/key assets to be protected
- Determine the mission impact of the loss or damage of that asset
- Conduct a threat analysis and perform assessment for specific assets
- Perform a vulnerability analysis and assessment to specific threats
- Conduct analytical risk assessment and determine priorities for each asset
- Be relatively low cost to train and conduct
- Make specific, concrete recommendations concerning countermeasures

This list is general in nature and may be adapted to meet the needs of a specific organization. Several other risk-assessment models exist today.

6.3.6 Risk Management Process

Risk management methodologies come in many shapes and forms, and all are useful. The basis of most risk methodologies includes a cycle of distinct elements, all of which must be reviewed individually to identify overall risk. The U.S. Government Accountability Office (GAO) risk management process is typical of these models and reinforces the recognition that risk management is a continuing cycle of interrelated actions rather than a single one-time process, as shown in Figure 6.23 U.S. GAO Risk Management Framework.

> *A detailed description and examples of application of the security risk assessment process can be found in the separate chapters on Security Risk Management and Enterprise Security Risk Management in the Guide to SRMBOK on Application and Case Studies.*

This process is described in more detail in AZ/NZS 4360:2004 (Figure 6.24) and in HB167:2006 Security Risk Management Handbook (Figure 6.25) (SRM companion guide to AS/NZS 4360:2004).

SRMBOK is consistent with the methodologies expressed in these documents and the methodologies therein are also similar to several risk methodologies, which include the following:

- Committe of Sponsoring Organizations of the Treadway Corporation (COSO) Enterprise Risk Management Integrated Framework

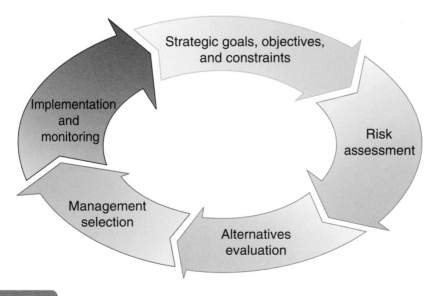

FIGURE 6.23   U.S. GAO Risk Management Framework[34]

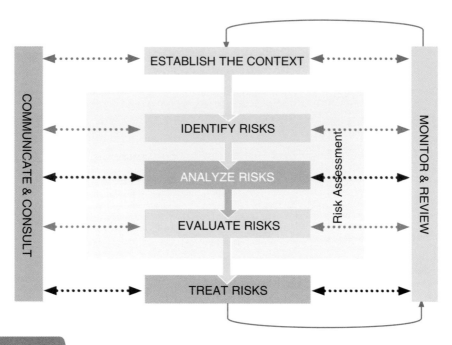

FIGURE 6.24 AS/NZS 4360:2004 Risk Management Process

- A Risk Management Standard (Association of Insurance and Risk Managers (AIRMIC), ALARM (The Public Risk Management Association), Institute of Risk Management (IRM) UK)
- The Orange Book Management of Risk – Principles and Concepts (HM Treasury UK)

6.3.6.1 Establish Terms of Reference. This step refers to the identification of objectives for the risk management process and or risk management assessment (Figure 6.26).

> A key element of Security Risk Management that distinguishes it from other forms of risk management is that the risk management process is often separated in practice into two elements—security risk assessment and Security Risk Management.

The reason for this separation lies in the following factors:

- The level of expertise required to conduct security risk assessment and to recommend specific treatments often requires the use of either an in-house adviser or external consultant.
- The application of risk management treatments is often the responsibility of line managers who are likely to have limited Security Risk Management experience and will be involved in the implementation of security measures recommended by the security risk assessment.

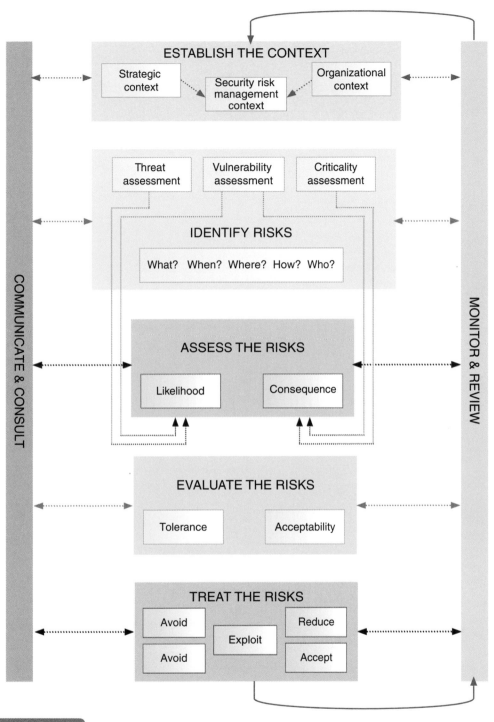

FIGURE 6.25 SRM process from HB167

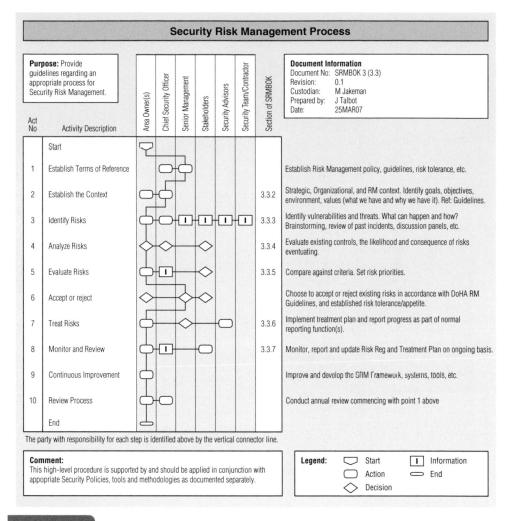

Security Risk Management Process

Purpose: Provide guidelines regarding an appropriate process for Security Risk Management.

Document Information
Document No: SRMBOK 3 (3.3)
Revision: 0.1
Custodian: M Jakeman
Prepared by: J Talbot
Date: 25MAR07

Act No	Activity Description	Section of SRMBOK	
	Start		
1	Establish Terms of Reference		Establish Risk Management policy, guidelines, risk tolerance, etc.
2	Establish the Context	3.3.2	Strategic, Organizational, and RM context. Identify goals, objectives, environment, values (what we have and why we have it). Ref: Guidelines.
3	Identify Risks	3.3.3	Identify vulnerabilities and threats. What can happen and how? Brainstorming, review of past incidents, discussion panels, etc.
4	Analyze Risks	3.3.4	Evaluate existing controls, the likelihood and consequence of risks eventuating.
5	Evaluate Risks	3.3.5	Compare against criteria. Set risk priorities.
6	Accept or reject		Choose to accept or reject existing risks in accordance with DoHA RM Guidelines, and established risk tolerance/appetite.
7	Treat Risks	3.3.6	Implement treatment plan and report progress as part of normal reporting function(s).
8	Monitor and Review	3.3.7	Monitor, report and update Risk Reg and Treatment Plan on ongoing basis.
9	Continuous Improvement		Improve and develop the SRM Framework, systems, tools, etc.
10	Review Process		Conduct annual review commencing with point 1 above
	End		

Column headers: Area Owner(s), Chief Security Officer, Senior Management, Stakeholders, Security Advisors, Security Team/Contractor

The party with responsibility for each step is identified above by the vertical connector line.

Comment:
This high-level procedure is supported by and should be applied in conjunction with appropriate Security Policies, tools and methodologies as documented separately.

Legend: Start · Information · Action · End · Decision

FIGURE 6.26 SRM process[3]

This of course is not the case in all organizations, many of which have high levels of expertise in-house. The separation of responsibilities often found in SRM, however, does differ from other areas of risk management, such as occupational health and safety (OHS), derivatives trading, or insurance buying whereby the party responsible for implementation usually has sufficient expertise to assess the risks.

6.3.6.2 Communicate and Consult. This step, like monitor and review, is a continuous and interactive element of all sections of the risk management process.

6.3.6.3 Establish Context. The importance of fully and comprehensively establishing the Security Risk Management context cannot be understated, and stakeholders should be engaged to identify the following:

- External context
- Internal context
- Security Risk Management context
- Process/program structure
- Evaluation criteria and risk appetite
- Security agendas of stakeholders
- Security business case

These concepts of the context are explored in greater detail throughout SRM body of knowledge (SRMBOK), however, the brevity of this section should not be taken to infer that it is a simple process. It is in fact difficult to overemphasize the importance of adequately preparing any security risk assessment by front-loading the process. Each step in the process is important, yet this foundational step of establishing the context is often glossed over by inexperienced practitioners in a desire to identify and treat the risks. Without sound analysis at this point, it is highly likely that the risk assessment and treatment plan will overlook or misjudge key risks.

6.3.6.4 Identify Risks. Risk identification normally flows from the context definition and is informed by threat, vulnerability, and criticality assessments, as well as historical information, management systems and program activities.

> *Refer to Section 6.2, Exposure, for additional information on this area.*

These activities associated with risk identification are treated in more detail in the section on exposures; however, it is in this area of the risk management process that they are developed into the actual risks for the organization, community, or individual. Prior to this phase, the conduct of threat, vulnerability, and criticality assessments have not yet made the leap to establishing key risks.

6.3.6.5 Analyze Risks

Risk register

The procurement, implementation, and ongoing maintenance of barriers such as IT security systems, fencing, guards, and the installation and maintenance of technical solutions can present significant immediate and ongoing costs to an organization. A risk register is a useful way of cataloging identified risks and measuring the cost of those risks materializing against the costs of preventing their occurrence. A risk register benchmarks the asset criticality against identified risks and provides a framework from which to allocate finite physical security resources and infrastructure funding.

srmbok

Security Risk Management·
BODY OF KNOWLEDGE

Example Risk Rating Matrix

		Consequence →				
People		Minor skills impact.	Minor impact to capability.	Unavailability of core skills affecting services.	Unavailability of critical skills or personnel.	Protracted unavailability of critical skills/people.
		Protracted unavailability of critical skills/people.	Injury requiring treatment by medical practitioner.	Major injury/ hospitalization.	Single death and/ or multiple major injuries.	Multiple deaths.
Information		Compromise of information otherwise available in the public domain.	Minor compromise of information sensitive to internal or sub-unit interests.	Compromise of information sensitive to this organization's operations.	Compromise of information sensitive to organizational interests.	Compromise of information with significant ongoing impact.
Property & Equipment		Minor damage or vandalism to asset.	Minor damage or loss of <5% of total assets.	Damage or loss of <20% of total assets.	Extensive damage or loss <50% of total assets.	Destruction or complete loss of >50% of assets.
Reputation		Local mention only. Quickly forgotten. Freedom to operate unaffected. Selfimprovement review required.	Scrutiny by Executive, internal committees or internal audit to prevent escalation. Short term local media concern. Some impact on local level activities.	Persistent national concern. Scrutiny required by external agencies. Long-term "brand" impact.	Persistent intense national public, political and media scrutiny. Long term "brand" impact. Major operations severely restricted.	International concern, governmental inquiry or sustained adverse national/ international media. "brand" significantly affects organizational abilities.
Financial		1% of Project or Organizational aAnnual budget.	2–5% of Project or Organizational annual budget.	5–10 % of Project or Organizational annual budget.	> 10% Project or Organizational annual budget.	> 30% of Project or Organizational annual budget.
Capability		Minimal impact on noncore business operations. The impact can be dealt with by routine operations.	Some impact on business areas in terms of delays, and systems quality but can be dealt with at operational level.	Impact on the organization resulting in reduced performance such that targets are not met. Organizations existence is not threatened, but could be subject to significant review or changed ways of operations.	Breakdown of key activities leading to reduction in performance (e.g., service delays, revenue loss, client dissatisfaction, and legislative breaches). Survival of the project/activity/ organization is threatened.	Critical failure(s) preventing core activities from being performed. The impact threatens the survival of the project or the organization itself.

Qualitative Likelihood	Quantitative Likelihood		Insignificant	Negligible	Moderate	Major	Extensive
Is expected to occur in most circumstances.	Has occurred on an annual basis in this organization in the past, or circumstances are in train that will cause it to happen.	**Almost Certain**	6	7	8	9	10
Will probably occur in most circumstances.	Has occurred in the last few years in this organization, or has occurred recently in other similar organizations, or circumstances have occurred that will cause it to happen in the next few years.	**Likely**	5	6	7	8	9
Might occur at some time.	Has occurred at least once in the history of this organization, or is considered to have a 5% chance of occuring in the next few years.	**Possible**	4	5	6	7	8
Could occur at some time.	Has never occurred in this organization but has occurred infrequently in other similar organizations, or is considered to have a 1% chance of occurring in the next few years.	**Unlikely**	3	4	5	6	7
May occur only in exceptional circumstances.	Is possible but has not occurred to date in any similar organization and is considered to have very much less than 1% chance of occurring in the short term.	**Rare**	2	3	4	5	6

Likelihood (vertical axis label)

Very High (VH)	Immediate action required by the Executive with detailed planning, allocation of resources and regular monitoring
High (H)	High risk, senior management attention needed
Medium (M)	Management responsibility must be specified
Low (L)	Monitor and manage by routine procedures
Very Low (VL)	Managed by routine procedures

FIGURE 6.27 Example of a 5 × 5 risk rating matrix

A risk register provides an overview of the following:

- The key risks to the organization—those that put in jeopardy the delivery of its medium/long term objectives or its ongoing survival
- The consequences of the risks materializing
- The impact and likelihood of the risk materializing
- The management and control mechanisms to administer risk mitigation strategies and contingency arrangements, if applicable, which would be invoked should the risk materialize
- A nominated person who takes responsibility for ensuring that the management and control arrangements are in place, are operating satisfactorily, and are being improved
- A brief statement of the further action necessary to minimize the risk event occurring and/or to mitigate its effects

6.3.6.6 Evaluate Risks. As noted previously, one of the most common risk evaluation techniques involves determining likelihood and consequence. Usually, these metrics are defined using one or more of the following three methods:

- **Qualitative**—using descriptive terms and phrases to assess and define risk
- **Quantitative**—using historical or calculated data
- **Combined qualitative/quantitative**—using numbers to provide ordinal or comparative assessment of likelihood, consequence, and/or risk

The latter is the most useful if it can be developed, as it not only allows historical data to be input into the analysis but also removes some of the subjectivity associated with the risk process. An example of a combined qualitative/quantitative matrix is shown in Figure 6.27.

Appendix M of HB 167:2006 provides a useful compilation of some other common parameters used in evaluating security risks. These have been expressed in the form of parameter (a) multiplied by parameter (b), although this does not necessarily imply that the terms should or could be mathematically combined in this manner. Often the basis of the measurements themselves will prevent any meaningful mathematical treatment of this nature. In such circumstances, the use of the multiplication symbol ($\times$) could be read as either a quantitative or qualitative combination of the parameters employed. A summary comparison of some benefits and problems with each of these approaches is presented in the table following the formulas.

Risk $=$ **Threat $\times$ Harm**
Where:
Risk $=$ the security risk
Threat $=$ a qualitative or semiquantitative measurement of the level of threat, e.g., rated from low to high
Harm $=$ the resulting impact when the threat occurs

Risk   = $T_L \times I$
Where:
Risk   =   the security risk
T_L =   the likelihood of the threat occurring
I   =   the impact of the threat occurring

Risk   = $S \times L_A$
Where:
Risk   =   the risk of an attack
S   =   the severity of an attack
L_A =   the likelihood of an attack

Risk   = $S \times L_A \times (1-E)$
Where:
Risk   =   the risk of an attack
S   =   severity of the attack
L_A =   likelihood of an attack
E   =   effectiveness of the security system or controls

Risk   = $S \times (L_{AX} \ L_{AS}) \times (1-E)$
Where:
Risk   =   the risk of an attack
S   =   severity of the attack
L_A =   likelihood of an attack being launched
L_{AS} =   likelihood of the attack being successful
E   =   effectiveness of the security system or controls

Risk   = $C \times T \times V$
Where:
Risk   =   risk associated with an adversary attack and/or system/asset failure
C   =   consequence(s), the negative outcomes associated with degradation or failure of the system or asset
Threat   =   threat, the probability or likelihood that a given attack scenario with the potential to disrupt systems or assets and cause undesirable consequences will occur
V   =   the vulnerability of the asset or system to the attack or failure

Risk   = $C \times L$
Where:
Risk   =   the risk of an event occurring with a definable consequence
C   =   the consequences should the event occur
L   =   the likelihood of the event occurring with those consequences

Risk = C × L × (1−E)

Where:

C   =   the consequences of the security risk event

L   =   the likelihood of the event occurring with the defined consequences

E   =   the effectiveness of the security control environment

Risk = C × L × V

Where:

C   =   the consequences of the security risk event

L   =   the likelihood of the event occurring with the defined consequences

V   =   the vulnerability of the asset/individual and the organization/community to the risk

Risk = Cr × L × V

Where:

Cr   =   the impact on an asset at that criticality level

L   =   the likelihood of the risk occurring with that criticality level impact

V   =   the vulnerability

Risk = (T × V) × Cr

Where:

T   =   the threat

V   =   the vulnerability

Cr   =   the criticality

Risk = T_L × V × Cr

Where:

T_L =   threat likelihood comprising: general threat likelihood + specific threat likelihood

V   =   vulnerability comprising: V = VG + Vs + VR

Where:

     VG = vulnerability to the general threat

     Vs = vulnerability to the specific threat

     VR = vulnerability to the specific and general threats.

Cr   =   criticality comprising: Cr = Cs + Cp + Co

     Where:

     Cs = social criticality

     Cp = personnel criticality

     Co = organizational criticality.

Table 6.2 Pros and cons of various risk measurement approaches

Approach	Benefits	Points to consider
Risk = Threat × Harm	Simple–requires examination of only two values.	Linkage between a level of threat and harm is not necessarily emphasized or direct. Threat is assumed to equate to likelihood. In this approach it does not equate to the likelihood of the harm. Requires the control framework to be considered implicitly in determining threat and harm to even approximate risk.
Risk = $T_L \times I$	Begins to introduce the concept of a potential event through the introduction of the likelihood of the threat occurring.	Does not adequately approximate the likelihood of the risk. Not necessarily a direct relationship between threat likelihood and impact. Requires consideration of the control framework to provide an approximate risk.
Risk = $S \times L_A$	As above	As above
Risk = $S \times L_A \times (1 - E)$	Requires the consideration of the effectiveness of the control environment. The $(1 - E)$ notation attempts to bring in concepts of vulnerability.	The likelihood remains the likelihood of the attack and not necessarily the likelihood of a successful attack.
Risk = $S \times (L_A \times L_{AS}) \times (1 - E)$	Considers the likelihood of the attack being successful. Improving the approximation of risk. Considers the effectiveness of control framework.	The likelihood is not a consideration of the likelihood of the consequences (severity) of the risk.
Risk = $C \times T \times V$	Begins to consider the relationship between some of the key factors in security risk.	May still be considering the likelihood of the threat and not necessarily the likelihood of the consequences.
Risk = Consequence × Likelihood	The standard definition of risk management. Considers the consequence of an event and the likelihood of the event occurring with those consequences.	Does not necessarily address how concepts of threat and vulnerability are factored into the analysis.

Approach	Benefits	Points to consider
Risk = C × L × (1 − E)	Begins to introduce the concepts of vulnerability through examining shortfalls in the control effectiveness. Also provides consideration around the suitability of current controls/barriers.	May require a subjective consideration of threat, vulnerability, and criticality in assessing consequence and likelihood.
Risk = C × L × V	Considers the impact of vulnerability on the risk.	May require a subjective consideration of threat and criticality in assessing consequence and likelihood. Does not attempt to assign vulnerability to just a likelihood or consequence concept.
Risk = Cr × L × V	Introduces the concept of criticality.	Assumes that a direct proportional relationship exists between consequence and criticality, which may not be present.
Risk = (T × V) × Cr	As above.	Assumes that there is a direct proportional relationship between consequence and criticality, which may not be present. Assumes that likelihood is a product of threat × vulnerability, which may be an incorrect assumption. Ignores the prospect that key elements of vulnerability will modify the consequence not necessarily the likelihood.
Risk = T_L × V × Cr	Allows for the overall impact of vulnerability over likelihood and consequence.	Assumes that criticality is directly proportional to consequence, which may not always be the situation. Assumes that threat likelihood is equivalent to risk likelihood, which may be an incorrect assumption.

6.3.6.7 Treat Risks. Risk response and controls include a range of measures. The objective is not to eliminate risks but rather to reduce risk to the point where it is (ALARP) as illustrated in Figure 6.43 and Figure 6.44.

Adapting the principles illustrated in Figure 6.7 with the addition of the 2 to 10 score in Figure 6.27 highlights the principles that are at play. Figure 6.28

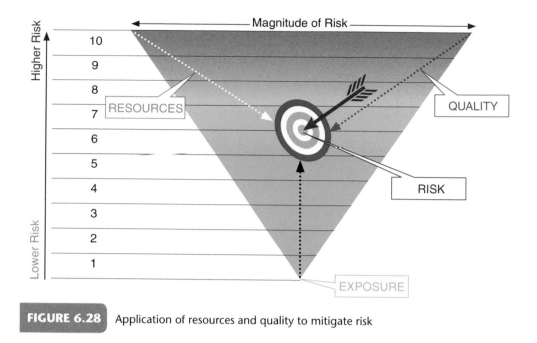

FIGURE 6.28 Application of resources and quality to mitigate risk

illustrates the dual role of applying risk treatments (resources) and ensuring that they are appropriate (quality) for the task at hand.

Risk Treatment Principles

Regardless of an organization's or individual's level of risk tolerance, the following few key paradigms should be recognized:

- **Do not accept unnecessary risk.** Unnecessary risk comes without a commensurate return in benefits or opportunities. The most logical options for accomplishing tasks are those that meet all business requirements with the least risk.

- **Accept risk only when the benefits outweigh the cost.** Risk is judged to be tolerable if the importance and benefits of the task are of such magnitude that acceptance of the risks associated with the task is justified. Risks are therefore tolerated in the conduct of the activity, with the intent to reduce the risk to a negligible level if and when this becomes practicable. Tolerance boundaries are only legitimately set by the decision maker with whom accountability lies.

- **Risk should be managed at the point at which it occurs.** Organizations should make risk decisions at the appropriate level. A fundamental principle of the methodology is that those accountable for the success or failure of the task must be included in the risk evaluation and decision process. For example, under the Convention on International Civil Aviation, the aircraft captain is the individual responsible for executing the mission and is authorized to accept risk up to the acceptable ALARP risk threshold. However, they are required to elevate decisions to the next level in the chain of command when it is determined that available risk treatment options, in the immediate operational context, will not reduce the residual risk to an acceptable level.

Security Risk Management Plan

The establishment of a risk management plan provides an organization with the executive support and impetus required to manage risk.

A risk management plan should incorporate strategies to reduce both the cost of risk management relative to identified threats and to assign the most appropriate risk treatment to each identified risk. The following hierarchy of controls provides a useful framework in that regard.

Principles of SRM Treatments

A key element of the design of SRM treatments involves the application of treatments that (in priority order) involve the objectives of deter, deny, delay, detect, and respond with respect to a potential attack.[1]

Deter

A deterrent factor is a device or barrier that displays its inherent asset protection capabilities to a potential malfeasant rendering an unauthorized action nonbeneficial, or it is a device or barrier that presents a likely consequence that would outweigh a perceived benefit for attempting an unauthorized action.

Deterrent factors can take many forms. Fencing, signage, visible guards, or a barking dog may deter unauthorized access to an asset. A deterrent device should be visible and applicable. That is, it should be an easily recognizable as a deterrent and should be contextually appropriate. Signage should also be credible. "Trespassers will be prosecuted" is a credible deterrent. "Beware of the crocodiles" may not be.

Similar considerations should be made in assessing the applicability of fencing and other physical deterrents. Civic planning regulations may prevent the erection of some types of fencing. Equally, some types of fencing may not be appropriate to some business environments. In some contexts, the use of cameras to prevent the theft of an asset such as merchandise may be illegal.

The cost of a deterrent must be relative to the cost of the loss on the protected asset.

The use of guards or guard dogs may be an appropriate deterrent factor. The risks associated with the potential loss or damage to a human or animal asset like a guard or guard dog may be more significant that the risks associated with the loss or damage of the asset in need of protection.

Deny

The denial of access by unauthorized parties to an asset is another mechanism used to promote security. Denial can take several forms including physical denial, electronic denial and proximity denial, e.g., relocation of an asset rendering it unavailable.

Delay

A delaying factor is a barrier or scenario that provides time for another protective measure to take effect should unauthorized access to an asset occur. Delaying factors are important to the security-in-depth concept. In the case of a barrier that prevents vehicular access but not human access, unauthorized entry to an area may be plausible but a speedy departure impossible, which increases the likelihood of apprehension or disruption.

Detect

Detection may occur in a variety of means, including alarms, system logs, direct observation, patrols, CCTV, or through signs of attempted entry. Detection may also occur before, during or after the person has actually committed an unauthorized or criminal act. Accordingly, once detected, it is important to assess the likely threat and risk being presented by the intruder/s as this will influence the nature of the response.

Respond

A response must be consistent and appropriate with the level of threat detected against the asset. The response should also be tempered by contextual considerations relevant to the organization and the asset. Training is crucial to the successful intervention in a security incident, and the apprehension of perpetrators as a response to a breach of security should take into account the consequences of that response. This is particularly pertinent in cases where an organization's reputation may be harmed by heavy handed treatment of malfeasance.

Recover

Recovery is the final barrier to mitigate the long-term consequences of any attack by returning to the desired levels of capabilities as quickly as possible. An effective recovery strategy does not depend on waiting until after the event—rather, planning for recovery measures tactics by measures such as off-site backups or insurance policies is an ongoing process irrespective of whether an event actually occurs.

> This is consistent with a long established and proven method for dealing with risks, which is to consider the issue in relation to four main activity areas: planning, preparedness, response, and recovery (PPRR), which is discussed in-depth in the chapters on activity areas and the Guides to SRMBOK on Resilience, Recovery and Continuity.

6.3.6.8 Different Tools for Costing Risk Treatments

Sensitivity Analysis

Sensitivity analysis is a useful technique to employ when evaluating the costs and/or benefits associated with various risk treatments. The technique involves taking a single variable, e.g., price, and examining the effect of changes in the selected variable on the likely performance of the treatment option or wider business unit/function. By examining the change that occurs, it is possible to arrive at some assessment of how sensitive changes are for the projected outcomes. When the benefit appraisal is positive, each input value can be examined to determine how much the estimated figure could be changed before the benefit became neutral or negative (a cost).

One form of sensitivity analysis is to pose a series of what-if questions. If we take the petty theft of goods for example, then we might ask the following questions:

- What if petty theft is 10% higher than expected?
- What if petty theft is five % lower than expected?
- What if the cost of the risk treatment, such as installing CCTV and warning signs, is reduced by 10%?
- What if the cost of the risk treatment is increased by 10%?

In answering these questions, it is possible to develop a better feel for the effect of forecast inaccuracies on the final outcome and, therefore, better substantiate the implementation of the risk treatment. One weakness, however, is that this technique does not consider the effect on projected outcomes of more than one variable at a time. Although only one variable is examined at a time, several variables considered important to the performance of the treatment option or wider business unit/function.

Scenario Analysis

Another approach that helps managers to gain a feel for the effect of forecast inaccuracies is to prepare projections according to different possible outcomes (Figure 6.29). For example, managers may wish to examine projected consequences prepared on the following basis:

- An optimistic view of likely events
- A pessimistic view of likely future events
- A most likely view of future events

A particular scenario can then be accepted and planning and resource allocation made on that basis. Alternatively, all of the scenarios can be mapped together and then smoothed to identify a middle ground, as shown in Figure 6.30.

This approach is open to criticism because it does not indicate the likelihood of each scenario occurring, nor does it identify the other possible scenarios that

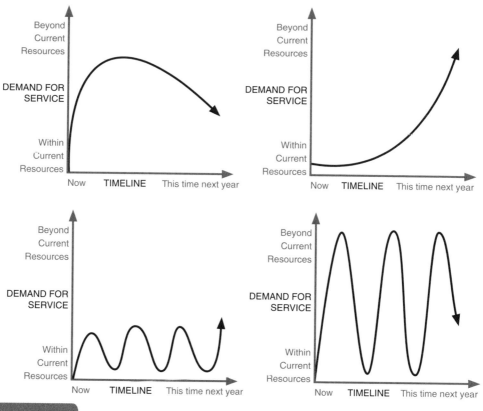

FIGURE 6.29 Scenario analysis based on alternative futures

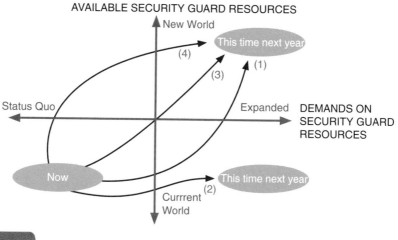

FIGURE 6.30 Allocating resources to possible future scenarios

might occur. Nevertheless, the portrayal of optimistic and pessimistic scenarios can be useful in providing some feel for the downside risk and potential upside associated with an event. Scenario analysis is unlike sensitivity analysis, in that it will involve changing many, variables simultaneously to portray a possible outcome.

Simulation

Simulation is a technique that is helpful in analyzing financial or program (time) models, in which the values of the variables may be uncertain. Variables in this context refer to risks, opportunities, costs, or duration. The objective of simulation is to obtain a distribution and its associated characteristics for the bottom-line performance figure (measure) it was derived from, considering the input variables in combination. The thinking behind simulation is similar to the idea of carrying out multiple what-if scenarios.

A common simulation technique is Monte Carlo modelling, which examines many what-if scenarios by accounting for a large number of possible values that each variable could take and weighting each value by the probability (likelihood) of the occurrence. For example, if the risk of intellectual property theft by an employee was estimated to cost the business between $500,000 and $1 million and had a probability of occurrence of 50%, then every other iteration would include the risk and the value assigned to the risk (that is, $500,000 and $1 million). The process is then repeated, commonly more than 5,000 times, to give 5,000 realistic possible outcomes of the cost of losing intellectual property by theft. The statistical data that describes each iteration is then aggregated and represented graphically by a histogram to show the range of possible financial loss outcomes, a probability distribution, and a cumulative frequency curve to show the likelihood of each loss as a percentage. In our intellectual property example, the Monte Carlo distribution might reveal an 80% confidence figure, which therefore represents an 80% chance that the loss would be $700,000. With this information, it is then possible to undertake further cost/benefit analysis of possible treatment options.

This approach provides greater insight into the risk associated with a given decision or option than a single value calculation based on the expected values for the uncertain variables.

6.3.6.9 Monitor and Review. The security risk environment is not constant. Organizations, communities, and individuals are also in continual flux. The monitoring of risk provides the capability to respond effectively to changing environments. The concept of "monitor and review" therefore becomes of critical importance to the conduct of Security Risk Management.

Continual monitoring and review of the following aspects should be occurring at all stages of security risk assessment:

- The changing strategic, organizational, and security risk contexts for changes that may impact the nature or level of risk to the individual or organization
- The incidence, nature, types, and impacts of security risk

- The changing acceptability or tolerance of risk by the individual, organization, community, or by their stakeholders
- The effectiveness of security risk controls
- The effectiveness of security awareness programs and other communications initiatives

The concept of monitor and review is based around the following needs to:

- Continuously examine the external and internal environments and reconsider the context and its effect on Security Risk Management
- Redevelop the analytical outputs of the Security Risk Management process to reflect the changing context
- Assess the efficiency and effectiveness of treatment plans in mitigating the risks identified
- Reevaluate the appropriateness of treatment activities to manage a dynamically changing risk environment
- Measure the effectiveness and success of communications and consultation activities undertaken
- Ensure that timely and adequate improvements are implemented
- Continuously examine the conduct of the Security Risk Management process and to adjust it to meet changing organizational needs and capability
- Ensure appropriate governance through reporting to appropriate authorities, regulators, boards, stakeholders, management, and staff as required
- Focus on both conformance and performance measurement

Types of Monitoring and Review

Monitoring and review may take several forms, including the following (among others):

- **Scanning** the internal and external environments for changing or emerging risk. The aim is to provide an early appreciation of emerging issues to allow sufficient time to act on them. Although virtually sine qua non at a strategic level, it should be adopted as a monitoring practice at all levels of the organization.
- **Periodic reviews** of processes, policies, practices, and systems as well as their risks and treatments. These reviews are often targeted at specific higher or changing risk issues, which include assurance activities such as control self-assessments. The aim is to ensure that treatment and control strategies continue to be relevant, efficient, and effective.
- **Continuous monitoring** on a frequent or ongoing basis, which often involves routine checking by the process operator's changes in risk level, control breakdowns, incident occurrence, or established indicators of these, e.g., alarm monitoring. The aim is to ensure that implemented treatments and controls remain effective and that new risks are not being created. This process will

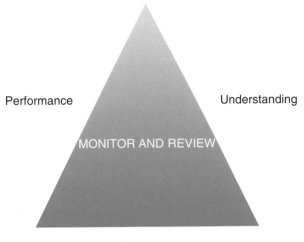

Performance   Understanding

MONITOR AND REVIEW

Assurance

FIGURE 6.31 Key elements of monitor and review processes

also provide input into maintaining the currency of any security risk registers that have been developed.

- **Systemic reviews** by internal or external audit teams to ensure compliance with internal and externally mandated requirements, and these reviews are highly selective in their focus. Reviews such as simulation exercises and penetration testing also provide awareness and training opportunities beyond the monitoring objectives.

Regardless of which type is undertaken, the key elements of a monitor and review process remain the same and should be based on the following (Figure 6.31):

- Understanding the changing context and organizational needs
- Measuring and reviewing the effectiveness of activities with a view to enhance organizational performance
- Assuring compliance and conformance with legislative and organizational requirements

Triggers for Monitoring and Review

AS/NZS 4360:2004 recommends that this monitoring and review should occur as a part of each phase of the risk assessment process. If this cannot occur, then the organization should at least ensure a review of security risk is undertaken in the following instances:

- Significant changes occur in the local security environment.
- Significant changes occur in the nature of security risk within similar industries or markets.

- The national security threat changes significantly.
- Significant changes occur to the organization's assets, e.g., the organization develops new intellectual property of commercial value.
- Management responsibilities change significantly, e.g., a business unit leader resigns.
- Structural or layout changes are made to the organization's premises or neighboring premises, which may require a realignment of security controls/barriers.
- New suppliers are appointed.
- New security-related technologies become available.
- Mergers and acquisitions are occurring.
- A security breach, failure, or near-miss occur.

Following any security breach, failure or near-miss, a post-event review should be conducted to do the following:

- Ensure that the incident and its aftermath are appropriately managed and the risk consequence is minimized
- Review to what extent the risk profile may have changed
- Identify any learnings from the response to, and recovery from, the event to determine the effectiveness of the current control framework and any additional treatment improvements required
- Communicate the importance of Security Risk Management where appropriate
- Investigate and identify the threat actors and pursue them if appropriate via administrative, civil, or criminal channels

6.3.7 Risk Appetite

Risk appetite (also referred to as risk preference, attitude, tolerance, or capacity) is the amount of risk a person or an entity is willing to accept in pursuit of value. Attitude to risk can be categorized as risk averse, risk neutral, or risk seeking, and the amount of risk a person or entity is likely to tolerate will vary because of a wide range of factors, which include the following:

- Expected outcomes (upside)
- Perceived exposure or losses (downside)
- Awareness of the actual risks (we do not know what we do not know)
- Previous experiences, whether successful or otherwise, and the level of extant knowledge pertinent to the successful management of a particular risk
- Resilience levels
- Personal beliefs and values
- Emotional state, e.g., anger tends to increase risk appetite

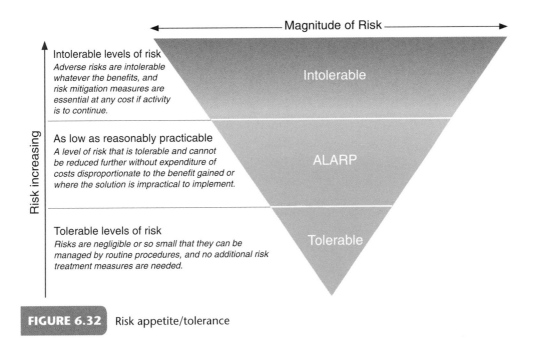

Magnitude of Risk

Risk increasing

Intolerable levels of risk
Adverse risks are intolerable whatever the benefits, and risk mitigation measures are essential at any cost if activity is to continue.

Intolerable

As low as reasonably practicable
A level of risk that is tolerable and cannot be reduced further without expenditure of costs disproportionate to the benefit gained or where the solution is impractical to implement.

ALARP

Tolerable levels of risk
Risks are negligible or so small that they can be managed by routine procedures, and no additional risk treatment measures are needed.

Tolerable

FIGURE 6.32 Risk appetite/tolerance

Once individuals and/or entities have determined their tolerance levels, the risk culture can be used to inform decision making, as it defines the boundaries around the acceptance of a given activity and provides guidance regarding what level of actions should be applied to maintain an acceptable balance of risk and reward.

HB 436:2004 Risk Management Guidelines, which is companion to AS/NZS 4360:2004, describes a common approach in terms of dividing risk appetite into three bands as follows (Figure 6.32):

- An upper band in which adverse risks are intolerable whatever benefits the activity may bring, and risk reduction measures are essential whatever their cost

- A middle band, or gray area, in which costs and benefits are taken into account and opportunities are balanced against potential adverse consequences

- A lower band in which positive or negative risks are negligible, or so small that no risk treatment measures are needed.

6.3.8 Swiss Cheese Model

James Reason developed the Swiss cheese model to illustrate how analyzes of major accidents and catastrophe tend to reveal multiple, smaller failures leading up to the actual hazard (Figure 6.33).[29]

Industry data and research conducted by Reason show that human error is the largest contributor to reduced dependability in most settings. In the SRM

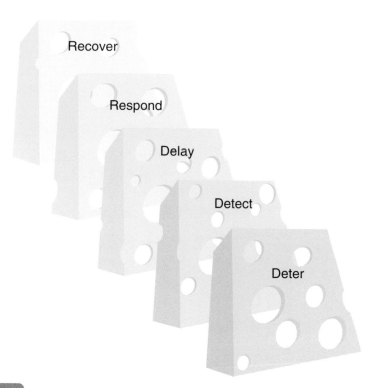

FIGURE 6.33 James Reason's Swiss cheese model illustrated using D3R2 security concepts

context this typically refers to the failure to identify, implement or maintain appropriate security control measures.

In the model, each slice of cheese represents a security barrier that is usually relevant to a variety of threats. The point is that no single barrier is foolproof. They all have holes, hence the name Swiss-cheese, and when the holes are allowed to align, a security risk event can occur. Any one of the slices is usually sufficient to prevent a security attack provided that its holes do not align (Figure 6.34).

The interdependent nature and benefits of redundant layers of protection associated with the Security-in-depth principle is illustrated by the Swiss cheese principle illustrated previously.

6.3.9 The Risk Bow-Tie

The risk bow-tie methodology is a structured approach to risk identification and management, which was developed initially by Shell Corporation. It can be represented in tabular format or, more typically, in a graphical presentation from which it draws its name (Figure 6.35).

At the center of the bow-tie diagram is the top event, which we do not want to happen, i.e., the attack. To the left is what might cause the event to occur (the

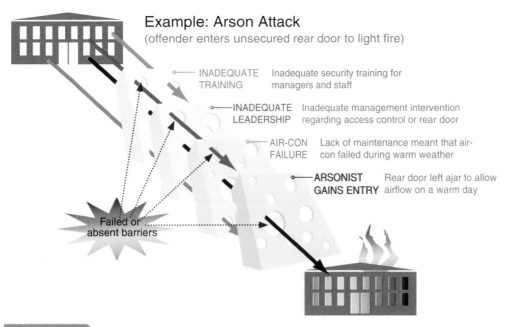

Example: Arson Attack
(offender enters unsecured rear door to light fire)

INADEQUATE TRAINING — Inadequate security training for managers and staff

INADEQUATE LEADERSHIP — Inadequate management intervention regarding access control or rear door

AIR-CON FAILURE — Lack of maintenance meant that air-con failed during warm weather

ARSONIST GAINS ENTRY — Rear door left ajar to allow airflow on a warm day

Failed or absent barriers

FIGURE 6.34 Example of Swiss cheese barriers and an arson attack using human factors analysis (Ref: Figure 5.5)

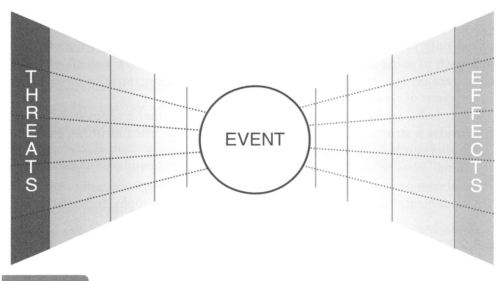

THREATS

EVENT

EFFECTS

FIGURE 6.35 Risk bow-tie

threat), and between the two are the preventive controls. The right-hand side contains details of the potential consequences and the mitigating barriers, which are illustrated as vertical green lines.

Illustrating this in more detail highlights the nature of the interrelations between various elements of the equation. This is shown in Figure 6.36.

Technology Controls	Deter	Delay	Detect	Respond	Recover
Security access systems	Yes	Yes	Partial	No	No
Intrusion detection and alarms	Yes	No	Yes	No	No
Mail screening	No	No	Yes	No	No
Password and encryption keys	Yes	Yes	No	No	No
Firewalls	Yes	Yes	Partial	No	No
Surveillance capability	Yes	No	Yes	No	No
Systems penetration testing	No	Yes	Yes	Yes	No
Panic alarms	No	No	No	Yes	No

6.4 RESOURCES

Quality Security Risk Management is dependent on the appropriate allocation of resources to tasks to mitigate risks. The best security plan (SRM treatment plan) will come to naught if resources are not available to implement it. Optimizing the use of available resources is a maxim of modern management and a fundamental of sound Security Risk Management.

6.4.1 Security Barriers

Judicious and effective procurement and contract management skills are essential in the operation and development of any organization.

In this context, the phrase "security barriers" refers to more than simply the construction of a fence or secure entry point. The coordination of an organizations personnel security with its physical security measures, its information security with its management agenda, and its information technology and communications security results in the creation of a series of integrated barriers that mitigated against an identified risk much more effectively than if any of these security elements operated in isolation. In the Security Risk Management vernacular, the banner under which these barriers are formed is known as Security Risk Management.

6.4.2 Types of Resources

Managers, individuals and governments will have widely varying levels of resources available. Fundamentally, they will all have access to the same resources.

6.4.2.1 Security Risk Management Resources. Resources for the mitigation of security risks are essentially the assets available to the organization that include the following:

- Physical property
- People

- Information
- Information and communications technologies

It should be noted that core functions, capabilities, and organizational reputation as well as financial reserves will come into play with deploying these assets; however, in the final analysis it will be these four elements that will enable any actual implementation.

6.4.2.2 Financial Resources. Management and deployment of financial resources are central to an entities risk management strategy. Although economic reserves are an essential element of long-term resilience, these reserves are not necessarily available as cash. They may come from a variety of sources, including cash-at-bank, insurance, additional equity funding, debt funding, grants, donations, or asset sales. In the SRM context, economic assets are less important for their own sake than for the capability that they can deliver via the judicious use of funds to source and deploy people and property, information, and ICT systems.

> *Financial resources are relevant to most areas of security risk mitigation. In SRM-BOK, however, the term is generally considered to be a measure of resource requirements rather than a true resource. Money alone will rarely mitigate risk (with the possible exception of elements such as ransom demands); it is typically more useful for quantifying and comparing cost/benefit of the application of more direct tangible resources, e.g., people, encryption software, and so on.*

6.4.3 Resource Attributes

Resources available to an organization to apply Security Risk Management treatments can be analyzed and configured based on the following three attributes:

- Availability
- Configuration
- Effectiveness

It is important to note that this is equally true for analysis of resource attributes available to a threat actor; however, ascertaining intelligence on these attributes in any meaningful fashion is likely to prove challenging if not completely beyond the scope of most entities.

6.4.4 Resource Allocation and Prioritization

The primary factors within an entities control are the allocation and relative prioritization of available assets. This is equally true of the implementation of risk mitigation controls or the conduct of intelligence gathering and risk analysis processes.

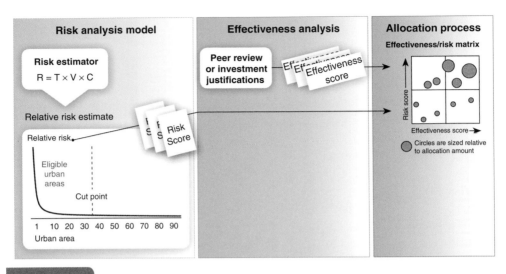

FIGURE 6.39 Overview of DHS' Urban Areas Security Initiative (UASI) grant determination process in fiscal year 2006 [34]

Resource allocation is discussed in more detail throughout SRMBOK, however the primary process is illustrated well in this example from the US Department of Homeland Security risk determination process illustrated in Figure 6.38: Overview of DHS' UASI Grant Determination Process in Fiscal Year 2006 below. In this instance, the formula R = T × V × C (Risk Rating = Threat × Vulnerability × Consequence) has been used to determine comparative risk levels. AS/NZS 4360:2004 and SRMBOK use the formula "likelihood × consequence" to evaluate comparative risk levels; however, the principle remains the same whatever methodology is applied.

> *The key lessons to draw from this process are that:*
> • *A level of analysis needs to be applied when considering the effectiveness of any given strategy*
> • *The bulk of resources should be applied to risks which are highly effective against higher rated risk levels*

6.4.4.1 Security-in-Depth. A thorough asset and threat identification process, which is consistent with an established context, is essential to the compilation of an appropriate physical security management plan. Best practice in Security Risk Management suggests that a security-in-depth approach to asset protection will provide the greatest security for an identified asset. Interlinked layers of security measures much like Swiss cheese layers (Figure 6.33: James Reason's Swiss-cheese model in Section 6.3.8) will provide mutually supporting layers of security as indicated in Figure 6.40.

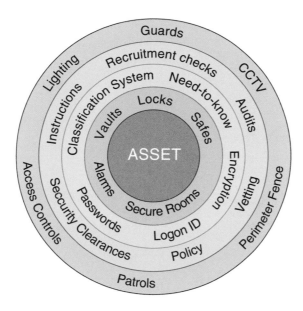

FIGURE 6.40 Example of security-in-depth

This concept is often used in Security Risk Management. In a threat assessment context, it provides a graphic depiction of existing countermeasures and other threat mitigation systems available in the formulation of a risk management strategy.

One limitation with the security-in-depth model is that it implies there is a single best-practice approach to layering security control measures. This is clearly not true as an organization's context will determine the type and ordering of security barriers. For example:

- In a military facility, items of value are protected behind locked doors with guards at the front gate.
- In an art museum, the external doors have locks, and most security guards patrol within the building.

This limitation can be overcome by following a hierarchy of controls in conjunction with security-in-depth.

6.4.5 Hierarchy of Controls

The hierarchy of controls is a risk management process most readily associated with the treatment of occupational health and safety issues; however, it has a much broader application in the implementation of control measures.

The hierarchy of control categorizes control measures in priority order that can be used to select and manage risk exposures. Hierarchy of controls (also referred to by the mnemonic "eliminate, substitute, isolate, engineer, administrative controls, and personal protection" (ESIEAP) has been adapted from the

Australian Safety and Compensation Council and can assist security practitioners with the selection and evaluation of control options to remove hazards at their source by doing the following:[52]

- **Elimination:** complete removal of the threat or risk exposure is the ideal control solution where this is practical. For example, it may be able to remove all risk of travel-related security risks by not traveling; however, if most of an organizations customers are overseas, the complete elimination of this risk is likely to be impractical.

- **Substitution:** involves replacing a hazardous substance, machinery, or work process with a nonhazardous or less hazardous one. Extending the travel security example, it might be possible to substitute the risk by meeting customers in a safer location.

- **Isolation:** involves separation of the risk from people by distance or the use of barriers. For example, it may be possible to isolate personnel from security threats when they travel by conducting meetings in a controlled environment, such as an airport business lounge.

- **Engineering controls:** may include modification of tools and equipment or the use of enclosures, barriers, or automation. In a security context, this might include boomgates, security barriers, armored vehicles, and firewalls.

- **Administrative controls:** where a risk cannot be eliminated or controlled by engineering, administrative controls should be used. Administrative controls mean introducing work practices or procedures that reduce risk. This might include revised timings, travel security training, and reducing the size of travelling parties.

- **Protect the asset:** as a last resort, where other measures are not practicable, it may be necessary to use measures such as personal protective equipment (PPE), which includes ballistic body armor or items such as secure briefcases as a last line of defense for sensitive documents while traveling.

> *This process of selecting a hierarchy of controls provides guidance when prioritizing treatments by selecting the most effective risk reduction methods.*
>
> *In some cases, it may be necessary to apply elements from each of the six ESIEAP elements. In other cases, it may be possible to reduce risk to ALARP by using only some measures.*

The principle of ESIEAP in security-in-depth is illustrated in Figure 6.41. The example in Figure 6.42 of the prioritization of risks associated with international operations highlights the principle that it may be necessary to apply several ESIEAP layers concurrently, much like a Swiss cheese model.

An example of using hierarchy of controls for security-in-depth for protection on information is provided in Table 6.5 below.

Table 6.5 Example of HCSD applied to information assets

Eliminate	Shred or destroy all nonessential sensitive files
Substitute	Use open source information where suitable
Isolate	Store all files in central location
Engineer	Store files in security containers and under alarm
Admin. controls	Security clearances, training, procedures, etc.
Protect	Protective markings on folders, lockable briefcases, etc.

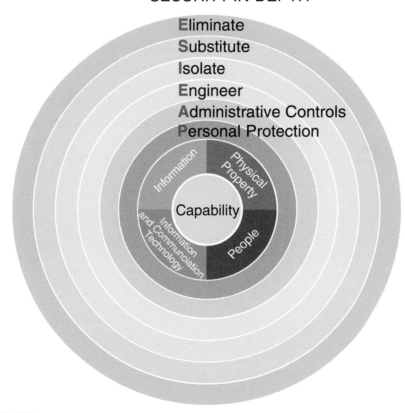

SECURITY-IN-DEPTH

FIGURE 6.41 Hierarchy of controls for security-in-depth (HCSD)

SECURITY-IN-DEPTH

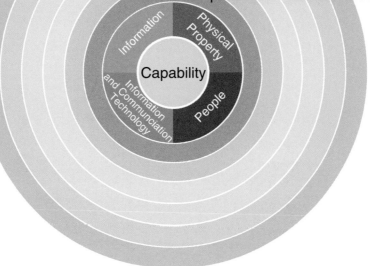

Eliminate—Cease oil exploration activities
Substitute—Operate in lower risk countries
Isolate—Locate staff outside high crime areas
Engineer—Fences, gates, armored vehicles
Administrative Controls—Policies, training
Personal protection—Ballistic vests

FIGURE 6.42 Example of HCSD for a multinational oil and gas explorer

6.5 QUALITY

> *The ISO 9000 series of quality management standards defines quality as: "The degree to which a set of inherent characteristics fulfills requirements".[53]*
>
> *(Standards Australia)*

This definition is also useful in the Security Risk Management context as the quality of a Security Risk Management system and its elements directly relates to assets protected, lives saved, businesses booming, and nation states flourishing.

The efficiency, effectiveness, and appropriateness of the collective elements, activities, and processes of SRM are what we broadly mean by quality in the SRM context. ISO 9000 offers additional clarity in achieving this through customer focus, leadership, broad staff involvement, systemic approach, continuous improvement, fact-based decision making, and mutually beneficial supplier relationships to provide a basis for the creation, progression, and management of quality systems. Decision makers should consider all of these quality factors when managing security or any other risks.

SRMBOK is concerned primarily with resilience or securing organizational capability. In many respects, however, the quality of security measures can be judged with respect to the ability to meet key organizational and individual needs. Security Risk Management systems can be evaluated through several prisms including the following:

- Aligned with community, organizational, and individual requirements or expectations
- Ability to identify and achieve ALARP levels of risk
- Appropriate to the threat
- Fit for purpose
- Effective
- Broadly supported
- Efficient
- Reliable

Each of these is covered in more detail below.

6.5.1 Defining Needs and Expectations

> *John Maclean is an elite sportsman—he has completed the Hawaii Ironman, swam the English Channel, completed the Molokai Ocean open water paddling world championships, and represented Australia at the Sydney Olympics.*[54] *He has done all this from a wheelchair as he is a paraplegic. John speaks about all people having needs and that there are different levels for different people.*
>
> *So what is a need? Simply put, a need is a requirement or a situation that requires a course of action. Moreover, this concept of level of needs focused on people can incorporate customer, organizational, and community needs. Indeed, in all relationships, whether one based on friendship or intimacy or one solely focused on business and productivity, transaction is conducted around needs. So, understanding the needs of people, stakeholders, and community enables individuals and organizations to relate to and with these groups more efficiently.*

6.5.1.1 What are Needs and Expectations. Abraham Maslow proposed a hierarchy of five levels of basic needs. In the levels of the five basic needs, which are illustrated in Figure 6.43, people have difficulty experiencing the second need until the demands of the first are satisfied, and have difficulty with the third until the second is satisfied, and so on. The first two elements of this hierarchy—physiological and safety requirements are (primarily) the domain of security risk management.

Like needs, expectations exist in all relationships or interactions between people, organizations, and communities. Often people are unaware of their expectations and may not articulate or communicate their requirements effectively. When expectations are not met, the reaction may be anger, frustration, or disappointment. These emotions can then impact the functioning of the relationship and prevent each side from successfully fulfilling their needs.

6.5.1.2 Individual Needs. These basic needs are as follows:

- Physiological needs—oxygen, food, water, and a relatively constant body temperature. These needs are the strongest because life ceases if a person is deprived of any of these.
- Safety needs—when all physiological needs are satisfied and are no longer controlling thoughts and behaviors, the needs for security can become active. Individuals typically have little awareness of their security needs except in times of emergency or raised threat levels.

6.5.1.3 Customer Needs. Vanessa Hall, in her work on trust outlines that a customer, will have needs and these needs combined with Maslow's Hierarchy of Needs may look like Figure 6.43.[55]

- Physiological needs—food, transport, housing, clothing
- Safety needs—security, product safety, wealth, family security
- Love/belonging—sense of community, part of a group, loved

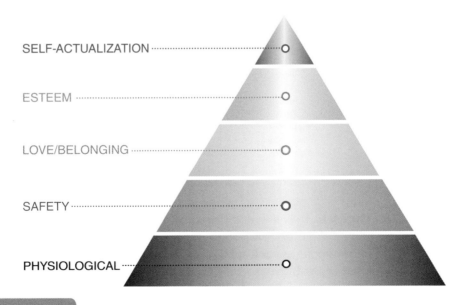

FIGURE 6.43 Maslow's hierarchy of needs

- Esteem—respect, recognition, accepted, confidence
- Self-actualization—creative, spontaneity, appreciate life, helping

In Security Risk Management terms, a customer focus refers to understanding an organization's internal and external environment. Governments, organizations, and individuals often observe their customers as their relevant minister, shareholders, clients, or interested parties.

In both the private and public sectors, elements of organizations often have internal customers. CCTV operators could include management and mobile guards in their customer base. Security vetting officers may consider recruitment officers to be their clients, and senior risk managers may recognize an organization's board of directors as customers.

These internal and external customer relationships should be taken into account when articulating an organization's internal and external context.

6.5.1.4 Organizational Needs.
Organizational objectives are usually stated explicitly in vision and mission statements. Organizational needs may be somewhat less explicit and should be established during the context setting phase of the risk assessment process.

Likewise, organizational expectations may be stated in the vision and mission statement yet actually expectations are realized through cultural conversations, which include what is said and what behaviors occur around the office. These expectations may run counter to what the expressed expectations are from a vision or mission statement. In Security Risk Management terms, awareness of these types of influences enables an understanding of the real risks associated with the organization.

6.5.1.5 Community Needs.
Community needs and expectations vary and again are established by context; however, key indicators of what a community needs and values can be found in the following:

- behaviors within that community
- legislated expectation, e.g., environmental protection acts
- community funded or supported activities, e.g., community action groups

6.5.2 As Low As Reasonably Practicable

The concept of ALARP revolves around practicality: Can anything be done about the risk at a cost that is less than the benefits achieved?

When risk reaches intolerable levels, the expectation is that risk will be reduced unless the cost of reducing the risk is grossly disproportionate to the benefits gained by accepting that risk. Where risks are close to the negligible level, then action might only be taken to reduce risk where benefits exceed the costs of reduction.

Although acceptable risk thresholds may vary with different activities, risks should be treated such that residual risks are ALARP. The basis for the ALARP judgment is that the risk should be treated to the point where the cost of more

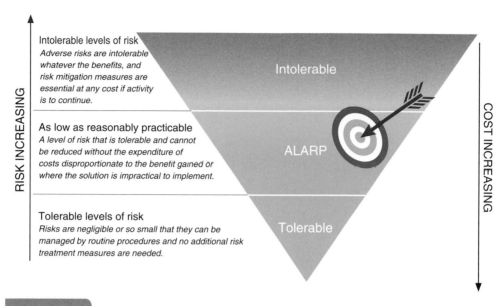

FIGURE 6.44 The concept of ALARP

treatment is excessive compared with the resulting value or opportunity realized through a reduction in risk (Figure 6.44). In extreme examples, it may not be possible to reduce a risk to reasonably acceptable levels for any amount of resource expenditure or opportunity realization, and in these cases, the risk treatment may be the abandonment of the activity, i.e., elimination of the risk by ceasing the activity.

> *In 1949, Lord Justice Asquith provided a definition of "reasonably practicable."*
>
> *"'Reasonably practicable' is a narrower term than 'physically possible' and it seems to me to imply that a computation must be made by the owner, in which the quantum of risk is placed on one scale and the sacrifice involved in the measures necessary for averting the risk (whether in money, time or trouble) is placed in the other; and that if it be shown that there is a gross disproportion between them – the risk being insignificant in relation to the sacrifice – the defendants discharge the onus on them. Moreover, this computation falls to be made by the owner at a point of time anterior to the accident."*
>
> *Source: Edwards v National Coal Board (1949) 1 KB 704 at 712, CA, per Asquith LJ*

The ALARP concept can also be described as the point whereby the trade-off between cost and benefit reached its optimal value in terms of reward for resources expended, as shown in Figure 6.45.

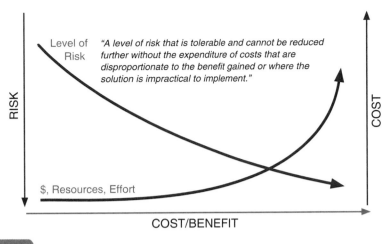

FIGURE 6.45   ALARP cost/benefit trade-off

6.5.3 Appropriate and Cost Effective

Historically, many security risk plans have been established with little regard to cost/benefit calculations and the dynamic nature of security threats an individual or organization may be operating in. For example, the cost/benefit of mandating that all employees must have armored vehicles would be completely inappropriate if only a small proportion of individuals are located in high-risk areas. However, conducting risk assessments at every location may not be cost effective or timely if it took more than 12 months or more to visit all the offices of a multinational organization.

Even if it is practical and cost effective to conduct security risk assessments and develop individual plans for each facility and project, any sudden increase in threat levels will necessitate an immediate review of security treatments. For example, if an issue-motivated group suddenly issues an edict that they intend to target your organization, the comparative threat level will make an unknown number of security measures inadequate overnight.

A more balanced approach is to establish a range of threat profiles and security specifications or postures that are adopted in any given threat environment.

> A security *specification* is a documented technical specification or other precise criteria used consistently as rules, guidelines, or definitions of characteristics to ensure that materials, products, processes, and services are fit for their purpose. Specifications should be determined and applied at the organizational level, implemented in a managed fashion, (e.g., through the development of policy and provision of concomitant funding), require a lead time to implement, and form the basis of review/audit activities.

For example, an Australian organization that operates in many overseas locations may decide that, based on the varying threat level at its different locations, the intruder alarm systems described in Table 6.6 are required as the minimum security specification in all of its buildings.

Many benefits are associated with the establishment of security specifications, including the following:

- Helps the organization's senior management make decisions about the level of risk the organization is prepared to accept, i.e., what is to be considered an acceptable or unacceptable risk
- Ensures consistency in security arrangements
- Embeds a culture of risk management

Table 6.6 **Example of threat-based organizational security specification**

Security Measure/Area Type	Threat Level				
	Low	Moderate	Medium	High	Extreme
Building Protection*	Commercial Grade with back-to-base monitoring	Commercial Grade with back-to-base monitoring	Type 2	Type 2	Type 1**
Intruder Resistant Area	Type 2 alarm system & peripherals				
Secure Room	Type 1 alarm system & peripherals				

NOTES:

*Sensor-activated halogen flood lighting should be installed at both the front and rear of the office/residence to illuminate the immediate grounds area. A command switch for the lighting shall be installed within the house for manual override or for manual use of the lighting.

**For all Type 1 security alarm systems (SAS):

- Detectors should cover all entrance and exit points. All perimeter doors should be protected with balanced magnetic reed switches. All SAS hardware is to be located in the controlled perimeter.
- A man-machine interface (keypad) should be located within the residence in close proximity to the main entry door and should provide for a 30-second delay on entry/exit. If power is lost to the residence, then an uninterrupted power supply (UPS) or battery back up system should be used to provide power to the SAS for a minimum of 4 hours.
- The SAS should be monitored by a host-country-accredited monitoring station, in accordance with Australian Standard (AS) 2201 or an equivalent specification.
- Written procedures should be in place in the event of an alarm. These may vary in accordance with operational requirements, but they must encompass instructions on contacting the staff and families, and a suitable response. Contingency plans should be put in place in the event of failure of the Type 1 SAS.

- Assists with the development of business cases as it defines the resources required for treating risk
- Directly links security control with the threat, thus ensuring that which is of key value to the organization has the most protection
- Allows for security reviews, audits, and plans to be based on comprehensive and expected specifications

Two minor challenges are associated with the application of security specifications by threat level. The first relates to a situation whereby threat information is being received from different sources. For example, if the threat levels from the two information sources are different, then it would be appropriate to assign a credibility and reliability rating (as per the Admiralty Scale) to these sources to determine the most likely threat level. If this approach fails to determine the threat level clearly, then prudence would suggest acting on the higher of the two levels. In those circumstances in which one supplier of threat assessments may rate an activity or location as three out of five and the other as three out of six, the solution is relatively simple. The following table suggests an equivalence system whereby the threat ratings can be aligned. Essentially, these three scales (1 to 4, 1 to 5, and 1 to 6) have been aligned to reflect a conservative view of the threat level interpretation. For example, if the "1 to 5" system moves from threat level 1 to level 2, the "1 to 4" system will already have the respective security measures at that level.

The second challenge involves a situation in which an organization is receiving threat information about multiple threat actors in the same location. For example, in the city of XYZ, the threat from issue-motivated groups (IMGs) may be at a low level 1, whereas the threat from violent crime (VC) may be at level 3, politically motivated violence (PMV) at level 2, and espionage at level 3 (see Table 6.8).

> A security posture is a practice or activity that can be implemented and/or modified at relatively short notice, e.g., locking doors and putting on additional guards, which can be undertaken against an agreed specification after changes to the threat level. A security posture at a higher threat level must build on the strengths of the posture implemented at the lower threat level.

Table 6.7 Threat-level equivalence matching

Threat Levels		
1	1	1
	2	2
2	3	3
3	4	4
4	5	5
		6

Table 6.8 Worked example of security specification for range of threat actors

			Threat Levels			
		1	2	3	4	5
Intruder Alarm System	VC	S	M	M	M	M-Crypt
	IMG		S	M	M	M-Crypt
	PMV			S	M	M-Crypt
	Esp.	S	M	M-Crypt	M-Crypt	M-Crypt

Practices or activities that fall within an organization's security posture are many and varied. Outlined below are some example practices that can be implemented or modified at short notice after changes to an organization's threat level. Following this is a worked example of a security posture for an airline carrier flying into a number of overseas locations with varying threat levels at the different locations (Table 6.9).

- Provision of threat-risk briefings
- Training, e.g., awareness, refresher, personal safety, group, emergency/evacuation, and so on
- Wearing/nonwearing of uniforms
- Wearing of passes and sign-in books
- Individual and/or group travel arrangements
- Deployment and positioning of bollards at road or building entry points
- Deployment of static and mobile security guards (foot and/or vehicle mounted)
- Graduated carriage of weapons (none, batons/cuffs, then firearms)
- Rules of engagement/orders for opening fire

> More detailed information on security specifications and postures is available in the Guide to SRMBOK on Security Specifications and Security Postures.

6.5.4 Leadership

The implementation, maintenance, and progression of risk treatments across an organization can only be achieved through sustained executive level commitment to Security Risk Management principles. Leaders within an organization should create an environment where people at all levels can contribute to the implementation of quality risk management outcomes.

Leadership commitment is required at every stage of the production of a quality security risk assessment process. Organizational leaders must have a clear

Table 6.9 Example of a threat-based organizational security posture

1	2	3	4	5
Safety Measure—Briefings				
During induction/ recruitment plus on an annual basis, all staff are to be briefed on local security plans and on protective security measures/ practices. Intelligence and staff safety summaries provided on each country as required but no less than quarterly.	All staff to be briefed on change of alert level and threat where known. All staff to be reminded to be vigilant/ inquisitive about strangers and to watch out for unidenti-fied or unattended packages and vehicles. Monthly intelligence and staff safety summaries provided on each country.	All staff to be briefed on change of alert level and threat where known. All staff to be advised of contingency and emergency response plans, and reminded to be particularly vigilant. Intelligence and staff safety summaries provided on each country as required but not less than weekly.	All staff to be briefed on change of alert level and specific threat. Intelligence and staff safety summaries provided on each country as required but not less than bi-weekly.	All staff to be briefed on change of alert level and specific threat. Intelligence and staff safety summaries provided on each country as required but not less than daily.
Safety Measure—Uniform				
No restrictions on the wearing of uniform except that security passes are not to be worn outside of airports.	No restrictions on the wearing of uniform except that security passes are not to be worn outside of airports.	No security restrictions on the wearing of uniform, unless the cabin crew manager imposes local restrictions.	No uniforms to be worn outside of airport precincts. Staff are to change within designated lounges.	Consider canceling flights until alert level lowers, otherwise as per alert level 4.
Safety Measure—Gatherings				
No restrictions.	As per alert level 1.	All travel to and from the airport to be undertaken as a group (in consultation with local police as necessary).	After disembarkation, all staff are to gather within the designated airport lounge until reembarkation.	Consider canceling flights until alert level lowers. Otherwise as per alert level 4.

1	2	3	4	5
Safety Measure—Training				
Basic aggression management training to be provided to all cabin crew after induction.	As per alert level 1.	Staff receive refresher training or more specialist aggression management training being provided.	As per alert level 3	As per alert level 3
Safety Measure—In-Flight				
As per current company flight operations policy.	As per current company flight operations policy.	As per current company flight operations policy. Pre-boarding cabin security check undertaken by contractors or as per alert level 1.	Additional resources provided to allow alteration of precision timing schedule to facilitate preboarding cabin security check to be undertaken by operating (outbound) cabin crew.	As per alert level 4.
Safety Measure—Other				
Institutionalizing a process to ensure all facilities and flight sectors are regularly assessed for weaknesses, and measures are taken to mitigate these.	Communications checked with emergency response arrangements. Contracted hotel is advised of heightened alert and asked to review its security.	All local leave outside of the secure hotel area is canceled. Contracted hotel is asked to employ additional security staff in hotel precinct. Company security to conduct on sight review. Consider arming flight crew.	Slipping is canceled, and crews move to transit patterns. Company aircraft to be guarded at all times while parked. Consider deploying a civilian security guard with cabin crew (or deploying with armed sky marshals). Local/airport security presence required.	Consider canceling flights until alert level lowers. Consider only flying if supported by armed sky marshals. Company aircraft to be guarded at all times while parked. Local/airport and company security presence mandatory.

understanding of their organizational environment. Every environment changes over time, which requires organizational leaders to review their environmental understanding constantly. The collection analysis and distribution of timely and accurate intelligence within an organization and an organizational commitment to receiving frank advice provides a platform for quality leadership and the creation of quality decision-making processes. Quality, fact-based decision making at all levels must be supported by quality implementation and review processes.

The production of quality implementation programs within an organization depends on the appropriate commitment of resources and effective communication in support of an implementation program from organizational leaders.

6.5.5 Staff and Stakeholder Involvement

As with the introduction of any new initiative at the organizational level, an effective communication and participation strategy will be needed in the coordination of plans and activities across the organization. Involvement of staff and stakeholders in the process, particularly from operational areas, is vital for achieving coordination and laying the foundations for integrated Security Risk Management outcomes.

Staff involvement should occur at various stages in the security risk assessment process, as follows:

- **Establishing a context.** This will assist organizational leaders and risk managers to understand an organizations internal and external environments across organizational strata. Consultation with staff will provide an insight into intraorganizational and client connectivity as it actually happens rather than how workflow or consultative mechanisms would ideally structure it. A consultative process of this nature will provide will provide the organization with a quality contextual assessment.

- **Threat assessment.** Providing an opportunity for staff to evaluate a threat assessment increases the quality of the assessment by affirming, or otherwise, identifying operational risks

- **Risk treatment implementation.** Promoting staff ownership of risk treatments through promoting participation in change management processes associated with the of risk treatments improves the quality and effectiveness of those treatments

- **Business continuity.** A quality response to the realization of an identified risk must include a detailed human resources plan and the commitment of staff to the resumption of operations following an adverse occurrence. To this end, staff consultation is essential.

6.5.6 Continuous Improvement

In this context, continuous improvement is a term that refers to the cyclical nature of quality Security Risk Management. It should be strategically integrated with an organization's corporate objectives to ensure that human resource management continues to evolve toward best practice.[56]

Every risk treatment process should include a review stage that establishes the effectiveness of the treatment and the processes that produced the treatment outcome. Continuous improvement programs also provide the impetus for an organization to conduct ongoing environmental assessments to monitor identified and emerging risks against an organization's internal and external context, and create new and progressive threat assessments to support the management of those risks. A continuous improvement program should include the following processes:

Plan: create a timeline of resources, activities, training, and target dates. Develop a data collection plan, the tools for measuring outcomes, and thresholds for determining when targets have been met.

Do: implement risk treatments and collect data.

Check: analyze results of data and evaluate reasons for variation.

Act: act on what is learned and determine next steps. If the risk treatment is successful, then ensure the treatment becomes an organizational norm. If it is not successful, then analyze sources of failure, design new solutions, and repeat the cycle.[57]

6.5.7 Capability Maturity Models

Defining quality is often, and perhaps most importantly, measured in terms of outcomes. It is important, however, to have some understanding of the underlying systems that contribute to those outcomes, in effect, another form of measuring lead indicators. One way in which we can gain some insight in this area and understand the pathway to improvement is through using capability maturity models.

The notion of maturity models is well developed and accepted. Each level is usually described in qualitative and semiquantitative terms, which enable organizations to assess themselves against agreed scales and set clear goals to move them toward higher levels of capability and maturity. Fully developed capability maturity models have had a proven effective in many disciplines, which help organizations to understand the degree of sophistication of a business management system as well as its reliability and effectiveness in meeting objectives. Many risk management capability maturity models have been proposed, which includes those Hillson, Hopkinson, and Chapman.[9]

The Software Engineering Institute at Carnegie-Mellon University developed a capability maturity model for software organizations that defines the following five levels of increasing capability and maturity:

- Initial (level 1)
- Repeatable (level 2)
- Defined (level 3)
- Managed (level 4)
- Optimizing (level 5)

The Risk and Insurance Management Society risk maturity model for Enterprise Risk Management uses the following seven core competencies or attributes to measure how well enterprise risk management is being embedded:[58]

1. ERM-based approach
2. ERM process management
3. Risk appetite management
4. Root cause discipline
5. Uncovering risks
6. Performance management
7. Business resiliency and sustainability

Another model proposed by Bosler et al,[59] adopts the following four levels:

- Level 1—Ad-hoc
- Level 2—Initial
- Level 3—Repeatable
- Level 4—Managed

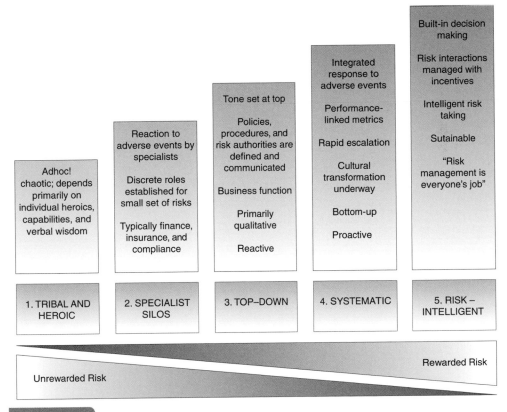

FIGURE 6.46 AESRM risk intelligence capability maturity model

Chapman proposes a risk management maturity model that involves the following four levels of maturity described as:[9]

- Level 1—Initial
- Level 2—Basic
- Level 3—Standard
- Level 4—Advanced

These levels are considered across the organizational attributes of culture, systems, experience, training, and management.

A recent study by Deloitte and Touche LLP in Canada commissioned by the Alliance for Enterprise Security Risk Management (AESRM, www.aesrm.org) as presented in The Convergence of Physical and Information Security in the Context of Enterprise Risk Management suggests a Risk Intelligence Capability Maturity Model as depicted in Figure 6.46. This capability maturity uses five levels of maturity. The study suggests that many organizations find themselves at level 2 relying on specialist silos such as security, finance, insurance, and compliance to manage risks on behalf of the enterprise.

6.5.8 The SRMBOK Capability Maturity Model

Ultimately, capability maturity models can be developed across a range of disciplines with a range of levels and indicators to demonstrate where an organization is in relation to its desired end states. With specific regards to Security Risk Management, SRMBOK recommends the following levels and indicators:

Level 1—INITIAL

The level 1 organization has a limited understanding of the benefits of Security Risk Management. SRM practices are adhoc, reactive, and unstructured; typically they show minimal or excessive security measures implemented after incidents and are unlikely to reflect the actual risks. Usually, little attempt is made to learn from the past or to prepare for future uncertainties.

Examples of level 1 maturity include the following:

- Identifying threats and hazards
  - Internal and external stakeholders are consulted on an adhoc basis concerning visible threats and hazards.
- Evaluating context
  - The internal and external risk contexts are not fully appreciated in all circumstances.
- Identifying risk
  - Identification of where, when, why, and how events could cause risk and resultant injury or illness occurs in a makeshift manner.
  - Existing risk controls to determine consequences and likelihood are evaluated informally.

- Estimation of risk impact against preestablished criteria is considered arbitrary, along with the nature and extent of possible risk treatments.
- Analysing risk
  - Each threat and hazard is treated as new risk, with existing controls and approach not formally known.
- Evaluating risk
  - Risk evaluation is based on adhoc assessment of impact.
- Controlling risk
  - Treatment options are limited, often with heavy reliance on particular types of control.
- Monitoring and reviewing threats and risk
  - The effectiveness of risk management processes is only reviewed as a result of inquiries or external attention.

Some practical ideas for improving maturity include the following:

- Attending and supporting training in threat and hazard identification and risk management.
- Becoming educated on common threats and hazards relevant to your worksite/systems of work/platforms, and so on.
- Asking your team to identify all the known and potential threats and hazards in your area, and creating a log.
- Distilling the range of known and unmitigated threats and hazards into a single list and either eliminating these or controlling them.

Level 2—BASIC
Risk Controllers

The level 2 organization is experimenting with the application of Security Risk Management usually through a small number of nominated individuals but has no formal or structured management systems in place. This organization has not yet effectively implemented SRM processes and is focused on threat mitigation, largely unaware of the potential opportunities of SRM.

To be at a level 2 maturity, appropriate practices and actions need to have been implemented. Examples include:

- Identifying threats and hazards
  - Hazards identification is managed through planned and mission-based processes.
- Evaluating context
  - Risk thresholds are set based on risk calculators.
- Identifying risk
  - The range of events that inform the identification of risk is limited to known risks.

- Analyzing risk
  - The likelihood and consequence of risk is evaluated in alignment with risk calculators.
- Evaluating risk
  - Determined risk is compared against acceptable thresholds, with decisions made regarding acceptability and the requirement for treatment.
- Controlling risk
  - Treatment occurs in alignment with the "hierarchy of threat and hazard control."
- Monitoring and reviewing threats and hazards and risk
  - Logs of risk decision making for activities are reviewed periodically.
  - Logs of threats and risks and the associated mitigation treatment are reviewed periodically.

Some practical ideas include:

- Inviting qualified threats and hazards and risk assessors to review your worksite.
- Reviewing your risk calculation methodology and how it can be used flexibly in a range of circumstances.
- Showcasing or acknowledging decisions that align with the intent of risk approaches and OHS responsibilities.
- Communicating the "hierarchy of control" and emphasizing how it is to be applied within your workplace.
- Checking that threat and hazard identification and risk management approaches align with compliance requirements.

Level 3—REPEATABLE

Risk Enhancers

The level 3 organization has built SRM systems into routine business processes in alignment with other management systems. Policies, procedures, and guidance exists for most threats, and the organization is aware of and pursuing opportunity realization through the SRM process. However, at this level it is likely to remain focused on loss mitigation. Generic security processes are formalized and widespread, although they may not yet be consistently applied.

To be at a level 3 maturity, appropriate practices and actions need to be implemented. Examples include:

- Identifying threats and hazards
  - Threat and hazard identification is supported by information and intelligence to enable decision makers to better appreciate the nature of threats and hazards present.
- Evaluating context
  - Risk thresholds are situational, with the intent of prevention and minimization.

- Identifying risk
  - A diverse range of events is considered to inform the identification of risk.
- Analyzing risk
  - The importance of risk analysis is understood, and risk calculation given rigorous consideration.
- Evaluating risk
  - Determined risk is compared against acceptable thresholds, with decisions made regarding acceptability and the requirement for treatment.
- Controlling risk
  - Treatment occurs in alignment with the "hierarchy of threat and hazard control."
- Monitoring and reviewing threats and hazards and risk
  - Logs of risk decision making for missions are reviewed systematically.
  - Logs of threats and hazards and the associated mitigation treatment are reviewed systematically.

Some practical ideas include:

- Reviewing threat and risk logs and associated elimination and control methods to identify any other opportunities for improvement.
- Improving linkages between threat and risk processes and other areas that can support risk mitigation, such as platforms, plant, infrastructure and equipment, contractors and suppliers, education, skilling, and awareness.
- Drawing a team together to find new innovations in risk treatment.
- Comparing threats and risks identified with other areas of the organization or the wider industry to highlight any gaps or areas of common concern for additional research.
- Reviewing project logs to ascertain nature of risk decision making and any changes that are required.
- Fine-tuning the understanding of acceptable and unacceptable risk decisions.
- Becoming more knowledgeable regarding "soft" threats and risks, and implementing new elimination and control mechanisms.

Level 4—OPTIMIZING
Risk Transformers

Level 4 organizations exhibit a culture in which Security Risk Management, resilience and opportunity realization are embedded and practiced at all levels. The organization has a proactive approach to SRM and actively uses it to improve capability, business processes, and competitive advantage. Security Risk Management is proactive, refined continually, and used consistently to manage opportunities as well as threats.

The relative focus on threat mitigation versus opportunity realization can be illustrated in Figure 6.47 with level 1 not shown on this graphic because of

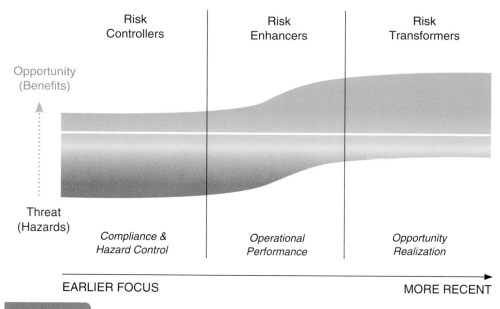

FIGURE 6.47 Security Risk Management maturity journey

the adhoc implementation and limited focus on both threat and opportunity. Examples include:

- Identifying threats and hazards
  - Lead indicators guide investigation of previously unidentified potential threats and hazards.

- Evaluating context
  - Context is considered beyond the organization to include the local community and wider industry.

Some practical ideas include:

- Monitoring threats and hazards and engaging in research or international benchmarking to find new solutions.
- Integrating greater sensitivity to community expectations within risk decision making.
- Encouraging a culture of mindfulness and constant "alert" to potential threats and hazards.
- Rewarding the identification of deviation from stated SRM standards and intent.
- Rewarding behavior that is courageous in the SRM integration principles.
- Being a mentor for balance and integrity between SRM and the organizational vision/mission.

Table 6.10 SRM capability maturity model

Level 1 INITIAL	Level 2 BASIC	Level 3 REPEATABLE	Level 4 OPTIMIZING
OVERVIEW			
Compliance only approach	SRM established for loss prevention	SRM built into routine business processes and management systems	SRM considered critical to competitive advantage and achievement of objectives
Risk appetite not defined	Shared but poorly articulated SRM tolerance	Comprehensive SRM policy and procedures	Security risk appetite and approach is documented and promulgated to all levels of the organization
No framework developed	SRM implemented at lower levels	Benefits recognized at all levels of the organization	SRM management systems demonstrate continuous improvement
No senior management support	Few policies and procedures		SRM proactive and focused on opportunity realization
No use of SRM to inform decision making			
CULTURE			
SRM implemented to meet minimum legislated requirements	SRM exposure defined	Proactive approach to SRM	SRM culture is lead by the Chief Executive
	Roles and responsibilities defined	Support for SRM at all levels of the organization	SRM information is used in decision making
	Basic SRM decision-making mechanisms	High-level security risks reviewed by senior management or board	SRM roles and responsibilities included in inductions, job descriptions, and performance appraisals
SYSTEMS			
SRM strategy and management systems non-existent or adhoc	SRM framework under development	Strategy and management systems documented and consistently applied	SRM framework and management systems are defined and benchmarked against best practice
	BCM and resilience not addressed	SRM framework in place and partially integrated with business continuity management (BCM)	Continuous improvement is evident at all levels
	Poor data collection and analysis		

Level 1 INITIAL	Level 2 BASIC	Level 3 REPEATABLE	Level 4 OPTIMIZING
EXPERIENCE			
Very limited understanding of SRM systems or terminology	Limited to small number of security practitioners	In-house core of experienced individuals, systems, and modeling	Organization has a depth of experience at all levels and experiences are analyzed and recorded as part of normal knowledge management processes
TRAINING			
Training implemented only to the level required by legislation	Training undertaken only by security practitioners	Organizational training needs analyzed and met Security training provided to staff at all levels	Training and education programs are based on robust and up-to-date training needs analysis Relevant training is provided to all levels of the organization
MANAGEMENT			
Management practices focused on meeting legislated requirements Response to critical incidents is the prime initiator for SRM	SRM management practices based on organizational management systems Most of SRM is reactive Security systems reviewed on adhoc basis	Guidance for SRM provided to all levels of management Resource allocation commensurate with risk Security plans reviewed at least annually	Guidance on SRM implementation is provided to all levels of the organization Lead indicators and benchmarks are established and monitored Resource allocation is monitored and optimized BCM and SRM are integrated and plans are reviewed and tested at least annually

6.5.9 Summary of Key Points

Although SRM resources are focused generally toward asset protection, the fundamental objective of Security Risk Management is described more accurately as "supporting organizational resilience to assist achievement of objectives." In practice, this usually means the protection of assets that support the maintenance of organizational function and capabilities.

A wide range of knowledge areas is required to manage any significant activity effectively. In the SRM context these are grouped under the following four categories:

- Exposure
- Risk
- Resources
- Quality

Collectively, these elements can be considered as the quadruple constraints of Security Risk Management because of the ability to trade-off one for another to achieve a desired level of risk.

> *Examples of developed Security Risk Management Maturity Models are provided in the Guide to SRMBOK Application and Case Studies.*

Operational Competency Areas 7

7.1 BUSINESS INTEGRATION

Abstract

This chapter addresses integration of security across a range of variables, which includes general management practice, quality systems, safety management, and financial systems, from three separate perspectives:

- Optimizing internal and external security interfaces
- Coordinating security domains, e.g., information, physical, personnel
- Aligning security with general management and organizational objectives

It considers balancing and integrating the quadruple constraints of Security Risk Management (SRM) as a core competency for Security Risk Management.

7.1.1 Introduction

The first and most important element of Security Risk Management (SRM) is understanding and recording organizational objectives. In this context, the term

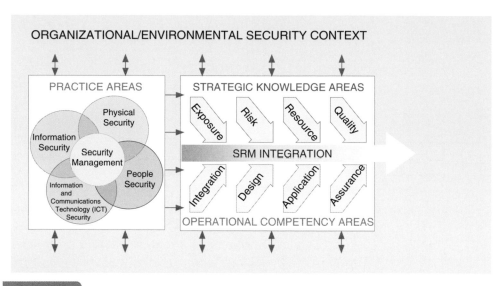

FIGURE 7.1 SRMBOK operational competency areas

"business integration" applies equally to not-for-profit organizations, government agencies, or for-profit corporations. It refers simply to the concept of business as an activity rather than as just a profit-motivated organization (Figure 7.1).

Integrating Security Risk Management practices into an organization is a task that requires the commitment of appropriate resources, wide-spread participation, and active management support. To ensure longevity in what is, in many cases, a cultural shift, it is essential that Security Risk Management processes are recognized by an organization as value adding, not simply as an additional cost.

An organization will derive the most significant value gains from Security Risk Management protocols that are integrated into an organization's existing functional processes. In simple terms, Security Risk Management theory and practice should be observed as an adjunct to current processes.

At the strategic level, integration can be achieved by identifying the following:

- Key performance goals
- The risks of not achieving those goals
- Any factors that may prevent those goals from being met

These three questions will help to develop a contextual baseline. As each asset and resource is identified, a threat assessment should take place and risk treatments progressed to secure them. This process highlights the association between an organization's operational risks and its strategic interests, which ensures that Security Risk Management is viewed as a value proposition.

7.1.2 Business Cases for Security

> *A business case can be defined as a "structured proposal for business improvement that functions as a decision package for organizational decision makers. A business case includes an analysis of business process performance and associated needs or problems, proposed alternative solutions, assumptions, constraints, and risk-adjusted cost/benefit analysis."* [60]
>
> (U.S. GOVERNMENT ACCOUNTING OFFICE)

7.1.2.1 Return on Security Investment (ROSI). Business cases can be built for many different purposes. Some are built for decision-support purposes, whereas others are built for business-planning purposes, e.g., to understand the implications of an action on next year's budgetary planning. The audience needs to understand clearly the case purpose to decide later, when they see the results, whether the case successfully meets the needs of those who must use the results. Once the business case purpose has been defined, metrics must be developed to determine whether subsequent recommendations are justified.

Processes are then designed and implemented to collect information relevant to these metrics for analysis. Decision makers examine the outcomes of various measured processes and strategies and track the results to guide the company and provide feedback. Thus, the value of metrics is in their ability to provide a factual basis for defining the following attributes:

- Success or otherwise of the business case initiative
- Strategic feedback to show the present status of the organization from many perspectives for decision makers
- Diagnostic feedback into various processes to guide improvements on a continuous basis
- Trends in performance over time as the metrics are tracked
- Feedback around the measurement methods themselves, and which metrics should be tracked
- Quantitative inputs to forecasting methods and models for decision-support systems

7.1.2.2 The Rule of Threes. Understanding how and why business cases get funded can be determined by the following:

1. Critical Success Factors
   - Awareness
   - Management commitment
   - Funding

2. How
  - Conditioning
  - Metrics and objectives
  - Presentation

3. Why
  - Reduce costs
  - Achieve profit/deliver on goals
  - Compliance/legislative

> *Additional guidance on ROSI is provided in the Guide to SRMBOK Application and Case Studies, as well as business case template examples.*

7.1.3 General Management Practice

Security Risk Management principles are difficult to institute from the ground up. Without a firm management commitment to funding and resourcing the administrative controls and physical barriers, the management of risk is an uphill battle. There is more to Security Risk Management than just funding and resourcing; The coordination of Security Risk Management practice areas (people, information, and physical) is also a key responsibility of management (Figure 7.2).

General management practices should reflect and support financial and physical risk programs. They should provide a framework that makes Security Risk Management a common philosophy at all levels of an organization and reward the participation in Security Risk Management methodologies.

7.1.4 Understanding and Leading the Security Risk Management Process

A complete assessment of an organization's context is a vital component of a well-structured and articulated design plan. Decision makers must be well versed in the internal and external machinations of their organization, which include

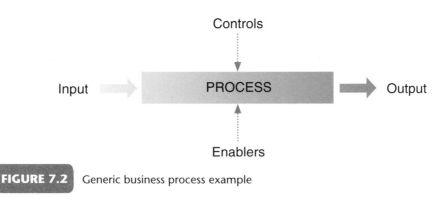

FIGURE 7.2 Generic business process example

how various tactical, operational, and strategic arms of their organization interface with clients, the community, legislative controls, and each other.

To provide a balanced approach to the design of a new Security Risk Management program, a design team should be formed that represents elements of an organization that both effect and are affected by security reforms.

It is important that an organization's executive strata own the design process to ensure that support for Security Risk Management principles flow from the top down. This stratum, chaired by the head of an organization, should consist of, but not be limited to the following examples:

- Chief Security Officer (CSO) or Chief Risk Officer (CRO)—This position will lead the discussion on the development of new Security Risk Management practices and the procurement of applicable systems

- Public Relations Manager—This person will advise the group on public relations (PR) issues regarding the implementation of Security Risk Management practices and postevent PR-related business continuity concerns

- Chief Financial Officer (CFO)—This officer will provide guidance regarding the financial viability of new Security Risk Management reforms and acquisitions, as well as the costs of their ongoing maintenance. The CFO should also provide the design team with a value assessment of new Security Risk Management practices against the loss of key assets or the degradation of key processes protected by the new security measures

- Human Resources Manager—This person will lead the discussion, with advice from the CSO, Chief Security Officer on human security issues, in particular the instigation of security focus recruitment mechanisms and vetting procedures and their impact on staffing levels or business continuity

- Chief Information Officer (CIO)—This individual will lead the discussion, with advice from the CSA, on issues concerning the development or acquisition of technological security solutions that impact of the electronic flow of information in or out of an organization, and postevent business continuity planning for information technology (IT) service provision to the organization.

- New Ventures Manager—A new ventures manager will provide input and advice to the design team on the positive or negative impact of Security Risk Management reforms on the flexibility of an organization to take advantage of new opportunities. This position will also lead the discussion on the management of positive risk

- Chief Legal Officer (CLO)—The CLO should provide advice to the Security Risk Management advisory group regarding the legal frameworks that relate to the implementation of new security measures and the responsibilities of the organization to comply with existing legislation

- Operational Representatives—A representative/s from the operational arms of an organization should also be present to provide renewed operational contextual advice to the group.

7.1.5 Organizational Requirements

Security Risk Management requirements will naturally differ from organization to organization in concert with contextual differences and identified risks. Although an organization of any size could benefit from a holistic threat assessment process, risk treatments will vary depending on the outcome of that assessment and the organization's size, structure, and operational environment.

7.1.6 Sustainability and Maintenance, Future Proofing

The implementation of a Security Risk Management process should not be considered a one off for an organization of any size or structure. Whereas physical barriers require maintenance, the applicability of physical, people, and information security controls must be reviewed regularly to ensure their resonance against contextually related threats.

7.1.7 Safety Management

The management of occupational health and safety issues is central to an organization's people security strategy. Safety management should not be targeted simply at ensuring the safety of employees but should also limit the risk of personal injury or collateral damage to the public and interlocutors. Even though preventing personal injury is important to the maintenance of an organizations public image, it also prevents costly litigation impacting on an organization's bottom line.

7.1.8 Quality Management Systems

From a business integration perspective, ensuring the quality of Security Risk Management systems is an ongoing process. Like any system, the quality of an outcome usually is dependent on the quality of the planning process. Security Risk Management is no exception. A quality risk assessment that provides an accurate précis of an organizations strategic, operational, and tactical level environment begins with a quality contextual assessment provided by knowledgeable and experienced staff and assisted by experienced Security Risk Management practitioners.

The establishment of a Security Risk Management advisory group under the risk council provides organizational decision makers with direction and guidance based on corporate knowledge and industry expertise. This group is particularly pertinent when dealing with the implementation of human resource management, financial management, or information and communications technology systems.

At the operational level, appropriately experienced members of a Security Risk Management advisory group should look to provide leadership in the acquisition and implementation of new systems to ensure compatibility with organizational goals and, if appropriate, existing systems.

At the tactical level, standard operating procedures regarding the use, alteration, and addition of new systems should be articulated to all staff to reduce the risk of unvetted processes impacting on organizational performance.

The promotion of feedback activities within an organization is arguably the most important part of any quality system. Providing operational and tactical level staff with communicative access to strategic level management, as well as regular planning and review activities that include broad consultation processes at all levels of an organization, is the best way to ensure that quality outcomes are being obtained and intellectual capital and the use and growth of corporate knowledge is maximized.

7.1.9 Financial Management

The integration of Security Risk Management into organizational financial management systems is critical to the success of Security Risk Management principles. Just as Security Risk Management helps to provide an organization with a clear view of risks, both positive and negative, financial management systems can provide an organization with benchmarks and quantitative data from which to measure the criticality of security risks. The ability to relate security exposures to financial activities, in particular loss exposures and opportunities, provides support for benchmarking security effectiveness and trends over time. Although not all security risks can be easily quantified, any work toward this goal can only provide additional benefits to an organization. Integration, or at least alignment, with existing financial and accounting systems is one of the key steps in this process. For example, the use of security job codes in a financial system can assist by identifying elements such as injuries caused by assault, versus just a worker's compensation claim. It can also be useful to identify and understand hidden costs such as any additional business rent attributable to a security-driven relocation to safer premises or the incremental cost of hiring a large four-wheel-drive or chauffeur-driven vehicle for safety reasons. Collectively, these costs can build a stronger picture of the real security impacts and benefits in financial terms.

From a traditional security viewpoint, senior management's primary decision-making role is to determine how much funding and other resources to allocate for "beefing up security" to some vaguely articulated industry standard level of practice. In the minds of management, the perceived link between security funding and the business mission (and the business bottom line) is tenuous at best. For example: "If I spend more money on computer security, my risk of intrusion will likely go down. But will this reduce any significant risks to my business mission? What risks will be reduced, and by how much?" With no clear benefit visible to management, the resulting security funding is typically inadequate to meet even the limited technical goals of the security experts.

For the most part, what is missing is an in-depth analysis of threats to the organization's mission and a corresponding cost/benefit analysis for risk-mitigation strategies and contingency planning.

Without an intimate cross-functional area understanding of the business mission and a detailed analysis of what needs to be protected and how, most organizations struggle with the value proposition that can be provided by well-considered security treatments.

Financial management systems that furnish senior management with a value determination based on the protection or benefits that SRM provides, rather than simply a raw cost of security measures, will assist decision makers to prioritize holistic Security Risk Management principles. Understanding the past security costs of a new project for example, can provide additional metrics to understand the return on investment (ROI) of future projects and to extrapolate the security risk/reward relationship in greater depth.

7.1.10 Summary—Business Integration

Firm management commitment is essential for the successful implementation of Security Risk Management practices.

The establishment of a dedicated Security Risk Management advisory team to act as a resource for organizational decision makers will add value to a Security Risk Management process.

Any Security Risk Management process should be augmented by the institution of a quality management system that incorporates a cross-organizational feedback process to ensure the use of corporate knowledge.

Financial assessments of a Security Risk Management processes should examine the value that Security Risk Management processes add to an organization rather than simply bottom-line expenses.

7.2 FUNCTIONAL DESIGN

7.2.1 Introduction

Functional design is an interdisciplinary process that aims to construct physical and virtual Security Risk Management systems that complement rather than restrict organizational goals. Producing a security framework that meets the operational needs of a particular organization, or that secures a particular asset, requires a sound understanding of an organization's interaction and dependence on internal and external stakeholders.

Requirements elicitation for a new system requires extensive involvement with stakeholders who usually have varying aims, backgrounds, and disciplines; this process is complicated even more if the system has critical security or other nonfunctional requirements. Established approaches to the elicitation and analysis of functional and nonfunctional requirements are very different—the former focusing on boundary behavior and the latter on threats to assets.

7.2.2 Functional Design of Security Treatments

Unlike most products and services, security systems often have little concern for consumer usability or ease of use. You cannot simply provide a security product to an end user and ask them for an assessment of its functionality. Unlike a sound system or a microwave, for example, in which a supplier can endorse a product as fit for purpose after consumers report back on features such as ease of use, maintainability, functionality, form, and styling, security products are functional only in the absence of failure. To this extent, their design needs to involve a focus on the difficulty of bypassing or defeating the product or system. Having an easily configured access control system or firewall is of little benefit if they are equally easily defeated. It is in often the testing to destruction of a security product that provides a true answer to how well the functional design meets requirements.

Equally, it is important to understand not only how a system will fail in the face of an attack but also how it will fail in the absence of an attack. Fire doors for example must fail to open if the power supply to a building fails, but an understanding of how they will fail in the event of simple mechanical failure is needed. Will users choose to chock open a main entry door if the door hinges seize one day, and if so, how does that affect the rest of the systems? Is this the only layer of defense, or will internal doors ensure an adequate level of protection?

Security Risk Management systems are designed to support organizational capabilities. The process of functional design involves integrating the application of a range of assets to provide functions or functionality, which then support organizational capabilities. In Figure 7.3, the term "functions" is used to refer

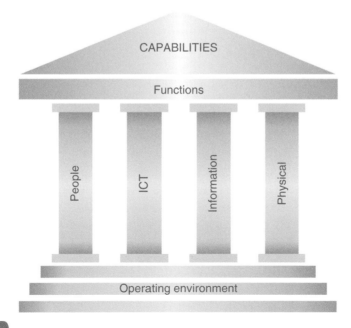

Role of functional design—linking assets to capabilities

to organizational functions; however, it is equally applicable to the subset of security-related functions.

A functional design process should draw on the contextual assessment as well as threat, vulnerability, and criticality assessments to provide an outcome oriented application of assets within a holistic risk program to ensure correct organizational fit with Security Risk Management systems.

Functional design is a truly interdisciplinary process. It requires expertise from all areas of Security Risk Management and organizational management to produce an appropriate, effective, and efficient system. It also requires multidisciplinary input to produce an integrated defense-in-depth outcome. Defense in depth, particularly using the eliminate, substitute, isolate, engineer, adminstrative controls, and personal protection (ESIEAP) model, provides an organization with a superior level of protection and the greatest flexibility in managing identified risks.

> Additional guidance on functional design is provided in Guide to SRMBOK Application and Case Studies, as well as a functional design template example.

7.3 IMPLEMENTATION MANAGEMENT

7.3.1 Introduction

Once a Security Risk Management plan has been devised and approved, it must be implemented. This process includes project management, procurement, contractor management, training, monitoring, procedure development, and the ongoing maintenance of systems and assets.

7.3.1.1 Context. The contextual environment in which Security Risk Management is being implemented will be critical to the manner and success of implementation. For example, if the introduction of Security Risk Management protocols into an organization is the result of an incident, it is likely to have crystallized support behind a security-based approach to business.

7.3.1.2 Structure and Size of an Organization. Smaller organizations and organizations with flatter management structures typically can institute governance reform measures more effectively than larger more hierarchically driven organizations.

7.3.1.3 Market Stability and Presence in that Market. Depending on organizational circumstance, market instability can be both a motivator and disincentive for the instigation of Security Risk Management reforms. Organizations that look to maintain flexibility and possibly market transience (short term profit driven) in a volatile marketplace and are less concerned about long-term security issues may shy away from Security Risk Management, whereas those that are looking to survive market volatility may be more inclined toward limiting security-related risks to their investments.

7.3.1.4 Organizational Leadership. The ability, experience, and knowledge base of an organization's leaders are obviously primary factors in the success or failure of implementing change of any kind into an organization. No "one size fits all" approach is available. Leaders must understand what change management strategies will work most effectively for their organization. Leaders must also be able to draw to their organization resources compatible with their Security Risk Management needs at the strategic, operational, and tactical levels.

Each of these factors contributes to the complexity of an organization's contextual environment and provides an insight into the internal and external risks faced by an organization. The implementation of Security Risk Management processes will be shaped by these complexities, and the success of Security Risk Management in an organization will be determined by how those processes fit with the identified contextual environment.

The structure of the implementation process is key to enhancing the likelihood of success of new Security Risk Management methodologies. Ideally, an implementation process should consist of several of the following main stages, managed to be mutually reinforcing:

- Organizational structure
- Training
- Quality management systems
- Project management
- Change management

The success of both change management and project management components of an implementation strategy are enhanced by the creation of an effective and sincere communication and feedback. This strategy should consist of a constant information and communication loop that manages the direction and promotes the success of both project management and change management programs by using human experiences and corporate knowledge.

7.3.2 Organizational Structure and Culture

Many corporate and government organizations have developed and implemented security and risk mitigation procedures to assist the management and control of key business outcomes both during and after risk events.

A significant body of research is available to suggest that a correlation exists between organizational structure and the culture that impacts on the potential of SRM solutions.

In his early management studies, Henri Fayol suggested that esprit de corps is a vital ingredient in any organization.[61] More recently, the New South Wales (NSW) Independent Commission Against Corruption (ICAC) stated that "... organizational culture has a strong influence on the way people (staff) act in their day-to-day work..."[62] and in specific reference to the security/risk industry, Her Majesty's Treasury (United Kingdom) states that "... an unhealthy corporate culture is an indicator for fraud potential..."[63]

Similarly, organizational structure can positively or adversely modify an organization's ability to identify and respond to risk. For instance, if the Security Risk Management function is relatively low in the management hierarchy and/or split across several different areas of the organization, it is unlikely that security will receive a high level of funding or coordination.

7.3.3 Training

The reason for training in all industry sectors is the development and maintenance of the knowledge, skill, and attitudes required by the individual to complete their job/task effectively and efficiently in a fast-moving economy. Training can be for people who already have employment or are about to enter the workforce, and it is not only for, security personnel who deal with SRM. The aim of the training process is to achieve a behavioral change in learners by giving them new skills, knowledge, and attitudes.

Training serves many important roles in an organization, not least of all as a driver of cultural change. As illustrated in Figure 7.4, training changes behaviors, which in turn modify attitudes, which in turn modifies culture.

Even though learning is a continuous process, training requires having a definite start and finishing point, which makes a training program successful. Training and learning are different parts of the same process, in that learning can occur through the process of training, and learning can be achieved by other means. Despite this, the process of becoming trained is a gradual process of inculcating correct (in this case security related) behaviors to the point at which they can be applied instinctively in response to an emergency or more mundane situation. This journey from "I don't know what I don't know" to becoming "unconsciously skilled" to the point of being able to react immediately and instinctively is illustrated in Figure 7.5.

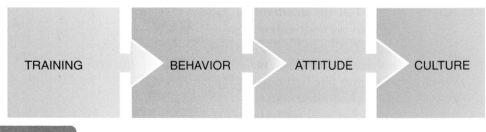

FIGURE 7.4 Training's impact on organizational culture

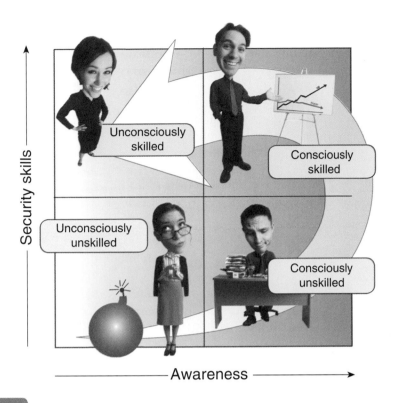

Security skills → (vertical axis)

Unconsciously skilled

Consciously skilled

Unconsciously unskilled

Consciously unskilled

Awareness →

FIGURE 7.5 Skill–awareness journey

7.3.4 Quality Management Systems (QMS)

Documenting standard operating procedures is a critical element of any management system, and Security Risk Management is no different in this respect. Figure 7.6 illustrates one aspect of the relationship between implementation, training, and strategic levels of Security Risk Management. Essentially, a risk assessment process drives the determination of a range of controls, which includes engineering, administrative, and other controls (refer to hierarchy of controls) that in turn require staff to be trained before they can be fully applied and implementation can be considered complete.

This view of management systems, although borrowed from the safety environment, is equally applicable to information security, general management, and a range of security applications with minor if any adaptation. The key elements are as follows:

- Strategy
- Operations
- Implementation

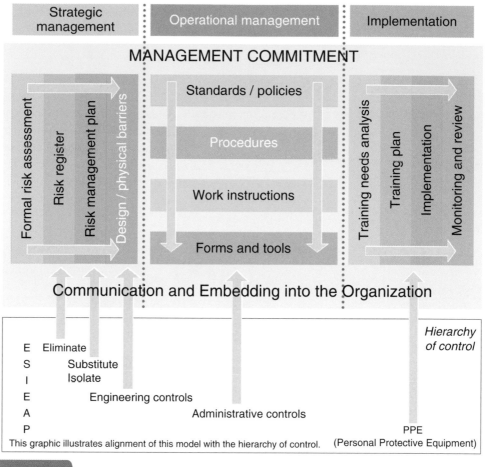

FIGURE 7.6 Example of linkages in an SRM framework

7.3.5 Project Management

Project management is the discipline of organizing and managing resources in such a way that these resources deliver all the work required to complete a project within defined scope, time, and cost constraints. A project is a temporary and one-time endeavor undertaken to create a unique product or service. This property of being a temporary and a one-time undertaking contrasts with processes, or operations, which are permanent or semipermanent ongoing functional work to create the same product or service repeatedly. The management of these two systems is often very different and requires varying technical skills and philosophy; hence, it requires the development of project management.

The first challenge of project management is ensuring that a project is delivered within the defined constraints. The second, more ambitious, challenge is the optimized allocation and integration of the inputs needed to meet those predefined objectives. The project, therefore, is a carefully selected set of activities chosen to use resources, e.g., time, money, people, materials, energy, space, provisions, communication, quality, and risk, to meet the predefined objectives.

An Overview of PMBOK Methodology

The Project Management Institute (PMI) published the first Project Management Body of Knowledge (PMBOK) in an attempt to document and standardize generally accepted project management practices. Currently in its third edition (2004), it provides a basic reference for project management. Although not without its critics, the PMBOK Guide is widely accepted to be the standard in project management. PMBOK recognizes five basic process groups and nine knowledge areas typical of almost all projects, programs, and operations. The five basic process groups are as follows:

- Initiating
- Planning
- Executing
- Controlling and monitoring
- Closing

An Overview of the PRINCE2 Methodology

PRINCE (Projects in controlled environments) is a structured method for effective project management. It is a de facto standard used extensively by the U.K. Government and is widely recognized and used in the private sector, both in the U.K. and internationally. PRINCE the method is in the public domain; it offers nonproprietary best-practice guidance on project management.

PRINCE2 defines 45 separate subprocesses (Figure 7.7) and organizes these into the following eight processes, which are all underpinned by the management of risk:

- Starting up a project (SU)
- Planning (PL)
- Initiating a project (IP)
- Directing a project (DP)
- Controlling a stage (CS)
- Managing product delivery (MP)
- Managing stage boundaries (SB)
- Closing a project (CP)

Other Project Management Methodologies

Of course, a wide range of other project management methodologies is available, such as the Berenschot model (Figure 7.8) and proprietary business models. Suffice to say, the most important issue is in choosing a methodology that suits your individual organization and applying it consistently across the organization.

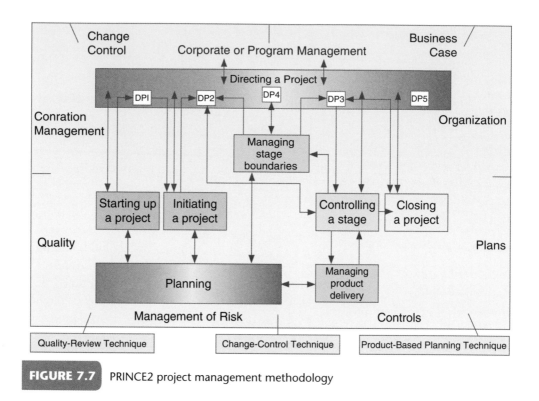

FIGURE 7.7   PRINCE2 project management methodology

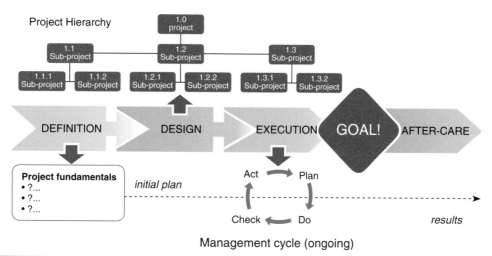

FIGURE 7.8   Berenschot project management methodology

Applying PM to SRM

Project management as a discipline has much to offer security practitioners in several areas, not least of all in regard to the implementation of security treatments many if not most of which, involve a "temporary endeavor using a multi-skilled team to create a unique product or service."

7.3.6 Change Management in SRM

The concept of change management describes a structured approach to transitions from a present to a desired state in individuals, teams, organizations, and societies. Traditionally, the term organizational change management was used to refer to this field of study. The most recent research points to a combination of organizational change management tools and individual change management models for effective change to take place.

In the early period of development of change management, much confusion existed between the process of developing a desired future state through programs such as Total Quality Management (TQM), Business Process Reengineering (BPR), or Six Sigma, and the process of managing the people side of change. Change management had been used as an umbrella term to refer to any activities related to change; however, it has one definition that is widely held: Change management is the process and tools for managing the people side of change.

Applying change management to new procedures, structures, and technologies was once thought to be an exercise in overcoming resistance to change. This older perspective on change management has shifted from one of managing resistance to building energy and engagement around a change. Change management is now viewed as a leadership competency rather than a reactive toolset for managing resistance from people.

7.3.7 Summary

The successful implementation of Security Risk Management processes has a significant bearing on their overall impact on an organization.

Managing both the physical implementation and integration of security measures and the education and support of an organizations human assets provide the best value outcome for an organization implementing Security Risk Management strategies.

This can be achieved by following suitable project management and change management paradigms.

7.4 ASSURANCE AND AUDIT

7.4.1 Introduction

> *Assurance can be defined as* "the confidence that may be held in the security provided by a system, product or process," *whereas audit may be described as* "the process of reviewing and evaluating compliance with applicable directives and regulations and/or the examination of records or accounts to check their accuracy." [38]

The ISO 9000 and ISO 14000 series of International Standards emphasize the importance of audits as a management tool for monitoring and verifying the effective implementation of an organization's quality and/or environmental policy. Audits are also an essential part of conformity assessment activities, such as external certification/registration and of supply chain evaluation and surveillance.

Traditional governance internal control and risk management guides are systems-based with a strong focus on legislative and regulatory compliance. Recent spectacular failures such as the Enron collapse, Barings Bank options trading losses and Enron indicate that having a compliance or risk management system is not synonymous nor a guarantee of sound corporate governance.

The proposed system of inherent controls is developed by refining and aligning current management practices. This means that a governance and assurance plan can be implemented within existing resources and without additional infrastructure. The leadership skill for the board and senior managers is to achieve an effective balance between inherent and formal control appropriate for their organization's level of control/risk maturity.

7.4.1.1 Principles of Assurance and Audit. The following principles describe the fundamental assumptions regarding audit and assurance processes outlined below:

- Establishing and maintaining control is the basis of sound business management.

- All critical management activities should be subject to periodic auditing to ensure that the management processes are being properly implemented and maintained.

- Audits should be conducted at all levels of the organization, including contractors.

- Maintaining effective management systems is about a demonstrated commitment by the most senior people in an organization to set performance and safety objectives, oversee planning and implementation, consider feedback from performance reviews, and continuously improve the system.

7.4.2 Assurance

> *"Assurance contributes to a reduction of risk, in so much as assurance reduces the uncertainty associated with vulnerabilities of the deliverable, and thus the potential vulnerability is reduced leading to a reduction in the overall risk...."*
>
> *(AS/NZS ISO/IEC 15443.1:2006)* [64]

Management systems are prone to failure and to security violations because of errors and vulnerabilities. These violations can be caused by human error, technology changes, poor functional design, or inadequate development processes, or can be a result of underestimating threats. System modifications, new flaws, and new attack methods are also frequently introduced, which increases the potential for vulnerabilities, failures, and security breaches. It can be determined therefore that errors, vulnerabilities, and risks will probably always exist and may change over time. Therefore, the errors, vulnerabilities, and risks will have to be managed on an ongoing basis within acceptable parameters, otherwise the deliverable assurance will change.

The task of security engineering and management is to manage the security risk by mitigating the vulnerabilities and threats with technological and organizational security measures to achieve a deliverable with acceptable assurance. Security management has an additional task of establishing acceptable assurance and risk objectives. In this way, the stakeholders will achieve reasonable confidence that the deliverable performs in the way intended or claimed with acceptable risk and within budget. From a security standpoint, this translates into confidence that the deliverable enforces the applicable security policy.

7.4.2.1 Benefits of Assurance. Assurance does not provide additional security controls in the truest sense, and it can be challenging for security practitioners to communicate the benefits of assurance processes. It may be argued that assurance contributes to the effectiveness of a security system; however, the assurance actually contributes no direct risk mitigation. Rather, it contributes to the following:

- The confidence that stakeholders may have in the Security Risk Management framework
- By identifying escalation factors and gaps in control systems, as shown in Figure 7.9.

As illustrated in Figure 7.9, many opportunities are available to prevent or treat threats before or after they eventuate. For example, the application of a threat barrier such as a boomgate will be effective in reducing illegal parking; however, an escalation factor such as high volume or exposure to salt air may cause the boomgate mechanism to fail because of corrosion. An escalation control to address this might include planned preventative maintenance schedules to prevent the escalation factor from causing a system breach, i.e., out of service boomgate. Similarly postevent barriers for an arson attack might include fire detection and sprinkler systems, which will also require preventative maintenance (escalation controls) to mitigate any escalation factors, e.g., salt, air, etc.

7.4.3 Audit

Audits are assessment processes that rate outcomes of management activities and direct attention to areas that could be improved. Audits are designed to promote and measure the management practices needed to establish and maintain effective work practices.

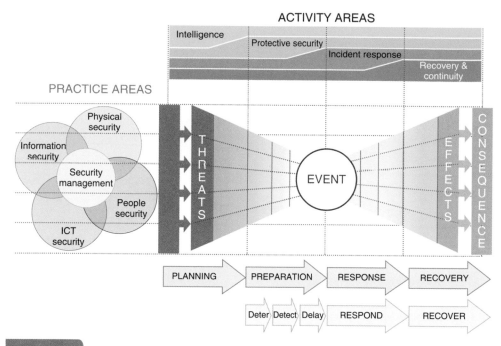

FIGURE 7.9 Risk bow-tie and role of assurance in identifying escalation factors

7.4.3.1 Audit Reports. When developing audit reports they:

- Should be clear, concise, and objective, i.e., identify what is good and what is not so good
- Should not be judgmental i.e., measure against agreed standards, not your own

7.4.3.2 Audit Findings. The quality of an audit finding may be judged with reference to the 4Cs:

- **Condition**—what is going on?
- **Criteria**—what should be going on?
- **Cause**—why is this happening?
- **Consequence**—what might happen if we do not fix it?

Ideally, all audit findings should contain all of the above elements. An example of this is provided in Figure 7.10.

7.4.3.3 Audit Recommendations. Recommendations for corrective action should comply as follows:

- Address the cause and diminish the effect for the matter noted
- Stand alone, i.e. still makes sense when read in isolation

- Start with an action word, e.g., "Replace…" not "Consider replacing…"
- Be doable
- Add value

It is important to either keep the number of recommendations to a minimum, as unnecessary recommendations destroy credibility, or prioritize them in order of importance (Figure 7.11).

Similarly, the quality of an audit recommendation can be judged with reference to "the 4 A's." All audit recommendations should conform as follows:

- **Actionable**—is it clear what to do?
- **Achievable**—how will you know when you have done it?
- **Appropriate**—does it address the cause rather than the condition?
- **Agreed**—do we all support this?

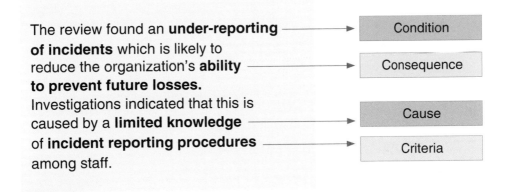

FIGURE 7.10 Example of an audit finding

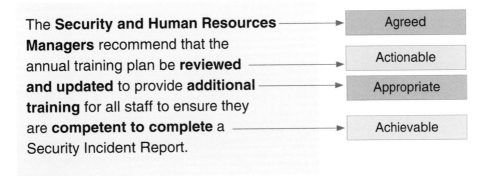

FIGURE 7.11 Example of an audit finding

7.4.3.4 Using Quantitative Measures. When figures are available, make sure they have the following 4 R's characteristics.

- **Relevant**—they must bear directly on the problem.
- **Reliable**—you must use figures whose authority can be demonstrated.
- **Representative**—you would not use basketball teams as your sole data in a survey of the average height of the population. The sample would be biased.
- **Readable**—put the figures in a form that is easy to read, e.g. graphs, tables, "S" can look like a "5."

Many inherent limitations exist with quantitative measures, not least of all the availability or reliability of such information. In some cases, information may be available but simply not relevant. For example, the incidence of car theft last year is of limited relevance if a car accessory supplier has launched a new low-cost but highly effective alarm system into the market this year. Even if you can identify exactly how many alarms have been installed, little information will be available to identify exactly how effective the alarms are in preventing thefts.

Another key limitation of quantitative data is that data are of most use when using the Law of Large Numbers. For example, an insurance company may be able to assess that it is likely, based on past data, that 32 homes will be broken into next month in your suburb. These data are of little if any value to you as a home owner in determining the actual risk to your home. Even as a rough guide, it is of little use without considering your home security system. Do you have a dog, an alarm, or deadlocks for example? Is your house surrounded by shrubs that a burglar could use to avoid detection?

7.4.4 Grading Performance

Audit processes should be conducted against defined criteria and ideally should use a formal documented audit instrument as part of a documented audit plan. Each measure should, where possible, be rated in an ordinal fashion. Table 7.1

Table 7.1 Example of audit performance rating scales

Range			Performance
Exemplary	High	10	Continuous improvement processes ensure sustained performance. Could be used as a benchmark. Excellent supporting documentation that is updated as part of continuous improvement. Consistent application of the requirements of the indicator over time. Based on current industry practice, the assessor cannot identify scope for improvement.

Range			Performance
	Low	9	Sustained performance in parts of the organization where the requirements of the indicator apply. Some minor problems may occur from time to time, but these are rare.
		8	Requirements of the indicator have been in place long enough to allow evaluation and review. Maintaining better than minimum requirement but room for improvement. Strong supporting documentation.
Satisfactory	High	7	Basic documentation supports the requirements of the indicator even through it may not be specified in the indicator itself. Continuous improvement processes developing. Monitoring procedures in place as part of continuous improvement.
	Low	6	Satisfies minimum requirements of the indicator. Basic documentation can be produced if specified in the indicator itself. Continuous improvement processes developing. Monitoring procedures in place as part of continuous improvement.
Inadequate	High	5	Basic requirements for the indicator are almost in place. Documents may be in draft form. Planning may have occurred, but plans are not fully implemented. Implementation of the basic requirements of the indicator are imminent.
		4	Preparation of consistent implementation is well under way. Early drafts of documents supporting the indicator may be available.
		3	Implementation may be adhoc.
	Low	2	Early progress toward implementation. Evidence of management commitment of resources to the requirements of the indicator.
		1	Some awareness and intention to implement. May be little action to implementation at this stage.
		0	No awareness/understanding of legislation, contractual obligations, or procedures as they apply to the indicator. No intention to implement the requirements of the indicator.

Note: Detail in this table is intended for guidance only. Other factors that influence the management system may be considered in the final decision on the score as long as the general intent within each range is maintained.

illustrates an example of a scoring system that offers options of a 1 to 3, 1 to 6, or 1 to 10 scoring system based on the guidance information provided in respective word pictures.

7.4.4.1 Summary. The principles underpinning an effective risk and control assurance framework are in essence standard management practices. Implementation, therefore, does not involve abandoning everything that is currently in place, but rather it entails refining and aligning current practices.

The establishment of a risk and control assurance framework without an underlying value system encourages compliance rather than commitment. A compliance culture is neither responsive to change, nor focused on innovation and performance improvement.

Activity Areas 8

8.1 INTRODUCTION

SRMBOK practice areas described several areas in which security practitioners operate, including management, information, information and communication technology (ICT), people, and physical security. This theoretical framework is useful as it shows the background from which industry professionals have developed. It also allows both the buyer of, and provider of, Security Risk Management (SRM) services an understanding of their strengths and skills within the context of the security risk requirement. Of course, another dimension to this, as discussed in the chapter on strategic knowledge areas, relates to the phases of likelihood and consequence management aligned with the planning preparedness, response, and recovery (PPRR) All-Hazards approach to risk management.

Aligning the PPRR model with SRM suggests four principle activity areas related to the phases of Security Risk Management. These range from threat assessment and preventative measures, such as security barriers, to emergency management and business continuity. Much like PPRR, none of these occur in isolation and should not be considered distinct and separate phases that conclude when the next phase begins. As illustrated in Figure 8.4, these four areas occur concurrently but with greater or lesser emphasis at different times.

One way of considering the management of security risks is to consider the issue in relation to the following four main activity areas as illustrated in Figure 8.1.

Preattack:

- Gathering and analyzing intelligence
- Implementing protective security controls

Postattack:

- Emergency response and incident management
- Business continuity and recovery management

All activities are critical to prevent the risk event from occurring and, failing this, to ensure the organization can minimize the consequences of the occurrence through rapid containment and organizational resumption.

Although these four elements tend to be viewed as discrete elements or phases of a process, they typically occur concurrently, with greater or lesser emphasis on the respective elements at any given point of the process as illustrated in Figure 8.2.

This view offers us an insight into the respective focus at different stages of Security Risk Management.

ORGANIZATIONAL/ENVIRONMENTAL SECURITY CONTEXT

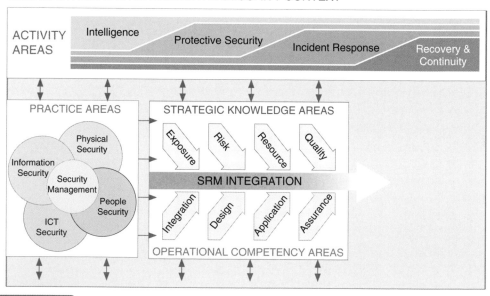

FIGURE 8.1 Activity areas

> *Activity areas are to a large extent aligned with risk treatment systems in so much as these four areas are the key groupings of activities used to mitigate security risks through the application of security controls.*

8.1.1 Comprehensive Approach

The above approach also permits a level of alignment with the comprehensive approach for emergency and disaster management arrangements, which embrace the aspects of PPRR as four aspects of emergency management, not as sequential phases (Figure 8.3).[65]

This approach is both easy to understand and intuitively appealing as it seems an eminently logical approach to prevent harm, or at least to mitigate the effects of an event with an effective and well-prepared response and recovery framework.

8.1.1.1 Prevention/Mitigation. Security personnel are well positioned to facilitate relationships with emergency response organizations who may play a crucial role in an emergency. They will also play a significant role in many mitigation practices particularly in relation to personnel and infrastructure protection, such as suspicious mail handling.

8.1.1.2 Preparedness. Security systems can facilitate significant aspects of preparedness measures. Senior security staff will contribute to the business impact analysis, and existing ultra high frequency (UHF) communications networks may be well suited to back up global system for mobile communications (GSM) and infrastructure-based systems.

Comparative allocation of resources at different activity phases

Intelligence	Protective Security	Incident Response	Recovery & Continuity

FIGURE 8.2 Level of effort for each element at different phases

PPRR Comprehensive Approach to Emergency Management

FIGURE 8.3 PPRR emergency management model

8.1.1.3 Response. Security personnel may play an important role in an emergency management plan (EMP) by providing response teams. These teams may assist by conducting the shutdown of a premises in an evacuation. Importantly, all security personnel will be trained in first aid and should coordinate casualty treatment and collection prior to emergency response organizations arriving.

8.1.1.4 Recovery. Although crisis and business continuity plans will be more focused on recovery than the EMP, the EMP will contribute to them at a local level. Thus, security functions within the organization must be geared to assisting these plans. Senior security personnel must be aware that the systems they put in place and the actions of their personnel during an emergency could have significant repercussions for recovery operations.

8.1.2 Alignment with Other Systems

The four activity areas can be considered as interwoven phases of Security Risk Management that have a degree of alignment with many other areas.

Figure 8.4 should not be taken to imply that a direct, simple, or immutable correlation exists between any of these elements. Indeed, it would be simplistic or misleading to suggest a direct alignment of intelligence with prevention or protective security with preparedness. In some contexts, intelligence will prove most useful for supporting preparedness; in others, it will be of greatest impact in defining the response phase of consequence management and so on for each of the

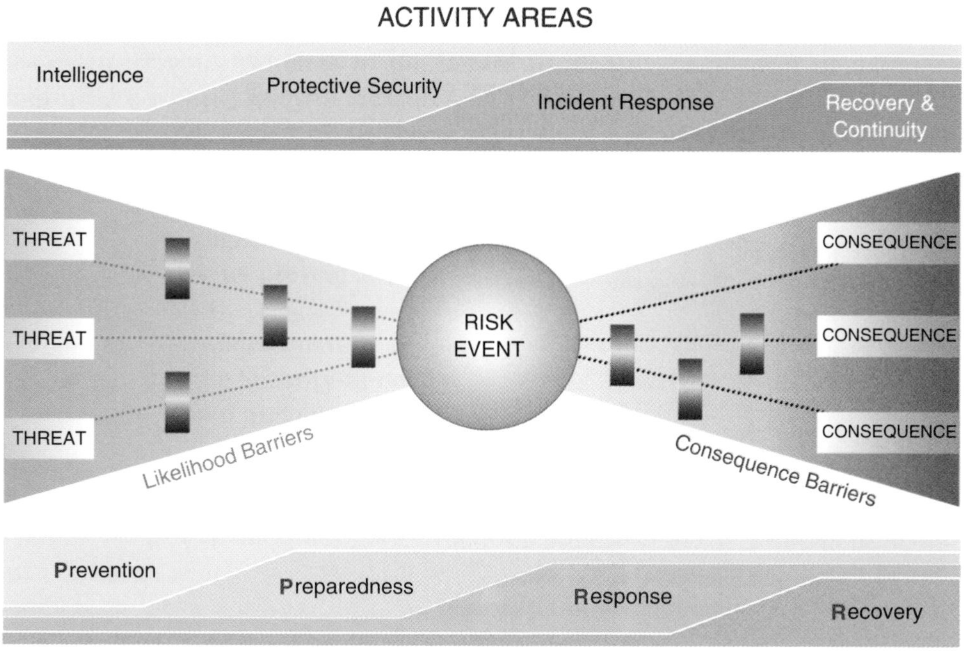

FIGURE 8.4 Alignment of activity areas with likelihood and consequence management

elements. Nonetheless, it is useful to consider this type of conceptual framework as part of a collective language if we are to achieve the best from each element.

The real benefit of models such as Figure 8.9 is that they allow managers and practitioners to coordinate a meaningful dialog for their own organization or circumstances, and to provide clarity around questions such as:

- Who is responsible for which phase?
- What is the key activity that we should/will be doing during each phase?
- How will those activities impact the other activity areas?
- What resources will the respective activity areas be able to provide, or not provide, by way of assistance?

This type of model is also instructive with a D3R2 model (deter, detect, delay, respond, recover) as described in HB167:2006 Security Risk Management Handbook.[1] Although response and recovery are reflected in the PPRR model (Figure 8.5), the elements of deter, detect, and delay are less immediately obvious. Given the nature of these activities, they align predominantly, although not exclusively, with the protective security activity area.

The term "activity areas" reflects the different phases of operations during the phases of the Security Risk Management activities.

It should be noted that the various activities do not stand alone and that all of them are happening at all phases of the Security Risk Management process.

For example, although the bulk of emergency response activities occur immediately after an event, some elements of emergency response occur at all stages.

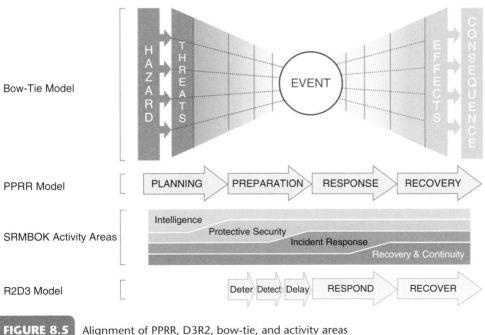

FIGURE 8.5 Alignment of PPRR, D3R2, bow-tie, and activity areas

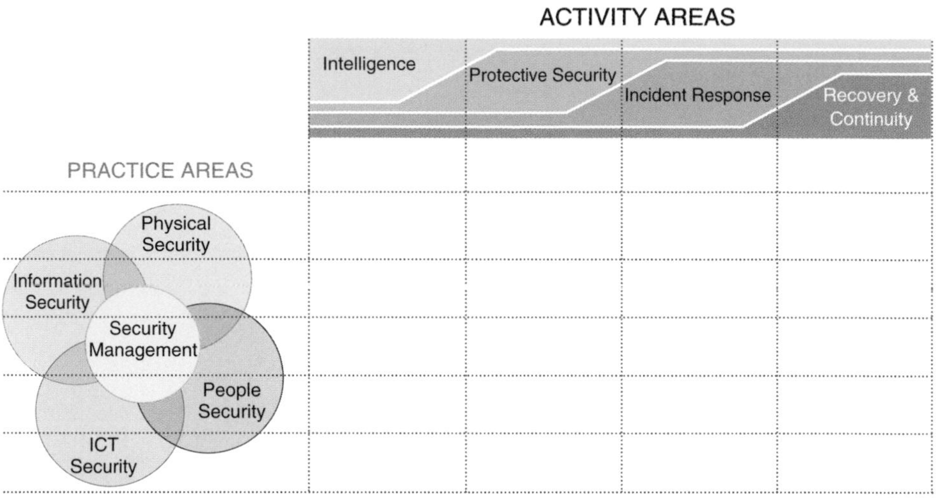

ACTIVITY AREAS

FIGURE 8.6 Practice areas complementing activity areas

For example, during the first stage of intelligence gathering, the planning and conceptualizing of emergency response activities is already underway. Similarly, security activities, such as access control for emergency teams and bystanders, must still occur during emergency response and recovery phases. It is simply that the security phases will involve a relatively smaller apportionment of resources and effort.

By aligning the junction of practice areas with activity areas (Figure 8.6), it is possible to establish a holistic view of the security functions and roles of an organization. This framework can assist managers and organizations to conduct a gap analysis so as to establish comparatively quickly which areas are strong and which need additional focus.

8.2 INTELLIGENCE

> "Intelligence is knowledge and foreknowledge of the world around us. It allows civilian leaders and military commanders to consider alternative options and outcomes in making decisions."[66]
>
> OPEN SOURCE: U.S. GOVERNMENT INTELLIGENCE COMMUNITY

At its simplest, intelligence can be described as the process of turning a sea of information into information you can visualize (Figure 8.7). Perhaps more importantly, it is the production of information that can be used to inform risk-based decision making. To be considered as intelligence, such information has to demonstrate characteristics such as credibility, timeliness, completeness, and fitness for purpose.

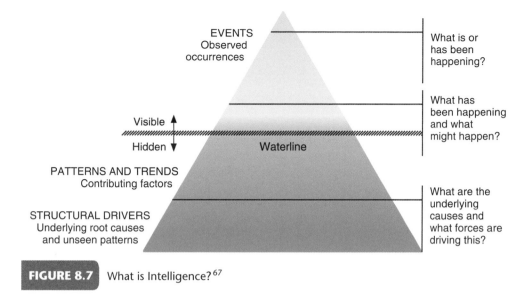

EVENTS
Observed
occurrences

What is or
has been
happening?

Visible ↑
Hidden ↓

Waterline

What has
been happening
and what
might happen?

PATTERNS AND TRENDS
Contributing factors

STRUCTURAL DRIVERS
Underlying root causes
and unseen patterns

What are the
underlying
causes and
what forces are
driving this?

FIGURE 8.7   What is Intelligence?[67]

8.2.1 Intelligence Process

Intelligence as a process is open to various interpretations and applications. Ephraim Kam comments: "The process of intelligence analysis and assessment is a very personal one. There is no agreed-upon analytical schema, and the analyst must primarily use his belief system to make assumptions and interpret information. His assumptions are usually implicit rather than explicit and may not be apparent even to him."[68]

8.2.2 The Intelligence Cycle

Despite Kam's misgivings, many principles are generally accepted regarding the gathering, interpretation, and dissemination of intelligence, which are usually described as an iterative process known as the intelligence cycle (Figure 8.8). Many open-source variants are used by government and private-sector organizations, such as that shown in Figure 8.9.[69]

Alternatively, the North Atlantic Treaty Organization (NATO) intelligence cycle comprises four phases (direction, collection, processing, and dissemination), whereas the intelligence cycle of the U.S. Central Intelligence Agency has five phases as illustrated in Figure 8.10.[69]

In reality, the intelligence process is probably not a cycle but rather a series of parallel activities, as collection and analysis, which are supposed to work in tandem, but in fact work more properly in parallel. Furthermore, the idea that decision makers wait for the delivery of intelligence before making policy decisions is equally incorrect as it is seldom that they can afford to wait the complete picture before acting. Simplistically stylized intelligence cycles also fail to account for either counter intelligence or covert action. The observation, orientation, decision, action (OODA) loop, developed by John Boyd and discussed

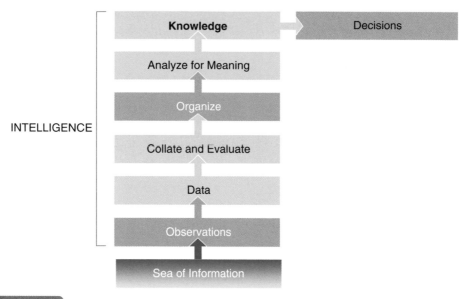

FIGURE 8.8 Intelligence process—converting information to decisions

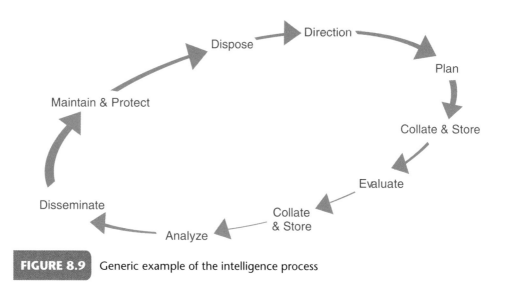

FIGURE 8.9 Generic example of the intelligence process

in the context of the intelligence cycle below, may come somewhat closer, as OODA is action oriented and spiraling, rather than a continuing circle.[70]

8.2.3 The OODA Loop

John Boyd created a model of decision and action, which was originally for air-to-air fighter combat, but it has proven useful in many areas of conflict. His

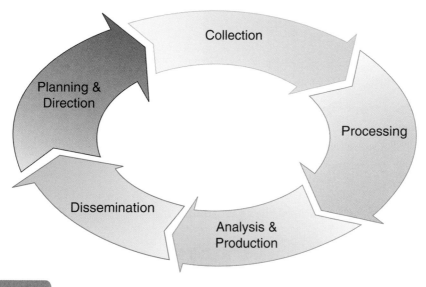

FIGURE 8.10 Intelligence cycle of the U.S. Central Intelligence Agency

model has the following four phases, which, although not usually stated in terms of the intelligence cycle, do relate to that cycle:

- **Observe:** become aware of a threat or opportunity
- **Orient:** put the observation into the context of other information
- **Decide:** make the best possible action plan that can be carried out in a timely manner
- **Act:** carry out the plan

After the action, the actor observes again, to observe the effects of the action. If the cycle works properly, the actor has initiative, and can orient, decide, and act even faster in the second and subsequent iterations of the Boyd loop. If the OODA process works as intended, the actor will get inside the opponent's decision-making loop because the actor's Boyd cycle dominates the opponent's, the actor is acting repeatedly, based on reasoned choices, whereas the opponent is still trying to understand what is happening.

Although Boyd treated his cycle as self-contained, it is reasonable to extend it to meeting the intelligence cycle. Observation can be an output of the collection phase, whereas orientation is an output of analysis. Eventually, actions are taken, and their results influence the senior decision makers.

A combination of the OODA process with the intelligence model in Figure 8.11 provides an enhanced way of managing the information development and dissemination process. The fourth component of Boyd's decision-action model, this being "Act—carry out the plan" directly links the implementation of activities in the intelligence process with the Risk Management Process, as shown in Figure 8.11.

A further consideration is the rate of refresh required to maintain the currency and accuracy of the intelligence. Significant factors to be considered relate to the volatility of the environment in which security is being considered, which include

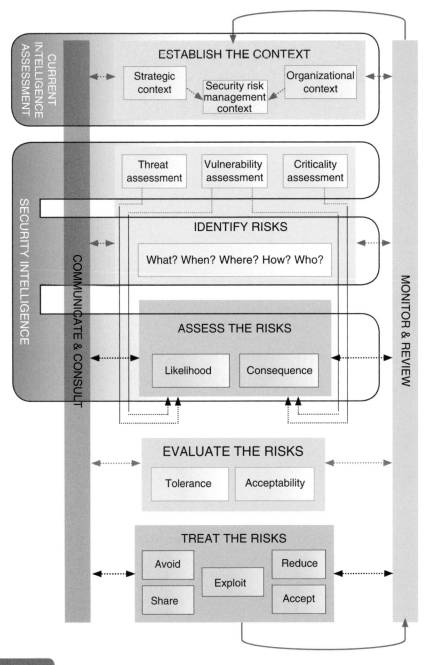

FIGURE 8.11 Linkages between intelligence process and the Risk Management Process

the characteristics of the entities providing the source of threat, such as capability to overcome security mitigations and the rate of change in the factors that may motivate them to conduct acts prejudicial to security. This element of the model is particularly relevant in the area of cyber security where attack techniques and security mitigations are in a constant race for supremacy (Figure 8.12).

8.2.4 Who Is Involved?

Intelligence activities are not just the domain of intelligence professionals. Even though most intelligence activities are conducted by operatives and analysts who would fit at the junction of the practice area of security management and the activity area of intelligence as illustrated in Figure 8.13, many other actors are involved in such activities to a greater or lesser degree.

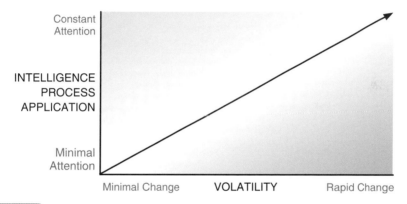

FIGURE 8.12 Effects of situational volatility on the intelligence process

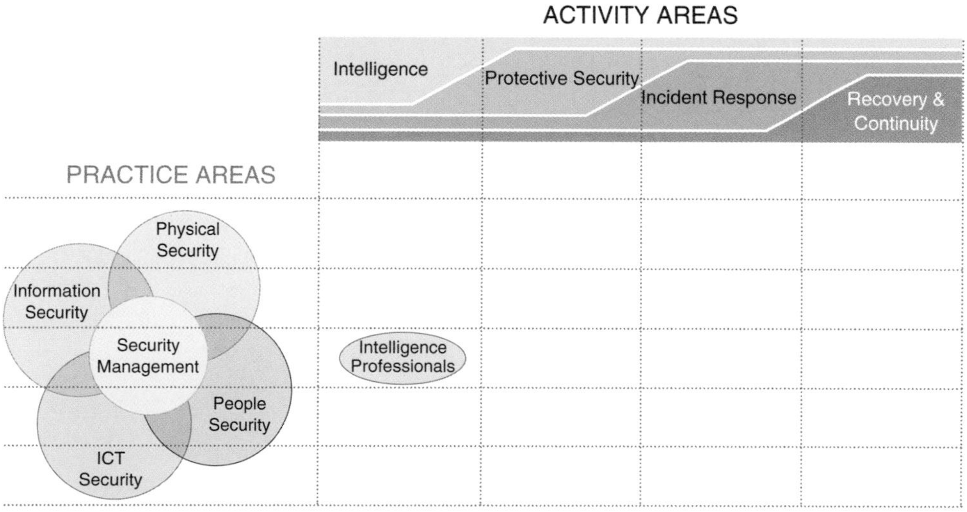

FIGURE 8.13 Intelligence professionals' place in practice and activity areas

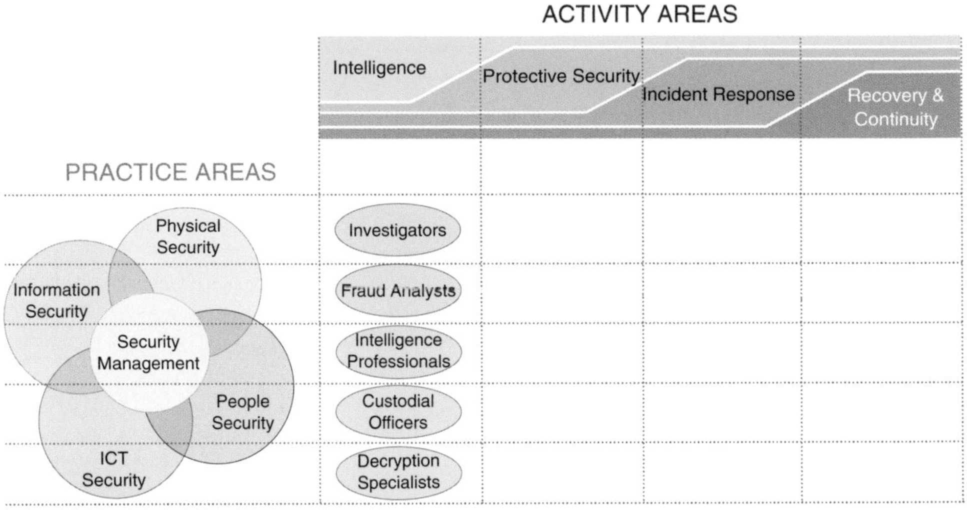

ACTIVITY AREAS

	Intelligence	Protective Security	Incident Response	Recovery & Continuity
PRACTICE AREAS				
	Investigators			
	Fraud Analysts			
	Intelligence Professionals			
	Custodial Officers			
	Decryption Specialists			

Physical Security · Information Security · Security Management · People Security · ICT Security

FIGURE 8.14 Examples of practitioner intelligence roles

This concept is equally applicable to private sector or government businesses. Although government organizations normally have access to greater resources and additional legislative powers compared with a private sector organization, significant amounts of intelligence are available as open-source intelligence (OSINT). Tools such as web search engines, credit reference checks, online databases, and streaming media, as well as subscription services from private OSINT providers, continue to make intelligence increasingly accessible.

> *Additional discussion of the intelligence process, tools and activities, as well as the issues and activities involved in setting up in-house corporate intelligence functions in support of Security Risk Management activities, can be found in the Guide to SRMBOK on Intelligence.*

Even though this is relatively self-evident, it is worth considering a small team of prison officers who collect intelligence within the prison system, who would reside at the junction of people, security, and intelligence. Similarly, the role of decryption specialists might sit at the junction of ICT and intelligence.

Figure 8.14 provides some examples of the different categories of security practitioners who might conduct intelligence activities.

8.3 PROTECTIVE SECURITY

Security practitioners need to cover a range of areas and activities at any given time that reflects the complex multifaceted nature of Security Risk Management responsibilities in the modern world. Although traditional security practices

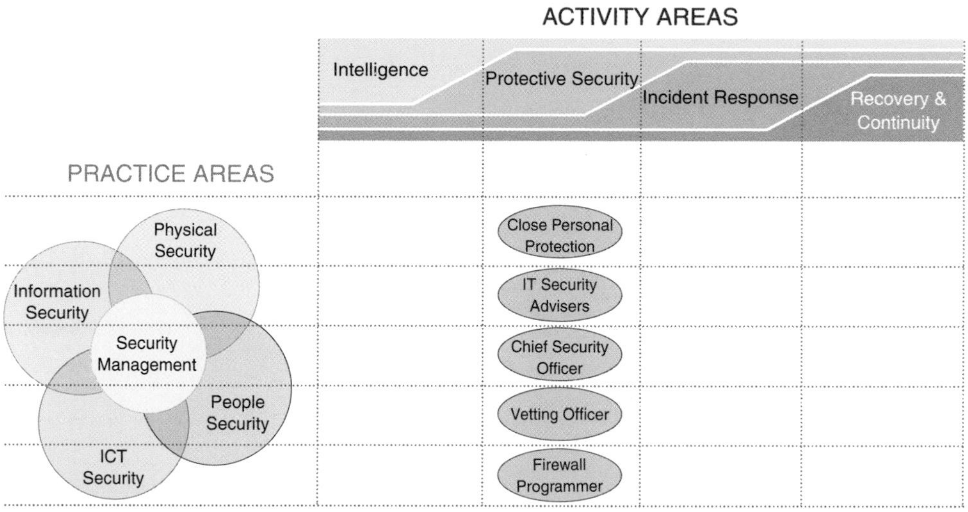

FIGURE 8.15 Examples of practitioner security roles

have focused primarily on the role of prevention, the security function is increasingly integrated into intelligence, response, and recovery practices.

Protective security in the context of a practice area is distinguished as being primarily involved in the preventative elements of risk management.

Almost everyone will have a security role at some point in their life, even if it involves only the protection of their own home or compliance with organizational security policies. The focus of this area is consideration of those who have a level of responsibility for security-related activities. Examples of some of these roles are provided in Figure 8.15.

8.4 RESPONSE

Incident and emergency response roles are normally considered to be the domain of agencies such as police, ambulance, and fire brigade. In this broader context, most elements of an organization will have a role in an emergency. At a individual level, of course, everyone has an interest in taking the immediate actions to safeguard themselves and those around them. This might involve rendering first aid, extinguishing a small fire, or simply going for help. At an organizational level, many groups will become involved in activities such as manning telephones, accounting for missing personnel, or assisting emergency services at the scene (Figure 8.16).

8.4.1 Emergencies

8.4.1.1 What is an Emergency?. Before we consider the role of SRM in emergency response management, it is worth defining the concept of an emergency, as each organization and specialist discipline describes hazardous events in

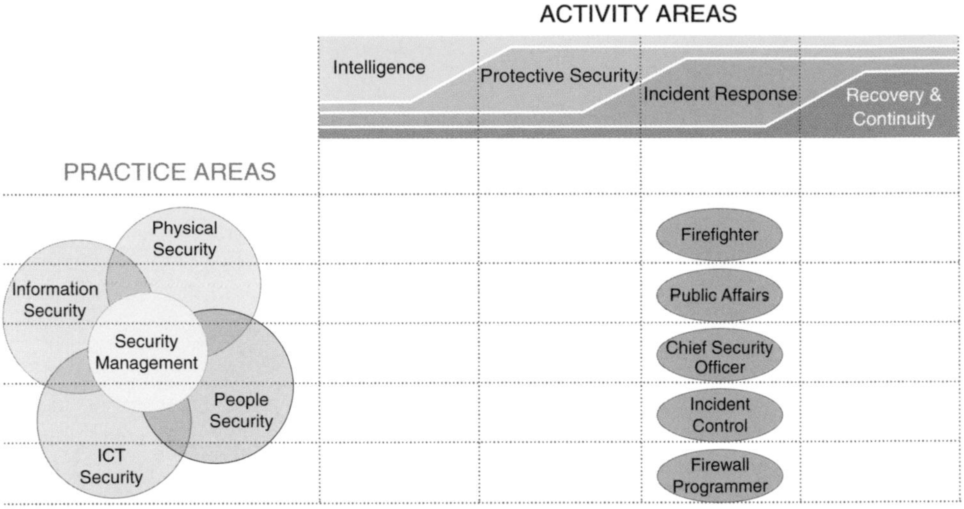

ACTIVITY AREAS

FIGURE 8.16 Examples of practitioner emergency response following a security incident

different ways. These examples include accidents, incidents, crises, emergencies, and disasters. Their descriptions also depend on the scale of the event and the terminology of the organization or community involved.

For example, a bus accident may be labeled an incident by emergency services, but it may be labeled a disaster by the local hospital. A general movement away from terms such as "disaster" toward the term "emergency" has occurred in Australia over the last few years, thus the term emergency is generally "...used in compound terms, such as emergency management, in preference to disaster. The terms disasterand disaster management are, however, still used in Australia to describe events of a truly disastrous nature."[65]

SRMBOK defines an emergency as an "event, actual or imminent, which endangers or threatens to endanger life, property or the environment, and which requires a significant and coordinated response."[65]

When an emergency occurs to an individual, group, or organization, it will generally require most of, if not all their attention. The situation or occurrence will tend to be localized, and although it is the focus of effort in that location, it typically will not affect operations on a national or global scale.

> **Emergency Management**
>
> *"A range of measures to manage risks to communities and the environment."*[71]

8.4.1.2 Why do Organizations Need to Manage Emergencies?. For an organization, be it corporate, government, or nongovernment, the ability to manage emergencies is essential. The ineffective management of an emergency can place personnel's health and well-being and an organizations infrastructure, profits,

and markets at risk. Furthermore, ineffective management of an emergency may lead its scope to grow to the point that it becomes a crisis.

8.4.1.3 What is Emergency Management?. Emergency management is the discipline that involves preparing, supporting, and rebuilding an organization when natural or man-made emergencies occur. It is a continual process by which all individuals, groups, and organizations manage potential emergencies in an effort to avoid or minimize the effects of the said emergencies. Effective emergency management relies on the thorough integration of emergency plans at all levels of an organization and with any external organizations who are stakeholders.

Although the relationships are significant, emergency management differs from crisis management and business continuity management. Emergency management has a more localized focus than crisis management, as crises comprise a danger to social, economic, political, or international affairs that leads to a decisive change. Likewise, business continuity is a process that allows an organization to continue functioning after, and ideally during, a disaster rather than simply being able to recover afterward. Clearly, whereas emergency management plans may need to form a part of larger crisis or business continuity plans, their focus is on dealing with the emergency itself. Thus, emergency management plans are created with concern for wider consequences but not to directly interact with those potential consequences.

The aims of any emergency management plan will focus on the health and safety of personnel and the preservation of infrastructure, and by doing so it will have many tangible effects. Emergency management plans will increase an organization's duty of care to employee health and safety. They will increase an organization's resilience to natural and man-made disasters, as well as to all levels of security threats. Emergency management plans will save an organization money by using cost-effective mitigation strategies prior to any emergency and by providing an initial focus for business continuity practices. Furthermore, by implementing an emergency management plan and thus exercising a degree of control over an emergency, it may be prevented from growing outside its local origins and growing into an organizational crisis.

Emergency management plans form an integral part of a comprehensive approach to Security Risk Management. As such, an organization that does not have emergency management plans, and thus has not accounted for the risk of emergencies, increases the risk to themselves.

8.4.2 The Comprehensive Approach

The term "comprehensive approach" from Emergency Management Australia (EMA) Manual 1 (concepts and principles) describes an approach that involves building emergency management arrangements and programs capable of dealing with a wide variety and scale of hazards that may affect organizations, communities and individuals irrespective of source.[71] These all hazard arrangements and programs must also provide for the performance of a range of tasks and be able to provide capabilities and conditions that allow those organizations, communities, or individuals to return as quickly as practicable and as closely as practicable to their desired condition or operations or existence.

EMA describes Australia's comprehensive approach to emergency management as recognizing the following four types of activities that contribute to the reduction or elimination of hazards and to reducing the susceptibility or increasing the resilience to hazards of a community or environment:[71]

- **Prevention/mitigation activities**—seek to eliminate or reduce the impact of hazards themselves and/or to reduce the susceptibility and increase the resilience of the community subject to the impact of those hazards
- **Preparedness activities**—establish arrangements and plans and provide education and information to prepare the community to deal effectively with such emergencies and disasters as may eventuate
- **Response activities**—activate preparedness arrangements and plans to put in place effective measures to deal with emergencies and disasters if and when they do occur
- **Recovery activities**—assist a community affected by an emergency or disaster in reconstruction of the physical infrastructure and restoration of emotional, social, economic and physical well-being

8.4.3 Emergency Response Management and SRM

Emergency response management is an integral component of comprehensive Security Risk Management as it has implications for crisis management and business continuity management. Also, just as security processes link into these aspects of risk management, security functions are important in an EMP.

The EMP will be closely integrated with crisis management plans and business continuity plans. Even though the lines where one plan ends and the others begin are blurry and may be different on a case-by-case basis, conceptually the differences are simple.

Emergencies are by definition more localized than crises. Thus, the EMP will deal with localized events. It may provide the foundation or first step of a crisis management plan, and ideally if conducted successfully, it may help prevent a crisis.

Likewise, the focus of the business continuity plan is on continuing business after and ideally during an emergency or crisis. Thus, the EMP must lead into the business continuity plan or it could even be considered phase 1 of the business continuity plan depending on its scope.

A very important area on which the EMP will focus, but crisis and business continuity plans may not, is the health and safety of personnel. By planning to ensure the health and safety of personnel, organizations fulfill their duty-of-care obligations, increase their resilience to disasters and threats, and save money through reduced employee absences.

The security functions within an organization will play an important role within all phases of emergency management planning and the EMP. Not only are many existing security functions well placed to facilitate parts of the EMP, but also an emergency is a time of security vulnerability, and a heightened state of alert may be required.

8.4.3.1 Emergency Management Team. It would be expected that at least one member of an organization's security staff be part of the emergency management team and intimately involved in the planning for and management of emergencies. This will enable security personnel and systems within the organization to assist in the coordination of mitigating, preparedness, and response measures.

Emergencies are simply out-of-course events, whether unexpected or predictable, that require the application of additional resources and management effort to return to the changed course or normal operations. Even though out-of-course events can never be totally prevented, their consequences (impacts) can be reduced by effective planning.

Emergency planning is designed to assist organizations assess and develop response plans to security-related events. It is not feasible to develop individual plans to respond to every single potential incident. Even if it could be done, having multiple plans is at the very least an administrative nightmare to keep them updated and a challenge to keep emergency responders current with all plans. More critically, it can lead to confusion during an emergency as to which plan to use. The challenge is to prepare a simple and effective plan that is sufficiently generic in nature to provide an effective response for any type or level of emergency.

Security risk assessments should already be in place and able to provide some insight into what type of security-related emergencies would warrant advance planning and investment in resources. Similarly, past incidents will provide guidance, as will experiences with other nonsecurity emergencies. A core concept in this section is that for most organizations, a security emergency management plan does not exist. Rather, the response to security incidents will be a subset of overall emergency management plan(s). Fire is fire, injuries are injuries, and so on. The key requirement is to ensure the security and emergency plans are fully integrated and tested. It is often at the seams or interfaces of countermeasures and plans that systems fail due to lack of coordination or oversight.

8.4.4 Effecting Emergency Management Planning

8.4.4.1 The Emergency Management Plan. An EMP describes the actions to be taken to protect employees, assets, and the public in times of crisis. The EMP is designed to equip an organization with an initial set of actions and decision-making processes that are to be followed in case of natural or man-made threats. EMPs normally cover four broad topic areas, which include preparing for foreseeable emergencies, establishing mitigation strategies, responding to an emergency, and recovering from an emergency.

To be effective, the EMP must be concise and easy to understand. As a governing principle, a one-page evacuation diagram on a notice board is far more valuable in an emergency than a 50-page written plan on a bookshelf.

8.4.4.2 Mitigation. This component of the EMP outlines those measures required to prevent an incident from occurring and if not, control an incident from escalating into a wider emergency or organization-wide crisis. Accordingly, it draws heavily on the barriers and treatments identified in the Security Risk Management plan and treatment plan. Mitigation strategies may include any number of measures that reduce the consequence (impact) of a situation escalating into an emergency.

Possible examples include the following:

- Building evacuation procedures
- Next of kin registers
- Telephone bomb threat guides
- Fire drills
- Insurance
- Cultivating strong relationships with local emergency services to ensure an effective response
- Encouraging a strong corporate culture that deters bullying, harassment, and assault
- Maintaining strong Security Risk Management representation on organization decision-making teams to ensure business operations do not increase the risk of emergencies
- Off-site information back-ups

8.4.4.3 Preparedness. In preparing for the management of an emergency, an organization must establish an emergency management team, write the EMP, train response staff in enacting the plan, test the plan, and make any necessary adjustments to the EMP. Preparation, although shown theoretically as the second step in emergency management, is actually a constant process of analysis and refinement. Any plan is only as good as the collective relevance of its content, and it is important to:

- Establish executive support and direction
- Define an emergency in terms of its potential affect on the organization
- Establish an emergency management team, responsible for responding before, during, and after an emergency
- Allocate resources to emergency planning, which include personnel, finance, and equipment
- Create a defined process for moving from normal operations to emergency mode

The above steps can be broken down even more into the following:

- **Review existing plans and procedures.** An analysis of any current EMP or similar policies, plans, and procedures to provide an ideal starting point.

- **Seek and gain support for upper management.** It is essential that those responsible for developing and implementing the EMP have not only the approval but also the resources, decision-making power, and support of local, regional, and whole-of-organization executives. It is important for executives to acknowledge their overall ownership of their organizations response, either positive or negative, in an emergency. In the worst case, executives may be held responsible for poorly planning for an emergency and be held accountable by internal and external stakeholders after an emergency.

- **Assign facilities or jurisdictions.** Planners must understand what areas are to be part of the EMP. For example, each regional office block of an organization may have their own EMP, which is to comply with the organization-wide EMP.

- **Identify resources.** There must be a clear understanding of what staff, equipment, and facilities are to be allocated to emergency response. Knowing what is available to respond to an emergency is essential, as an organization can only plan to respond with resources that are guaranteed to be available.

- **Conduct a business vulnerability analysis.** By evaluating the strengths and weaknesses of an area of responsibility, planners can identify key business areas which require significant attention during an emergency. For example, during a bomb threat, is the risk associated with 30 grams of explosive in a letter bomb greater or less than the risk of panic during an evacuation of a 30-storey office block?

- **Develop emergency management team.** First, the appointment of an overall emergency management leader should be established. Often, the Security Risk Management supervisor is ideal for this role. The EMP coordinator should be able to liaise readily with management and employees at all levels of the organization. The emergency management team should consist of managers from such section as information technology, human resources, communications, medical, legal, transport, public relations, security, and occupational heath and safety.

During the planning phase, the following major planning considerations must be addressed:

8.4.4.4 Decision Flow. To allow for rapid decision making, normal organizational processes may have to be replaced by expedited systems. Accordingly, the decision flow should be modified to include only the information inputs and decision outputs that are required to prevent, respond, and recover from an emergency, such as:

- What are the circumstances in which an emergency is to be declared?
- Who can declare an emergency?

- Who is in charge during an emergency?
- What redundancies are built into the system to allow for decision makers who are unavailable?
- Under what circumstances is the end of an emergency declared?
- Who can declare an end of emergency and return to normal operations?

8.4.4.5 Communications. Usual forms of communications, such as GSM mobile phones, cannot be guaranteed in an emergency. In a widespread emergency, such as a terrorist attack or riot, mobile phone communications are the first to become clogged with overuse. Furthermore, as many emergencies create a collapse in essential services, the power supply to fax, phone, and Internet may not be available. As a result, it may be necessary to procure alternative communications and reserve them for emergency use.

Alerts, Alarms, and Warnings

A system of easily disseminated and understood emergency notifications is needed to inform staff and the public of what action to take. Key examples may be fire alarms, natural disaster warnings, or evacuation alerts. These signals can be disseminated via any number of ways, such as siren, automated Short Message Service (SMS), loud speaker, or automated phone message.

Shutdown and Evacuation

Procedures must be created to determine when a facility shut down and/or evacuation is required. These may be emergency specific. For example, in the event of a cyclone or mass riot, security risk managers may receive ample notice to provide for a preemptive decision on whether to stay or go. Aspects to consider include how and who may be involved in the relocation as well as, how to maintain essential business services, shelter facilities, and site security post evacuation.

Response Teams

The level of emergency response capability within an organization will depend on the emergency, size of the organization, and skills held within the staff base. Creating and training response teams to likely emergencies is arguably the most important part of the EMP process. Determining how the response teams are to remain current in their training and testing is also critical.

Stakeholders

Determining how, and on what, stakeholders are to be informed before, during, and after an emergency is essential. Often, the impact of the emergency itself is not as catastrophic as the media, regulator, shareholder, or staff reaction.

It is essential that the EMP is considered a living document and that the preparation phase of emergency management is a process of continuous improvement.

8.4.4.6 Response. The EMP is activated once the individual or position authorized to declare an emergency notifies all concerned parties of the emergency. This may take the form of a security guard informing the security supervisor of an incident and the security supervisor hitting the corresponding alarm. Depending on the incident, there may or may not be time to meet with managers, emergency services, and staff. Before pending industrial action for example, there may be time to determine the actions to be taken well in advance. However, in the event of an incident without warning, like a terrorist attack, immediate action must be taken. In this scenario, the EMP must be enacted without consultation.

In considering whether to initiate the EMP, the authorized staff must consider the benefits of a mass activation versus the potential effects of mass panic. As highlighted above, the risks associated with the fear of a bomb may outweigh the risk associated with a small amount of explosives detonating in an isolated area. Therefore, in some cases, notifying key emergency response staff and organizational leaders may need to occur before a mass notification. Conversely, in a localized incident, perhaps only staff in the affected area should be notified, which allows the remaining workforce who are not at risk to continue daily operations.

Once the EMP has been initiated, it should not be revoked until the organization is ready to return to normal operations. In a localized and simple emergency, this may occur straight away. If, however, substantial destruction occurs, the emergency response may continue into the recovery phase.

8.4.4.7 Recovery. The recovery phase of an EMP can be considered the first step in a business continuity or crisis recovery plan as it deals with the immediate resumption of essential business operations. Once this has been achieved, the EMP is canceled. However, a crisis management plan may continue for long periods, as it deals with whole of business survival issues. For example, during a chemical spill, emergency response will be implemented until the threat to life and critical infrastructure is controlled. The crisis management plan, however, will cover how the organization deals with the far-reaching consequence of the incident, such as the overall ability of the organization to recover from the crisis.

Using first aid as an example, the recovery phase begins once the casualty is breathing, arterial bleeding has stopped, and is conscious. The recovery phase is complete once professional emergency services are on the scene and take control of the incident. If the casualty's condition deteriorates, then the process returns to the response phase. So too, during a terrorist attack, after a bomb goes off, the recovery phase may not be able to commence until mass panic is controlled and secondary detonations from fuel storage areas are prevented.

8.4.5 Tips and Tricks with Emergency Plans

Table 8.1 Tips and tricks with emergency plans

Creation of the plan	Often, the first downfall of an EMP is the manner in which it was created. If the planning team did not have access to all the stakeholders or was unable to get them to review the plan prior to publication, then the plan will inevitably have holes.
Creating stakeholder interest	Money talks. A simple cost/benefit analysis of how effectively managing an emergency will save money will often be enough to stir executive interest. Equally important is defining the role that both senior and junior management will have in the planning process. Once information has been collected, the planning team should be able to work out the detail with planned review steps, rather than constant referral to stakeholders.
Top-down planning/ bottom-up refinement	How often have operations level staff complained that management have made a decision without realizing the full implications. The draft plan should be written in such a way that it can be easily modified after user input and testing.
Testing the plan	The plan should be tested at each stage of development, which includes war gaming the plan by working through it step by step with a member of the planning team playing "devil's advocate" and asking what if questions. It also includes rehearsing the plan after it has been briefed and actively collecting criticism during these rehearsals to refine the plan.
Communications	Very few plans will work with no communication. Even a fire drill requires an alarm to be sounded. Typically, the more complex a plan, the more communication is required. Thus, poorly developed communication procedures can easily cause a plan to fail.
Internal communications	As discussed, mobile phone networks are often the first to fail in an emergency. Likewise, line communication and power systems cannot be guaranteed. For these reason, the plan may need to include redundancy in the communication systems used. Equally valuable is the production of a plan, which once implemented, requires minimal communication.
External communications	Aside from emergency services, many people and organizations may need to be communicated with in an emergency. Possibly the most important of these is the media. Media coverage, whether positive or negative, has the power to turn on or off assistance or to determine whether an emergency will grow into a crisis. For this reason, a member of the emergency management team must be appointed as a spokesperson. Ideally, they will have some training in dealing with the media and be able to produce key themes and messages with which to brief the media.

Briefing and training	As mentioned, a one-page diagram on the back of a door is generally far more use in a emergency than a 50-page document on a shelf. However, regardless of how easily decipherable a plan is, during an emergency it is too late for personnel to work out what their role is to play. This is as true for an employee whose only responsibility is to walk calmly down the fire stairs as it is for a key member of the emergency management team.
A picture tells a thousand words	For a plan to be implemented properly, it must be clearly and easily understood. Many plans will involve a series of stages that can easily be depicted in a diagram. These diagrams can then be placed in common areas as reminders. Diagrams are also an effective way to judge whether a plan is too complex. If the diagram that describes the plan is too complex, then the plan is probably too complex.
Induction training	All personnel must understand their role in an emergency for the plan to work safely and effectively. Most organizations have some form of induction training for staff when corporate policies and occupational health and safety (OHS) briefs are delivered. What better time to brief the emergency management plan and ensure that all personnel are aware of it from their first day at work?
Periodic training and testing	Obviously, having a detailed knowledge of the emergency management plan is not a priority for most members of an organization. Thus, periodic training, rehearsing, and testing is required to ensure personnel know what to do. Rehearsing and testing serves as an excellent opportunity to collect the information required to refine and update plans as simple things like the refurbishing of an office space could necessitate changes
Flexibility	No plan will ever be perfect in all situations, and every situation cannot be predicted. Overly prescriptive plans, or plans with too many decision points that originates from one or multiple sources, are prone to failure
Contingencies	A flexible plan is not one that is vague. It is one that has redundancy and built in contingencies. If plan A is unworkable in a given situation, then the plan stipulates a clear process to switch to plan B
Decision making	All emergency decisions must stem from a central point. Having one person in overall charge with a team working for him or her to collect information results in faster decisions. Everyone must know who the decision maker is, and just as importantly who is next in line to be the decision maker if the original person is unavailable. As a rule, in an emergency, an organization should operate like a country under martial law with clear and accountable lines of authority with the power to take sweeping immediate actions if necessary. This power should be clearly specified, and commanders must be held accountable for any actions taken during the emergency; that is, actions must be defensible in the cool light of day with hindsight after the emergency is concluded

Checklist for Emergency Plans

- Do you have a written emergency plan? ☐

- Does everyone (who needs to) know how to find it? ☐

- Has everyone been briefed or trained in their roles? ☐

- Is it simple and flexible enough to be applied to any type of emergency (fire, flood, bomb threat, assault)? ☐

- Does it cover both evacuation and shelter in place strategies? ☐

- Is it integrated with other risk management plans (safety, security, business continuity, and disaster recovery, etc.)? ☐

- Is your plan reviewed at appropriate intervals (at least annually) to ensure it is still accurate and relevant? ☐

- Does your plan include a site map which identifies key areas (e.g., assembly areas, exits, fire protection devices, medical facilities)? ☐

- Does your plan explain the steps to be taken in the event of the different types of emergencies? ☐

- Does your plan nominate the staff or staff positions that make up the emergency response team? ☐

- Does your emergency team meet regularly to practice and discuss the emergency plan? ☐

- Do members of your emergency management team meet frequently to ensure all persons are aware of their roles? ☐

- Do you have an annual plan for different types of emergency exercises? ☐

- Do you critique evacuation exercises and provide feedback to participants on the success of the exercises? ☐

- Have all staff, customers, residents, and so on been trained in their roles during an emergency? ☐

- Is there a training plan to support ongoing skill maintenance of emergency responders and other stakeholders? Is it up to date and being worked as per the plan? ☐

- Do you have multiple methods of communicating to all personnel about specific items and activities they should watch for in relation to the security and safety of their area of responsibility? ☐

8.5 RECOVERY AND CONTINUITY

Security management does not stop with prevention and response. No matter how well threats are identified and addressed, vulnerabilities managed, and access controls implemented, prudent risk management dictates that you assume that an incident will occur. An all-hazards approach acknowledges that out-of-course events are not limited to security breaches. Any number of events, which include natural disasters, power failures, hardware malfunctions, and software bugs can all disrupt an organization's ability to function.

> "Business continuity management provides the availability of processes and resources in order to ensure the continued achievement of critical objectives"
>
> *(HB 221:2004 HANDBOOK - BUSINESS CONTINUITY MANAGEMENT)*

Business continuity management (BCM) involves developing and applying the practices that develop resilience. This process involves preparing for potential disruptions and creating strategies for organizations, individuals, and/or communities to restore capabilities. It is likely to include elements such as:

- Business impact analysis
- Preparation and execution of recovery plans
- Establishment and mobilization of alternate sites or facilities
- Restoration or replacement of existing facilities

Business continuity, like each of the previous three activity areas, is a discipline and complex skill set in and of itself, which many practitioners will choose to specialize. As with other areas of security management, a significant amount of overlap exists among business continuity, other activity areas, and practice areas.

It is an activity that is to a certain extent, ongoing through the life cycle of an organization as that organization prepares for potential major incidents and deals with the minor challenges of normal operations. However, this phase is more typically considered to be the relatively extended period of restoration following the immediate emergency response measures after an incident. As such, it is likely that all areas of an organization will have a role to play in this regard, even if it is only the restoration of their own business functions.

Business continuity management has often been confused with the information technology (IT) driven scenarios of ensuring that computer and network systems are designed with a high level of availability (Figure 8.17). This has led to the implementation of contingency systems and switched networks that will enable the business to continue to operate in the event of a disaster befalling the computer center, such as power failure or fire (which together are defined more accurately under the heading of disaster recovery).

It is important to understand that business continuity is not just about the recovery of information technology systems or services; it is an organization-wide discipline concerned with the continuity of the business. As such, it is essentially a business issue and should be viewed in that context.

Disaster recovery refers to ability of the business to recover from specific incidents, which include the provision of facilities and services to enable the business to continue to function. A key component of disaster recovery is often

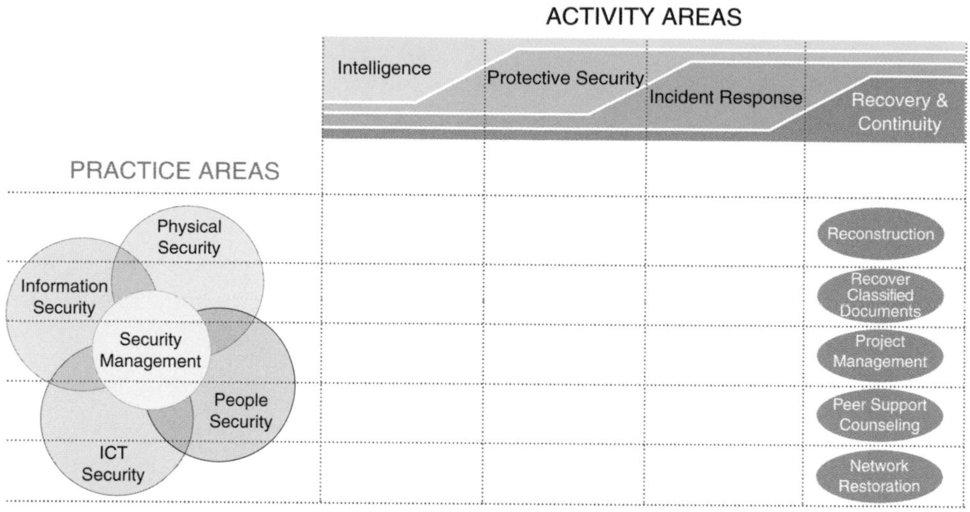

ACTIVITY AREAS

FIGURE 8.17 Examples of practitioner roles in business continuity

the provision of the critical IT applications and infrastructure necessary to support the recovery of the critical business processes.

Underpinning recovery is crisis management, which ensures that the most appropriate personnel are brought together to manage the immediate effects and wider implications of the incident. The information that they are provided with from the business facilities, IT, and others will enable decisions to be made on what should be recovered, how this will be accomplished, and when it will be done.

8.5.1 The Benefits of Business Continuity Management

In addition to the protection of the business, many benefits can be achieved through having a structured and consistent business continuity process. Some more general benefits are detailed as follows:

- **Regulatory requirements:** In some industries, a recovery capability is becoming a mandatory requirement. For example, regulators such as the Bank for International Settlements stipulate that financial organizations require sufficient continuity and security controls to meet the business requirements. Failure to demonstrate tested recovery facilities could result in heavy fines. Within the service community, there is an obligation to provide continuous services, e.g., hospitals, emergency services (police, fire, and ambulance services), and prisons.

- **Positive marketing of contingency capabilities:** Being able to demonstrate effective BCM capabilities will enable an organization to provide high service levels to clients and customers, and thus win business.

- **Competitive advantage:** Service organizations, such as suppliers of outsourced computer facilities, are increasingly being asked by business partners, customers, and stakeholders to demonstrate their contingency provision and may not be invited to tender for business unless they can demonstrate appropriate recovery capabilities. In many cases, this is a good incentive for customers to continue a business relationship and becomes a part of the competitive advantage used to win or retain customers.

- **Insurance:** Effective business continuity management can help the organization demonstrate to underwriters or insurers that they are proactively managing down their business risks. The ability to recover the business and to mitigate losses is often a requirement of the policy. Therefore, the risk to the insurer of an organization with comprehensive business continuity plans is lower, and the premiums should reflect this. Alternatively, the organization may feel comfortable in reducing cover or self-insuring in certain areas as a result of limiting potential losses.

8.5.2 A General Approach to BCM

Numerous standards and methodologies have been developed for the preparation and maintenance of business continuity plans (BCP). These standards tend to follow the same structure with similar activities, albeit in a different order. This methodology adopts the better practices from each of these to assist organizations with developing a business continuity management methodology applicable to their own organizations (Figure 8.18).

8.5.2.1 Overview. Each of these components is discussed in detail below.

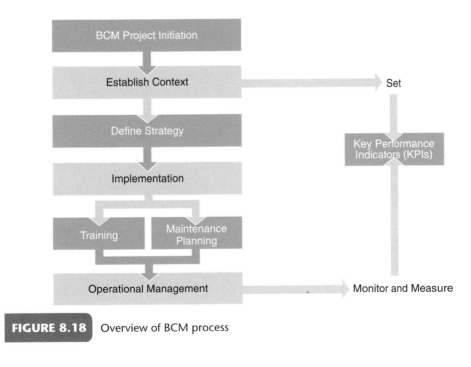

FIGURE 8.18 Overview of BCM process

BCM Project Initiation

The project initiation phase ensures parties involved in the process of developing the plans are fully involved in setting the expectations and objectives of the project. The deliverable from this phase is the project document that will include the following:

- Objectives
- Individuals' responsibilities and contact details
- Project plan and major milestones. This will identify the input required from individuals during the course of the project
- Risks and issues affecting the successful completion of the project
- Deliverables
- Quality criteria

Establish Context

The next phase of the project is to establish the context for business continuity management within the organization. This activity will provide the high-level statement of the business objectives and measurement indicators.

Asset Definition

It is essential that all company assets are identified that together support the business process, which include the following:

- Key personnel and responsibilities
- Business processes
- Technical services, including computer systems, networks, information feeds, and so on
- Data
- Facilities and premises
- Support services
- Literature

The information gathered will form the basis of an asset register, which must be maintained as part of the ongoing maintenance activity.

Policy

A high-level policy will capture the corporate view on business continuity management. This document is not all encompassing, rather, it is a concise view of the approach that will be taken, the key business activities that will be maintained, and the board commitment to maintenance of the plans and supporting infrastructure.

The policy provides the foundation for an organization's business continuity capability, development, implementation and maintenance.

Key Performance Indicators

KPIs are established to demonstrate the ongoing commitment to and maintenance of continuity infrastructure. These indicators address all aspects of the plans and recovery procedures, to ensure that they are continuously monitored, measured, and maintained.

To ensure that the plans are maintained and can be demonstrated as being current (both to auditors and third parties—clients and investors), the KPIs include objectives such as the following:

- A clearly defined, documented and approved BCM assurance management process and frequency (cycle)
- Review and agreement by key personnel
- A clearly defined and documented monitoring, evaluation and review process for its BCM KPIs
- Clearly defined, documented, and approved management information assurance reports

In particular relation to the key business objectives:

- What outputs or deliverables (i.e., products or services) are required to meet these business objectives?
- When do the business objectives need to be achieved?
- Who needs to be involved, both internally and externally, to achieve the business objectives?
- How are the business objectives going to be achieved?

Additional KPIs applicable to the organization may be defined during the course of the project.

Define Strategy

Definition of the strategy is a key aspect of the process; it will ensure that best use is made of available resources and will enable all participants to be aware of their responsibilities and objectives.

Business Impact Analysis (BIA)

The BIA underpins the whole business continuity management process. It consists of techniques and methodologies required to identify, quantify, and qualify the impacts on an organization of a loss of, interruption to, or disruption of key business processes or their supporting infrastructure.

Risk Assessment

A major part of business continuity management is understanding the likelihood of business assets being affected by an incident that will disrupt the business processes. Understanding the risks will enable an effective risk mitigation strategy to be defined through defining and implementing an appropriate control and recovery infrastructure.

Strategy

Defining the recovery strategy is an essential step in the overall business continuity planning process (Figure 8.19).

In the context of continuity, strategy concerns the determination and selection of alternative operating methods to be used to maintain the organization's business process following an incident, to an acceptable level. Experience and good practice clearly identify that the early provision of an organizational (corporate) business continuity strategy will ensure that activities are aligned with and support the organization's overall strategy. When developing a strategy, the following three levels of strategic planning need to be considered:

- Organization (overall) business continuity strategy
- Process level strategy
- Resource recovery strategy

Organizational Strategy

An organizational (corporate) continuity strategy is key to ensuring resilience and high reliability of the continuance of the organization's business process at an acceptable minimum level, and it should be viewed as a living document.

Process Level Strategy

The process level strategy is a documented framework focused on the resilience and high reliability of an organization's business processes from both an organizational and an industry perspective.

Resource Recovery Strategy

A resource recovery strategy concerns the deployment of appropriate resources as part of the business continuity strategy. This type of strategy provides the practical link between the BIA and the plans.

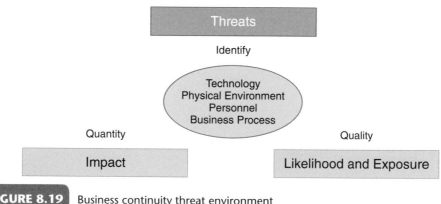

FIGURE 8.19 Business continuity threat environment

When developing any level of BCM strategy, many strategic options should be considered. These include the following:

- Doing nothing
- Processing transfer—switching operation to alternative sites
- Termination or change of business process
- Taking out insurance to cover the loss of service
- Loss mitigation or minimising the risk of a disruptive event

Implementation

The implementation phase takes the objectives of the strategy and develops the business infrastructure to ensure the objectives of the policy are met.

Develop Business Continuity Plans

A plan does not provide a competence or capability; it provides the approach to establishing an effective capability. Although the plan is important, it is an outcome of the more important planning process and a blueprint to kick-start the response to a business continuity incident.

The plans identify the required facilities, technical infrastructure, key responsibilities, and processes that will be required to position the business to recover from disruptive events, both small and catastrophic.

Implementation Planning

Implementation planning considers those aspects of the infrastructure that must be revised to support the plan. This plan will address key aspects of the business including the following:

- Premises
- Facilities
- Support services
- Technical services
- Personnel responsibilities

The planning phase must take into account other strategies and development plans to ensure that they are fully integrated and effective use is made of available resources.

Implementation

The implementation of the recovery infrastructure is essentially aimed at the following two key aspects:

- Reduction of the risk of a disruptive event occurring through the implementation of protection or contingent systems
- Recovery systems and processes to ensure that recovery can be achieved within a required time and that disruption is kept to a minimum

Develop Recovery Procedures

The recovery procedures are essential to ensuring that the services and systems are recovered in the order that will prove most effective to the business such that key business processes are maintained. The procedures, however, must allow for a degree of flexibility to enable the recovery manager to make key tactical decisions during the recovery process, which may develop as a result of market status or other external influences.

Crisis Management Planning

The ability to achieve effective crisis management and business continuity during an incident requires strong leadership and coordination between the people responsible, individual site or building crisis management and business crisis management (Figure 8.20). Another critical aspect of an organization's crisis capability is the competence of the crisis management team. This team must include effective communication paths at all levels:

- Longer term strategic business planning
- Near term tactical response to events or incidents
- Operational management and recovery of the environment

Failure to put in place an effective and fit-for-purpose crisis management capability and team will expose an organization's brand to unnecessary financial, credit, reputation, regulatory, legal, market, and operational risk.

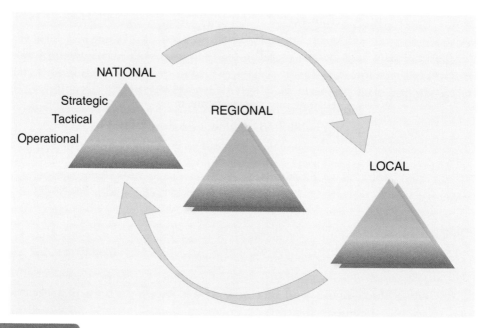

FIGURE 8.20 Crisis management planning

Initial Testing

The final stage of the implementation phase is to test the recovery and continuity infrastructure. An initial test will address the technical infrastructure and will, for example, confirm that data can be recovered, networks switched, and systems rebuilt. It is also essential at this stage to conduct walk throughs of the procedures and review the staff awareness, i.e., Do they know what is expected of them? Initial testing objectives must be classed as one of the KPIs.

Training and Awareness

Creating and embedding a BCM culture within an organization may be a lengthy process. It may encounter a level of resistance that should not be underestimated. Success within an organization is primarily dependent on the following:

- Business continuity management becoming an integral part of the organization's strategic and day-to-day management ethos
- Education, awareness training, and participation being used to effect cultural change (merely documenting a strategy and plan represents a narrow and limited method of developing a culture)
- Preparation and delivery of a program to create corporate awareness and enhance the skills, knowledge, and experience required to implement, maintain, manage, and execute
- A vision statement and the visible proactive support from the organization's executive, senior, and middle management
- Ownership of the various parts of the organization where operational risk originates and resides (not just within facilities or IT)
- Commitment to maintaining and reviewing the organization's policy, strategies, framework, plans, and solutions on a regular basis
- Appreciation and recognition of the importance of business continuity to the organization and the role of individuals within it
- Communication to all external stakeholders and third parties (sourced service providers) on whom the organization depends, of the importance of continuity to the organization and their role in both normal and incident situations

In addition to the general education and awareness program outlined above, specific training will be required for key figures in the organization. These individuals include the recovery manager, the crisis manager, and the business unit leaders. It should be noted that the key roles identified above may not necessarily be board appointees. They will, however, have the authority to make key tactical decisions or have direct access to decision makers during a recovery episode.

Maintenance Planning

Organizations exist in a dynamic environment and are subject to change in people, processes, supplies, market, risk, environment, geography, and business strategy. To ensure that business continuity continues to reflect the nature, scale, and complexity of the organization it supports, a clearly defined and documented maintenance program must be established. Any changes, internal or external, that have an impact on the organization must be reviewed.

Review and Audit Planning

The audit process plays a key role in ensuring that an organization has a robust and effective business continuity capability. Like planning, implementation, and maintenance, the audit requires interaction with a wide range of managerial and operational roles from both a business and technical perspective. The purpose of an audit is to assess an organization's existing competence and capability, verify it against predefined criteria, and deliver an audit report detailing the findings, conclusions, and recommendations.

Testing Plans

The initial testing will confirm that the infrastructure and processes are suitable for the business objectives at that time. An ongoing program of testing must also be defined to exercise the plans over a continuous period, ensuring that all changes have been included and are fully operational.

The testing program should include the following areas:

- Technical recovery testing—at least monthly
- Desktop plan and process reviews—quarterly
- Full simulation—annually.

The results and actions that occur must be captured in a report that itself is considered a KPI.

Change Management

A key feature of the BCM process as identified earlier is the ability to capture changes and properly reflect them in the plans, recovery processes, and technical infrastructure. A centralized method for capturing changes and ensuring that they are properly signed off by the appropriate individuals must be established. Again, having a fully operational and managed change process in place must be considered a KPI.

Operational Management

The final phase of the business continuity planning process is to make the management systems, testing plans, and operational infrastructure operational. The responsibility for management and maintenance of the plans must be assigned and the reporting schedule defined.

Release to operational management is identified as an agreed change and signed off by the project manager as a final milestone.

8.5.3 Standards

Some standards that cover information security management and business continuity are provided below for reference.

ISO/IEC AS/NZS 17799:1:2001	Information Technology – Code of Practice for Information Security Management
AS/NZS 7799:2:2003	Information Security Management – Specification for Information Security Management Systems
AS/NZS HB 221:2004	Handbook – Business Continuity Management
AS/NZS HB 231:2005	Information Security Risk Management Guidelines
BS PAS 56	Business Continuity Institute – Guide to Business Continuity Management
AS/NZS 4360:2004	Risk Management

8.6 SUMMARY OF KEY POINTS

By aligning the junction of practice areas with activity areas, we can establish a holistic view of the security functions and roles of an organization. This framework can assist managers and organizations to conduct a gap analysis relatively quickly and to establish which areas they are strong in and where they need to focus efforts. An example is provided in Figure 8.21 below.

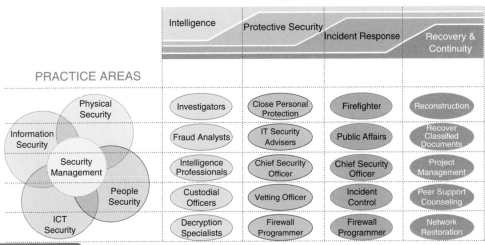

FIGURE 8.21 Indicative examples of practitioner/activity roles

A small group of specialists will spend most of their professional lives in roles that could be placed within this practice/activity area matrix. Most personnel in most organizations, however, will not have dedicated roles within this framework as part of their day-to-day activities. That being said, everyone has a role to play in reporting unusual incidents (intelligence), following security procedures, and assisting as required in any post-event scenario (Figure 8.18).

A detailed evaluation form to check your organization's business continuity and resilience maturity is provided in chapter 13.

Security Risk Management Enablers

9

9.1 INTRODUCTION

At its simplest, Security Risk Management (SRM) involves protecting assets by identifying risk and by applying resources to mitigate those risks. To achieve this, many enabling elements are required, which can be grouped into the following five areas:

- Regulation and policy
- Training and implementation
- Operations and application
- Governance and assurance
- Sustainability and resilience

The relationship among enablers, inputs, controls, processes, and outputs is shown graphically in Figure 9.1.

9.1.1 Regulation and Policy

Regulation and policy are systems that form the broader legislated and organizational environment. These enablers are used as key strategic shapers of the operating environment (Figure 9.2).

ORGANIZATIONAL/ENVIRONMENTAL SECURITY CONTEXT

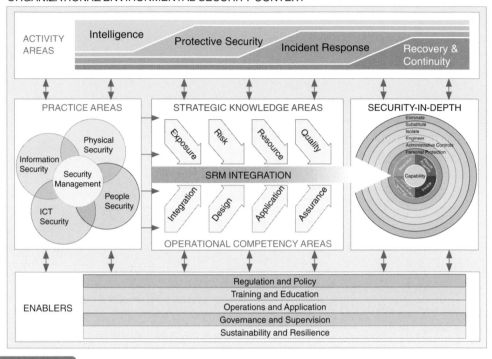

FIGURE 9.1 Security Risk Management enablers

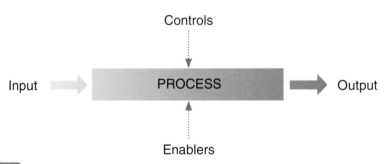

FIGURE 9.2 Relationship of enablers to the risk management process

These terms have been used here to refer broadly to the decision-making frameworks, which provide the fundamental building blocks for the Security Risk Management application. Although different organizations will use these terms slightly differently, they have been applied within this context to refer primarily to mandatory or recommended guidelines, respectively.

"Regulation" includes all forms of governmental legislation, common law, and regulations, as well as organizational overtly stated internal compliance requirements, procedures, audit criteria, and so on.

"Policy" includes all forms of both stated and unstated requirements and expectations of governments and organizations. It may include public policy announcements, internal policy statements, or cultural norms, which constitute normal practice.

Although relatively blunt instruments, these items form the principle context within which Security Risk Management measures are applied and to a certain extent will also shape the threat or exposure environment. The prominence of these enablers cannot be understated, as each of the four following SRM enablers will be expected to work within the structure laid down by regulation and policy.

9.1.2 Training and Implementation

Training and implementation are the areas in which the "rubber hits the road" in terms of applying Security Risk Management systems. Once the policy environment has been established and key objectives defined, little actual success can be achieved without communicating and training individuals and organizational units in the process aspects of the relevant Security Risk Management systems. Similarly, project management methodologies and general management practices are required to ensure that the more tangible security measures are correctly implemented.

This education process refers not to the training of security practitioners but more particularly, in the SRM body of knowledge (BOK) context, to the development of organizational capability at all levels based on a sound framework of training needs analysis and training delivery programs to sustain organizational capability. This process is the cornerstone for delivery of each of the subsequent enablers and can be considered a prerequisite even to the implementation of any element of the system, be that physical, information based, or conceptual implementation programs.

9.1.3 Operations and Application

The ongoing implementation and application of SRM practices and systems is perhaps the fundamental measure of enabling protective practices in the real world. A combination of design, delivery, and maintenance activities is critical in this area.

Much has been written on this area in broader areas of management and financial disciplines in particular; however, it is important to observe that some key differentiators of SRM operations include the fact that security is an enabler to all areas of an organization, and similarly it relies on all management disciplines in differing measures depending on the context.

In particular, Security Risk Management is closely aligned with occupational health and safety (OHS) risk management. This alignment is clearly evident in the case of physical security information security practices; however, even information security is at its core related to protecting the information to protect persons from harm or loss.

Many management practices can be considered a core business; however, only a handful of operational activities can truly be considered life threatening if the ongoing application or delivery of their outcomes should fail. Security is one such area, and the enabler of ongoing operations and application is in the point where stakeholders will start their inquiries in the event of any perceived or actual failure.

9.1.4 Governance and Accountability

Governance and accountability are the twin frameworks to:

- Establish oversight and management systems within regulatory/policy requirements
- Ensure that those frameworks are applied as intended

The word "governance" has Latin origins, which suggest a concept of steering. Although several interpretations are commonly applied to the use of the word "governance", depending on the context, this sense of steering is particularly relevant to the multifaceted and diverse Security Risk Management environment. Governance as a steering or guiding force assists with providing direction and yet permits organizations and individuals to apply Security Risk Management practices and activities in a manner that befits the relevant threat environment in which they may find themselves.

Given the often life and death nature of security risks, steering alone will not be sufficient to ensure that duty-of-care obligations are met. This instance?? is where the matching concept of accountability is so essential. Providing that individuals and indeed organizations are adequately trained, they can rightly be held accountable for the outcomes of their actions and inactions.

9.1.5 Sustainability and Resilience

Although similar in concept to business continuity, the term "sustainability and resilience" is used here to refer to the broader collective of organizational measures, systems, and treatments and, to a large extent, the organizational culture, mission, and values.

It should be noted that resilience is not, in this context, a goal in itself, but rather it is an underlying enabler to support the protection of assets and the maintenance of ongoing capabilities. The twin concepts of sustainability and resilience are simply those characteristics that enable an organization, community, or individual to continue on in the face of adversity.

> The United Nations (UN) International Strategy for Disaster Reduction defines "resilience" as "The capacity of a system, community or society potentially exposed to hazards to adapt, by resisting or changing in order to reach and maintain an acceptable level of functioning and structure. This is determined by the degree to which the social system is capable of organising itself to increase its capacity for learning from past disasters for better future protection and to improve risk reduction measures."

Inherent in this notion is the concept of organizational culture and ongoing capability to learn, grow, and adapt based on previous and likely events.

9.2 SUMMARY OF KEY POINTS

Developing any management system or sustained societal capability requires several underpinning enablers. Security Risk Management is no different in this respect, and we do not intend the above list to be either restrictive or mandatory. Rather, it provides a framework that can be used to assess governance and Security Risk Management systems, which are covered in later chapters.

Enablers are simply logical groupings of core organizational capabilities that can assist organizations to reach their goals—in this case by supporting the application of security systems. Some key points to consider are as follows:

- Regulation and policy, although limited in many respects, form the basis for all other enablers.

- A robust training system is core to the development of organizational capability at all levels, never more so than in the case of Security Risk Management, which frequently requires rapid decisions and immediate actions in the face of infrequently encountered high-risk situations. It is the cornerstone for delivery of each of the subsequent enablers.

- Many management practices can be considered a core business. Security is one of a small group, which can be life threatening if SRM application should fail or be perceived to fail.

- Governance mechanisms in SRM need to be sufficiently flexible to allow individuals to meet specific and variable threats, therefore, accountability at all levels will be essential if SRM practices are to be successful.

- Managers and SRM practitioners alike may face challenges in allocating resources associated with prioritizing conflicting requirements.

Asset Areas 10

10.1 WHAT IS AN ASSET?

The concept of an asset is essentially linked to ideas of value. Cash, motor vehicles, and buildings are typically examples in a financial or accounting context. This limited definition is usually broadened to include people and intangibles, such as reputation, intellectual property, and organizational functionality.

> *An asset is any item or process that an individual, community, or government values and is important to supporting their expected outcomes and objectives.*[72]

The precise definition is probably less important than the ability of stakeholders to reach a consensus on this matter. The way in which various organizations and individuals use the term "asset" can in fact lead to confusion in many instances.

In this section, we offer the following two views of assets:

- A general overview regarding what constitutes an asset
- A framework that practitioners and organizations can adapt for the purposes of providing alignment with other definitions or frameworks

10.1.1 A Traditional View

A traditional view of assets might include people, information, property, economic assets, and reputation. As illustrated in Figure 10.1, the economic benefits might in fact simply be a measure of the correct application of assets, such as people, information, and property, which sustains a strong reputation in the marketplace.

We might describe this view of assets as people, information, and property that deliver benefit.

10.1.2 An Emerging View

Fundamentally, what constitutes an asset relates predominantly to what is valued. This simple truism underpins the more complex concept of values—an area often rooted in organizational, individual, or community culture. Our cultural perspectives shape our values and subtly, but importantly, shape what we consider to be an asset. A very simple example of this would be a tribal culture that

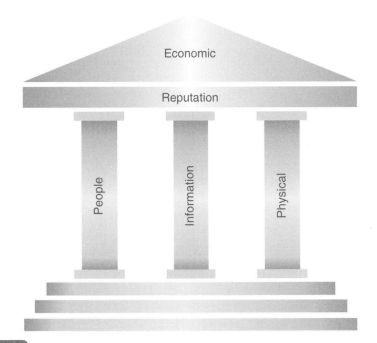

FIGURE 10.1 The link between assets and economic value

does not value money. Similarly, different societies, organizations, and individuals place different values on human life.

It is likely that in an increasingly interconnected world with rapid technological advances, our understanding and definition of the very term "assets" will be subject to subtle redefinition. Recent reductions in the cost of manufactured goods and the increasing value of information services is changing the way that we evaluate the concept of assets.

Another definition of asset might therefore involve "something that we require to sustain capabilities." This framework, as illustrated in Figure 10.2, recognizes the increasing importance of information-related technologies versus simply the information or the physical aspects of the technology. Information and communications technology (ICT) is used to refer to the confluence of a range of disciplines to provide a concept that is greater than the sum of its parts. It also reflects that these categories align with the areas that practitioners typically identify their area of expertise.

This might otherwise be expressed in the following definition.

> *Assets are people, information, property, and information and communication technologies that are valued or relied on to build and sustain capabilities.*

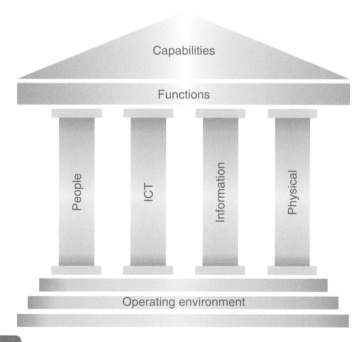

FIGURE 10.2 Assets supporting functions that deliver capabilities

10.2 KEY ASSET GROUPS

Security Risk Management body of knowledge (SRMBOK) proposes that the following four categories of assets can be applied as a framework to identify the elements that deliver capabilities and the principle objective:

- Physical property
- People
- Information
- ICT

As illustrated in Figure 10.3, capability is the core objective or requirement that is supported by the interaction of and coordinated application of people, information, ICT, and physical security resources. Although asset areas can be grouped in many ways, the above categories provide at the very least, one way in which we can consistently analyze and evaluate the interaction and performance of security resources and related assets. Each of these areas is discussed in detail in the following sections.

The protection of these four categories of assets is an important element of sustaining organizational resilience. In addition, these assets are also the primary resource categories that can be used to provide security risk mitigations.

10.2.1 Physical Property

As illustrated in Figure 10.4, physical assets can include tangible and intangible assets. Tangible physical assets are easily understood as they include the generally understood assets of property and physical goods. Intangible physical assets

Asset Areas

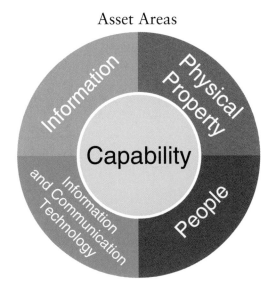

FIGURE 10.3 Key asset categories required to deliver capabilities

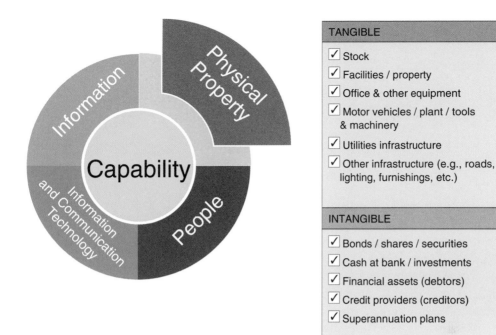

TANGIBLE

- ✓ Stock
- ✓ Facilities / property
- ✓ Office & other equipment
- ✓ Motor vehicles / plant / tools & machinery
- ✓ Utilities infrastructure
- ✓ Other infrastructure (e.g., roads, lighting, furnishings, etc.)

INTANGIBLE

- ✓ Bonds / shares / securities
- ✓ Cash at bank / investments
- ✓ Financial assets (debtors)
- ✓ Credit providers (creditors)
- ✓ Superannuation plans

FIGURE 10.4 Example of physical assets

include items such as cash, bonds, and financial assets. Even when they have an actual manifestation, e.g., bank notes and share certificates, the real worth of the asset lies in the underlying value rather than the physical presence of a banknote.

10.2.2 People

People include employees, contractors, visitors, customers, and suppliers in the broadest sense. People are in fact the essential underlying asset group that lead to the creation of all other asset groups through the concerted application of human endeavor (Figure 10.5). In this sense, people are the primary asset; however, from the Security Risk Management perspective, all assets are of value and need to be applied in a consistent and unified manner.

10.2.3 Information

Information assets as illustrated in Figure 10.6 include structural, relational, and human categories of information. These categories can include hard copy, electronic, conceptual, or any form of information that can be stored, retrieved, and used, whether it is currently accessible or not, which include information retained within an individuals' conscious or unconscious brain. In its broadest

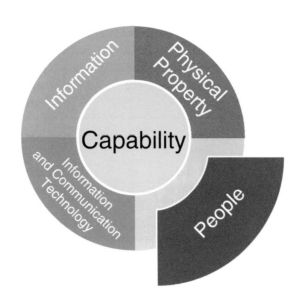

TANGIBLE

- ✓ Employees / staff
- ✓ Subcontractors
- ✓ Owners / shareholders

INTANGIBLE

- ✓ Customers
- ✓ Suppliers
- ✓ Financiers
- ✓ Regulators
- ✓ Visitors
- ✓ Community
- ✓ Others

FIGURE 10.5 Example of people assets

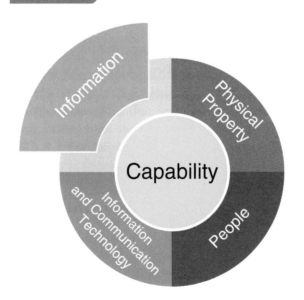

STRUCTURAL

- ✓ Commercially sensitive / classified
- ✓ Intellectual property
- ✓ Information systems data
- ✓ Management processes
- ✓ Organizational philosophy / culture

RELATIONAL

- ✓ Customer relations / arrangements
- ✓ Supplier relations / arrangements
- ✓ Financial relations / arrangements
- ✓ Licensing / franchising
- ✓ Distribution channels
- ✓ Company name / brand

HUMAN

- ✓ Know-how / expertise
- ✓ Innovative capacity
- ✓ Learning & development ability
- ✓ Diversity / demographics

FIGURE 10.6 Examples of key information asset groups

Table 10.1 Common ICT assets

Asset Name	Asset Name	Asset Name
Data centers	Server application software	Fax machines
Servers	End-user application software	Removable media (tapes, floppy disks, CD ROMs, DVDs, portable hard drives, PC card storage devices, USB storage devices, and so on)
Desktop computers	Development tools	Power supplies
Mobile computers	Routers	Uninterruptible power supplies
Personal digital assistants (PDAs)	Network switches	Fire suppression systems
Cell phones	Smart cards	Air conditioning systems
Air filtration systems	Enterprise management tools	Partner collaboration application
Other environmental control systems	File sharing	Partner cryptographic keys
Source code	Storage	Partner credit reports
Employee passwords	Telephony	Public cryptographic keys
Employee private cryptographic keys	Virtual private networking (VPN) access	Supplier collaboration application
Computer system cryptographic keys	Employee biometric identifiers	Supplier cryptographic keys
Microsoft Windows® Internet Naming Service (WINS)	Collaboration services (for example, Microsoft SharePoint®)	Website sales application
E-mail/scheduling (for example, Microsoft Exchange®)	Network infrastructure design	Website marketing data
Instant messaging	Internal Web sites	Customer credit card data
Microsoft Outlook® Web Access (OWA)	Employee ethnographic data	Customer contact data
Active Directory® directory service	Domain name system (DNS)	Dynamic Host Configuration Protocol (DHCP)

sense, it can include the information contained within complex structures such as DNA or organic cells. Much of this information is not necessarily immediately accessible; however, our quanta of information continues to grow through both incremental development and ongoing research.

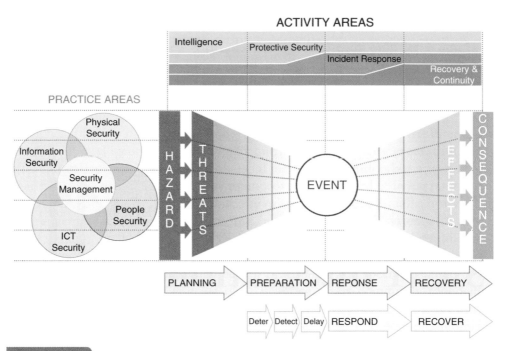

FIGURE 11.1   Integration of practice areas with activity areas and bow-tie

ORGANIZATIONAL/ENVIRONMENTAL SECURITY CONTEXT

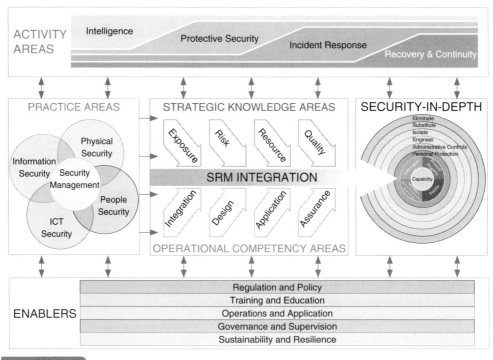

FIGURE 11.2   SRMBOK organizational resilience model

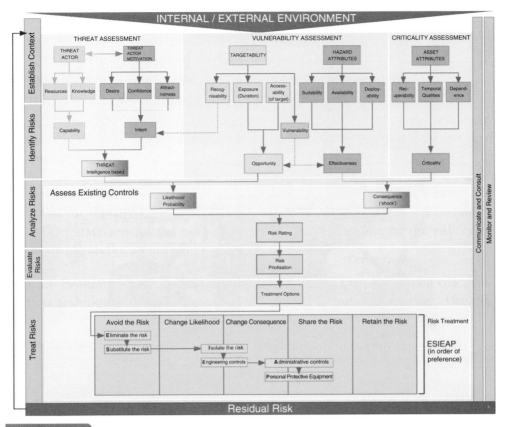

FIGURE 11.3 Expansion of AS/NZS 4360:2004 Risk Management Process for Security Risk Management

Figure 11.3 illustrates the application of some core concepts that underpin Security Risk Management, such as threat assessment, vulnerability assessment, and so on, and how they interact with the AS/NZS 4360:2004 Risk Management Process. This figure also includes and integrates other methodologies, such as CARVER + SHOCK, where CARVER stands for:

- **Criticality**—measure of public health and economic impacts of an attack
- **Accessibility**—ability to physically access and egress from a target
- **Recoverability**—ability of system to recover from an attack
- **Vulnerability**—ease of accomplishing an attack
- **Effect**—amount of direct loss from an attack as measured by loss in production
- **Recognizability**—ease of identifying a target

Additional details regarding the meaning and application of each element of Figure 11.4 can be found in the Lexicon at the end of this document and throughout the text.

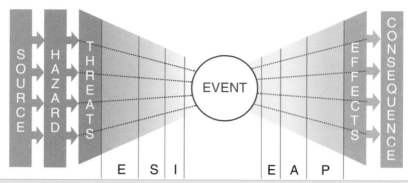

Note: The alignment of ESIEAP with Bow-tie is provided as an INDICATIVE MODEL ONLY. ESI will not always align with likelihood management nor will EAP necessarily be associated with consequence management. In some cases, however, it may prove useful to consider bow-tie in alignment with ESIEAP for discussion purposes.

FIGURE 11.4 Conceptual alignment of bow-tie with eliminate, substitute, isolate, engineer, administrative controls, and personal protection (ESIEAP)

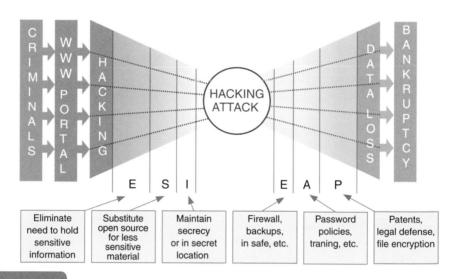

FIGURE 11.5 Indicative example of alignment of ESIEAP with bow-tie to protect data

> The illustration in Figure 11.5 is an example only. It should not be taken to suggest that ESI is always on the left-hand side of the bow-tie or that EAP is always on the right-hand side. In practice, it is possible to develop a range of examples that might have ESIEAP barriers on the left-hand side and more ESIEAP barriers again on the right-hand side.

11.1 SRM INTEGRATION WITH ENTERPRISE RISK MANAGEMENT

Enterprise risk management (ERM) refers to the methods and processes used by enterprises, as opposed to particular business units or cross-unit functions, to manage risks or seize opportunities related to the achievement of their objectives (Figure 11.6). ERM is evolving to address the needs of various stakeholders, who want to understand the broad spectrum of risks that face complex organizations to ensure they are appropriately managed. Regulators and debt rating agencies have increased their scrutiny on the risk management processes of companies.

ERM provides an holistic framework for managing risk, which typically involves identifying particular events or circumstances relevant to the organization's objectives (risks and opportunities), assessing them in terms of likelihood and magnitude of impact, determining a response strategy, and monitoring progress. By identifying and proactively addressing risks and opportunities,

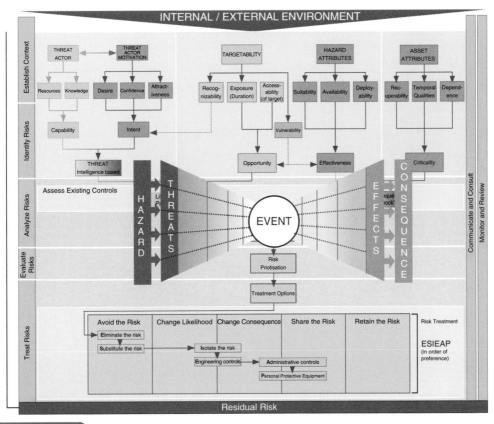

FIGURE 11.6 Alignment of bow-tie with SRMBOK risk management model

business enterprises protect and create value for their stakeholders, which include owners, employees, customers, regulators, and society overall. As such, security risk management is a subset of the broader enterprise risk management function.

11.2 ERM FRAMEWORKS

Organizations by nature manage risks and have a variety of existing specialized departments or functions (risk functions) that identify and manage particular risks. However, each risk function varies in capability and how it coordinates with other risk functions. A central goal and challenge of ERM is improving this capability and coordination while integrating the output to provide a unified picture of risk for stakeholders and improving the organization's ability to manage the risks effectively.

Two early ERM frameworks have been developed by the Risk and Insurance Management Society (RIMS) and the Committee of Sponsoring Organizations of the Treadway Commission (COSO). Each describes an approach for identifying, analyzing, responding to, and monitoring risks or opportunities within the internal and external environment facing the enterprise. Management selects a risk treatment/response strategy for specific risks identified and analyzed, which may include the following:

- **Accept:** no action is taken, due to a cost/benefit decision
- **Avoidance:** exiting the activities giving rise to risk
- **Reduction:** taking action to reduce the likelihood or impact related to the risk
- **Share or insure:** transferring or sharing a portion of the risk, to reduce it

Monitoring is typically performed by management as part of its internal control activities, such as review of analytical reports or management committee meetings with relevant experts, to understand how the risk response strategy is working and whether the objectives are being achieved.

11.2.1 RIMS Risk Maturity Model for Enterprise Risk Management

ERM as defined by RIMS is "the culture, processes and tools to identify strategic opportunities and reduce uncertainty." According to the RIMS Risk Maturity Model for ERM, the following seven core competencies or attributes measure how well ERM is embraced by management and ingrained within the organization. A maturity level is determined for each attribute, and ERM maturity is determined by the weakest link.

- **ERM-based approach**—Degree of executive support for an ERM-based approach within the corporate culture. This goes beyond regulatory compliance across all processes, functions, business lines, roles, and geographies. Degree of integration, communication and coordination of internal audit, information technology, compliance, control, and risk management.

- **ERM process management**—Degree of weaving the ERM process into business processes and using ERM process steps to identify, assess, evaluate, mitigate, and monitor. Degree of incorporating qualitative methods supported by quantitative methods, analysis, tools, and models.

- **Risk appetite management**—Degree of understanding the risk–reward trade-offs within the business. Accountability within leadership and policy to guide decision making and attack gaps between perceived and actual risk. Risk appetite defines the boundary of acceptable risk, and risk tolerance defines the variation of measuring risk appetite that management deems acceptable.

- **Root cause discipline**—Degree of discipline applied to measuring a problem's root cause and binding events with their process sources to drive the reduction of uncertainty, collection of information, and measurement of the controls' effectiveness. The degree of risk from people, external environment, systems, processes, and relationships is explored.

- **Uncovering threat sources and gauging risks**—Degree of quality and penetration coverage of risk assessment activities in documenting risks and opportunities. Degree of collecting knowledge from employee expertise, databases, and other electronic files to uncover dependencies and correlation across the enterprise.

- **Performance management**—Degree of executing vision and strategy, working from financial, customer, business process, and learning and growth perspectives, such as Kaplan's balanced scorecard or similar approach. Degree of exposure to uncertainty or potential deviations from plans or expectations.

- **Business resiliency and sustainability**—Extent to which the ERM process's sustainability aspects are integrated into operational planning. This example includes evaluating how planning supports resiliency and value. The degree of ownership and planning beyond recovering technology platforms. Examples include vendor and distribution dependencies, supply chain disruptions, dramatic market pricing changes, cash flow volatility, and business liquidity.

11.2.2 COSO ERM Framework

The COSO Enterprise Risk Management-Integrated Framework published in 2004 defines ERM as "a process, effected by an entity's board of directors, management, and other personnel, applied in strategy setting and across the enterprise, designed to identify potential events that may affect the entity, and manage risk to be within its risk appetite, to provide reasonable assurance regarding the achievement of entity objectives."

As can be observed from Figure 11.7, the COSO ERM framework has eight components and four objectives categories. It is an expansion of the COSO Internal Control-Integrated Framework published in 1992 and amended in 1994.

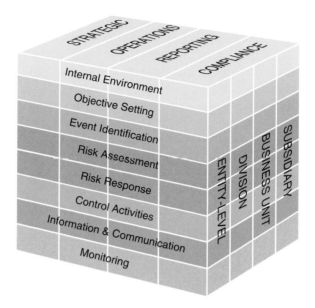

FIGURE 11.7 COSO Enterprise Risk Management Framework

Components	Objectives
• Internal environment • Objective setting • Event identification • Risk assessment • Risk response • Control activities • Information and communication • Monitoring	• Strategy—high-level goals, aligned with and supporting the organization's mission • Operations—effective and efficient use of resources • Financial reporting—reliability of operational and financial reporting • Compliance—compliance with applicable laws and regulations

11.3 IMPLEMENTING AN INTEGRATED ERM PROGRAM

11.3.1 Structuring for Success

Organizational design approaches to risk management vary from centralization at the corporate level or decentralized among divisions or processes, depending on the nature of the risks in question and the organizational preferences of management. Although there is no right way or wrong way to organize, the following principles have emerged:

• Centralized risk management tends to focus on risks that affect the achievement of key corporate objectives and strategies, and significantly affect most if not all functions and processes (for example, organizational reputation).

These risks may be referred to as enterprise-wide risks. Accountability for enterprise-wide risks may reside with the Corporate Executive Officer (CEO) and the board of directors, although responsibility for their management may be dispersed throughout the organization. Other risks that may be managed centrally include those that require specialized skill sets that cannot be duplicated at the division level or those that require partnering or contracting at the corporate level.

- Decentralized risk management pushes the responsibility of risk management to those who live with it day to day. Risks that may be best managed in this way are division or process-level risks, which are those that are significant only within a particular process but nonetheless affect the organization's ability to implement successfully its overall strategies.

- Regardless of whether risks are managed in a centralized or decentralized manner, or with a hybrid of these structures, a new organizational trend is to create ERM program offices and appoint Chief Risk Officers (CROs) who are responsible for developing, advising, and managing enterprise risks.

Experience shows that many leaders believe ERM is important—and potentially a competitive differentiator—but many of them remain largely unable to translate risk information into the action steps that can drive business value. The next section describes a proposed implementation model designed to extend the value enhancement process.

11.3.2 Five Steps to Implementing ERM

For organizations choosing to implement ERM, the following steps provide a simplified view of the task of implementing ERM; the implementation process does not occur overnight. ERM is a journey and these steps provide a practical starting point.[75]

STEP 1: Conduct an enterprise security risk assessment (ESRA)

Using the business strategy as a context, an ESRA identifies and prioritizes the organization's risks and provides quality inputs for purposes of formulating effective risk responses, which include information about the current state of capabilities around managing the priority risks. If an organization has not prioritized its risks, ERM becomes a tough sell because the value proposition can only be generic. Identifying gaps relating to the entity's priority risks provides the basis for improving the specificity of the ERM value proposition. So, avoid endless dialogs about ERM: Get started by conducting an ERA to understand the risks inherent in your business model.

STEP 2: Articulate the ERM vision and value proposition using gaps around the priority risks

This step provides the economic justification for going forward. The ERM vision is a shared view of the role of risk management in the organization and the capabilities needed to manage its key risks. A working group of senior executives should be empowered to:

- Articulate the role of risk management in the organization
- Define relevant goals and objectives for the enterprise as a whole and its business units

To accomplish this task, management needs a reliable fact base grounded in specific capabilities that must be developed to improve risk management performance. This is where a gap analysis becomes handy. To illustrate, view the following steps:

- Begin with prioritizing the critical risks and determine the current state of capabilities around managing those risks. This step is an ERA, as discussed in Step 1. Once the current state of capabilities is determined for each key risk, the desired state is assessed with the objective of identifying gaps and advancing the maturity of risk management capabilities to close those gaps. Risk management capabilities include the policies, processes, competencies, reports, methodologies, and technology required to execute the organization's risk response.
- ERM infrastructure consists of the policies, processes, organizational structure, and reporting in place to instill the appropriate oversight, control, and discipline around continuously improving risk management capabilities. Examples of elements of ERM infrastructure include, among other things, an overall risk management policy, an enterprise-wide risk assessment process, presence of risk management on the board and CEO agenda, a chartered risk committee, clarity of risk management roles and responsibilities, dashboard and other risk reporting, and proprietary tools that portray a portfolio view of risk. Here is the message: The greater the gap between the current state and the desired state of the organization's risk management capabilities, the greater the need for ERM infrastructure to facilitate the advancement of those risk management capabilities over time.

STEP 3: Advance the risk management capabilities of the organization for one or two priority risks

This step focuses the organization on improving its risk management capabilities in an area where management knows improvements are needed. Like any other initiative, ERM must begin somewhere. Many possible starting points are available. Examples include the following:

- Compliance with Sections 404 and 302 of the Sarbanes–Oxley Act
- One or two priority financial or operational risks based on the enterprise-wide risk assessment results (see Step 1), for example, operational risk in a financial institution
- Regulatory compliance risks and/or governance reform issues

- Integration of ERM with the management processes that matter, for example, strategic management, annual business planning, new product launch or channel expansion, quality initiatives, capital expenditure planning, and performance measurement and assessment. Regardless of where an organization begins its journey, the focus of ERM is the same—to advance the maturity of risk management capabilities for the priority business risks.

STEP 4: Evaluate the existing ERM infrastructure capability and develop a strategy to advance it

It takes oversight, control, and discipline to advance the capabilities around managing the critical risks. The policies, processes, organization, and reporting that instill that oversight, control, and discipline is called ERM infrastructure. The purpose of ERM infrastructure is to eliminate significant gaps between the current state and the desired state of the organization's capabilities around managing its key risks. We provided some examples of ERM infrastructure above when discussing Step 2.

Other examples include a common risk language, knowledge sharing of best practices, common training, a chief risk officer or equivalent executive, definition of risk appetite and risk tolerances, integration of risk responses with business plans, and supporting technology. ERM infrastructure facilitates three very important things with respect to ERM implementation. First, it establishes fact-based understanding about the enterprise's risks and risk management capabilities. Second, it ensures there is ownership over the critical risks. Finally, it drives closure of unacceptable gaps. ERM infrastructure is not a one-size-fits-all model. What works for one organization might not work for another. The elements of ERM infrastructure vary according to the techniques and tools deployed to implement ERM, the breadth of the objectives addressed, the organization's culture, and the extent of coverage desired across the organization's operating units. Management should decide the elements of ERM infrastructure needed according to these and other relevant factors.

STEP 5: Advance the risk management capabilities for other key risks

After the first four steps are completed, it will often be necessary to update the ERA for change. Once a refined definition of the priority risks is available, based on the updated ERA, management must determine the current state of the capabilities for managing each risk and then assess the desired state. The objective is the same as with the one or two priority risks addressed in Step 3, that is to advance the maturity of the enterprise's capabilities around managing its key risks. In taking this step, management broadens the enterprise's focus to other priority risks. Improving risk management capabilities is the objective. For each priority risk, management evaluates the relative maturity of the enterprise's capabilities. From there, management needs to make a conscious decision: How much added capability do we need to achieve our performance goals and objectives continually? Improvements in risk management capabilities must be designed and advanced, they must be consistent with the organization's finite resources and management's assessment of the expected costs and benefits. The goal is to identify the organization's most pressing strategic exposures and uncertainties and then to focus the improvement of capabilities for managing them.

The ERM infrastructure management has chosen to put in place drives progress toward this goal. Companies in the early stages of developing their ERM infrastructure often set the foundation with a common language, a risk management oversight structure, and an enterprise-wide risk assessment process. Some companies have applied ERM within specific business units. And a few companies have evolved toward more advanced stages, such as the management of market and credit risks in financial institutions as well as the management of compliance risks in regulated industries. Wherever a company stands with respect to developing its risk management, directors and management would benefit from a dialog around how capable the entity's risk management needs to be with respect to each of its priority risks using the business strategy as a context.

The capability maturity model provides a scale for evaluating the maturity of an organization's risk management capabilities. The model provides five states for rating the process capability, ranging from initial to optimizing. It is a powerful tool for rating the enterprise's capabilities in strategically vital risk areas, identifying gaps based on the level of capability desired in specific areas, and shifting the dialog on operating metrics to incorporate appropriate emphasis on process maturity. The ERM infrastructure ensures that the rating process is fact based and conducted with integrity by the participating risk owners.

11.3.3 Common Challenges in ERM Implementation

Various consulting firms offer suggestions for how to implement an ERM program. Common topics and challenges include the following:

- Identifying executive sponsors for ERM
- Establishing a common risk language or glossary
- Identifying and describing the risks in a risk inventory or risk register
- Implementing a risk-ranking methodology to prioritize risks within and across functions
- Establishing a risk committee and/or CRO to coordinate certain activities of the risk functions
- Establishing ownership for particular risks and responses
- Demonstrating the cost/benefit of the risk management effort
- Developing action plans to ensure the risks are appropriately managed
- Developing consolidated reporting for various stakeholders
- Monitoring the results of actions taken to mitigate risk
- Ensuring efficient risk coverage by internal auditors, consulting teams, and other evaluating entities

11.3.4 ERM Key Success Factors

Organizations evolving toward ERM should keep in mind that it is a journey not a destination. ERM can potentially represent a sea change in organizational behavior, which requires a process of building awareness, developing buy-in, and ultimately driving the acceptance of ownership throughout the entity. Change enablement is, therefore, a significant aspect of an ERM initiative because everyone's perspective about risk varies. To help ensure success, keep in mind the following first principles when implementing ERM:

- Develop a compelling business case that links the ERM agenda to real priority business needs; garner support from the top, and manage progress against milestones over time

- Obtain agreement on risk management objectives and the appropriate ERM infrastructure; consider relevant cultural issues, and focus on enterprise-wide application

- Integrate risk management with the strategy-setting and business planning process and implement early an effective enterprise-wide risk assessment process

- Clarify process ownership issues around who:
  - Makes decisions with respect to the desired risk management capabilities
  - Is responsible for designing the improved capabilities to close significant gaps
  - Monitors progress and performance

- Remember the purpose of ERM infrastructure is to provide the appropriate oversight, control, and discipline around continuously improving risk management capabilities

- Align the ERM framework with criteria against which it is possible to benchmark the organization's ERM capabilities and progress.

Key Questions to Ask

Key questions for board members:

- Does management involve the board timely during the strategy-setting process, including when making decisions to accept or reject risk? For example:
  - Are you satisfied with the substance of the board-level dialogue regarding "risk appetite," i.e., executive management's "view of the world," which drives the organization's strategic choices?
  - Are you confident the company is not taking significant risks without the board's knowledge, e.g., is an operating unit's superior returns relative to its competitors a result of taking significantly greater risks than competitors?
- Does the board understand the priority business risks and how those risks are addressed? Are the risks on a list? Is there sufficient time during board meetings to discuss them?
- Is the board satisfied with the reports it receives?

Key questions for management:

- Do you understand the significant uncertainties or soft spots inherent in your organization's strategies for achieving its business objectives and performance goals? Have you communicated these uncertainties to the board?
- Are you highly confident that your organization is managing all potentially significant business risks? Do you periodically revisit your risk assessments to determine whether changes have occurred?
- Is an effective oversight structure established to:
  - Clarify roles, responsibilities, responsibilities, and accountabilities with respect to risk management?
  - Monitor risk owner performance?
  - Ensure that improvements in risk management capabilities are on schedule?

11.4 SUMMARY OF KEY POINTS

- The fundamental paradigm shift from asset protection to organizational resilience with sustaining capability as the key driver is likely to impact significantly on the way we allocate and prioritize security measure in coming decades.

- Exposure, risk, resources, and quality need to be traded off to achieve an optimal balance.

- Boards or their equivalent structures at the head of organizations need to ensure they have sufficient oversight and knowledge of the respective elements of the organizations Security Risk Management framework to ensure that duty-of-care obligations to shareholders, stakeholders, and employees are adequately met.

- Although SRM resources are focused generally toward asset protection, the fundamental objective of Security Risk Management is better described as "supporting organizational resilience to assist achievement of objectives." In practice, this usually means the protection of assets that support the maintenance of organizational function and capabilities.

- The principles underpinning an effective risk and control assurance framework are in essence standard management practices. Implementation, therefore, does not involve abandoning everything that is currently in place, but rather entails refining and aligning current practices.

- SRM body of knowledge (SRMBOK) approaches SRM from the perspective of a practitioner. Key practice areas are protective security, physical security, information security, information and communications technology security, and people security.

  These practice areas have been selected because:
  - By aligning the junction of practice areas with activity areas, we can establish a holistic view of the security functions and roles of an organization. This framework can assist managers and organizations to conduct a gap

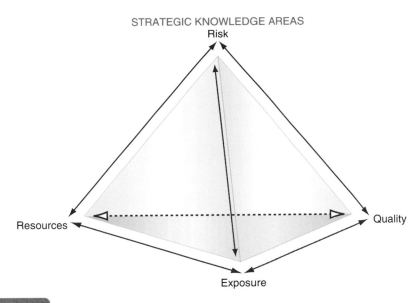

STRATEGIC KNOWLEDGE AREAS

Risk

Resources

Quality

Exposure

FIGURE 11.8 Quadruple constraints of Security Risk Management

analysis to quickly establish which areas they are strong in and where they need to focus efforts (Figure 11.8).

- Assets (property, people, information, and ICT) are defined by their sense of being valued and their role in generating capabilities
- Enablers are simply logical groupings of core organizational capabilities, which can assist organizations to reach their goals—in this case by supporting the application of security systems.

- Properly implemented, Security Risk Management should be integrated as part of broader enterprise risk management activities. ERM can help organizations pursue strategic growth opportunities with greater speed, skill, and confidence by aligning the organization's risk taking with its core competencies and risk appetite. Markets notice strategically focused organizations and will differentiate these organizations by the quality and extent—real or perceived—of their risk management capabilities.

SRM Lexicon 12

This lexicon attempts to set forth definitions of common terminology used in Security Risk Management (SRM). Several terms are shown with multiple definitions where appropriate.

12.1 INTRODUCTION

One key challenge associated with communicating security risks is that the language used is often based on commonly used "plain English" terms and expressions to add clarity. In some respects, this strategy is counter-productive, as everyday languages are an evolving work in progress. Defining the difference among similar terms such as threat, risk, peril, hazard, and vulnerability is an ongoing challenge partly because of an increasing general use of these terms that results in a variety of subtly different applications. This general usage is, on the whole, a benefit to the application of Security Risk Management processes; however, it can result in many potentially confusing definitions.

Other disciplines, such as medicine, have largely overcome this challenge by using static terminology based on Latin and Greek terminology. Although this approach is useful for a highly skilled practitioner, it introduces its own challenges in terms of communicating with the layperson.

Each of these approaches (general language versus static terminology) can work equally well, but for an individual without experience in applying Security Risk Management, either approach can be a source of confusion.

Security Risk Management has evolved from several different disciplines and generally uses terms from common language; however, many lexicons and glossarics exist across the collective discipline of risk management. Accordingly, this lexicon has based terms on these existing documents and attempts to add value by using graphic elements to illustrate the relative linkages and relationships between each.

12.2 ILLUSTRATIONS

The conceptual relationships shown in Figure 12.1 are extracted from Figure 11.3 and are aligned with several other disciplines. Readers are encouraged to consider these graphics within the context of terms provided in the lexicon.

The following models are of course not intended to be the only way of considering these terms and processes, but they may prove useful to many readers when conducting security risk assessments and developing security plans. The relationship of terms and how to apply this framework as well as examples are explored in greater detail throughout the SRM body of knowledge (BOK) but more particularly in a separate Guide to SRMBOK on Security Risk Assessment

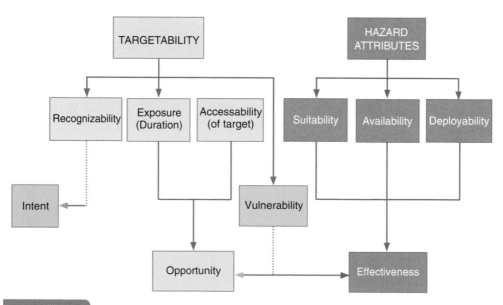

FIGURE 12.1   Relationship of defined terms in vulnerability assessment

and Management, where examples are also provided of how these might be applied to either asset classes or at the enterprise level.

Figure 12.1 highlights some of the complexity and interconnectedness of the many elements of vulnerability assessment. Vulnerability in this figure is shown as a direct function of asset targetability and is an input to both the opportunity that an attacker may have as well as the effectiveness of any particular attack.

The diagram also highlights that the relative attractiveness of a target is an input to an attackers intent. For example, a highly visible petrochemical plant that is beside a main road is likely to provide a more visible/attractive target than one in a remote location. Its attractiveness as a target may also shape the intent of the attacker in terms of whether they choose one target or another, and indeed what they seek to achieve from the attack. Attractiveness in this case is of course from the attacker's perspective. Just how attractive it will be depends on many factors, but it is primarily related to the goals and motivations of the attacker.

Another key point to note is that some elements are binary in nature; that is, they are either there or they are not. For example, a hazard must be suitable, available, and deployable all at the same time if it is to be effective. Nuclear weapons, for example, are highly suitable as terrorist weapons but are difficult to deploy and of very limited availability. Improvised explosive devices based on products such as ammonium nitrate fuel oil (ANFO), however, are suitable, readily available, and easily deployable, which makes them very common for this type of attack.

Similarly, the targetability of an asset is based on the twin attributes of accessibility and exposure. For a hacker seeking to penetrate a commercial database, it must be both accessible in some way, e.g., via a virtual private network, and there must be a level of exposure. Exposure can take many forms, but perhaps the simplest example might be the duration of which the virtual private network gateway is open. If a particular gateway is only open for 3 minutes per day for a routine data transfer, it is obviously more difficult for an attacker to even detect the opening, much less exploit it, than if it is open 24 hours per day.

Figure 12.2 provides a degree of structure and categorization to the generally accepted terms of intent and capability as drivers or measures of threat. This concept is explored in greater detail in the Guide to SRMBOK on Security Risk Assessment and Management, where many matrices are provided at each step to assist SRM professionals to incorporate a level of granularity at each step (if so desired). For example, a 5 × 5 matrix (similar to Figure 6.9) based on resources and knowledge can be a useful tool for prioritizing effort on mitigating the capability of a category or group of offenders. For example, it may be useful as a tool to help prioritize prosecution efforts based on which of two organized crime groups with similar intent actually has the greatest capability.

The criticality of an asset is a function, at least in this model, of three elements. The recoverability of an asset relates to its ability to return to a normal course after an attack (Figure 12.3). The temporal qualities of an asset relate to

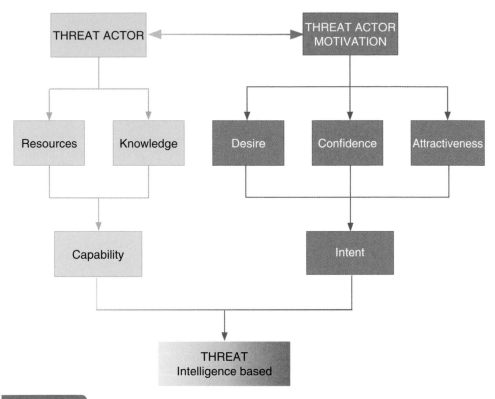

FIGURE 12.2 Relationship of defined terms in threat assessment process

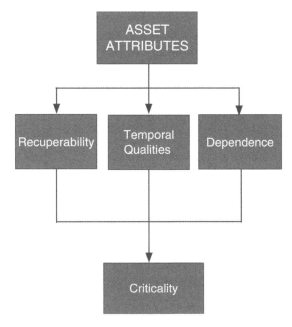

FIGURE 12.3 Relationship of defined terms in criticality assessment

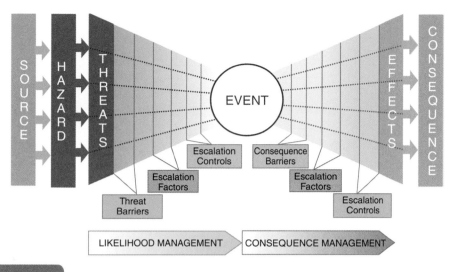

FIGURE 12.4 Relationships of defined terms

its characteristics in time. For example, a building that is likely to be required for 100 years is likely (usually) to be more critical than a big-top circus tent that is only required for 10 days. Similarly, the degree of dependence that is placed on an asset, perhaps related to function, extant dependencies, reputation, or other qualities, will also contribute to an assessment of the criticality of an asset (Figure 12.4).

12.3 NOTES TO READERS

We have endeavored wherever possible to use the most appropriate but succinct existing definitions, which are referenced and acknowledged accordingly.

Where appropriate, we have chosen to adapt or combine existing definitions to create one that we believe is most suitable for security risk management.

Where we believe it of benefit to readers, we have included more than one definition. In this situation, the additional definitions will provide either additional insights or shaping statements to provide context; some definitions may be more useful for readers from different backgrounds or environments. In some instances, we have also included other definitions for completeness where a degree of conflict remains or alternative views surround the term.

In the event that we have provided definitions from several sources, the primary definition that we use when referring to the term throughout SRMBOK is definition number one (1).

12.4 DEFINITIONS

Accessibility (of Target)

The extent to which an asset may be approached by physical or virtual means, such as on foot, in a vehicle, or via a denial of service attack over the Internet.

A highly accessible target, other things being equal, may be more vulnerable to attack than a target that is largely inaccessible (see SRMBOK SRM Process Flow).

See Asset, Attack, Target, and Vulnerability.

Administrative Controls

Administrative controls consist of the policies, procedures, standards, and baselines that make up an organization's security program.

See also Control, Organization.[74]

Admiralty Scale

A rating system for intelligence information based on the quality and validity of the information and its source.[1]

All-Hazards Approach

The principle that controls should be designed and applied in such a way as to deal with all types of threats using the same set of management arrangements to address the mitigation of initial impacts, secondary consequences, and cascading events.

> Note 1: This approach recommends the use of a single set of management and response systems for response to security incidents regardless of their nature or cause.

As Low As Reasonably Practicable (ALARP)

The principle that risks should be treated such that residual risks are as low as reasonably practicable.

> Note: The basis for the ALARP judgment is that the risk should be treated to the point where the cost of more treatment is excessive compared with the resulting reduction in risk, no additional treatment is possible, or the risk is negligible.

Asset

1. People, information, property, or information and communication technologies that are valued or relied on to sustain capabilities.
2. An item or process that an individual, community, or government values and is important to supporting the expectations of those people's, organizations', or governments' outcomes and objectives.[1]

See also Business Continuity, Capability, Organization

Asset Attractiveness

Relates to how the threat source views the asset in terms of the activity that they want to undertake. For example, the attractiveness of an asset to a graffiti vandal, where a major consideration would be that many people see the graffiti, is different to the attractiveness of an asset for a person wanting to commit extortion or sabotage. You would expect the saboteur or extortionist to have a greater understanding of the operation of a facility or asset than the vandal.[1]

Asset Attributes

The qualities of an asset that would help to determine the nature and extent of an impact following an event or incident. These qualities include recoverability (the capacity for an asset to be restored and made functional again), temporal qualities (the speed with which an asset can be restored), and criticality (the importance of the asset to business continuity). See SRMBOK SRM Process Flow.

See also Asset, Criticality, Event, Impact, Incident, Recoverability, Temporal Qualities

Assurance

A process that provides confidence that planned objectives will be achieved within an acceptable degree of residual risk.[75]

See also Residual Risk, Risk

Attack

Deliberate and targeted release of a hazard against an asset, organization, capability, or project.

See also Asset, Capability, Hazard, Organization, Project

Attack Vector

The method or means of attack, e.g. improvised explosive device or social engineering.

Audit and Review

A Security Risk Management exercise conducted across any or all domains of security practice with the objective of establishing (a) opportunities for improvement and (b) compliance with organizational expectations and standards.

See also Organization, Protective Security, Security Risk Management

Availability

The extent to which a threat actor can gain access to a hazard. A hazard that is suitable and deployable may not be effective if a threat actor cannot gain access or ready access to it (see SRMBOK SRM Process Flow).

See also Deployability, Effectiveness, Hazard Attributes, Suitability

Example 2: An assailant breaches the perimeter of a building. Even if security guards intervene before anyone is injured, a breach of a security barrier has occurred.

See also Barriers, Compromise, Controls, Event, Impact

Business Case

A usually documented proposal outlining an intended course of action and identifying costs and benefits. Generally seeks an approval and/or budget allocation.[72]

Business Continuity

The uninterrupted availability of all key resources to support essential business processes.[78]

See also Criticality, Impact, Recoverability, Resources, Temporal Qualities

Business Continuity Management

Business continuity management provides the availability of processes and resources to ensure the continued achievement of critical objectives.[79]

See also Criticality, Impact, Recoverability, Resources, Temporal Qualities

Business Continuity Planning

An interdisciplinary peer mentoring methodology used to create and validate an exercised logistical plan for how an organization will recover and restore partially or completely interrupted critical function(s) within a predetermined time after a disaster or extended disruption.[80]

Business Integration

The integration of sound Security Risk Management principles with the business functions of an organization. Indicators that business integration has occurred may include the following:

- The creation of a senior management position with responsibility for Security Risk Management in the organization
- A direct reporting line from the Security Risk Manager to the Chief Executive Officer (CEO) or head of the organization
- The inclusion of Security Risk Management objectives in performance appraisals for senior managers in the organization
- Evidence of a sound Security Risk Management program

See also Protective Security, Security Risk Management

Business Intelligence

A business management term that refers to applications and technologies, which are used to gather, provide access to, and analyze data and information about their company operations. Business intelligence systems can help companies have a more comprehensive knowledge of the factors that affect their business, such as metrics on sales, production, and internal operations. They can help companies to make better business decisions. Business intelligence should not be confused with competitive intelligence, which is a separate management concept.[81]

See also Competitive Intelligence

Capabilities

1. The ability to apply assets predictably and effectively to execute a specified course of action in support of objectives.
2. The combination of competence, knowledge, skill, resources, systems, and structures necessary to provide the capacity (either implied or demonstrated) to execute a particular course of action and deliver a specified level of performance in pursuit of organizational objectives, now and/or in the future.

See also Business Continuity, Organization

Capability

1. The capacity or ability of a threat actor to implement an attack, i.e., materialize a threat into an event.
2. The ability of a suitably organized, trained, and equipped entity to address, penetrate, or alter systems and/or to disrupt, deny, or destroy all or part of a critical infrastructure.[38]
3. The ability, experience, and knowledge of a person, process, or information to undertake the stated or claimed activity. This is commonly used in relation to the capability of a threat source.[1]

Note: A capability may or may not be accompanied by an intention.

See also Attack, Intent, Threat Actor

Chief Security Officer (CSO)

The highest ranking executive officer within an organization who has responsibility for overall management of security affairs. Usually reports to the most senior manager in an organization (Chief Executive Officer or equivalent).

Collateral Exposure

Is the "exposure arising out of a proximal relationship with the victim of a security breach" or incident.[1]

C3—Command, Control, and Communications

1. In military systems, the capabilities required by commanders to accomplish their assigned missions.
2. The use of communications systems in the exercise of command and control.[82]

Community

A group of people with a commonality of association and generally defined by location, shared experience, or function.[72]

Compartmentalization of Information

A process or policy where access to information is granted to persons who directly need to know certain elements of a larger store of information to perform specific tasks.

See also Isolate within Hierarchy of Controls

Competitive Intelligence

Process of gathering and analyzing information on the external competitive environment.[83]

See also Business Intelligence, Industrial Espionage

Compromise

1. Modification or misuse of assets or capabilities whether deliberate or accidental.
2. Interception, copying, distribution, uncontrolled promulgation, or alteration of information (with or without the knowledge of its custodian).
3. Application of undue influence to an individual that results in a security breach.

   Note 1: May involve consequential loss; however, access to the information (whether altered or not) by the custodian is retained.

   Example 1: Release or misuse of sensitive information.

   Example 2: Compromise of an individual to gain advantage or sabotage organizational assets/capability.

   See also Asset, Capability

Confidence

The extent to which a threat actor believes they have the capacity and competence to achieve a particular objective. Confidence and desire, when combined, equate to intent (see SRMBOK SRM Process Flow).

See also Confidence, Desire, Intent, Threat Actor

Conformance

A compliance approach to monitoring.[1]

Consequence

1. The collective sum of all impacts to the capabilities of an organization(s), including long-term and indirect effects such as combined health, economic, and psychological impacts (see SRMBOK SRM Process Flow).

2. The ultimate and overall organizational "... outcome of an event expressed qualitatively or quantitatively, being a loss, injury, disadvantage or gain. There may be a range of possible outcomes associated with an event".[1]

> Note: In this context, consequence is synonymous with shock as used in the "CARVER + Shock" vulnerability assessment model.

> Example 1: A hacker attack may lead to the loss of data as an impact. The end consequence of the operational, reputation, and administrative burden may result in long-term consequences, such as increased insurance premiums or ultimately the bankruptcy of the organization.

> Example 2: An impact of a bomb attack may include the loss of a life. The overall consequences of this event could include (a) long-term effects on the victim's family and (b) loss of ongoing organizational capabilities if the employer could not replace staff because of lost confidence in their ability to protect staff.

> See also Attack, Event, Impact, Loss, Shock

Consequence and Impact Statement

An evaluation of the consequences of an identified threat occurring and an analysis of the likely impact of those consequences on the asset.

Context

A summary of the key internal and external issues that could influence the risks under examination or decisions about those risks.[1]

> See also Geopolitical Risk, Geo-Strategic Environment, Risk, Transnational and Extra-jurisdictional Risks

Continuous Improvement

Continuous improvement is both a mind-set and a range of techniques to review and evaluate work processes. As a mind-set, it is a way of approaching work so that a culture of innovation and creativity is encouraged. As a range of techniques, continuous improvement includes approaches such as benchmarking, reengineering, quality management, organizational reviews, performance management, and so on.[56] Continuous improvement as a concept reinforces the cyclical nature of quality Security Risk Management.

Controls

1. Process, policy, device, or other action that acts to minimize negative risk or enhance positive opportunities.[1]

2. A process, exercised by an entity's board of directors, management, and other personnel, which is designed to provide reasonable assurance regarding the achievement of objectives.[75]

3. Controls include all existing, proposed, and potential systems, procedures, physical measures, and so on to mitigate risk (Figure 12.6).

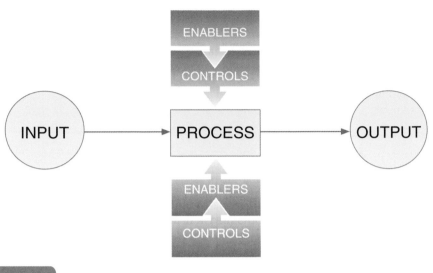

Relationship of controls to enablers in SRM processes

Note 1: They are known as likelihood controls when addressing likelihood management (left-hand side of bow-tie) and consequence controls when addressing consequence management (right-hand side of bow-tie).

Note 2: Countermeasures are a subset of controls that include only those controls that mitigate adverse consequences.

Note 3: Controls may be used to refer to existing or proposed risk treatment measures.

See also Attack, Barrier, Consequence, Control, Hazard, Hierarchy of Controls, Safeguards, Target, Threat

Corporate Governance

A system by which an organization is directed and controlled. Corporate governance activities include direction, executive action, supervision, and accountability.

Countermeasure

1. Individual, discreet, and independent security measures[84] or controls applicable to specified threats.[1]
2. Measures the controls and treatments for risks and/or vulnerability. The four types at the tactical level are as follows:
   - Deterrent controls reduce the likelihood of a deliberate attack.
   - Preventive controls protect vulnerabilitys and make an attack unsuccessful or reduce its impact.
   - Corrective controls reduce the effect of an attack.

- Detective controls discover attacks and trigger preventive or corrective controls.
- Financial controls include insurance and contingent finances.

  Note: Although countermeasures are designed to be applied for specific threats, this does not preclude them from providing protection from additional unspecified or unknown threats (Ref: All Hazards approach).

  See also Control, Risk Treatment Options, Threat

Crime Prevention Through Environmental Design (CPTED)

A multidisciplinary approach to deterring attacks by moderating behavior using strategies that aim to influence the offender decisions that precede criminal acts.

  Note1: This approach is typically applied to the built environment (physical security); however, the concept has much to offer other practice areas.

Critical Incident Management

The policies, plans, structures, and processes by which the response to abnormal conditions is commanded, coordinated, and controlled.[1]

Critical Infrastructure

Infrastructure that, if destroyed, degraded, or rendered unavailable for an extended period will impact on social or economic well-being or affect national security or defense.[1]

  See also Asset Attributes, Consequence, Criticality, Impact

Critical IT and Communications Infrastructure

Information technologies and communication networks that, if destroyed, degraded, or rendered unavailable for an extended period would significantly impact on the operations of an organization.

Criticality

1. The extent to which an asset, or a component part of an asset, is essential to supporting organizational capabilities (see SRMBOK SRM Process Flow).
2. The importance or dependence that an organization has on a person, function, process, item, or infrastructure or specific facility.[1]

  See also Asset, Business Continuity, Recoverability

Current Risk

Risk rating (consequence and likelihood) of a risk event when considered with existing controls in place (Figure 12.7).

  Note: Current risk will vary dynamically based on the application of controls and any variations in exposure, whether created by internal organizational activities,

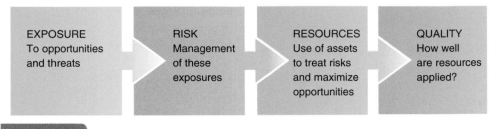

| EXPOSURE To opportunities and threats | RISK Management of these exposures | RESOURCES Use of assets to treat risks and maximize opportunities | QUALITY How well are resources applied? |

FIGURE 12.7 Relationship of exposure, current risk, and residual risk

e.g., new project or additional travel, or by the external environment, e.g., transnational security issues or political changes.

See also Control, Impact, Likelihood, Risk

Customer

An individual, organization, or other body that derives a benefit from an asset. Customers may be internal or external.[1]

Decision Making

The process by which information is analyzed, options formulated, and a preferred option(s) identified for subsequent action. Typically decision making is informed (makes use of available information) or uninformed (makes use of gut feel).[1]

Deployability

The extent to which a hazard may be moved to a position from which an effective attack may be launched on a target (see SRMBOK SRM Process Flow).

See also Attack, Hazard, Target

Design Basis Threat (DBT)

1. A threat against which an asset must be protected and on which the protective system's design is based. It is the baseline type and size of threat that buildings or other structures are designed to withstand. The design basis threat includes the tactics aggressors will use against the asset as well as the tools, weapons, and explosives employed in these tactics.

2. The assumed threat or design basis for establishing security specifications and systems. This threat is usually the most likely credible realistic threat—not just the worst-case scenario.

   Example: Part of the physical DBT for an office building in a major city might include protection against a 120-kg vehicle-borne improvised explosive device (IED). Although a worst-case scenario might involve a nuclear attack, it is neither a credible threat nor cost/effective to defend against nuclear attack. Nor is such a threat likely (for most organizations) to be a practical benchmark for the construction of threat barriers.

See also Context, Threat.

Desire

The extent to which a threat actor wishes to achieve a particular goal, such as an attack on an asset. Desire and confidence are subsets of threat actor motivation; when combined, they represent the intent of a threat actor to undertake an activity such as an attack.

Example: A threat actor may be driven by the desire to overthrow an incumbent government. This overarching motivation needs to be considered in light of the immediate intent before the actual threat can be established. In practice, the threat actor is likely to manifest such a long-term motivation in a range of short-term intents, which include the desire to use deadly force such as bomb attacks to raise their profile in the media.

See also Asset, Attack, Confidence, Threat Actor, Threat Actor Motivation

Dynamic Pressures

Social, community, market, and organizational forces that act on root causes that allow or increase their potential to become threats or hazards.[1]

Effect

1. Any impact on assets, objectives, or outcomes whether, adverse or beneficial, whole or in part, that result (in this context) from a security event or incident.
2. The outcome following the occurrence of an event.[1]

Note: Impact is the (relatively) immediate short-term result of an event or incident with relatively little if any effect on organizational capabilities. The collective and ultimate result of the impact(s) that results in an effect on organizational capabilities is defined as a consequence.

Example: Loss of revenue, injury to personnel, increased costs, diversion of resources, timing of activities, damage to environment.

See also Asset, Asset Attributes, Consequence, Criticality, Effectiveness, Incident, Recoverability, and Temporal Qualities

Effectiveness

1. Ability of a hazard to be employed in a manner that achieves the objectives of a threat actor when released against an asset, organization, or capability.
2. The collective indication of hazard attributes (suitability, availability, and deployability) in light of the vulnerability of a targeted asset.

See also Asset, Attack, Capability, Hazard, Hazard Attributes, Target, Threat, Threat Actor, Vulnerability

Emergency

An event, actual or imminent, that endangers or threatens to endanger life, property, or the environment, and that requires a significant and coordinated response.[65]

Emergency Management

1. The organization and management of resources and responsibilities for dealing with all aspects of emergencies, in particularly preparedness, response, and rehabilitation. Emergency management involves plans, structures, and arrangements established to engage the normal endeavors of government, voluntary, and private agencies in a comprehensive and coordinated way to respond to the whole spectrum of emergency needs. This strategy is also known as disaster management.[85]

2. A range of measures designed to manage risks from disasters and emergencies. It involves developing and maintaining arrangements to prevent or mitigate, prepare for, respond to, and recover from emergencies and disasters.

See also Asset Attributes, Criticality, Pandemic, Protective Security, Recoverability, Temporal Qualities

Emergency Risk Management

Risk management associated with low probability, extreme consequence events.

Engineering Controls

Engineering controls help reduce exposure to potential hazards either by isolating the hazard or by removing it from the work environment. Engineering controls include mechanical ventilation and process enclosure. They are important because they are built into the work process.[86]

Controls that isolate or remove the blood borne pathogens hazard from the workplace. Examples include needle-less devices, shielded needle devices, blunt needles, and plastic capillary tubes.[87]

Safety devices that reduce the size of minimum separation distances. Such devices include sandbags, earth berms, and aluminum shields.[88]

See also Control, Hazard, Physical Security, Risk Treatment Options

Enterprise Security Risk Management

An enterprise (or company) is comprised of all the establishments that operate under the ownership or control of a single organization. An enterprise may be a business, service, or membership organization; it may consist of one or several establishments and operate at one or several locations.[89]

Enterprise Security Risk Management is Security Risk Management that covers an entire enterprise, as opposed to particular business units within an enterprise. For example, a multinational resources company may have an enterprise Security Risk Management plan that covers all of its business units, in every country in which it operates. The same company may have Security Risk Management plans for specific business units and specific facilities, which reflect the environment within which these units operate.

See also Security in Depth, Security Risk Assessment, Security Risk Assessment – Asset and Project Based, Security Risk Assessment – Enterprise, Security Risk Management, Security Risk Management System

Environmental Security

1. The security that is inherent in the physical surroundings in which a facility or functional unit is located, such as on ships, on aircraft, and in underground vaults, where locations by their nature provide a certain amount of protection against exploitation of compromising emanation even before other protective measures are implemented.[91]

2. The application of electrical, acoustic, physical, and other safeguards to an area to minimize the risk of unauthorized interception of information from the area.[91]

3. Protection of the natural environment.

4. Protection of assets from man-made threats that result from deterioration of the natural environment, e.g., people trafficking or civil unrest associated with deforestation, global warming, and so on.

See also Security in Depth, Security Risk Assessment, Security Risk Assessment – Asset and Project Based, Security Risk Assessment – Enterprise, Security Risk Management, Security Risk Management System

Escalation Control

A protective measure recommended or in place to prevent a threat from increasing the risk caused by loss or failure of threat barriers/controls. These may be hardware, e.g. secondary blast walls, but will generally be procedural barriers, e.g., maintenance, audit.

See also Barrier, Bow-Tie, Consequence, Control, Escalation Factors, Hazard, Recoverability, Threat

Escalation Factors

Conditions that lead to increased risk caused by loss or failure of barriers or controls, e.g., inadequate maintenance, fatigue, or failure to audit or inspection treatments or controls.

See also Barrier, Bow-Tie, Consequence, Control, Escalation Factors, Hazard, Recoverability, Threat

Evaluation Criteria

Criteria such as risk consequence and likelihood levels that are used to determine risk tolerance, appetite, and the need to treat or not.[91]

Event

1. Occurrence of a particular set of circumstances.[92]
2. The key activity that must occur to have an impact on assets (for example, explosion, theft, hacker attack).

   Note 1: In the security context, this will normally mean any occurrence that has potential to cause personal injury, disease or death, or property damage. Event is used to refer to both potential (eg. hypothetical occurrences) and actual occurrences (eg. incidents).

   Note 2: An out-of-course event is any event that is not part of the normal circumstances under which the organization functions, or does not usually occur when the organization is functioning.[93]

   See also Consequence, Criticality, Impact, Incident, Probability, Recoverability

Events and Mass Gatherings

See Special Events and Mass Gatherings.

Expected Loss or Expected Value Approach

The evaluation of risk based on the dollar variation that results as a consequence of the risky events.

Typically calculated using probability expressed as a percentage multiplied by the likely cost. For example, a retailer may consider, perhaps based on historical records, that they have a 90% probability of losing $10,000 to shoplifters in any given year and a 10% probability of having $50,000 worth of goods shoplifted. The resultant formula may look like:

$(0.9 \times \$10,000) + (0.1 \times \$50,000) = \$14,000$ ($9,000 + $5,000) as an expected loss for the year.

See also Consequence, Return on Security Investment

Explosive

A chemical composition where the chemical bonds can be relatively easily broken, which causes the material to become a gas. What differentiates an explosive is the rate at which the change from solid/liquid to gas occurs. In a fire, the solid material is converted to gas at a very slow rate; in an explosion, the rate of change is measured in terms of thousands of meters per second.

Exposure

The time frame (in terms of both duration and frequency) in which an asset is exposed to potential threats or opportunities. This will influence:

1. The degree to which a resource is open to, or attracts, these threats or opportunities,[94]
2. The plausible maximum consequence that develops from a risk without regard to controls, and[94]

3. The susceptibility to gain or loss from a particular event.

> Note: Exposure is a function of the entity's interaction with the prevailing environment, whereas the actual level of risk will be determined by their vulnerability, susceptibility, accessibility, or time in that environment (duration and frequency), as well as the quality and resourcing of controls.

> Example 1: Exposure may be increased if an employee increases his or her frequency of business travel. In practice, this may increase risk by increasing the likelihood. It is not, however, automatically synonymous with risk as the organization may increase resources applied to protect that person or improve the effectiveness (quality) of existing controls, which thereby results in a lower overall risk.

> Example 2: Exposure may also vary by increasing or decreasing either the duration (days, weeks, months) or the opening hours of a nightclub, festival, or sporting event. In the former example, the risk may be unchanged—until one introduces the concept of duration, which considers whether we are concerned about the risk during 1 day or the risk of an incident anytime in the next 10 years.

See also Exposure Timeframe, Frequency, Impact, Likelihood, Probability, Risk, Risk Rating and Figure 12.7, Relationship of Exposure, Current Risk and Residual Risk

Facility

Any physical infrastructure.[1]

Frequency

Frequency refers to the expected number of times a task is actually conducted, e.g., travel, trade shows, or the application of threat barriers (such as security patrols).

See also Accessibility of Target, Asset Targetability, Exposure (Duration), Likelihood, Probability, Recognizability, Risk

Functional Design

A formal documentation of a proposed system's capabilities, processing methods, and points of integration that serves as the basis for approval and work initiation.[95]

See also Information Security, Physical Security

Geopolitical Risk

Those aspects of the geostrategic environment that present the chance of something happening that will have an impact on objectives. These aspects may include indirect influences and effects (such as a feeling of insecurity on the part of a population following a high-profile terrorist incident in a foreign country), or more direct risks (such as a disruption to an organization's supply chain following a terrorist incident in a foreign country).

See also Geo-Strategic Environment, Maritime Security, Pandemic, Transnational and Extra-Jurisdictional Risks

Geostrategic Environment

The broad, transnational environment within which an organization operates, and that includes regional and international economic, environmental, political, security, jurisdictional, and social influences. These influences are relevant to an organization because they represent the external environment within which an organization operates.

See also Maritime Security, Pandemic, Transnational, and Extrajurisdictional Risks.

Harm

The environmental, physical, emotional, economic, social, political, and other intangible consequences that could result from a real or potential occurrence of the security threat being considered.[1]

Hazard

1. Something that has the potential to impact (ie. cause harm) an asset adversely if not controlled or if deliberately released or applied, e.g., explosives, biohazards, flammable liquids, firearms, Trojan, virus, and.

2. An object or "situation with a potential for harm in terms of human injury or ill-health, damage to property, damage to the environment, or a combination of these" or other assets (Figure 12.8).[96]

   Note: Although a hazard is by its nature inherently dangerous, normal management practices are usually sufficient to ensure that it is not released against organizational assets. In the Security Risk Management context, it will normally require the intervention of a Source or Threat Actor to deploy it in such a way as to cause harm or create an out-of-course event.

   See also Availability, Bow-tie, Consequence, Deployability, Effectiveness, Event, Hazard, Impact, Opportunity, Suitability.

Hazard Attributes

In the SRM Process, hazard attributes are comprised of suitability, availability and deployability. When combined, these attributes equate to the effectiveness of a hazard.

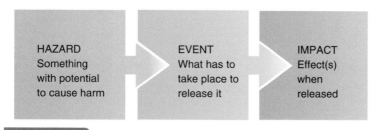

FIGURE 12.8 Relationship of hazard, event and impact

Example: In the context of a weapon, fertilizer-based improvised explosive devices are highly suitable, deployable, and available. Improvised nuclear devices by comparison might be considered to be highly suitable, moderately deployable, but unavailable.

See also Availability, Consequence, Deployability, Effectiveness, Event, Hazard, Impact, Opportunity, Suitability

Hierarchy of Controls (HOC)

The hierarchy of controls is a term which refers to using the most effective means possible to control hazards in priority order starting with (i) the most effective measures that eliminate hazards to (vi) the least satisfactory that achieve only limited protection.

Abbreviated as ESIEAP the order of effectiveness to control hazards is as follows:

- Eliminate the risk, eg. cease conducting the activity
- Substitute the risk for a lower risk using a different product or process
- Isolate the asset from harm
- Engineering controls to protect against the hazard, e.g., boom gates
- Administrative controls using training, policy, rosters, and so on to change how work is done
- Protect the asset, e.g., personal protective equipment (PPE) such as gloves, helmets and vests

See also Administrative Controls, Asset, Control, Hazard

Hoax

An item or threat that does not actually represent a hazard. Appropriate and practiced bomb threat analysis and unattended item procedures will help in determining whether an item or threat represents a hazard. If an item is thought to be suspicious, it is usually beyond the capability of an organization to determine whether the contents are live explosives or hoax material. This analysis will be conducted by the investigating emergency services who will examine the contents after the item has been dismantled. The term "hoax" should not be used until after the incident is concluded and the summary report has been promulgated.

Home-Based Work

An agency may approve or authorize an employee to carry out his or her duties while based at his or her place of residence.[97]

See also Compromise, Personnel, Physical Security, Protective Security Review, Security in Depth

Human Factors

Study of interfaces between humans, their environment, and technology. In particular, how humans interact physically and psychologically in relation to particular environments, activities, or systems, which include reactions and preferences with respect to sensory stimuli.

Human Security

1. Protection of communities and individuals from internal political violence.[98]
2. The complex of interrelated threats associated with civil war, genocide, and the displacement of populations.

   Note 1: Whereas national security focuses on the defense of the state from external attack, and people security focuses on the protection of individuals from other individuals, human security is about protecting individuals and communities from any form of political violence.

   Note 2: The UNDP's 1994 Human Development Report's definition of human security includes threats in the areas of economic security, food security, health security, environmental security, personal security, community security, and political security.

   See also Personal Protective Practices, People

Iconic Status

A position of significant prestige, esteem, and widespread recognition of an entity as being unique.

Impact

See Consequence

Implementation Management

1. Management of the process of taking a change and making it a permanent part of the system. A change may be tested first and then implemented throughout the organization.[99]
2. The mechanisms, competencies, relations, or skills developed to influence, supervise, monitor, or automate the process as well as the results of policy execution.[100]

   See also Project, Protective Security Review, Treatments, Vulnerability Analysis

Improvised Explosive Device (IED)

A device fabricated in an adhoc manner that contains explosive components designed to, or capable of, causing unlawful injury or damage.[101]

Incident

1. Any unplanned event resulting in, or having a potential for, injury, ill health, damage, or other loss.[96]

2. Any event that has actually occurred and has actually resulted in an impact (for example, injury, death, theft, property damage).

   Note 1: An incident must occur before consequences are realized in any meaningful form.

   Note 2: An incident is a breach that results in impact(s) and/or consequence(s).

   See also Breach, Event, Near-Miss Incident

Incident Reporting

Reporting, analysis, and data management associated with security incidents.

Industrial Espionage

Unlawful espionage conducted for commercial purposes, as distinct from national security purposes. The term is distinct from legal and ethical activities, such as examining corporate publications, websites, patent filings, and the like to determine the activities of a corporation (this is normally referred to as competitive intelligence). Instead, it describes unethical or illegal activities, such as theft of trade secrets, bribery, blackmail, technological surveillance, and even occasional violence. As well as spying on commercial organizations, governments can also be targets of commercial espionage, e.g., to determine the terms of a tender for a government contract so that another tenderer can underbid.[102]

See also Business Intelligence, Competitive Intelligence

Information

1. Data that have been processed and presented in a form suitable for human interpretation, often with the purpose of revealing trends or patterns.[103]
2. Information is the result of processing, manipulating, and organizing data in a way that adds to the knowledge of the person receiving it.[104]

   See also Information System, Knowledge

Information and Communications Technologies (ICT)

Those elements at the confluence of information and communications whether physical, conceptual, or electronic.

   Examples: Physical (e.g., routers, phone scramblers) conceptual (e.g., software, encryption algorithms) or electronic (e.g., radio waves, photon transfer).

Information Security

1. The adoption of measures to prevent the unauthorized use, misuse, modification, or denial of use of information, knowledge, facts, data, or capabilities.
2. That part of security concerned with the protection of confidentiality, integrity, and availability of information assets. Information security requires a combination of safeguards from errors, unauthorized data access, and replication

and equipment failures in addition to backup and recovery procedures as well as physical security.

See also Compromise, Information, Information System, Knowledge, Personnel Security, Physical Security

Information Systems

1. A system for managing and processing information, usually computer based.
2. A functional group within a business that manages the development and operations of the organization's information.[105]

See also Information, Knowledge, Organization

Information Transfer

The manner in which information is transferred from one party to another.

> Note: Typically in communications, these transfers are viewed seen as push (information dispersal), pull (information gathering), or push-pull (dialog).[1]

Insurance

1. Promise of reimbursement in the case of loss; paid to people or companies so concerned about hazards that they have made prepayments to an insurance company.
2. Policy: written contract or certificate of insurance; "you should have read the small print on your policy."
3. Indemnity: protection against future loss.[106]

See also Frequency, Loss, Probability, Risk

Intellectual Property (IP)

1. A creation of the intellect that has commercial value, including copyrighted property such as literary or artistic works, and ideational property, such as patents, appellations of origin, business methods, and industrial processes.[107]
2. Intellectual property represents the property of your mind or intellect. In business terms, this term also means your proprietary knowledge.[108]

See also Asset, Compromise, Information, Information Security, Intruder, Knowledge

Intelligence

The value-added output that develops from the activities of the collection, evaluation, analysis, integration, interpretation, and dissemination of available information, which is pertinent to an organizations decision-making processes.

A body of evidence and the conclusions drawn that is acquired and furnished in response to the known or perceived requirements of consumers. It is often derived from information that is concealed or not intended to be available for use by the acquirer.[109]

Intent

1. The intended immediate outcome of an attack.
2. The confidence to carry out the stated or postured claim as well as the desire to carry out the action or activities. The outcome following the occurrence of an event.[1]

> Example: The overall motivation behind an attack may be to achieve political control of a country. The intent of an attack, however, may be to inflict damage on infrastructure and inflict casualties that will embarrass the incumbent government and/or create civil unrest.

See also Attack, Capability, Confidence, Desire, Motivation, Threat, Threat Actor, Threat Actor Motivation

Interdependency

The nature of a relationship between two parties.[1]

Intruder

Person(s) (offenders) who deliberately enter the organization (or data systems) without authorization, whether physically or electronically.

See also Trespasser

Investigations

An examination or enquiry into something, especially a detailed one that is undertaken officially.[110]

See also Compromise, Event, Incident, Intruder, Protective Security Review, Trespasser

Key Control

Controls or groups of controls that are believed to be maintaining an otherwise intolerable risk at a tolerable level.

Adequacy of risk management, control, and governance processes is present if management has planned and designed them in a manner that provides reasonable assurance that the organization's objectives and goals will be achieved efficiently and economically.

The effectiveness of risk management, control, and governance processes is present if processes are operating in a manner that provides reasonable assurance that the organization's objectives and goals will be achieved.[111]

Key Points

Locations (physical or virtual) of equipment or systems that are vital to continuing essential operations and would be difficult to replace or repair readily.

Includes where material of a highly classified, vital, or valuable nature is stored or used. Often identified through a formal business impact analysis.

See also Business Continuity, Hazard, Impact

Knowledge

1. General awareness or possession of information, facts, ideas, truths, or principles.[110]
2. In the SRM process, one of the attributes of a threat actor, the other is resources. A threat actor's knowledge and resources combine to establish a capability.

See also Capability, Knowledge, Resources, Threat Actor, Threat Actor Attributes

Likelihood

1. Used as a general description of probability or frequency.[112]
2. The qualitative of semiquantitative assessment or estimation of whether an event will occur, i.e., the most credible expected frequency of an event occurring.
3. Unless otherwise defined in a particular risk assessment, the default use of this word shall be applied as applying either over the course of 1 year or the life of the project, whichever is the lesser.

Note 1: To be most effective, likelihood needs to be defined across a specific scope such as a period of time, e.g., 6 hours, 10 days or 2 years, or number/frequency of events, e.g., per 100 times the activity is performed.

Note 2: In a security context likelihood is often assessed by using intelligence, review of incident reports and/or threat assessment (TA).

See also Event, Frequency, Incident, Risk, Suitability

Likelihood of Occurrence

An assessment based on, in the case of natural disaster, historical occurrences or in the case of human or manufactured threats, intent and capability analysis.

Loss

1. Any negative consequence or adverse effect, financial or otherwise.[112]
2. Removal or denial of utility of an item from an organization (whether temporary or permanent, critical or noncritical) including loss of data integrity by modification or destruction, theft of equipment, delays or denials of service, or loss of life.

Note: Loss can be measured and expressed as a physical entity or asset, or as a reduction of quality.

See also Consequence, Hazard, Impact, Peril

Mail Bomb

An explosive or incendiary device sent through postal or courier systems. As the delivery, identification, assessment, and response options differ from bombs placed on the site by an offender, they have different risk mitigation considerations.

Maritime Security

Maritime security is concerned with the prevention of intentional damage through sabotage, subversion, or terrorism. Maritime security activities include the following:

- Port security
- Vessel security
- Facility security[113]

See also Asset, Attack, Aviation Security, Hazard, Protective Security

Mass Transit Security

Protective security with a particular focus on the issues and challenges posed by mass transit systems, which can include confined spaces that are difficult for responding emergency services agencies to access, as well as mass casualties following an attack on patrons of the mass transit system.

See also Asset, Attack, Hazard, Protective Security, Travel Security

Mixed Access Areas

1. Areas within an organization or facility that may be accessed by members of the public and by personnel working with or for the organization.
2. Areas within an organization or facility that may be accessed by personnel that have different levels of access privileges.

See also Asset, Intruder, Organization, Personnel, Threat Actor

Model

A representation of a set of components of a process, system, or subject area, generally developed for understanding, analysis, improvement, and/or replacement of the process. A representation of information, activities, relationships, and constraints.

Near-Miss Incident (NMI)

1. An incident that, but for separation in time or space, could or would have involved personnel or assets of the organization or community in question. This type of information is particularly useful when building threat profiles or analyzing risks.
2. An incident that did not result in an impact; however, it would be likely to have in other circumstances. If it were not for some separation in time or space,

the NMI could or would have involved an impact on function, capability, or assets.

NMI reporting and analysis is particularly useful when building threat profiles or analyzing risks.

Example: A bomb attack at a shopping center that a staff member had visited 30 minutes before the blast occurred. In this instance, no impact occurred on the individual or organization; however, only a 30-minute window of time separated the person from injury. Reporting and analysis of this information may be useful to assist with optimization of resources for future protection.

See also Asset, Capability, Event, Impact, Incident, Threat

Offender

Individual or group that causes negative consequences by deliberate breach of security.

See also Intruder, Threat Actor, Trespasser

Opportunity

1. A chance, especially one that offers some kind of advantage.[110]

2. An uncertain event with a positive probable consequence. Related to risk.

See also Probability, Risk[114]

Organization

1. A group of people and facilities with an arrangement or responsibilities, authorities, and relationships.[112]

2. A company, corporation, firm, enterprise, institution, or other legal entity or part thereof, whether incorporated or not, public or private, that has its own function(s) and administration.[96]

See also Asset, Personnel

Organizational Experience

The level of extant corporate knowledge pertinent to the successful management of a particular risk.

Organizational Flexibility

The ability of an organization to respond positively to identified risks and ensure an accepted level of business continuity should a risk materialize.

Organizational Fragility

The level of residual strength or resilience of an organization's financial physical or intellectual resource base should an identified risk materialize.

Pandemic

Existing in the form of a widespread epidemic that affects people in many different countries.[110]

People

Unless otherwise stated, the term is used generically to apply to all categories of humanity.

See also Personnel, Human Security

People Security

1. Those elements of security associated with protection of humans (usually in groups).
2. Those elements of security where human(s) are the key element in applying or breaching security.

See also Human Security

Perception

1. An individual's interpretation of sensory information received.[1]
2. The process of selecting, acquiring, interpreting, analyzing, and organizing sensory information.[1]

Peril

Cause of loss.[115]

See also Hazard, Impact, Loss

Personal Protective Equipment (PPE)

1. Equipment worn by people as a barrier between themselves and the hazard(s).[96]
2. Protective clothing, helmets, goggles, or other gear designed to protect the wearer's body or clothing from injury by electrical hazards, heat, chemicals, and infection, for job-related occupational safety and health purposes, as well as in sports, martial arts, and combat. Personal armor is combat-specialized protective gear.[116]

See also Barrier, Hazard, Hierarchy of Control, Protective Equipment, Security-in-Depth

Personal Protective Practices (PPP)

Those security measures that are within the scope and control of an individual and are intended to protect themselves or others from physical violence, theft, predatory behavior, and the loss or anxiety associated with them.

See also People Security, Travel Security

Personnel

1. Unless otherwise stated, the term is used generically to apply to all persons within a particular community/organization being considered, whether they are staff or contractor, and it may also apply in some circumstances to other categories of personnel that the organization has a prevailing influence over or responsibility for (for example, visitor or conference delegate).

2. The people employed in an organization, business, or armed force.[110]

See also Organization, People

Personnel Security

1. That part of security concerned with the assessing and vetting personnel whether preemployment or for managing their clearances/authorization to classified material.

2. The process of maintaining the integrity of information held about those personnel.

See also Personnel, Protective Security

Physical Security

1. The part of protective security concerned with the provision and maintenance of a safe and secure environment for the protection of agency employees and clients, as well as physical measures designed to prevent unauthorized access to official resources and to detect and respond to intruders.[97]

2. That part of security concerned with physical measures designed to:
   - Safeguard assets and personnel
   - Prevent unauthorized access to equipment, facilities, material, and documents
   - Safeguard them against espionage, sabotage, damage, and theft

See also Assets, Personnel, Protective Security

Piracy

The taking and using of copyright or patented material without the legal right to do so.[110]

See also Compromise, Information and Intellectual Property

Post Blast

If a bomb explodes, that is, a risk is realized, then damage and possibly injuries will result. The site will probably be a crime scene, and business continuity/resumption, staff support, and related business plans will be implemented.[t]

---

[t] The Australian Bomb Data Center defines a bombing as "An incident involving the use of one or more improvised explosive devices (IED) which has functioned. Military explosive ordnance which may not be improvised but which has been used in an illegal manner is also included in this definition." http://www.afp.gov.au/services/operational/abdc/abdc_incident_types.

Probability

A measure of the chance of an occurrence expressed as a number between 0 and 1.[112]

Statistical or quantitative assessment of the frequency with which an event might occur. Often used interchangeably with likelihood.

See also Event, Frequency, Incident, Likelihood

Protective Equipment

Equipment used as the final barrier between assets and hazard(s).

> Note: This might include PPE such as helmets, goggles, or body armor, as well as nonpersonal protective equipment for protecting assets, such as hardened pick-resistant briefcases (classified information), strongboxes (cash in transit), or cable locks (laptops).

See also Hierarchy of Controls (HOC), Personal Protective Equipment (PPE)

Protective Security

1. Blanket term applied to all elements of Security Risk Management that are used to protect assets, functions, capability, or continuity principally involving the conceptual/virtual frameworks, philosophies, and activities that can be used to protect assets of any type.

2. The total concept of measures, concepts, and systems applied across information, people, physical, and information and communications technology security.

See also Asset, Capability, Continuity, Security Risk Management

Protective Security Review (PSR)

Review of existing security measures whether by physical inspection or examination of records, procedures, and systems (such as a site security review).

See also Risk Rating, Risk Prioritization, Risk Treatment Options, Security Risk Management

Quality

The degree to which a set of inherent characteristics fulfills requirements.[117]

RAG Modeling

Restricted access group or "RAG modeling" refers to the practice of grouping and managing access in three main categories as follows:

1. Restricted access areas for managers and members of staff (trusted individuals)

2. Accompanied access areas where visitors and trusted individuals are permitted under controlled circumstances, such as under escort

3. Group access areas where access is relatively uncontrolled, such as parks and other public areas

It is can also be illustrated on site maps, induction manuals, or in document file covers using red, amber, and green colors.

Recognizability

1. One aspect of asset targetability (the others being exposure and accessibility).

2. An asset may be part of a nation's critical infrastructure, or it may be critical to the business continuity of an organization, but if this status is not apparent to potential threat actors, then the asset may be less likely to be targeted.

3. Certain assets are deemed to have iconic status. Damage to or destruction of these assets could potentially have a significant psychological impact on a nation's population. The damage or destruction of certain assets could even have an international impact.

For example, the destruction of water supply infrastructure might have a critical impact on a country's economy; however, it may not be less obvious or recognizable as a target of attack compared with a landmark building located in a central business district location.

See also Accessibility (of target), Asset, Asset Targetability, Business Continuity, Exposure (duration), Impact, Threat Actor

Recommendations

Recommendations will usually follow on from security review findings, and when approved they will lead to implementation of treatments. The quality and comprehensiveness of recommendations should be considered by how well they address the following 4 As:

- **Actionable**—Is it clear what to do?
- **Achievable**—How will you know when you have done it? What are the metrics to define success?
- **Appropriate**—Does it address the cause rather than the condition? Is it aligned with organizational objectives?
- **Agreed**—Do all the members of the review team support this? Will it be palatable to stakeholders and achievable by budget holders?

An example is shown in Figure 12.9.

See also Security Review Findings, Risk Prioritization, Risk Rating, Risk Treatment Options

Recoverability

1. Ability to restore capabilities or assets in timely, cost-effective fashion after an attack.

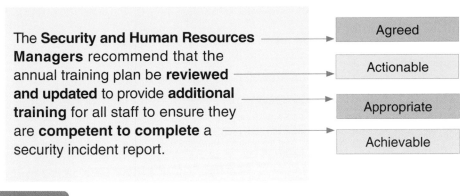

The **Security and Human Resources Managers** recommend that the annual training plan be **reviewed and updated** to provide **additional training** for all staff to ensure they are **competent to complete** a security incident report.

- Agreed
- Actionable
- Appropriate
- Achievable

FIGURE 12.9 Example recommendation

Example: It may be possible to replace a damaged plant and equipment relatively quickly, but personnel with specialist knowledge may be challenging to heal or replace in timely fashion (if at all).

One attribute of an asset, in the SRMBOK SRM Process Flow (the others being temporal qualities and criticality), which refers to the capacity of an asset to be restored to a functional state in a timely and cost-effective manner.

See also Asset, Asset Attributes, Business Continuity, Criticality, Impact, Temporal Qualities

Red Team

1. The process and/or group(s) associated with assessing vulnerabilities and limitations of security measures, structures, or asset protection systems from an attacker's perspective.

2. In vulnerability assessments and exercises, "red teaming" refers to the work performed to provide an adversarial perspective, especially when this perspective includes plausible tactics, techniques, and procedures (TTPs) as well as realistic policy and doctrine.

   Noun: Group of subject matter experts and stakeholders brought together for the purposes of brainstorming, identifying, and analyzing possible threat scenarios and controls predominantly from an adversarial perspective.

   Verb: Process of analyzing and documenting vulnerabilities, controls, and treatments within a defined scope.

   See also Vulnerability

Residual Exposure

The total plausible maximum consequence that develops from a risk after proposed controls are put in place.

See also Control, Impact, Organization, Risk, Residual Risk

Residual Risk

1. Risk remaining after implementation of risk treatment.[112]
2. An assessment of the projected likely risk estimated to remain after application of planned risk treatments.

   Note: Residual risk is always referred to in SRMBOK as estimated risk after future risk treatments have been implemented. Once the risk treatments are in place, the actual risk at that time will be the current risk.

   See also Protective Security, Risk Treatment Options, Treatments, Figure 12.7: Relationship of Exposure, Current Risk and Residual Risk

Resilience

1. The ability to resist being affected or to recover from an event.[1]
2. The capacity of an organization, system, community, individual, or society potentially exposed to hazards to adapt, by resisting or changing, to reach and maintain an acceptable level of capabilities, function, and structure.[118]

   Note: Resilience is related to existing controls and the capacity to reduce or sustain harm.[119]

Resources

A capacity, tool, asset, or commodity available to or drawn on by an organization whether used for Security Risk Management or for achievement of organizational objectives. Risk treatment options in particular may require expenditure on the part of an organization.[120]

   Note: Resource can also be a threat actor attribute, the other being knowledge. Resources available to a threat actor can be tangible, such as weapons and other equipment, or intangible, such as laundered funds.

   Example: Resources may be tangibles, such as financial, personnel, and property, or may be intangible such as intellectual property.

   See also Asset, Knowledge, Organization, Risk Treatment Options, Threat Actor

Return on Security Investment (ROSI)

ROSI can be defined in both soft and hard terms. Calculating ROI for events that are prevented is difficult, because it is difficult to trace cause and effect—did a bomb not destroy the organization's head office because of SRM, or because the organization was not targeted in the first place? The ROI in this sense is difficult to quantify, and so metrics are likely to give way to adjectives such as good, high, and effective.

An alternative, more difficult way of calculating ROI has been developed for the IT industry. In simplified terms, this equation is:

$$C - ALE = ROSI$$

where C is the cost required to recover from any number of impacts and ALE is the annual loss expectancy.

ROSI is also subject to the law of diminishing returns—returns are likely to increase sharply with each additional dollar spent but eventually taper off and plateau.[121]

See also Event, Incident, Impact, Loss

Risk

1. The chance of something happening that will have an impact on objectives.[112]

   Although risk is normally used to refer to negative consequences, it can also refer to positive outcomes (i.e., maximizing benefits and gains). In the security context, it is used primarily, but not exclusively, to refer to loss control.

2. Risk is a theory that denotes a potential negative impact to an asset or some characteristic of value that may develop from some present process or future event. In everyday usage, risk is often used synonymously with the probability of a loss or threat. In security risk assessments, risk combines the probability of an event occurring with the impact that event would have and with its different circumstances.[122]

   See also Consequence, Exposure, Impact, Residual Risk, Risk Prioritization, Risk Treatment Options

Risk Appetite

The amount of risk a person or an entity is willing to accept in pursuit of value. Attitude to risk can be categorized as risk averse, risk neutral, or risk seeking, and the amount a person or entity is likely to tolerate will vary because of a wide range of factors.

Also referred to as risk preference, attitude, tolerance, or capacity.

Risk Aversion

A term used to describe the unwillingness of an organization or individual to engage in any activity where uncertainty is involved.

See also Consequence, Exposure, Impact, Residual Risk, Risk Prioritization, Risk Treatment Options

Risk Management

1. The culture, processes, and structures that are directed toward the effective management of potential opportunities and adverse effects.[1]

2. A strategy for helping policy makers make decisions about assessing risk, allocating resources, and taking actions under conditions of uncertainty.[34]

Risk Measurement

Risk is usually measured in terms of the chance of an event happening that will have an impact on objectives. It is measured in terms of consequences (how harmful it is) and likelihood (how likely the threat is to succeed).[112]

The expression of risk in either a qualitative, semiquantitative, or fully quantitative context. This may be either:

- Qualitative—usually expressed within a matrix
- Semi-quantitative—often expressed as a percentage of exposure levels
- Quantitative—often expressed as a ratio or percentage having derived data from other systems

> Note: Risk should normally be capable of being expressed or described succinctly using the CASE risk statement model.

> See also Consequences, Impact, Likelihood, Risk, Risk Statement, Threat

Risk Prioritization

The sequential categorization of the relative importance of risk to an organization to optimize the allocation of resources to the highest priority risks.

One of the final steps in the Security Risk Management process. Prioritization of risks will be a function of many considerations, which include capability, impact, and business continuity. Available resources will be devoted to risk treatment options on the basis of risk prioritization.

> See also Business Continuity, Capability, Impact, Risk Treatment Options

Risk Rating

A rating based on likelihood and consequence to indicate how significant each potential risk is to an organization.

The risk rating may be expressed in several ways, for example, by using qualitative terms such as severe, high, major, and significant or semiquantitatively, using a numeric scale.[97]

Risk Statement

A short statement to identify a specific risk in descriptive or explanatory fashion. Risk statements should normally include at least the following elements as summarized in the acronym CASE (Table 12.1):

- **Consequence**—what is the impact of this risk?
- **Asset**—what asset(s) are at risk?
- **Source**—what are the source(s) or threat actors of this risk eventuating?
- **Event**—how would the source apply the hazard against the asset?

> Note 1: This does not address likelihood or consequence. These terms are considered in security risk analysis

> Note 2: Refer to Figure 12.11 Example of Security Review Finding for an example of another risk statement based on a risk finding.

> Example 1: Compromise of (consequence) classified information (asset) because of theft (event) by criminal elements (source).

Table 12.1 Example of alignment of defined terms to the risk statement

An issue-motivated group	Source
has indicated a willingness to engage in violent protest	Intent
and has access to, and knowledge of	Capability
explosives.	Hazard
They have identified a well-staffed office building,	Assets
which has parking underneath	Vulnerability
and where vehicle entry barriers are	Likelihood barriers
poorly maintained and often out of order, which makes it easier	Escalation factor
to detonate a vehicle-borne IED beneath the building.	Event
This location was selected because fire and ambulance	Consequence barriers
are distant from the office, which thereby enables maximum	Escalation factor
injury to personnel and damage to property	Impact
that result in significant loss of organizational capability.	Consequence

Example 2: Failure to protect (consequence) personnel (assets) against terrorist (source) attack (event) using an improvised explosive device (hazard).

Example 3: Failure to prevent an issue-motivated group (source) that has indicated intent (threat) to detonate (event) explosives (hazard) outside the street-level office window (vulnerability) leading to injuries (impact) to personnel and property (asset) with a long-term reduction in profitability and viability of the organization (consequence) because of an inability to attract and retain staff.

See also Asset, Consequence, Event, Hazard, Impact, Risk, Source

Risk Treatment

1. Process of selection and implementation of measures to modify risk.[112]

2. Process of selection and implementation of measures to modify risk—this can include avoiding, modifying, sharing, or retaining risk.[97]

   Note 1: The term "risk treatment" is sometimes used for the measures themselves.[112]

   Note 2: Risk treatments may also be a source of risk if they introduce new risks.

   See also Residual Risk, Risk Treatment Options, Treatments

Root Causes

Underlying conditions that may generate threats, hazards, and other sources of risk. Within a security context, this may include factors such as social and economic conditions, such as poverty, injustice, political aspirations, and alienation.[1]

Root Cause Analysis

1. Application of investigative and analytical techniques to identify the conditions and preconditions that permit and/or initiate an undesired event or state.[123]

2. Root cause analysis is the process of learning from consequences. The consequences can be desirable, but most root cause analysis deals with adverse consequences.[124]

See also Event, Incident, Probability

Safeguards

Administrative, physical, or technical controls designed to provide protection against threats and reduce identified vulnerabilities. Examples of safeguards could include biometric devices for user authentication, terminals that log off automatically, performing background checks on key personnel, and having an emergency response plans.

See also Administrative Controls, Barriers, Controls, Threat, Vulnerability

Security

Security is the condition of being protected against danger or loss. It is achieved through the mitigation of adverse consequences associated with the intentional or unwarranted actions of others.

In general usage, security is a concept similar to safety, but as a technical term security means that something is not only secure but also it has been secured. In this context, security refers to the measures used to protect sensitive organizational assets that collectively create, enable, and sustain organizational capability. Such assets will differ depending on the nature of the organization's activities, but typically they include classified or sensitive information as well as physical assets of value, people, unique processes, alliances/partnerships, and intellectual capital.

Individuals or actions that encroach on the condition of protection cause a breach of security.

See also Asset, Barrier, Business Continuity, Capability, Enterprise Wide Security Management, Organization, Personnel, Risk Assessment, Security Risk Management System, System, Treatments

Security Breach

An accidental or unintentional failure to observe the security procedures or policy whether or not it results in an security incident.

> Example 1: Leaving a classified file unattended would be a security breach even if the information was not compromised and no incident or impact occurred.

Example 2: Leaving a password written down on a computer monitor would be a security breach. If someone later used that password to access user accounts, that would constitute a security incident.

See also Compromise, Consequence, Event, Impact, Security Breach

Security Framework

An overall model for developing comprehensive security programs. In a broad sense, a security framework underpins the enterprise approach to security. A security framework should include considerations of information, personnel, and physical security along with sound Security Risk Management principles and practices.

See also Enterprise Security Risk Management, Information Security, Personnel Security, Physical Security, Protective Security, Security Risk Management, Security Risk Management Framework, Security Risk Management System

Security Incident

1. A security breach, violation, or event that results in negative consequences.

2. A security incident is regarded as any event or circumstances that involve or affect the individual, community, or organization that causes or is likely to cause a loss (physical or otherwise), disruption, or fear from the deliberate activities of other parties. Where impacts are, or could potentially be realized against people, property, or information.[1]

See also Compromise, Consequence, Event, Impact, Security Breach

Security-in-Depth

1. A system of multiple layers, in which security countermeasures are employed to support mutually and complement each other, whereby each layer provides a level of protection for inner layers as well as key assets.

2. The proposition that multiple layers of security are better than a single protection mechanism. The layers may be technological, procedural, policy, or other elements that work in coordination to provide redundant and mutually supportive security measures (as shown in Figure 12.10).

See also Hierarchy of Control, Swiss-Cheese Model

Security Manager

The designated manager responsible for advice, development, and in some instances the application of security measures in an organization.

See also Chief Security Officer, Protective Security

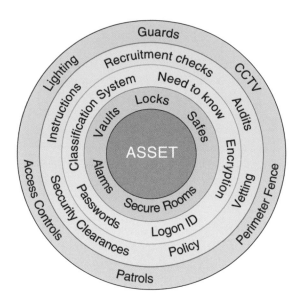

FIGURE 12.10 Conceptual example of security-in-depth

Security Posture

A practice or activity that can be implemented and/or modified at relatively short notice, e.g., locking doors, putting on additional guards, and that can be under-taken against an agreed specification after changes to the threat level. A security posture at a higher threat level must build on the strengths of the posture implemented at the lower threat level.

Security Review Findings

The documented findings of a formal risk review or security audit that describe deficiencies, vulnerabilities, and/or opportunities for improvement.

Such findings should include four elements; the quality and comprehensiveness of a finding may be judged with reference to the following 4Cs:

- **Condition**—What is going on? What circumstances were found?
- **Criteria**—What should be going on (per procedures, objectives, etc.)?
- **Cause**—Why is this happening and what is the underlying root cause?
- **Consequence**—What might happen if we don't address it?

An example of how to apply the 4Cs in a security review finding is provided in Figure 12.11.

See also Recommendations, Consequence, Protective Security, Protective Security Review, Risk Prioritization, Risk Rating, Vulnerability

Security Risk

A security risk is any event that could result in the compromise of organizational assets. The unauthorized use, loss, damage, disclosure, or modification

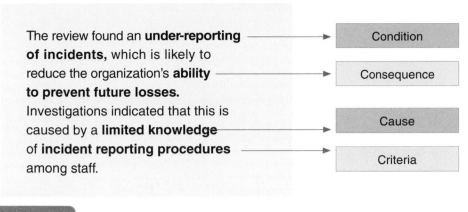

The review found an **under-reporting of incidents,** which is likely to reduce the organization's **ability to prevent future losses.** Investigations indicated that this is caused by a **limited knowledge** of **incident reporting procedures** among staff.

Condition

Consequence

Cause

Criteria

FIGURE 12.11 Example of security review finding

of organizational assets for the profit, personal interest, or political interests of individuals, groups, or other entities constitutes a compromise of the asset and includes the risk of harm to people. Compromise of organizational assets may adversely affect the enterprise, its business units, and their clients. As such, consideration of security risk is a vital component of risk management.

Security Risk Analysis

The process of making an assessment of security risks that considers how likely is it that an event will result in a particular consequence (usually the most credible or worst case consequence).

See also Consequence, Risk

Security Risk Assessment (SRA)

A formal process of security risk analysis to document security related risks over a defined scope of location/s and/or activities and in the light of organizational criteria.

See also Protective Security, Risk, Security Risk Management

Security Risk Assessment—Asset or Project Based

An SRA with a specific and restricted scope to focus on specific assets and/or projects at a high level of detail. This level of granularity can assist security managers and senior managers to manage specific risks and threats.

Note: An SRA—Enterprise may provide the context for an SRA—Asset/ Project Based.

See also Enterprise Security Risk Management, Security in Depth, Security Risk Assessment, Security Risk Assessment—Enterprise, Security Risk Management, Security Risk Management System

Security Risk Assessment—Enterprise

An enterprise security risk assessment (ESRA) covers an entire enterprise (as opposed to particular business units or assets within an organization) with the key objective being to protect organizational capabilities.

Example: A multinational resources company may conduct an ESRA, which considers all business units, activities, and projects globally to identify and treat systemic vulnerabilities. The same organization may also conduct security risk assessments that reflect the environment within which specific business units or facilities operate.

Note: An enterprise is an organization comprised of all the establishments that operate under the ownership or control of a single entity. An enterprise may be a business, service, government department, or membership organization; consist of one or several establishments; and operate at one or several locations.[125]

See also Enterprise Security Risk Management, Security in Depth, Security Risk Assessment, Security Risk Assessment—Asset and Project Based, Security Risk Management, Security Risk Management System

Security Risk Landscape

A map of potential security exposures and/or their sources, of an individual, community, or organization.[1]

Also known as a Security Risk Universe

Security Risk Management

Security Risk Management is the culture, processes, and structures that are directed toward maximizing benefits and minimizing adverse effects associated with the intentional and unwarranted actions of others against organizational assets.[u]

See also Assets, Business Continuity, Impact, Personnel, Risk Management

Security Risk Management Body of Knowledge (SRMBOK)

An all-encompassing term that describes the sum of knowledge regarding readily accepted traditional practices, recent innovations, and research within the evolving field of Security Risk Management.

Security Risk Management Framework (SRMF)

The inter-relation and interaction of elements of an organization's management system concerned with managing security risk. Includes elements such as policy, procedures, and standards and is usually capable of being represented in graphical format for descriptive purposes.

See also Administrative Controls, Organization, Risk

---

[u]Adapted from AS/NZS4360:2004 Risk Management Standard and Schneier (2006).

Security Risk Management Process

1. A logical process that may be used to assess and quantify risk, and may provide management with cost-effective solutions to security risk reduction using available resources.[126]

2. Systematic application of management policies, procedures, and practices to the tasks of communicating, establishing the context, identifying, analyzing, evaluating, treating, monitoring, and reviewing risk.[3]

3. A process that can be broken down into the following six basic steps:
   - Gather information
   - Identify the risks
   - Analyze the risks
   - Assess and prioritize the risks
   - Treat the risks (and prepare the security plan)
   - Monitor the risk environment and evaluate the security plan.[127]

   See also Administrative Controls, Security Review Findings, Security Risk Analysis, Security Risk Assessment, Security Risk Management, Security Risk Management Framework, Security Risk Management System

Security Risk Management System (SRMS)

The elements of an organization's management system concerned with managing security risk. Elements can include strategic planning, decision-making, policy arrangements, quality management systems and other processes for dealing with security risks.

   See also Enterprise Security Risk Management, Organization, Risk, System

Security Risk Management—Toolbox

The Security Risk Management methodologies, systems, procedures, and risk treatment options that can be applied to aid Security Risk Management for organizations.

   See also Administrative Controls, Security Review Findings, Security Risk Analysis, Security Risk Assessment, Security Risk Management, Security Risk Management Framework, Security Risk Management System

Security Specifications

1. A documented technical specification or other precise criteria used consistently as rules, guidelines, or definitions of characteristics to ensure that materials, products, processes, and services are fit for their purpose. Specifications should be determined and applied at the organizational level, should be implemented in a managed fashion (for example, through the development of policy and provision of concomitant funding), should require a lead time to implement, and should form the basis of review/audit activities.

2. Required security procedures or management controls that govern information, personnel, and physical security for an organization.[128]

See also Administrative Controls, Compromise, Information Security, Personnel Security, Physical Security, Security Risk Management

Security System

A security system consists of a series of countermeasures.

For example, an alarm system might consist of a detection device, siren, flashing light, and control room notification device.

See Security Risk Management System (SRMS).

Security Training Programs

Training programs designed to provide personnel with the knowledge and skills necessary to adhere to security specifications set by the organization and to contribute to the security of the organization. Security training programs can be divided into the following two main categories:

- Programs designed to provide security training for personnel that do not perform roles specifically related to the provision of security services and security risk management. The aim of these programs is to:
  - Develop security awareness in personnel
  - Provide the security-related skills and knowledge needed by personnel to perform to perform their specific role within the organization
- Programs designed to provide security training for personnel that perform roles specifically related to the provision of security services and Security Risk Management. These programs would need to include the generic content that is provided to all personnel, along with the security knowledge and skills that enable them to perform their security function.

See also Security Manager, Security Standards

Severity

Severity is also often referred to as consequence. It is derived from the costs of the loss(es) being incurred or the loss most likely to be incurred as a result of the security breach / event.

See also Consequence, Loss, Security Breach, Security Incident

Shock

Combined health, economic, and psychological impacts of an attack, or the shock attributes of a target. (As outlined in "CARVER + shock" methodology)

See also Attack, Consequence, Impact, Target

Significant Organizational Infrastructure

The facilities, systems, supply chains, information technologies, and communication networks that, if destroyed, degraded, or rendered unavailable for an extended period, would have a significant negative impact organizational goals.

Source

Initiator of the release of a hazard.

> Note: In the context of Security Risk Management, source is usually considered to involve human intervention (whether groups or individuals). Extreme weather, systems failure, and so on may constitute vulnerabilities that can increase the exposure to risk events. For example, extreme weather events, such as cyclones, may result in civil unrest that in turn becomes the source of security threat.

> See also Exposure, Hazard, Risk, Threat Actor, Vulnerability

Special Events and Mass Gatherings

A nonroutine activity within a community that brings together a large number of people.

> Note: Emphasis is not placed on the total number of people attending but rather the impact on the community's ability to respond to a large-scale emergency or disaster or the exceptional demands that the activity places on response services. A community's special event requires additional planning, preparedness, and mitigation efforts of local emergency response and public safety agencies.

> Mass gatherings are a subset of special events. Mass gatherings are usually found at special events that attract large numbers of spectators or participants.[129]

Stakeholders

Those people and organizations who may affect, be affected by, or perceive themselves to be affected by, a decision, activity, or event.

Stakeholders include anyone with an interest or influence in the organization or community, or projects or issues associated with parts thereof. This group could include, but is not be limited to the board, management, employees, citizens, local communities, unions, shareholders, families, media, lobby groups, customers, suppliers, government, and regulators.[1]

Suitability

One attribute of a hazard (the others being availability and deployability). To be effective, a hazard must have the capacity to achieve the objective(s) of the threat actor in question. This will partly be dependent on asset targetability and asset attributes.

For example, a shoulder-fired ground-to-air missile may be suitable for an attack on aircraft flying at low altitude, but it is unlikely to be as suitable for an attack on a water-storage facility.

See also Asset, Asset Attributes, Asset Targetability, Attack, Availability, Hazard, Threat Actor

Supply Chain Protection

The management of upstream and downstream relationships with suppliers and customers to create enhanced value in the final market place at less cost to the supply chain as a whole.

Susceptibility

The likelihood and consequence of being harm by a threat.[1]

Swiss Cheese Model

Swiss cheese model is based on the work of James Reason (1990), which suggests that in any given circumstance, several barriers are in place (each of which has vulnerabilities or inadequacies). However, before an incident can occur, all the holes must line up to allow the risk to materialize (shown in Figure 12.12).

System

A combination of related elements organized into a complex whole.[120]

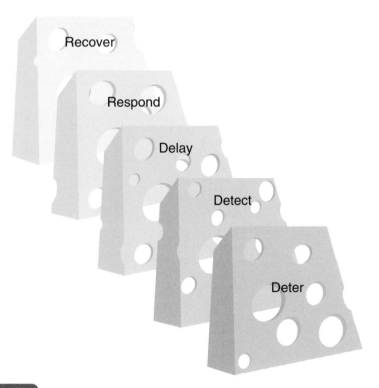

FIGURE 12.12 Swiss cheese model

Target

The asset that a threat actor intends to attack.

See also Asset, Asset Targetability, Attack, Intent, Threat Actor, Vulnerability

Targetability

1. Asset targetability is a function of the recognizability, exposure (duration) and accessibility of a target (see SRMBOK SRM Process Flow).

2. The extent to which an asset may sustain a deliberate and targeted release of a hazard. An asset that could only be attacked through a wide scale and indiscriminate attack would have a low targetability.

See also Asset, Hazard, Target

Temporal Qualities

Qualities of an asset that can be defined with reference to or limited by time.

Example: Loss of a mission-critical server that is required to have 100% uptime would be likely to have greater impact on an organization than one that could be offline for several days. This impact would be varied depending on the timeframe involved in replacing or restoring it.

Example: The loss of an asset such as a circus tent, which had in any case, only a limited life-span would be likely to be less significant than loss of a similar structure which was expected to have a 100-year life-span.

Temporal qualities are one attribute of an asset (the others are recoverability and criticality) that helps to determine the impact on an organization and on business continuity if that asset was destroyed or compromised.

See also Asset, Asset Attributes, Business Continuity, Criticality, Impact, Recoverability

Threat

1. "A source of harm that is deliberate or has intent to do harm" and has the (demonstrated or likely) capability to do so either now or in the future.[97]

2. An indication of something impending that could attack the system. Includes strategic threats, such as a regional conflict, or tactical threats, such as impending physical attack.

Threats are usually measured in terms of intent and capability. The term includes known (stated or assessed intention or determination to inflict pain, loss, or punishment on someone or something) or unknown (undeclared, hidden, or potential) threats. Malicious threats, such as system hacks, data destruction, data modification, theft of IP, bomb threats, sabotage, or fraud, can be categorized within a range going from rational (obtaining something of value) to irrational (attack against of assets without benefit).

Note 1: Threat as defined by [CERT 1993] includes "any circumstances or event that has the potential to cause harm to a system or network." That means, even the existence of an (unknown) vulnerability implies a threat by definition.

Note 2: Threats can be nonmalicious and include human error, hardware/software failures, and so on, or natural events as hurricanes, earthquakes, fires, or man-made events.

3. Anything that has the potential to prevent or hinder the achievement of objectives or disrupt the processes that support them.[1]

4. A source of risk when armed with a hazard has the potential and intent to harm.

See also Attack, Capability, Intent, Loss

Threat Access

The degree (actual or perceived) to which a threat can interact with a target.[1]

Threat Actor

Human beings, whether individuals or groups, that cause a hazard to be released, i.e., that cause a threat to materialize. These threats include intruders, criminals, disgruntled employees, foreign intelligence services, terrorists, and issue-motivated groups.
    Also known as Threat Agent or Source.
    See also Attack, Confidence, Desire, Hazard, Intent, Knowledge, Resources

Threat Actor Attributes

In the SRM process flowchart, threat actor attributes are comprised of resources and knowledge that when combined, describe the capability of a threat actor.
    See also Capability, Intent, Threat, Threat Actor, Threat Actor Motivation

Threat Actor Motivation

In the SRM process flowchart, threat actor motivation is composed of desire and confidence that when combined, describe the intent of a threat actor.
    See also Capability, Confidence, Desire, Intent, Threat, Threat Actor, Threat Actor Attributes

Threat Assessment (TA)

1. Systematic assessment of threat including identification, analysis, and evaluation based on evidence and conducted using a repeatable logical process that may involve high-level context analysis or more specific detailed analysis of an organization, facility, or event.

2. Evaluation and assessment of the intentions of people who could pose a hazard to a resource or function, how they might cause harm, and their ability to carry out their intentions—threats must be assessed to determine what potential exists for them to actually cause harm.[97]

Verb: To analyze or assess threat or potential threat.

Noun: An assessment of the likelihood of an incident or event to occur. Usually presented on a qualitative or semi-quantitative rating, e.g., 1, 2, 3, 4, 5 or low, medium, high, extreme.

Threat is usually assessed based on the attributes of the potential attacker in the context of the potential target. The following attributes, for example, might be among those considered when making a threat assessment.

See also Attack, Hazard, Target, Threat, SRMBOK SRM Process Flow

Intent	What outcome does the offender seek to achieve?
Capability	How capable are the offenders of initiating the event and do they have requisite skills, knowledge, abilities, and resources?
Motivation	What motivates the offenders and what is their level of commitment?
Impact	What is the likely impact, i.e., benefit, to the offender?
Difficulty	What is the degree of difficulty or personal risk to the offender?

Threat Identification

1. A précis of the origin and form of particular threat.
2. An objective assessment of possible scenarios where deliberate or accidental harm may befall an asset.

See also Red Team

Transnational and ExtraJurisdictional Risks

Transnational and extrajurisdictional risks are related to the concepts of geostrategic environment and geopolitical risk. It is, however, more narrowly focused. Whereas the terms geostrategic and geopolitical take into account strategy, politics, economics, and geographic considerations (such as sea lane choke points), transnational and extrajurisdictional risks refer to political, economic, and legal risks.

For example, when information is transmitted over the Internet, it may be routed through and/or stored on multiple servers in multiple foreign countries. Such information may be affected by the legislation enacted in various jurisdictions, which can lead to problems and complications regarding privacy and intellectual property. Risks such as these are covered by the term "transnational and extrajurisdictional risks," but they would generally not be considered under the rubric of the terms geostrategic environment and geopolitical risk.

See also Geo-Strategic Environment, Maritime Security, Pandemic, Transnational and Extra-Jurisdictional Risks

Travel Security

Protective measures for the safekeeping of people, property, and information while temporarily based, or in transit outside their normal area of operations.

See also Geo-Strategic Environment, Geo-Strategic Risk, Personnel Security, Personal Protective Practices, Threat, Threat Actor, Threat Assessment

Treatment Options

Potential risk mitigation strategies.
  See also Treatments

Treatments

Controls that are proposed (i.e., not yet existing) to reduce or mitigate the likelihood or consequence of an event occurring, that is, to reduce the residual risk.
  Process of selection and implementation of measures to modify risk.

> Note 1: The term "risk treatment" is sometimes used as a noun to refer to the actual measures.

> Note 2: Risk treatment measures can include avoiding, modifying, sharing, or retaining risk.

> (ISO/IEC Guide 73, in part)

See also Consequence, Controls, Likelihood, Residual Risk, Risk Rating, Risk Treatments

Trespasser

Person(s) who accidentally and/or unknowingly breach an organization's premises (or data systems) without authorization (whether physically or electronically).

> Note: Trespasser is an entity without intent to commit an offence, e.g., hikers walking onto a mining lease or visitors who may be lost within a facility.

See Also Intent, Intruder, Organization

Unattended Item

An item whose presence is not readily explained and that could contain a hazard.

Unsafe Conditions

1. Environmental circumstances or state of affairs to which an asset, organization, or capability has or could be exposed where the risk has not yet been reduced to as low as reasonably practicable (ALARP).
2. Conditions that allow hazards/threats to manifest.[1]

  See also As Low as Reasonably Practicable (ALARP)

Vulnerability

1. The degree of susceptibility and resilience to hazards.[97]
2. Vulnerability is a multidimensional concept that involves exposure, sensitivity, and resilience. Vulnerability can increase through cumulative events or

when multiple stresses weaken the ability of a person, organization, or community to buffer itself against future adverse events.

3. A weakness that can be exploited by an adversary to gain access to an asset. For example, vulnerabilities might include, but are not limited to, building characteristics, personal bahaviors, properties of equipment, and security practices and procedures.[38]

4. An exploitable weakness or deficiency of an asset (facility, entity, system, information, or person) that can create "windows of opportunity," which could:

   • Allow a threat to materialize
   • Increase the likelihood of attack
   • Increase the consequence of an attack

These include the conditions determined by political, economic, social, technical, or legal factors and processes, which increase the susceptibility of an organization or community to the impact of hazards.

Note 1: Vulnerabilities may affect the likelihood and/or consequences of an attack.

Note 2: Vulnerability comprises resilience and susceptibility. Resilience is related to existing controls and the capacity to reduce or sustain harm. Susceptibility is related to exposure.

Example: Typical vulnerabilities in an ICT environment might include access points to the internet. Failure caused by design flaws or incorrect firewall configuration could for example lead to successful hacking, i.e., increased consequence.

Example: Financial difficulties constitute vulnerability in an individual and might increase the likelihood of an attempt to compromise information that they have access to.

Example: In a physical environment, vulnerability might include ground floor windows without security treatments. Associated risks might include theft from break in, which would be more likely to occur and more likely to succeed if windows have no security treatments. (In this example, consequence remains unchanged—the consequence of a break and enter will be no greater or lesser whether the offender enters by a window, door, roof, or other means.)

See also Attack, Consequence, Exposure, Hazard, Impact, Likelihood, Organization, Threat

Vulnerability Analysis / Assessment

1. A determination of the susceptibility of the asset to a particular threat that involves the identification, exploration, and evaluation of the weaknesses that could be exploited by threat actors.

2. The process (verb) or outputs (noun) associated with reviewing assets and/or security systems to identify weaknesses. Usually conducted from a greenfield perspective (baseline) to identify how they could fail or could be successfully attacked.

Note: Vulnerability assessment may be conducted by attackers to identify potential opportunities; however, the process in this context is usually used to refer to the assessment process used as part of a security risk assessment to identify treatment measures.

See also Asset, Attack, Effectiveness, Opportunity

Sample Templates | 13

The following range of sample templates have been designed to allow individuals to capture information pertinent to their own organizational context, including:

- Security risk registers
- Risk treatment forms
- An outline security plan
- Day-to-day operational governance registers
- A property selection and security planning checklist
- An example commitment statement to security and risk management
- A bomb threat checklist
- A bomb threat room search checklist card
- Detailed evaluation criteria for business continuity plans

13.1 SECURITY RISK REGISTER FORM (EXAMPLE 1)

Example based on AS/NZS 4360:2004

Security Risk Register

| | Date: | |
| | Assessed by: | |

Function or activity:								
Ref.	**The risks**		**Likelihood and Consequence of event happening**		Adequacy of existing controls	Consequence rating	Likelihood rating	Level of risk	Risk priority
	What can happen? How can it happen?	Consequences	Likelihood					

13.2 SECURITY RISK REGISTER FORM (EXAMPLE 2)

Risk Register

Date of assessment:

Compiled by:

Reviewed by:

Risk category			**Treatment options**	**Risk**	**Monitoring and comments**
Ref	Description	Level		After treatment	

13.3 RISK TREATMENT SCHEDULE (EXAMPLE 1)

Risk Treatment Schedule and Plan

Date:

Assessed by:

Function or Activity:

The risk priority order from risk register	Possible treatment options	Preferred options	Risk rating after treatment	Result of cost benefit analysis	Person responsible for implementation of option	Timetable for implementation	How will risk and the treatment options be monitored?
				A: Accept B: Reject			

13.4 RISK TREATMENT SCHEDULE (EXAMPLE 2)

Risk Treatment Schedule and Plan

Date of assessment:

Compiled by:

Reviewed by:

Risks (in priority order)	Risk treatments	Residual risk	Person responsible for implementation	Date/time for implementation	How will risk and the treatment be monitored?

13.5 OUTLINE SECURITY PLAN

The following framework may be used as a guide for preparing a security plan.

Introduction	A statement from the organization head (or equivalent) outlining the importance of the plan and why it must be supported.
Statement of purpose	This makes explicit the relationship between organizational security practices and the corporate plans and business objectives (in other words, what is valuable to the organization and how its protection will help to achieve desired outcomes). If the review and planning process has been triggered by a specific event (security incident, new legislation, new function, etc.), this should be spelled out.
Security environment	This provides a summary of the threat assessment and the organization's current exposure as well as a general assessment of current security management arrangements.
Objectives	These are clear, concise statements about what the security plan is designed to achieve. They should be related to the organization's corporate objectives.
Security strategies and actions	These outline the strategies to be introduced or maintained to achieve the desired corporate security outcomes. This section should describe the security treatments (actions) to be implemented and the implementation strategy. For instance, if a security awareness session for employees handling security classified information is one of the treatments, describe how this is to be achieved and who is responsible.
Residual risks	Residual risks should be estimated, described, and rated to guide priorities for monitoring risks and evaluating treatments.
Timetable	The timetable could be included as part of the previous section or could be summarized and appear separately. Regardless of where the indication of time frames is provided, the plan should provide information about significant steps in the implementation of risk treatments.
Resources	This part should document the security budget and determine the cost of the recommendations or options.

13.6 DAY-TO-DAY OPERATIONAL GOVERNANCE REGISTERS

Record of Current Security Instructions

Note: A record of CURRENT security orders and instructions, e.g., security practices and procedures and relevant annexes and audit plans, should be included in this register.

Serial no.	Title	Reference no.	Date of origin	Amendment status	Location

Security Surveys, Inspections, Reviews, Advisory Visits, Classified Holding Musters, & Random Spot Checks

Note: 1. Results of random spot checks on classified document holdings, should be included in this section of the register.
2. Reference to security surveys, inspections, and in-house reviews should be included in this section of the register.
3. Records of inspections and walk testing of Intrusion alarm systems should be included in section B.4 – record of intrusion alarm systems.

Date	Type of check	Conducted by	Result	Action/comments

Record of Security Containers (Combination Operated)

Note: 1. Under NO circumstances are actual combinations to be entered in this section.
2. Combinations are only to be changed by the custodian or other authorized combination holder.

Bldg	Room	Custodian	Container class/type	Container serial no	Date combination changed	Date next change due	Location of written duplicate	Date of last service	Next service due

Record of Security Containers (Key Operated)

Note: 1. Security keys are to be signed for in the security key register.
2. Security containers located within a work/storage area must only be serviced/repaired by an SCEC-endorsed locksmith.

Bldg	Room	Custodian	Container class/type	Container serial no	Location of duplicate	No. of keys held

Record of Access Controls (Combination)

Note: 1. Under NO circumstances are actual combinations to be entered in this section.
2. Combinations are only to be changed by the custodian or other authorized combination holder.
3. Details of access controls (keys) are to be recorded in the security key register.

Bldg	Room	Door	Access control type	Custodian	Date combination changed	Date next change due	Location of written duplicate	Date of last service	Next service due

Record of Intrusion Alarm Systems (IAS)

Type of IAS	Date installed	Tested	Accreditation certificate	Maintenance conducted	Remarks

Security Key Register

Note: 1. The register should be checked against key holdings biannually
2. Record keys issued on a permanent or temporary basis

Location	Custodian	Key serial no	Copies	Item (container/ door)	Signatory	Comments

Building Patrol Listing

Building no.	Location	Sensitive documents	Sensitive equipment	Sensitive fixed disk info. systems	IAS yes/no	Freq. of patrols (2, 4, or 8 hourly)	Remarks/action

Record of Occasional Access to Classified Material through Approved Limited Higher Access

Note: Details of access to sensitive information by staff whose security clearance does not normally permit, but have limited higher access as specifically authorized, are to be recorded in this section.

| Date | Personal particulars | | | Signature | Authorization | | Action/task remarks |
	Staff name	Clearance level held	Clearance level granted		Authorized by	Position	

Record of Security Cleared Staff

Note: 1. A record of CURRENT security clearances for staff must be retained in this register.
2. A record of CURRENT security clearances held by visitors may be included on a separate page in this register. Details of the company facility or business unit holding primary responsibility for the visitor clearance should be included.

Staff member's full name	Security clearance level	Date granted	Location where working	Transfer date (if applicable)	Limitations/ remarks

Record of Staff Traveling Overseas

Note: Record details of staff traveling overseas for business or private reasons and briefings given, as appropriate, in this section.

Staff member's full name	Depart date	Return date	Country/ies visited	Business (B) or private (P)	Date of pre-visit briefing	Date of debriefing	Comments comment

Record of Security Education/Training

Note: Frequency of training is as important as the nature of training.

Date	Subject matter	Presenter	Attendees	Remarks

Record of New Starter Briefing/Debriefings

Note: Record details of new starter briefings/debriefings given to individuals in this section of the register.

Name	Date briefed	Date debriefed	Topics covered	Comments

Master Record of Classified Document Registers

Note: 1. Very highly sensitive documents are to be recorded in separate registers to those used to register other classified documents.
2. Musters of all documents are to be conducted when custodians change, as noted in section A.6

Location	Custodian	Serial no. of register	Date opened	Date closed	Purpose (see Note 1)

Record of Privately Owned Computers Processing Company Information

Note: This record is to be accompanied by all letters of accreditation/authority.

Date of authority/ accreditation	Reference for authority/ accreditation	Name of computer owner	Type of equipment	Location of equipment	Classification of data being processed

Record of Security Incidents

Note: All security-related incidents and breaches involving sensitive materials or direct access to classified material are to be recorded or referred to in this section. Should the subject matter be classified, only reference details are to be provided thus negating the requirement to classify this register. Building insecurities including perimeter doors and windows should not be included, unless direct access to classified material is involved. Include details of corrective action taken.

Date	Reference	Details and action taken	Reported to?

13.7 PROPERTY SELECTION AND SECURITY PLANNING CHECKLIST

Property Details

Property type:	
Property address:	
Review date:	
Reviewer:	

Building Information Requirements

Checklist	Comments
What are the base rental costs?	
• Basic $ per sqm per annum	
• Estimated outgoings per annum	
• Car parking licenses $ per annum	
• Total year one rent including outgoings, car parking, off-site storage facilities, etc.	
What is the lease term? Are there any option periods?	
What are the lease conditions? Is a draft lease available?	
What is the rent review period and process? (Defined formula is preferred over market review.)	
Is the landlord offering incentives?	
• Contribution to fit-out	
• Rent-free periods	
• Waive make-good	
Are there any attached agencies involved in the leasing arrangement?	
• Names	
• Subtenancy area wanted	
• Status of agreement	

Approach Philosophy

The security approach is to select an office within the perimeter of a building and and to protect the information, staff, and clients within the area by means of physical barriers (walls and doors), locks, access control, security alarm system, procedural measures, and an effective response to an incident.

General

The office area should be wholly located within the perimeter of a building and not located on the external perimeter of the building.

- Secured (lockable) points of entry and other openings
- Intended office walls can be repaired or replaced by us at a later date
- An effective means of limiting entry and access to authorized people only
- All staff requiring frequent entry must hold an appropriate security clearance
- A security alarm system (SAS).

Features to Avoid

The following features should be avoided if at all possible:

- **Large expanses of external wall glazing**—This is the largest source of injury in most bomb blasts that affect modern buildings. Illustrating this terrible truth is the fact that glass injuries were reported over half a kilometer away in the Oklahoma bombing. If it has to be used, the glazing needs to be designed properly. With use of the correct laminated glass and balanced framing, windows can be made to deform in their frames rather than to blow into a million fragments that kill and maim.
- **Roof glazing and atria above public areas**—Should they shatter, the shards of glass can prove lethal to those below, so ideally the glass and framing must be designed to stay intact.
- **Deep surface modeling of facades and overhangs**—Building features like terraces and a balcony trap blast forces and magnify their effect. These must be avoided on the building perimeter.

Exterior Environment

A close look should be taken at the environment surrounding any proposed new location. For instance, the ground floor of the building has a convenience store only open during normal business hours versus a store selling alcohol or a medical facility that may open late or 24 hours.

Checklist	YES	NO	N/A	Comments
Is there police support for tenants? What are police/building owner relations like?	☐	☐	☐	
Is there roof top or underground access to the building?	☐	☐	☐	
Are there other facilities near the proposed site and who occupies them (e.g., a police or fire station, an Israeli or U.S. Embassy)?	☐	☐	☐	
Are there any obvious hazards nearby (e.g., is there a petrol station, shipping facility, train line on which a train carriage can carry a very large amount of explosive material)?	☐	☐	☐	
Is there vehicle parking? What type (multi story, curb-side, underground, open space, etc.)?	☐	☐	☐	
Does the building have a 24-hour concierge or 24-hour guarding/receptionist?	☐	☐	☐	
Are there access roads? What type?	☐	☐	☐	
Are there other buildings in the immediate vicinity? How far away and how tall are they?	☐	☐	☐	
Are the neighbors/building tenants a cause for concern?	☐	☐	☐	
Do neighboring buildings have external closed-circuit television (CCTV) cameras and external guarding?	☐	☐	☐	
Is there a local police station? How far away?	☐	☐	☐	
Are crime statistics and other data available?	☐	☐	☐	
Can we get a map of the building and immediate grounds and a building floor plan?	☐	☐	☐	
Are there roadways/natural curves making direct entry at speed difficult?	☐	☐	☐	
Are there waterways and vegetation near the perimeter? If so, please describe.	☐	☐	☐	
Are there fences, stonewalls, gates, roadblocks, chicanes, etc. surrounding the perimeter?	☐	☐	☐	

External Walls

Building overhangs should be avoided.

Checklist	YES	NO	N/A	Comments
Are internal office partition walls in place? Are they made of glass or plasterboard/timber, etc.?	☐	☐	☐	
Are there any openings on the office perimeter walls and within the office area, e.g., service points and entries, inspection covers, water and sewerage, vertical building risers, air-conditioning intakes?	☐	☐	☐	
Do the office perimeter walls extend from the base of the floor to the underside of the above slab or secured roof structure and provide a tamper-evident barrier?	☐	☐	☐	
Is there any external cladding present on these walls? (A secondary hazard in the event of a blast.) How are the walls constructed (concrete, brick, masonry, steel frame, and glazing)?	☐	☐	☐	
Are there any structures against or in close proximity to the walls that could be used to gain access to the roof or other floors?	☐	☐	☐	

Alcoves or areas of reduced visibility that could provide a hiding place for intruders should be eliminated, especially in public areas that are adjacent to the office, such as public toilets, kitchens, cleaning rooms, building risers, and power/utilities areas.

Openings

Every building exit/entrance point and wall opening (whether building opening or grounds) is a potential weak point that degrades perimeter protection and is a vulnerability to the security and safety of the office.

Checklist	YES	NO	N/A	Comments
Are there exit and entry points? How many? (include fire exits that are egress only).	☐	☐	☐	
Are there any building or office facades on the perimeter walls (as this can lead to a wall collapse in the event of any extreme pressure overload from an explosive device)?	☐	☐	☐	
Are there any building balconies for the office that allow for entry and exit? These should be included as an opening and are critical in the evaluation of any office security and safety.	☐	☐	☐	

Vehicle Entry

Vehicle access control is both critical and essential. Vehicle entry should be restricted to building occupants only where possible, with all nonoccupants required to park outside the building.

In high threat areas all vehicles entering any multilevel car park (where possible) should be quarantined in a sterile area adjacent to the entry—but far enough away to reduce potential damage—and inspected for explosives before being allowed entry.

Checklist	YES	NO	N/A	Comments
Will existing barriers in place stop a four-wheel-drive-type vehicle moving at the speed limit?	☐	☐	☐	
If there is ANY public parking located less than 5 m from the structural pillars of the building?	☐	☐	☐	

Between the Office Perimeter and any Public Access Point

Ideally, any office or building should incorporate a sufficient distance from the building to any public vehicle access point (setback) to ensure a minimum safety distance for potential vehicle-borne explosive devices.

Checklist	YES	NO	N/A	Comments
Is the distance (in meters) from any office windows/perimeter wall/reception area to the street kerb side parking and to any other unrestricted public vehicle parking area (vertically and horizontally) less than 30 m?	☐	☐	☐	
Is there a blast wall or earthen bund greater than one meter surrounding the building?	☐	☐	☐	
Does the traffic circulation and parking on the roads surrounding the office and building present a problem?	☐	☐	☐	
Is parking supervised?	☐	☐	☐	
Are visitors' parks more than 30 m from the building?	☐	☐	☐	
Is there closed-circuit television (CCTV) or manned surveillance of the parking areas that are controlled by the building management or owner?	☐	☐	☐	
Are any vehicles entering building car parking already screened/checked for explosives?	☐	☐	☐	
Would we be able to put company signage in the entrance area of floor office area reflecting our office location and tenancy?	☐	☐	☐	

Lighting

Office area and perimeter building lighting should be installed at any proposed new sites, complete with back-up power supply. Lighting should provide illumination of the office and immediate surrounding office area. It should also include the surrounding area of the building.

A night-time assessment of the proposed site is required to determine the adequacy of lighting and the building/office environs during that time. Night-time white lighting of the building/office perimeter and car parking area should as a rule of thumb reach a 5-lux level of illumination. This is the equivalent of a well-lit residential street.

Checklist	YES	NO	N/A	Comments
Is there night-time lighting of the office and building perimeter? Please describe (halogen, fluorescent, spot or flood lighting, movement activated or on a timer or light sensor).	☐	☐	☐	
Is the lighting controlled? How? This should be checked and verified.	☐	☐	☐	
Is there ample lighting provided at building and office entry points (including fire exit doors) and in public gathering places such as car parks and courtyards?	☐	☐	☐	

Windows and External glazing

Checklist	YES	NO	N/A	Comments
Are the windows treated in any way against explosion such as blast screens, film or curtains, etc.? Are there any types of glazing used on the office and building perimeter windows—plate glass, toughened glass, laminated glass, double glazing polycarbonate, etc.?	☐	☐	☐	
Is the glass fixed into the window frames? How— silicone/right angle brackets/rubber moldings? What type of frame construction is used—steel, timber, or aluminum?	☐	☐	☐	

Doors

Checklist	YES	NO	N/A	Comments
Are they solid or hollow core timber doors? What are they made from—steel, timber, steel cladding glass, and aluminum?	☐	☐	☐	
Do the perimeter doors open outward?	☐	☐	☐	
Are the door hinges screw-fixed to the frames with a minimum of three hinges per door?	☐	☐	☐	
Are there double doors located on the proposed office area perimeter? (An inactive leaf of a double door should be secured with a pair of leading edge internal flush bolts or some other locking system.)	☐	☐	☐	

Locks and Keys

Checklist	YES	NO	N/A	Comments
Are there locks fitted to the doors and windows? What type(s) of locks (mortise locks, rim locks, key in knob locksets)? If unsure, please take photos and return to Canberra.	☐	☐	☐	
Are key(s) available? What types?	☐	☐	☐	
How are the doors keyed? Are they all keyed alike? Is there a master key and where is it held?	☐	☐	☐	
When was the last time the locks and key lock cylinders were changed?	☐	☐	☐	

Underground and Roof Access

Checklist	YES	NO	N/A	Comments
Is there access to the roof internally and how is the access controlled?	☐	☐	☐	
Is the roof accessible from nearby buildings or structures?	☐	☐	☐	
Is there underground access to the building? From where and how many?	☐	☐	☐	

Guarding

Checklist	YES	NO	N/A	Comments
Is there a 24-hour or daytime guard service or receptionist? If so, are regular patrols of the building perimeter and building internal office areas conducted? What are the roles and responsibilities of the guarding force, e.g., building evacuation and notification of tenants?	☐	☐	☐	
Do building guards patrol the building/office and building grounds any time? What else are the guards responsible for?	☐	☐	☐	
Are the guards armed? What types of guards are there—military, police, private?	☐	☐	☐	
Are building entrances monitored by guards?	☐	☐	☐	
Is there any form of metal detection, or other screening used—guards, sniffer dogs, etc.?	☐	☐	☐	
Are bags searched on entry?	☐	☐	☐	
Is there a storage facility for bags once they have been searched, to leave bags at the entry prior to building access?	☐	☐	☐	

Security Systems

Checklist	YES	NO	N/A	Comments
Is a CCTV camera surveillance system installed in the building and office area?	☐	☐	☐	
Does the camera cover the external grounds of the building?	☐	☐	☐	
Is the CCTV monitored? What response instructions are there?	☐	☐	☐	
Is a security alarm system installed inside the area? Does it cover windows and all door access points? Please note make and model number of the alarm system and where alarm panel/computer located.	☐	☐	☐	
Does the building have a security control center? Staff and procedures documented? Permanent link to the local police force or private guard force?	☐	☐	☐	
Is there an electronic access control system such as a card reader or card swipe reader to gain access into the proposed office area? If so who controls the issuing of cards and where is the access panel/computer located?	☐	☐	☐	

Fire and Services

Checklist	YES	NO	N/A	Comments
What type of fire protection is available?	☐	☐	☐	
Is it tested? How often?	☐	☐	☐	
Is emergency power available in the building?	☐	☐	☐	
Is there an alternative supply of potable water?	☐	☐	☐	
Access to power/heating/air conditioning plants, gas mains, water supplies, as well as electrical and telecommunications services should be secured. Is it and if so how?	☐	☐	☐	

Access

Checklist	YES	NO	N/A	Comments
Are there separate elevators feeding basement/car park areas and upper office floors? For example, is there a goods-only lift?	☐	☐	☐	
In larger buildings, do elevators feed segmented floors, such as one group servicing floors 1–9 and a second elevator servicing floors 10–19?	☐	☐	☐	
Are electronic access controls available in the elevators?	☐	☐	☐	
Is building car parking controlled? If so how?	☐	☐	☐	
Is there any public car parking within the building?	☐	☐	☐	
Do delivery vehicles gain access to the site for drop off and pick up? Is it within the footprint of the building perimeter?	☐	☐	☐	
Are there vehicle barrier systems, such as bollards, planters, or high curbs, that currently exist and are used to limit direct curbside public vehicle access to the front of the building?	☐	☐	☐	
Is pedestrian access to the building controlled, If so, how?	☐	☐	☐	
Are there free public areas within the building that are not controlled or monitored?	☐	☐	☐	
Are there appropriate signage indicating evacuation points for the office? And for directing visitors to appropriate areas and entry/exit points?	☐	☐	☐	

13.10 SAMPLE BOMB THREAT ROOM SEARCH CHECKLIST

After completion of search, tape this page to the wall immediately outside the room door.

If a Suspicious Item is Found

Do NOT touch or move it.

Call your building warden or security manager on _____

Report what you have found.

    Description _____

    Location _____

Nearest telephone extension _____

Wait for instructions.

Areas to be Searched

Room/building/specific space/equipment within room

Search Pattern

Start search from the doorway.

Move to the right continuously, search around the walls and floor until you return to the door.

Search false ceilings last.

Key Search Points

All packages/bags identified	☐	Rubbish bins checked	☐
Bookcases checked	☐	Window sills checked	☐
File cabinets checked	☐	Desks checked	☐
Ductwork checked	☐		

Remember To:

Open all windows.

Close all curtains.

Secure any sensitive/classified material.

Stay off the phone unless making a report.

Stay in your office and search your area.

Do NOT turn off any electrical devices.

Room Search Details

Time _____ Date _____ Conducted By _____

Searched ☐   **Not Searched** ☐   **Nothing Found** ☐   **Item Found** ☐

13.11 EVALUATION CRITERIA FOR BUSINESS CONTINUITY AND ORGANIZATIONAL RESILIENCE

Introduction

Business continuity management is, as the title implies, designed to improve the ability for the executive to continue to manage their business under adverse conditions, whereas organizational resilience provides a measure against which to gauge the ability to return to business as usual.

It is reasonable to assume that all businesses will vary in detail, and so it is reasonable to assume that no two business continuity management plans or organizational resilience measures will be the same. The most complete evaluation of these areas will occur by testing them with as much reality as possible against the success criteria set within the individual organization. The best guidance for the production of your own organization-specific program is to have reviewed and addressed, where relevant, all issues to a reasonable degree.

These evaluation criteria has been produced by the Business Continuity Institute (BCI), in cooperation with the DTI, CCTA, and the Loss Prevention Council. The criteria can be reproduced providing the source is acknowledged. For more information, contact the Institute on +44 (0) 870 603 8783 or visit the BCI website at www.thebci.org.

Users wishing to complete the scoring system should estimate the degree to which they comply with the guidance by marking the boxes provided as shown with the figure 1 or 0. Where 1 represents compliance with the statement.

Not at all	Partially	Largely	Fully
0	0	1	0

These boxes appear at the right-hand end of the line adjacent to each significant heading and subheading. This document is linked to a spreadsheet, which will be updated automatically from the scores placed in the boxes and will produce a final analysis of the effectiveness of the continuity management process being assessed. Those users wishing to use the spreadsheet to develop a numerical score should enter the number 1(one) in the corresponding cell. The spreadsheet will calculate a resultant score that can be used to show where the application of the recommended practice can be improved.

The document is presented in 10 principal sections, each of which addresses a significant part of the process. The 10 sections are generally in sequential order rather than in order of importance, and it may be necessary to iterate between sections during a business continuity program.

Subject Area Overview

Subject Area	Title and Description
1	**Project Initiation and Management** Establish the need for a business continuity plan (BCP), including obtaining management support and organizing and managing the project to completion within agreed on time and budget limits.
2	**Risk Evaluation and Control** Determine the events and environmental surroundings that can adversely affect the organization and its facilities with disruption as well as disaster, the damage such events can cause, and the controls needed to prevent or minimize the effects of potential loss. Provide cost/benefit analysis to justify investment in controls to mitigate risks.
3	**Business Impact Analysis** Identify the impacts resulting from disruptions and disaster scenarios that can affect the organization and techniques that can be used to quantify and qualify such impacts. Establish critical functions, their recovery priorities, and interdependencies so that the recovery time objective can be set.
4	**Developing Business Continuity Strategies** Determine and guide the selection of alternative business recovery operating strategies for the recovery of business and information technologies within the recovery time objective, while maintaining the organization's critical functions.
5	**Emergency Response and Operations** Develop and implement procedures for responding to and stabilizing the situation following an incident or event, including establishing and managing an emergency operations center to be used as a command center during the emergency.
6	**Developing and Implementing Business Continuity Plans** Design, develop, and implement the business continuity plan that provides recovery within the recovery time objective.
7	**Awareness and Training Programs** Prepare a program to create corporate awareness and enhance the skills required to develop, implement, maintain, and execute the business continuity plan.
8	**Maintaining and Exercizing Business Continuity Plans** Preplan and coordinate plan exercises, and evaluate and document plan exercise results. Develop processes to maintain the currency of continuity capabilities and the plan document in accordance with the organization's strategic direction. Verify that the plan will prove effective by comparison with a suitable standard, and report results in a clear and concise manner.

9	**Public Relations and Crisis Communication** Develop, coordinate, evaluate, and exercise plans to handle the media during crisis situations. Develop, coordinate, evaluate, and exercise plans to communicate with and, as appropriate, provide trauma counseling for employees and their families, key customers, critical suppliers, owners/stockholders, and corporate management during crisis. Ensure all stakeholders are kept informed on an as-needed basis.
10	**Coordination with Public Authorities** Establish applicable procedures and policies for coordinating response, continuity, and restoration activities with local authorities while ensuring compliance with applicable statutes or regulations.

Each of these areas is discussed below.

Project Initiation and Management

Establish the need for a business continuity plan (BCP), which includes obtaining management support as well as organizing and managing the project to completion within agreed on time and budget limits.

This topic must address:

- Lead sponsors in defining objectives, policies, and critical success factors
- Scope and objectives
- Legal and requirements reasons
- Case histories
- Coordinate and organize/manage the BCP project
- Understand the difference between disaster recovery, response, mitigation/avoidance, contingency planning, business continuity, and crisis management
- Oversee the BCP project through effective control methods and change management
- Present (sell) the project to management and staff
- Develop project plan and budget
- Define and recommend project structure and management
- Manage the process

The planning process should demonstrate evidence of work done in the following areas.

Establish the Need for Business Continuity

Not at all	Partially	Largely	Fully
0	0	0	0

Has the need for business continuity been established, by reference as appropriate to the following?

- Reference relevant legal/regulatory/statutory/contractual requirements and restrictions
- Reference relevant regulations of industry trade bodies or associations, where appropriate
- Reference current recommendations of relevant authorities (define these)
- Relate legislation, regulations, and recommendations to organizational policy
- Identify any conflicts between organizational policies and relevant external requirements
- Identify any audit records
- Propose methods, which may include a BCP, to resolve any conflicts between organizational policies and relevant external requirements
- Identify business practices, e.g., just-in-time inventory, that may adversely impact the organization's ability to recover following a disaster event

Communicate the Need for a Business Continuity Plan

Not at all	Partially	Largely	Fully
0	0	0	0

Has the need for a business continuity plan been communicated throughout the organization, as evidenced by the following?

- Develop awareness by means of formal reports and presentations
- State the benefits of the BCP and relate the benefits to organizational mission, objectives, and operations
- Gain organizational commitment to the BCP project
- Develop a mission statement/charter for the BCP project

Involve Executive Management in the BCP Project

Not at all	Partially	Largely	Fully
0	0	0	0

Have steps been taken to involve executive management in the BCP project? Such as follows:

- Explain executive management's role in the BCP project
- Explain and communicate management's accountability and liability

Establish a Planning/Steering Committee: Roles and Responsibilities, Types of Organization, Control and Development, and Membership

Not at all	Partially	Largely	Fully
0	0	0	0

Has a planning/steering committee been set up and a plan developed, as below?

- Select appropriate personnel
- Define their roles and responsibilities
- Develop an overall project plan with realistic time estimates and schedule
- Develop a suitable set of objectives for the BCP

Develop Budget Requirements

Not at all	Partially	Largely	Fully
0	0	0	0

Have budget requirements been addressed in the following respects?

- Clearly define resource requirements
- Obtain estimates of financial requirement
- Verify the validity of resources requirements
- Validate the estimates of financial requirements
- Negotiate resource and financial requirements with management

Identify Planning Team(s) and Responsibilities

Not at all	Partially	Largely	Fully
0	0	0	0

Have planning teams been set up with appropriate responsibilities?

- Emergency management/crisis response/crisis management team
- Business continuity planning teams (multilocation, multidivisions, etc.)
- Recovery/response and restoration teams

Develop and Coordinate Action Plans

Not at all	Partially	Largely	Fully
0	0	0	0

Have appropriate action plans been developed and coordinated?

Develop Project Management and Documentation Requirements

Not at all	Partially	Largely	Fully
0	0	0	0

Have all project management and documentation requirements been established and agreed within the organization?

Report to Senior Management and Obtain Senior Management Approval/Commitment

Not at all	Partially	Largely	Fully
0	0	0	0

Has an appropriate reporting system been set up and senior management commitment obtained?

- Set up a schedule to report the progress of the BCP project to senior managers
- Develop regular status reports for senior management that contain concise, pertinent, accurate, and timely information on key parameters of interest or information which senior management should be made aware of

Project Management

Not at all	Partially	Largely	Fully
0	0	0	0

Have suitable project management procedures, with the following characteristics, been put in place?

- Identify and develop business continuity plan phases similar to classic project plan phases, e.g., problem investigation, problem definition, feasibility study, systems description, implementation, installation, and review
- Establish business continuity plan project characteristics: goals, tasks, resources, time schedules, and critical success factors
- Execute generally accepted responsibilities of a business continuity planning project manager:
  - Define the business continuity planning project
  - Assess the business continuity planning project risk
  - Organize the business continuity planning project
  - Plan the business continuity planning project in detail, including time management and project scheduling
  - Monitor and manage the business continuity planning project activities

- Track and report the business continuity planning project progress
- Manage change associated with the business continuity planning project

Risk Evaluation and Control

Determine the events and environmental surroundings that can adversely affect the organization and its facilities with disruption as well as disaster, the damage such events can cause, and the controls needed to prevent or minimize the effects of potential loss. Provide cost/benefit analysis to justify investment in controls to mitigate risks.

This topic must address the following:

1. Understand the function of probabilities and risk reduction/mitigation within the organization
2. Identify potential risks to the organization, as well as the probability and consequences
3. Identify outside expertise required
4. Identify vulnerabilities/threats/exposures
5. Identify risk reduction/mitigation alternatives
6. Identify credible information sources
7. Interface with management to determine acceptable risk levels
8. Document and present findings

The planning process should demonstrate evidence of work done in the following areas.

Understand Loss Potentials

Not at all	Partially	Largely	Fully
0	0	0	0

To what extent have steps been taken to identify and understand the potential for loss, by the following means?

- Identify threats from both internal and external sources. These should include, but not be limited to, the following:
  - Natural, man-made, technological, or political disasters
  - Accidental versus intentional
  - Internal versus external
  - Controllable risks versus those beyond the organization's control
  - Events with prior warnings versus those with no prior warnings
- Determine the probability of events
  - Information source reliability
  - Information credibility

- Create methods of information gathering
- Develop a suitable method to evaluate probability versus severity
- Establish ongoing support of evaluation process
- Identify the relevant key security and legislative issues
- Establish cost/benefit analysis to be associated with the identified loss potential

Determine the Organization's Vulnerability to Loss Potentials

Not at all	Partially	Largely	Fully
0	0	0	0

Has the organization's vulnerability to loss potentials been fully determined?

- Identify primary threats the organization may face and secondary/collateral events that could materialize because of such threats, e.g., hurricane threat could result in several events, including high winds, flood, fire, building and roof collapse, etc.
- Select vulnerabilities most likely to occur and with greatest impact.

Identify Controls and Safeguards to Prevent or Minimize the Effect of the Loss Potential

Not at all	Partially	Largely	Fully
0	0	0	0

Are adequate controls and safeguards in place against the effect of the loss potential?

- Location(s) and security considerations. The actions taken and facilities installed to reduce the probability of occurrence of incidents that would impair the ability to conduct business.
- Physical protection
  - Understand the need to restrict access to buildings, rooms, and other enclosures where circumstances demand a three-dimensional consideration
  - Understand the need for barriers and strengthened structures to deter willful and accidental and/or unauthorized entry
- Physical presence
  - Understand the need for the use of specialist personnel to conduct checks at key entry points
  - Understand the need for manned and/or recorded surveillance equipment to control access points and areas of exclusion

- Logical protection
  - Understand the need for system-provided protection of data stored, in process, or in translation
- Location of assets
  - Understand the inherent protection afforded key assets by virtue of their location relative to sources of risk
- Location: physical construction, geographic location, corporate neighbors, facilities infrastructure, community infrastructure
- Protection: detection, notification, suppression
- Security and access controls, tenant insurance, leasehold agreements
- Personnel procedures
- Procedural controls
- Information backup and protection
- Information security: hardware, software, data, network
- Preventive maintenance and equipment preplanning
- Utilities: duplication of utilities, redundancies in utilities
- Interface with outside agencies
- Services: electricity, air conditioning, water, communications, maintenance, equipment replacement and spares, documentation

Evaluate, Select, and Use Appropriate Risk Analysis Methodologies and Tools

Not at all	Partially	Largely	Fully
0	0	0	0

Have appropriate risk analysis methodologies and tools been evaluated and adopted?

- Identify alternative risk analysis methodologies and tools
  1. Qualitative and quantitative methodologies
  2. Advantages and disadvantages
  3. Reliability/confidence factor
  4. Basis of mathematical formulas used
- Select appropriate methodology and tool(s) for company-wide implementation

Identify and Implement Information-Gathering Activities

Not at all	Partially	Largely	Fully
0	0	0	0

Have appropriate and consistent information gathering methods been established?

- Develop a strategy consistent with business issues and organizational policy
- Develop a strategy that can be managed across business divisions and organizational locations
- Employ credible information sources
- Create organization-wide methods of information collection and distribution
  1. Forms and questionnaires
  2. Interviews
  3. Meetings
  4. Documentation review
  5. Analysis
- Use software, where appropriate

Evaluate the Effectiveness of Controls and Safeguards

Not at all	Partially	Largely	Fully
0	0	0	0

Has the effectiveness of controls and safeguards been reviewed?

- Develop communications flow with other internal departments/divisions
- Establish business continuity service level agreements for both supplier and customer organizations and groups
- Develop preventive and preplanning options
  1. Cost/benefit analysis
  2. Implementation priorities, procedures, and control
  3. Testing program
  4. Audit functions and responsibilities
- Understand options for risk management and selection of appropriate or cost-effective response, i.e., risk avoidance, transfer, or acceptance of risk
- Develop interface with suppliers and utilities
- Develop security practices
- Identify methods to minimize the effects of the loss potential
- Brief participants, ensuring they understand their objectives and reporting structure

Risk Evaluation and Control

Not at all	Partially	Largely	Fully
0	0	0	0

Have all risks been evaluated and suitable controls put in place?

- Establish disaster scenarios based on risks to which the organization is vulnerable. The disaster scenarios should be based on these type of criteria: severe in magnitude, occurring at the worst possible time, resulting in severe impairment to the organization's ability to conduct business.

- Evaluate risks and classify them according to relevant criteria, including risks under the organization's control, risks beyond the organization's control, threats with prior warnings (such as tornadoes and hurricanes), and threats with no prior warnings (such as earthquakes).

- Evaluate the impact of risks and threats on those factors essential for conducting business operations, which include the availability of personnel, availability of information technology, availability of communications technology, status of infrastructure (including transportation), and so on.

- Evaluate controls and recommend changes, if necessary, to reduce impact caused by risks and threats.
    1. Controls to inhibit impact threats: preventive controls (such as passwords, smoke detectors, and firewalls)
    2. Controls to compensate for impact of threats: reactive controls (such as hot sites).

Security

Not at all	Partially	Largely	Fully
0	0	0	0

Have possible security threats and counter measures been identified?

- Identify the organization's possible security exposures, which include the following specific categories of security risks:
    1. Physical/plant security
    2. Information security—computer room and media storage area security
    3. Communications security—voice and data communications security
    4. Network security—Intranet security, Internet security
- Advise on feasible, cost-effective security measures required to prevent/reduce security-related risks and threats

Backup and Restoration Procedures

Not at all	Partially	Largely	Fully
0	0	0	0

Are backup and restoration procedures in place for all vital records?

- Identify vital record needs in the organization, including paper and electronic records
- Evaluate existing backup and restoration procedures for vital records
- Advise on and implement feasible, cost-effective backup and restoration procedures for all forms of the organization's vital records

Business Impact Analysis

Identify the impacts resulting from disruptions and disaster scenarios that can affect the organization and techniques that can be used to quantify and qualify such impacts. Establish critical functions, their recovery priorities, and interdependencies so that a recovery time objective can be set.

This topic must address the following items:

1. Identify organization functions
2. Identify knowledgeable and credible functional area representatives
3. Identify and define criticality criteria
4. Present criteria to management for approval
5. Coordinate analysis
6. Identify interdependencies
7. Define recovery objectives and timeframes, including recovery times, expected losses, and priorities
8. Identify information requirements
9. Identify resource requirements
10. Define report format
11. Prepare and present analysis

The planning process should demonstrate evidence of work done in the following areas.

Establish the Project

Not at all	Partially	Largely	Fully
0	0	0	0

Has the project been established on a sound basis?

- Identify and obtain a project sponsor for the business impact analysis (BIA) activity
- Define objectives and scope for the BIA project
- Choose an appropriate BIA project planning methodology/tool
- Identify and inform participants of the BIA project and its purpose

- Identify training requirements
- Establish a training schedule and undertake training
- Ensure the project leader has a sound understanding of the purposes of the organization
- Obtain agreement on final project time schedule and initiate the BIA project

Assess Effects of Disruptions, Loss Exposure, and Business Impact

Not at all	Partially	Largely	Fully
0	0	0	0

Have the effects and impacts of potential disruptions been properly assessed?

- Effects of disruptions
  - Loss of assets: key people, physical assets, information, and other intangible assets
  - Disruption to the continuity of service and operations
  - Violation of law/regulation
  - Public perception
- Impact of disruptions on business
  - Financial
  - Customers and suppliers
  - Public relations/credibility
  - Legal
  - Regulatory requirements/considerations
  - Environmental
  - Operational
  - Personnel
  - Other resources
- Determine loss exposure
  - Quantitative
    - (a) Property loss
    - (b) Revenue loss
    - (c) Fines
    - (d) Cash flow
    - (e) Accounts receivable
    - (f) Accounts payable
    - (g) Legal liability
    - (h) Human resources
    - (i) Additional expenses/increased cost of working

- Qualitative
  - (a) Human resources
  - (b) Morale
  - (c) Confidence
  - (d) Legal
  - (e) Social and corporate image
  - (f) Financial community credibility

Business Impact Analysis Considerations: Quantitative and Qualitative Methods

Not at all	Partially	Largely	Fully
0	0	0	0

Has a full business impact analysis been carried out, addressing both quantitative and qualitative aspects?

- BIA data collection methodologies
  - Finalize an appropriate data collection method, e.g., questionnaires, interviews, workshop, or an agreed combination)
  - Recommend and obtain agreement as to how potential financial and nonfinancial impact can be quantified and evaluated
  - Identify and obtain agreement on requirements for nonquantifiable impact information and gain agreement
  - Develop questionnaire (if used) and completion instructions
  - Determine data analysis methods (manual or computer)
- Data collection via questionnaires
  - Understand the need for appropriate design and distribution of questionnaires, including explanation of purpose, to participating departmental managers and staff
  - Understand the role of, and manage, project kick-off meetings to distribute and explain the questionnaire
  - Understand the role of and support respondents during completion of questionnaires
  - Review completed questionnaires and identify those requiring follow-up interviews
  - Conduct follow-up discussions when clarification and/or additional data is required
- Data collection via interviews only
  - Understand the need for consistency, with the structure of each interview predefined and following a common format
  - Ensure the base data to be collected at each interview is predefined

- Understand the need for initial interview to be reviewed and verified by the interviewee
- Schedule follow-up interviews, if initial analysis shows a need to clarify and/or add to the data already provided
- Data collection via a workshop
  - Understand the need for, and set a clear agenda and set of objectives
  - Identify the appropriate level of participating management and obtain agreement
  - Choose appropriate venue, evaluating location, facilities, and staff availability
  - Act as facilitator and leader during discussions:
- Ensure workshop objectives are met
- Ensure all issues outstanding at the end of the workshop are identified and agree responsibility for their resolution on
- Business impact analysis report
  - Prepare draft BIA report containing initial impact findings and issues
  - Issue draft report to participating managers and request feedback
  - Review manager feedback and, where appropriate, revise findings accordingly or add to outstanding issues
  - Schedule a workshop or meeting with participating manager(s) to discuss initial findings, when necessary
  - Ensure original findings are updated to reflect changes that developed from these meetings
  - Prepare final business impact analysis report according to organization or house standards
  - Prepare and undertake formal presentation of business impact analysis findings to peers and executive bodies

  Note: It is essential that the BIA report is presented to the Board of Directors in a format that is compatible with their corporate standards. No separate standard is nominated for the format or distribution of BIA reports, and these reports are expected to vary between companies.

Define Criticality of Business Functions and Records, and Prioritize

Not at all	Partially	Largely	Fully
0	0	0	0

Has the criticality of business functions and records been defined and have priorities established?

- Establish the definition of criticality and negotiate with management single or multiple levels of criticality
- Identify critical functions

- Business functions
- Support functions
- Interdependencies
- Identify vital records to support business continuity and business restoration
- Prioritize critical business functions

Identify Business Processes

Not at all	Partially	Largely	Fully
0	0	0	0

Have business processes as well as their inter-relationships and interdependencies been identified?

- Inter-relationship between the business processes
- Process dependencies
  - Intradepartmental
  - Interdepartmental
  - Technology

Determine Recovery Timeframes and Minimum Resource Requirements

Not at all	Partially	Largely	Fully
0	0	0	0

Have recovery timeframes and resource requirements for business critical functions been determined?

- Determine recovery windows for critical business functions based on level of criticality
- Determine the order of recovery for critical business functions, and support functions and systems based on parallel and interdependent activities
- Determine minimum resource requirements for recovery and resumption of critical functions and support systems
  - Internal and external resources
  - Owned versus non-owned resources
  - Existing resources and additional resources required

Determine Replacement Times

Not at all	Partially	Largely	Fully
0	0	0	0

Have replacement timetables been established for the following?

- Equipment
- Key staff
- Raw materials/subassemblies
- Other

Developing Business Continuity Strategies

Determine and guide the selection of alternative business recovery operating strategies for recovery of business and information technologies within the recovery time objective, while maintaining the organization's critical functions.

This topic must address:

1. Understand available alternatives, their advantages, disadvantages, and cost ranges, including mitigation as a recovery strategy
2. Identify viable recovery strategies with business functional areas
3. Consolidate strategies
4. Identify off-site storage requirements and alternative facilities
5. Develop business unit consensus
6. Present strategies to management to obtain commitment

The planning process should demonstrate evidence of work done in the following areas.

Identify Business Continuity Strategy Requirements

Not at all	Partially	Largely	Fully
0	0	0	0

Have all business continuity strategy requirements been identified?

- Review business recovery issues
  - Timeframes
  - Options
  - Location
  - Personnel
  - Communications
- Review technology recovery issues for each support service
- Review nontechnology recovery issues for each support service, including those support services not dependent on technology
- Compare internal/external solutions

- Identify alternative recovery strategies
  - Do nothing
  - Defer action
  - Manual procedures
  - Reciprocal agreements
  - Alternative site or business facility
  - Alternative source of product
  - Service bureau
  - Consortium
  - Distributed processing
  - Alternative communications
  - Mitigation
  - Preplanning
- Compare internal and external solutions
- Assess risk associated with each optional recovery strategy

Assess Suitability of Alternative Strategies Against the Results of a Business Impact Analysis

Not at all	Partially	Largely	Fully
0	0	0	0

Has the suitability of alternative strategies been assessed against the business impact analysis?

- Effectively analyze business needs criteria
- Clearly define recovery planning objectives
- Develop a consistent method for evaluation
- Set baseline criteria for options

Prepare Cost/Benefit Analysis of Recovery Strategies and Present Findings to Senior Management

Not at all	Partially	Largely	Fully
0	0	0	0

Has a cost/benefit analysis of recovery strategies been prepared and presented to senior management?

- Employ a practical, understandable methodology
- Set realistic time schedules for evaluation and report writing
- Deliver concise specific recommendations to senior management

Select Alternate Site(s) and Off-Site Storage

Not at all	Partially	Largely	Fully
0	0	0	0

Have appropriate alternative site(s) and off-site storage been selected and agreed?

- Criteria
- Communications
- Agreement considerations
- Comparison techniques
- Acquisition
- Contractual consideration

Understand Contractual Agreements for Business Continuity Services (BCS)

Not at all	Partially	Largely	Fully
0	0	0	0

Has an appropriate framework for BCS contractual agreements been prepared?

- Understand and prepare requirements statements for use in formal agreements for the provision of continuity services
- Formulate any necessary technical specifications for use in invitation-to-tender format
- Interpret external agreements proposed by suppliers in relation to the original requirements specified
- Identify specific requirements excluded from any standard agreements proposed
- Understand and advise on the inclusion of optional elements and those that are essential

Enterprise-Wide

Not at all	Partially	Largely	Fully
0	0	0	0

Have enterprise-wide plans for business continuity been drawn up?

- Develop, implement, and exercise enterprise-wide plans for business continuity to emphasize coordination of business unit continuity, information technology, and communications technology recovery and continuity
- Develop, implement, and exercise enterprise-level crisis management plans for media handling, crisis communications, and so on

Business Unit Plans

Not at all	Partially	Largely	Fully
0	0	0	0

Have business unit plans for business continuity been drawn up?

- Develop, implement, and exercise business unit response, recovery, resumption, restoration, and return plans
- Designate and obtain approval for recommended staff and access to essential equipment resources for work area recovery sites

Emergency Telecommunications

Not at all	Partially	Largely	Fully
0	0	0	0

Have appropriate strategies and arrangements for voice and data communications been developed?

> Note: This area of contingency planning requires a thorough understanding of the installed telecommunication systems, the business continuity planner is strongly urged to include telecommunications or communications expertise when dealing with this area.

- Voice communications
  - Develop strategies to recover/restore voice communications
  - Make arrangements with local and long distance phone service providers for voice communications recover, e.g., alternate exchanges, alternate routing, dial backup, foreign exchanges, and so on
- Data communications
  - Develop, implement, and exercise plans to recover/restore data communications
  - Evaluate and select appropriate arrangements with local, long distance, and global telecommunications network service providers for data communications recovery strategies and action plans

Emergency Response and Operations

Develop and implement procedures for responding to and stabilizing the situation following an incident or event, including establishing and managing an emergency operations center to be used as a command center during the emergency. This topic must address:

1. Identify potential types of emergencies and the responses needed, e.g., fire, hazardous materials leak, and medical
2. Identify the existence of appropriate emergency response procedures

3. Recommend the development of emergency procedures where none exist
4. Integrate disaster recovery/business continuity procedures with emergency response procedures
5. Identify the command and control requirements of managing an emergency
6. Recommend the development of command and control procedures to define roles, authority, and communications processes for managing an emergency
7. Ensure emergency response procedures are integrated with requirements of public authorities (refer also to subject area 10, coordination with public authorities)

The planning process should demonstrate evidence of work done in the following areas.

Identify Components of Emergency Response Procedure

Not at all	Partially	Largely	Fully
0	0	0	0

Have the various components of an emergency response procedure been identified and put in place?

- Reporting procedures
  - Internal (escalation procedures)
    - Local
    - Organization (decision-making process)
  - External (response procedures)
    - Public agencies and media
    - Suppliers of products and services
- Pre-incident preparation
  - By types of disaster
    Acts of nature
    Accidental
    Intentional
  - Management continuity and authority
  - Roles of designated personnel
- Emergency actions
  - Evacuation
  - Medical care and personnel counseling
  - Hazardous material response
  - Firefighting
  - Notification
  - Other

- Facility stabilization
- Damage mitigation
- Testing procedures and responsibilities

Develop Detailed Emergency Response Procedures

Not at all	Partially	Largely	Fully
0	0	0	0

Have detailed emergency response procedures been worked out?

- Protection of personnel
  - Recognize and understand the value of supplementing any relevant statutory precautions
  - Identify options for immediate deployment and subsequent contract
  - Provide for communication with staff, next-of-kin, and dependents
  - Understand implications of statutory regulations
- Containment of incident
  - Understand the principles of salvage and loss containment
  - Understand options available to supplement the efforts of the emergency services in limiting business impact
  - Understand possibilities within business functions to limit the impact of a disaster, within statutory constraints
- Assessment of effect
  - Analyze the situation and provide effective assessment report
  - Estimate the event's direct impact on the organization
  - Communicate situation to employees at involved facility and any other organization locations
  - Demonstrate awareness of the likely media interest and formulate a response in conjunction with any existing public relations and/or existing marketing unit
- Decide optimum actions
  - Understand the issues to be considered when recommending or making decisions on recovery options
  - Understand the roles of the emergency services
  - Maintain principles of security, especially in regard to the disposal of stored/archived materials or damaged materials with retained value

Identify Command and Control Requirements

Not at all	Partially	Largely	Fully
0	0	0	0

Have all command and control requirements been identified?

- Designing and equipping the emergency operations center
- Command and decision authority roles during the incident
- Communication vehicles, e.g., radio, messengers, and cellular telephones
- Logging and documentation methods

Command and Control Procedures

Not at all	Partially	Largely	Fully
0	0	0	0

Have all command and control procedures been established?

- Opening the emergency operations center
- Security for the emergency operations center
- Scheduling the emergency operations center teams
- Management and operations of the emergency operations center
- Closing the emergency operations center

Emergency Response and Prioritization

Not at all	Partially	Largely	Fully
0	0	0	0

Have emergency response and prioritization procedures been developed and tested?

- Develop, implement, and exercise emergency response and prioritization procedures, including determination of priorities for actions in an emergency
- Develop, implement, and exercise prioritization procedures such as first aid and medical treatment. Identify location and develop procedures for transportation to nearby hospitals

Salvage and Restoration

Not at all	Partially	Largely	Fully
0	0	0	0

Has a salvage and restoration reaction team been assembled and has a strategy for initial on-site activity defined?

- Assemble reaction team
  - Understand the need for effective diagnosis of incident by telephone

- Understand the need for effective assembly of relevant resources at the affected site
- Develop internal escalation procedures to provide required level of resources on-site as incident/response develops
- Define strategy for initial on-site activity
  - Understand the need to identify immediate loss mitigation and salvage requirements
  - Understand the need for and, if necessary, prepare an action plan for site safety, security, and stabilization
  - Identify appropriate methods for protection of assets on-site, including equipment, premises, and documentation
  - Recognize potential need to establish liaison with external agencies, e.g., statutory agencies, emergency services such as fire departments and police, insurers, loss adjusters, etc., and specify type of information these agencies may require
  - Understand business requirements and interpret them to aid physical asset recovery
  - Establish procedures with public authorities for facility access

Developing and Implementing Business Continuity Plans

Design, develop, and implement the business continuity plan that provides recovery within the recovery time objective.

This topic must address:

1. Identify the components of the planning process
   a. Planning methodology
   b. Plan organization
   c. Direction of efforts
   d. Staffing requirements
2. Control the planning process and produce the plan
3. Implement the plan
4. Test the plan
5. Maintain the plan

The planning process should demonstrate evidence of work done in the following areas.

Determine Plan Development Requirements

Not at all	Partially	Largely	Fully
0	0	0	0

- Have planning aids been selected?
- Have specific tools been selected?
  - Job descriptions
  - Action plans
- What checklists are in use?
  - Matrices and flowcharts
  - Forms
  - Information database
  - Other supporting documentation

Define Recovery Management and Control Requirements

Not at all	Partially	Largely	Fully
0	0	0	0

- Is there an agreed definition of a disaster?
  - Differentiate between an interruption and a disaster
  - Suggest severity criteria that may be used to create a definition
  - Design escalation criteria
- Is there an agreed approach to key phases of recovery, and is that approach documented?
- Is there an agreed recovery team concept?
  - Team description
  - Team organization
  - Responsibilities
- Recovery coordinator
- Group coordinators
  - Support staff
  - emergency operations center
- Is there an established procedure to shift from emergency response plan to business continuity plan?

Identify and Define the Format and Structure of Plan Components.

Not at all	Partially	Largely	Fully
0	0	0	0

Are procedures in place to ensure business continuity using a format suitable for use under emergency conditions?

- Is the plan adequately designed and structured?
  - Identify examples of alternative plans and structures
  - Define how plan structure is tied to the organization

- Document structure and design of departmental continuity plans
- Ensure built-in mechanisms to ease maintenance
- Plan and implement the gathering of data required for plan completion
- Have tasks and responsibilities been allocated?
  - Differentiate between recovery teams and departmental teams
  - Identify tasks to be undertaken
  - Identify necessary teams to perform required tasks
  - Assign responsibilities to teams
  - Identify and list key contacts, suppliers, and resources

Draft the Plan

Not at all	Partially	Largely	Fully
0	0	0	0

- Have appropriate tools been selected for plan development and maintenance?
- Is there a business continuity plan, ensuring adequate and appropriate involvement of personnel required to implement the plan?
- How is data gathered to ensure the plan is complete and accurate?

Define Business Continuity Procedures

Not at all	Partially	Largely	Fully
0	0	0	0

- How is information cataloged?
  - Identify and confirm information and documentation critical to the organization's key business
  - Select or recommend appropriate methods of business backup
  - Determine which information should be duplicated
  - Establish duplication or replication methods
  - Set up regular schedules for duplication
  - Quantify storage requirements
  - Identify suitable storage facilities
  - Establish schedules for safe transfer of information to suitable storage facilities
  - Understand retention periods
  - Identify key suppliers
- Are there adequate protection and replication strategies?
  - Define assumptions that govern the choice of replication and storage strategies

- Define program for replication and storage of specific classes and types of information
- Understand the advantages and disadvantages of
- Duplication methods
- Replication methods
- Storage methods
  - Understand the advantages and disadvantages of available protection methods
  - Predict shelf-life of stored information
  - Understand suitable treatment that may be required during storage, according to the media used and environmental conditions
- Is there adequate information recovery?
  - Recommend suitable procedures, taking into account:
    - Most suitable sequence of recovery
    - Compatibility of reading and writing equipment and storage media
    - Timeframes determined by the business requirements
    - Timeframes determined by the legislative requirements
    - Requirements of daily or weekly routines, where applicable
  - Identify recovery or starting point for processing or handling information
  - Develop a reasonable set of assumptions, taking various realistic scenarios into account
- Are there optional business methods?
  - Recommend alternative ways to conduct business when normal resources are unavailable following a disaster or other disruptive event that will be effective until recovery procedures are successfully completed
  - Recommend methods/procedures to transfer business functions from alternative, temporary, or emergency operation into the new/replaced/reinstalled service

Damage Assessment

Not at all	Partially	Largely	Fully
0	0	0	0

- How is damage assessment carried out?
  - Create an action plan for assessing damage
  - Understand economics of repair versus replacement
  - Understand the capabilities of salvage specialists in selecting and applying relevant methods of contamination analysis

- Understand the criteria for selecting appropriate subcontractors for salvage operations
- Clearly relate damage assessment to business continuity of organization
- Is there a strategy for restoration?
  - Employ a logical but relevant and practical approach to business recovery requirements
  - Demonstrate ability to reduce consequential losses
  - Agree on restoration methods for business assets, e.g., equipment, electronics, documents, data, furnishings, premises, plant, computers, and so on
  - Understand the approval process for restoration and especially the implications of warranties
  - Define a strategy for restoration

Critical Resource Acquisition

Not at all	Partially	Largely	Fully
0	0	0	0

Are procedures in place for the acquisition of critical resources at short notice?

Security

Not at all	Partially	Largely	Fully
0	0	0	0

Have physical security procedures been addressed in the plan?

Human Resource and Personnel Considerations

Not at all	Partially	Largely	Fully
0	0	0	0

Have human resource and personnel considerations been included in the plan?

Develop General Introduction or Overview

Not at all	Partially	Largely	Fully
0	0	0	0

Does the plan have a general introduction containing the following topics?

- General information
  - Introduction
  - Scope

- Objectives
- Assumptions
- Responsibility overview
- Testing
- Maintenance
- Plan activation
  - Notification
    - Primary
    - Secondary
  - Disaster declaration procedures
  - Mobilization procedures
  - Damage assessment concepts
    - Initial
    - Detailed
    - Team members
- Team organization
  - Team description
  - Team organization
  - Team leader responsibilities
- Policy statement
- Emergency operations center

Develop Administration Section

Not at all	Partially	Largely	Fully
0	0	0	0

Are the organization and administrative functions addressed?

- Have recovery functions for specific support functions been identified?
  - Personnel/human resources
  - Security
  - Insurance/risk management
  - Equipment/supplies purchasing
  - Transportation
  - Legal
- Is a public relations/media communications coordinator included?
  - Qualifications
  - Responsibilities

- Are other specialist coordinator/team responsibilities identified?
  - Relations/liaison with regulatory bodies
  - Investor relations
  - Relations with other involved groups, e.g., customers and suppliers
- Is there a vital records management and recovery program?
- Are action plans included?
  - Recovery team
    - Personnel
    - Responsibilities
    - Resources
  - Department/individual plans
  - Checklists
  - Technical procedures

Develop Business Operations Plan

Not at all	Partially	Largely	Fully
0	0	0	0

- Is there a plan for the operating units?
  - Essential business functions
  - Information protection and recovery
  - Activation actions
  - Disaster site recovery/restoration actions
  - End-user computing needs
- Is there an adequate vital records program?
- Are action plans in place?
  - Recovery team
    - Personnel
    - Responsibilities
    - Resources
- Do action plans address the following?
  - Specific department/individual plans
  - Checklists
  - Technical procedures

Develop Information Technology Recovery Plan

Not at all	Partially	Largely	Fully
0	0	0	0

- How is the recovery site activated?
  - Management
  - Administration/logistics
  - New equipment
  - Technical services
  - Application support
  - Network communications
  - Network engineering
  - Operations
  - Intersite logistics and communications
  - Data preparation
  - Production control
  - End-user liaison
- Are end-user requirements recorded?
- Is there a vital records program?
- Are action plans in place?
  - Recovery team
    - Personnel
    - Responsibilities
    - Resources
- Do action plans address the following?
  - Specific department/individual plans
  - Checklists
  - Technical procedures

Develop Communication Systems Plan

Not at all	Partially	Largely	Fully
0	0	0	0

- Is there a voice communications recovery plan?
  - Phone lines, including in-bound lines and fax lines
  - Voice mail, voice response units, and other voice-based services
  - Alternate arrangement for automated voice response during of a disaster
- Is there a data communications recovery plan?
  - Data communications with mainframe-based information systems
  - Local area network (LAN) recovery for work area recovery
  - Wide area network (WAN) recovery for restoring global connectivity

- E-mail, shared software, and other data communications-based work support
- Is detailed and up-to-date documentation available for voice and data communications networks throughout the enterprise?

Develop End-User Applications Plans

Not at all	Partially	Largely	Fully
0	0	0	0

- Is the plan adequately designed and structured?
  - Identify examples of alternative plans and structures
  - Define how plan structure is tied to the organization.
  - Document structure and design of departmental continuity plans
  - Ensure built-in mechanisms to ease maintenance
  - Plan and implement the gathering of data required for plan completion
- Is there an agreed approach to key phases of recovery; document agreed approach?
- Have tasks and responsibilities been allocated?
  - Differentiate between recovery teams and departmental teams
  - Identify tasks to be undertaken
  - Identify necessary teams to perform required tasks
  - Assign responsibilities to teams
  - Identify and list key contacts, suppliers, and resources

Implement the Plan

Not at all	Partially	Largely	Fully
0	0	0	0

- Is there an education program?
  - Standard guidelines for developing and implementing continuity plans
  - Staff roles and responsibilities defined in the continuity plans
  - Procedures to be followed by employees throughout the organization
  - Training and awareness presentations to management and staff
- Are the required tasks completed?
  - Acquiring additional equipment
  - Contractual arrangements
  - Preparing backup and off-site storage

- Have test plans, schedules, and reporting procedures been developed?
- Have maintenance, updating, and reporting procedures been developed?

Continuity Actions and Procedures

Not at all	Partially	Largely	Fully
0	0	0	0

Are continuity action plans in place?

Establish Plan Distribution and Control Procedures

Not at all	Partially	Largely	Fully
0	0	0	0

- Are procedures established for distribution and control of business continuity plans?
- Are procedures established for distribution and control of results of plan exercises?
- Are procedures established for distribution and control of plan changes and updates?

Awareness and Training Programs

Prepare a program to create corporate awareness and to enhance the skills required to develop, implement, maintain, and execute the business continuity plan.

This topic must address:

1. Establish objectives and components of training program
2. Identify functional training requirements
3. Develop training methodology
4. Develop awareness program
5. Acquire or develop training aids
6. Identify external training opportunities
7. Identify vehicles for corporate awareness

The planning process should demonstrate evidence of work done in the following areas.

Define Training Objectives

Not at all	Partially	Largely	Fully
0	0	0	0

Have training objectives been defined?

Develop Various Types of Training Programs

Not at all	Partially	Largely	Fully
0	0	0	0

Have all forms of training been considered?

- Computer based
- Classroom
- Test based

Develop Awareness Programs

Not at all	Partially	Largely	Fully
0	0	0	0

Has an awareness program been developed for the following departments?

- Management
- Team members
- New staff orientation

Identify Other Opportunities for Education

Not at all	Partially	Largely	Fully
0	0	0	0

Have all opportunities for education been explored?

- Professional business continuity planning conferences and seminars
- User groups
- Industry associations
- Publications

Maintaining and Exercising Business Continuity Plans

Preplan and coordinate plan exercises, and evaluate and document plan exercise results. Develop processes to maintain the currency of continuity capabilities and the plan document in accordance with the organization's strategic direction. Verify that the plan will prove effective by comparison with a suitable standard, and report results in a clear and concise manner.

This topic must address:

1. Preplan the exercises
2. Coordinate the exercises

3. Evaluate the exercise plans
4. Exercise the plans
5. Document the results
6. Evaluate the results
7. Update the plan
8. Report results/evaluation to management
9. Understand strategic directions of the business
10. Attend strategic planning meetings
11. Coordinate plan maintenance
12. Assist in establishing audit program for the business continuity plan

The planning process should demonstrate evidence of work done in the following areas.

Establish an Exercise Program

Not at all	Partially	Largely	Fully
0	0	0	0

Is there an established exercise program that addresses the following points?

- Effectively analyze complex issues
- Employ a logical, structured approach
- Develop an exercise strategy that
  - Does not put the organization at risk
  - Is practical, cost-effective, and appropriate to the organization
  - Ensures a high level of confidence in recovery capability
- Create a suitable set of exercise guidelines

Determine Exercise Requirements

Not at all	Partially	Largely	Fully
0	0	0	0

Is there an adequate definition of the exercise requirements addressing the following points?

- Define exercise objectives and establish levels of success
- Identify types of exercises, and their advantages and disadvantages
  - Simulations and walk-throughs
  - Modular
  - Functional

- Announced
- Unannounced
- Establish and document scope of the exercise
- Exercise growth or expansion
- Exercise frequency
- Logistics and preplanning

Develop Realistic Scenarios

Not at all	Partially	Largely	Fully
0	0	0	0

Have realistic exercise scenarios been prepared?

- Create exercise scenarios to approximate the types of incidents the organization is likely to experience and the problems associated with these incidents
- Train team members in new roles and decision-making falling outside the normal requirements of their permanent positions
- Exercise opening and communications, as well as logging and documentation requirements for the emergency operations center
  - Reconstruction
    - Damage assessment
    - Facility
    - Equipment
    - Environment
    - Salvage/restoration (specialist services)
    - Insurance

Establish Exercise Evaluation Criteria and Document Findings

Not at all	Partially	Largely	Fully
0	0	0	0

Are there adequate criteria for evaluation and documentation of the results of the exercise?

- Observation
- Documentation
- Evaluation—expected versus actual results
- Plan update requirements

Create an Exercise Schedule

Not at all	Partially	Largely	Fully
0	0	0	0

Is there a nominated schedule for the exercise?

- Develop a progressive, incremental schedule
- Set realistic time scales
- Allocate appropriate and realistic resources

Select Exercise Method

Not at all	Partially	Largely	Fully
0	0	0	0

Has an exercise methodology been selected?

- Understand different methods of exercising
- Identify advantages and disadvantages of alternate exercise methods
- Select a sound and appropriate exercise method
- Define controls and responsibilities
- Document the exercise specifications and circulate to all parties

Define Exercise Objectives

Not at all	Partially	Largely	Fully
0	0	0	0

Are the exercise objectives specified?

- Clearly define exercise objectives and scope
- Ensure objectives do not put the organization at risk
- Brief participants, ensuring they understand the objectives and their roles

Prepare Exercise Control Plan and Reports

Not at all	Partially	Largely	Fully
0	0	0	0

Are control plans and reporting methods specified?

- Create realistic exercise scenarios appropriate to the organization
- Define assumptions and describe limitations

- Identify resources required to conduct the exercise
- Identity exercise adjudicators (umpires)
- Provide an inventory of items required for the exercise and specifications for the exercise environment
- Provide a timetable of events
- Provide an alternate exercise plan to ensure that value is gained from the exercise in the event of adverse circumstances

Conduct and Manage Exercises

Not at all	Partially	Largely	Fully
0	0	0	0

How will the exercise be conducted?

- Conduct and manage each exercise
- Audit exercise actions

Post-Exercise Reporting

Not at all	Partially	Largely	Fully
0	0	0	0

How will post exercise reports be distributed?

- Provide a summary of events for participants
- Provide a cogent, comprehensive summary with recommendations, commensurate with levels of confidentiality requested by exercise umpire/adjudicator or as specified by the subject organization

Feedback and Monitor Actions Resulting from Exercise

Not at all	Partially	Largely	Fully
0	0	0	0

How will feedback and corrective action programs be monitored?
- Ensure that scheduled plan maintenance addresses all documented recommendations
- Identify actions and owners for recommendations; confirm owner acceptance
- Confirm time schedules for completing or reviewing agreed actions
- Monitor (and escalate where necessary) progress to completion of agreed actions
- Identify recommendations that require specific verification through exercising

Establish Review Criteria

Not at all	Partially	Largely	Fully
0	0	0	0

What criteria are established for the review of plan details.

- Periodic review
- Key change events
- Exercise results

Define Plan Maintenance Scheme and Schedule

Not at all	Partially	Largely	Fully
0	0	0	0

Is there a schedule for the maintenance of the plan?

- Define ownership of plan data
- Analyze sensitivity of particular elements to change
- Develop suitable timeframes for amendment and/or review
- Prepare maintenance schedules and review procedures

Maintain the Plan

Not at all	Partially	Largely	Fully
0	0	0	0

Are plan maintenance procedures in place?

- Select tools
- Monitor activities
- Establish update process
- Audit and control

Formulate Change Control Procedures

Not at all	Partially	Largely	Fully
0	0	0	0

Are adequate change control procedures in place?

- Analyze business changes with business continuity planning implications
- Set guidelines for feedback of changes to planning function

- Develop change control procedures to monitor changes
- Create proper version control; develop plan reissue, distribution, and circulation procedures
- Understand the potential implications of change on the plan and, therefore, the requirement for exercising as required

Establish Status Reporting Procedures

Not at all	Partially	Largely	Fully
0	0	0	0

Are adequate status reporting procedures in place?

Establish Plan Distribution and Control Procedures

Not at all	Partially	Largely	Fully
0	0	0	0

Are adequate documentation control procedures in place?

- Select support tools for the maintenance process
  - Understand the advantages and disadvantages of word-processing plans
  - Understand the advantages and disadvantages of software-support tools
  - Understand maintenance implications when selecting support tools, e.g., questionnaires, database based, or with combined features
- Integration with organization awareness programs
  - Identify and integrate the various factors that influence the orientation and effectiveness of the business continuity program
  - Integrate and establish input to any existing organization orientation training programs
  - Integrate and arrange liaison functions with key business users

Set Audit Objectives and Scope

Not at all	Partially	Largely	Fully
0	0	0	0

Have audit objectives been nominated?

- Understand the different audit options and methods
- Understand possible viable structures for a business continuity plan, and the methods of controlling such a plan
- Understand the essential characteristics of a viable business resumption plan
- Recommend and agree on objectives and scope for the audit

Assess and Select Audit Method

Not at all	Partially	Largely	Fully
0	0	0	0

Has an audit methodology been nominated?

- Determine whether to conduct a preliminary study and identify appropriate method, e.g., by use of questionnaires, interviews with key personnel
- Develop a schedule of audit activities
- Assess resource requirements for the audit activities
- Prepare an audit plan
- Prioritize audit area
- Be aware of available techniques for auditing business continuity plans and select appropriate techniques to achieve the audit objectives

Audit the Administrative Aspects of the Business Recovery Program

Not at all	Partially	Largely	Fully
0	0	0	0

Has the business recovery program been nominated?

- Devise a schedule to audit any or all the following
  - Awareness and training
  - Documentation
  - Organization
  - Vital records
  - Stand-by facilities
  - Maintenance
  - Contracts, Service Level Agreements (SLAs), or other commitments
  - Backup regimes
  - Suppliers
  - Exercises
  - Logistics

Audit the Plan's Structure, Contents, and Action Sections

Not at all	Partially	Largely	Fully
0	0	0	0

Has the plan structure been audited?

- Determine whether a section in the plan addresses recovery considerations
- Evaluate the adequacy of emergency provisions and procedures
- Recommend improved positions if weaknesses exist

Audit the Plan's Documentation Control Procedures

Not at all	Partially	Largely	Fully
0	0	0	0

Has the plan documentation control procedure been audited?

- Determine whether the plan is available to key personnel
- Review update procedures
- Demonstrate that update procedures are effective
- Examine the provision of secure backup copies of the plan for emergency use
- List those individuals with copies of the plan
- Ensure that plan copies are current

Public Relations and Crisis Coordination

> Note: Details of this subject area vary from country to country and from industry to industry. The following basic components should be considered in addition to those specific to your country and/or industry.

Develop, coordinate, evaluate, and exercise plans to handle the media during crisis situations. Develop, coordinate, evaluate, and exercise plans to communicate with and, as appropriate, provide trauma counseling for employees and their families, key customers, critical suppliers, owners/stockholders, and corporate management during crisis. Ensure all stakeholders are kept informed on an as-needed basis.

This topic must do the following:

1. Establish public relations programs for proactive crisis management
2. Establish necessary crisis coordination with external agencies
3. Establish essential crisis communications with relevant stakeholder groups
4. Establish and test media handling plans for the organization and its business units

The planning process should demonstrate evidence of work performed in the following areas.

Identify Components of Proactive Public Relations Program

Not at all	Partially	Largely	Fully
0	0	0	0

Is there an adequate public relations program?

- Internal (corporate and business unit level) groups
- External groups
- External agencies

Identify External Agencies with Which Liaison is Required

Not at all	Partially	Largely	Fully
0	0	0	0

Are all relevant external agencies identified?

- Local/state/national emergency services
- Local/state/national civilian defense authorities
- Local/state/national weather bureau
- Other governmental agencies as appropriate

Identify Stakeholder Groups and Establish Essential Communications Plans

Not at all	Partially	Largely	Fully
0	0	0	0

Are all relevant stakeholder groups identified?

- Owners/shareholders
- Staff and their families
- Key customers
- Key suppliers
- Corporate/headquarters management
- Other stakeholders

Establish and Exercise Media Handling Plans

Not at all	Partially	Largely	Fully
0	0	0	0

Have the media handling plans been exercised?

- Policies and procedures for media handling
- Plans and preparations for media handling
- Implement and exercise media handling plans

Coordination With Public Authorities

> Note: Details of this subject area vary from country to country and from industry to industry. The following basic components should be considered in addition to those specific to your country and/or industry.

Establish applicable procedures and policies for coordinating continuity and restoration activities with local authorities while ensuring compliance with applicable statutes or regulations.

This topic must do the following:

1. Coordinate emergency preparations, response, recovery, resumption, and restoration procedures with public authorities
2. Establish liaison procedures for emergency/disaster scenarios
3. Maintain current knowledge of laws and regulations concerning emergency procedures

The planning process should demonstrate evidence of work performed in the following areas.

Identify Applicable Laws and Regulations Governing Emergency Response

Not at all	Partially	Largely	Fully
0	0	0	0

Have all appropriate legal and regulatory requirements been addressed?

- Gather/identify sources of information on applicable laws and regulations
- Gather disaster recovery, environmental cleanup, and business resumption requirements

Identify and Coordinate with Agencies Supporting Disaster Recovery and Business Continuity

Not at all	Partially	Largely	Fully
0	0	0	0

Have all relevant support agencies been identified?

- Identify statutory requirements for the industry in which the organization participates

- Identify and coordinate with public agencies providing disaster assistance (financial and resources); establish liaison procedures
- Work with statutory agencies to conform to legal and regulatory requirements

Develop, Implement, and Exercise Plans to Meet Statutory Requirements

Not at all	Partially	Largely	Fully
0	0	0	0

Have all statutory requirements been addressed within the plan?

- Ensure that plans conform to statutory requirements
- Ensure that plan execution is coordinated with public authorities where necessary or required under law, e.g., during a disaster caused by terrorism, bombing, or other criminal activities that require intervention by public authorities
- Periodically review liaison procedures

Supporting Excel Spreadsheet

The following pages in text format correspond to the Microsoft Excel spreadsheet also available with this document.

Users wishing to complete the spreadsheet should insert the number 1 (one) in the cell corresponding to the tickbox in the main text.

The spreadsheet will provide a score for each section plus an aggregate score for the whole ten sections.

Each section is shown with a minimum target score roughly equal to 75% of the available points. This score should be taken as being largely compliant with the best practice for the development of business continuity management plans.

Business Continuity Management—Evaluation Score Sheet

(To complete the score sheet, enter the figure 1 in the box that corresponds to your estimate of readiness for each topic.)

Section 1. Project Initiation and Management

		Not at all	Partially	Largely	Fully
1	Establish the need for business continuity				
2	Communicate the need for a business continuity plan				
3	Involve executive management in the Business Continuity Plan (BCP) Project				
4	Establish a planning/steering committee: roles and responsibilities, etc.				
5	Develop budget requirements				
6	Identify planning team(s) and responsibilities				
7	Develop and coordinate action plans				
8	Develop project management and documentation requirements				
9	Report to senior management and obtain senior management approval/ commitment				
10	Project management				
	Score for each item in Section 1 =	0	0	0	0
	(Target score 30 points)				

Section 2. Risk Evaluation and Control

		Not at all	Partially	Largely	Fully
1	Understand loss potentials				
2	Determine the organization's vulnerability to loss potentials				
3	Identify controls and safeguards to prevent or minimize the effect of the loss potential				
4	Evaluate, select, and use appropriate risk analysis methodologies and tools				
5	Identify and implement information gathering activities				
6	Evaluate the effectiveness of controls and safeguards				
7	Risk evaluation and control				
8	Security				
9	Backup and restoration procedures				

Score for each item in Section 2 =

Not at all	Partially	Largely	Fully
0	0	0	0

(Target score 27 points)

Section 3. Business Impact Analysis (BIA)

		Not at all	Partially	Largely	Fully
1	Establish the project				
2	Assess effects of disruptions, loss exposure, and business Impact				
3	Business impact analysis considerations: quantitative and qualitative Methods				
4	Define criticality of business functions and records, and prioritize				
5	Identify business processes				
6	Determine replacement times				

Score for each item in Section 3 =

Not at all	Partially	Largely	Fully
0	0	0	0

(Target score 20 points)

Section 4. Developing Business Continuity Strategies

	Not at all	Partially	Largely	Fully
1 Identify business continuity strategy requirements				
2 Assess suitability of alternative strategies against the results of a business impact analysis				
3 Prepare cost/benefit analysis of recovery strategies and present findings to senior management				
4 Select alternate site(s) and off-site storage				
5 Understand contractual agreements for business continuity services				
6 Enterprise-wide				
7 Business unit plans				
8 Emergency telecommunications				
Score for each item in Section 4 =	0	0	0	0

(Target score 24 points)

Section 5. Emergency Response and Operations

	Not at all	Partially	Largely	Fully
1 Identify components of emergency response procedure				
2 Develop detailed emergency response procedures				
3 Identify command and control requirements				
4 Command and control procedures				
5 Emergency response and prioritization				
6 Salvage and restoration				
Score for each item in Section 5 =	0	0	0	0

(Target score 20 points)

Section 6. Developing & Implementing Business Continuity Plans

	Not at all	Partially	Largely	Fully
1 Determine plan development requirements				
2 Define recovery management and control requirements				
3 Identify and define the format and structure of plan components				
4 Draft the plan				
5 Define business continuity procedures				
6 Damage assessment				
7 Critical resource acquisition				
8 Security				
9 Human resource and personnel considerations				
10 Develop general introduction or overview				
11 Develop administration section				
12 Develop business operations plan				
13 Develop information technology recovery plan				
14 Develop communication systems plan				
15 Develop end-user applications plans				
16 Implement the plan				
17 Continuity actions and procedures				
18 Establish plan distribution and control procedures				
Score for each item in Section 6 =	0	0	0	0

(Target score 16 points)

Section 7. Awareness and Training Programs

	Not at all	Partially	Largely	Fully
1 Define training objectives				
2 Develop various types of training programs				
3 Develop awareness programs				
4 Identify other opportunities for education				
Score for each item in Section 7 =	0	0	0	0

(Target score 12 points)

Section 8. Maintaining & Exercising Business Continuity Plans

		Not at all	Partially	Largely	Fully
1	Establish an exercise program				
2	Determine exercise requirements				
3	Develop realistic scenarios				
4	Establish exercise evaluation criteria and document findings				
5	Create an exercise schedule				
6	Select exercise method				
7	Define exercise objectives				
8	Prepare exercise control plan and reports				
9	Conduct and manage exercises				
10	Post-exercise reporting				
11	Feedback and monitor actions resulting from exercise				
12	Establish review criteria				
13	Define plan maintenance scheme and schedule				
14	Maintain the plan				
15	Formulate change control procedures				
16	Establish status reporting procedures				
17	Establish plan distribution and control procedures				
18	Set audit objectives andscope				
19	Assess and select audit method				
20	Audit the administrative aspects of the business recovery program				
21	Audit the plan's structure, contents, and action sections				
22	Audit the plan's documentation control procedures				
	Score for each item in Section 8 =	0	0	0	0

(Target score 16 points)

Section 9. Public Relations and Crisis Coordination

		Not at all	Partially	Largely	Fully
1	Identify components of proactive public relations program				
2	Identify external agencies with which liaison is required				
3	Identify stakeholder groups and establish essential communications plans				
4	Establish and exercise media handling plans				
	Score for each item in Section 9 =	0	0	0	0

(Target score 12 points)

Section 10. Coordination With Public Authorities

		Not at all	Partially	Largely	Fully
1	Identify applicable laws and regulations governing emergency response				
2	Identify and coordinate with agencies supporting disaster recovery and business continuity				
3	Develop, implement, and exercise plans to meet statutory requirements				
	Score for each item in Section 10 =	0	0	0	0

(Target score 9 points)

	Not at all	Partially	Largely	Fully
The combined readiness score =	0	0	0	0

Total points scored	0

Each Section must meet the target score;

Total points scored should exceed 270, that is 75% of the possible 360 points

About the Lead Authors | 14

14.1 Julian Talbot, CPP

Julian is a Certified Protection Professional (CPP) with more than 20 years of international security risk management experience, including development of security management budgets up to $60 million. He has held roles as Manager of Security in Australia and South East Asia, including for the Australian Government's most extensive international network (Austrade) with offices in 60 countries, and for Australia's largest natural resources project, Woodside's $20 billion North West Shelf Venture.

He is the Practice Leader for Risk Management with Jakeman Business Solutions Pty Ltd. which is a specialist business strategy and risk management company based in Canberra, Australia. Recent projects have included enterprise security risk assessments and multi-year security risk management plans for a range of multi-billion dollar organizations.

Julian holds a Master of Risk Management, is a Fellow of the Risk Managment Institution of Australasia, an Assistant Regional Vice President with ASIS International (the worlds largest organization for security professionals), a Director with the Risk Management Institution of Australasia, a Director of the Australian Institute of Professional Intelligence Officers, and a Research Associate with the Australian Homeland Security Research Center.

14.2 Dr Miles Jakeman

Miles is the Managing Director of the Citadel Group Limited. His key skills cover business strategy, program management, and security risk management. Over a 20-year career, Miles has worked with the Australian Department of Defense, the Australian Security Intelligence Organization (ASIO), and the Australian Federal Police, as well as with multinational companies. In all of these capacities, Miles has provided advice on security and risk issues, including representing countries in ministerial level forums.

Miles is a member of the Australian Institute of Company Directors (AICD) and the ACT Capital Angels, a preferred Risk Management Supplier to the Australasian Business Travelers' Association, an Associate of the Asia-Pacific Cabin Safety Working Group, and an Associate of RMIA. Miles has a PhD on the topic of Islamic intellectuals in Indonesia and their links to the country's political power centers and extremist religious groups. He also holds a Bachelor of Science (Honors) and a Graduate Diploma (Asian Studies). He speaks two foreign languages and received a University of New South Wales commendation in 1990 for academic excellence during his postgraduate studies.

Bibliography and Other References

1   Standards Australia/Standards New Zealand (2006), *HB 167:2006 Handbook Security Risk Management*, Standards Australia, Sydney.

2   Myers, D (2001), Do We Fear the Right Things?, APS Observer, December.

3   AS/NZS4360: 2004 Risk Management Standard and Schneier (2006).

4   HB167: 2006 Security Risk Management.

5   Committee Draft of ISO/IEC Guide 73 Risk management—Vocabulary.

6   Roper, C (1999), *A Risk Management for Security Professionals*, Butterworth-Heinemann, Boston, M.A

7   Bernstein, P (1996), *Against the Gods*, John Wiley and Sons, New York.

8   Kurzweil, R (2007), *The Singularity is Near*, Penguin Group, New York.

9   Chapman, R (2006), *Tools and Techniques of Enterprise Risk Management*, John Wiley and Sons, West Sussex, U.K.

10 Knight, R. and Pretty, D (2000), *The Impact of Catastrophes on Shareholder Value*, Oxford Executive Research Briefings, University of Oxford, U.K.

11 Blueler, M (1978), *The Schizophrenic Disorders: Long-Term Patient and Family Studies*, Yale University Press, New Haven, C.T.

12 Garmezy, N (1981), Children under stress: Perspectives on antecedents and correlates of vulnerability and resistance to psychopathology (pp. 85–105). In A.I. Rabin, J.A. Aranoff, M. Barclay, and R. Zucker (Eds.) Further Exploration in personality. Wiley-Interscience, New York.

13 Hamel, G and Valikangas, L (2003), *The Quest for Resilience*, Harvard Business On Line, Available at http://doi.contentdirections.com/mr/hbsp.jsp?doi=10.1225/R0309C.

14 *ibid*, p. 2.

15 Weick, K and Sutcliffe, K (2001), *Managing the Unexpected: Assuring High Performance in an Age of Complexity*, John Wiley and Sons, San Francisco, C.A., p. 146.

16 *Weaving the Net: Promoting the Mental Health and Wellness through Resilient Communities*, Mental Health Council of Australia with Dr. Stephen Mugford and Steve Rohan-Jones, November 2006.

419

17 Model developed by o2c http://www.o2c.com.au

18 Seville E (200), *Resilience Management: A Framework for Evaluating and Improving Organizational Resilience,* Resilient Organizations Research Report 2007/01.

19 Rochlin, G (1998), Defining 'high reliability' organizations in practice: A taxonomic prologue, (p. 15) in Roberts, K (Ed) *New Challenges to Understanding Organizations,* Macmillan Publishing Company, New York.

20 Starbuck, WH and Milliken, FJ (1988), Challenger: Fine-tuning the odds until something breaks, *Journal of Management Studies,* 25 (4), pp. 319-340.

21 ThinkExist (2006), Available at http://thinkexist.com/quotation/we_are_what_we_repeatedly_do-excellence_then-is/12820.html.

22 Lafrance, Y 2004, Psychology: A precious security tool GSEC certification Practical Assignment 1.4b, SANS Institute, Available at http://www.sans.org/reading_room/whitepapers/engineering/, Accessed 24 September 2007.

23 Reason, J (1997), *Managing the Risks of Organizational Accidents,* Ashgate Publishing, London, U.K.

24 Weick, K and Sutcliffe, K (2001), *Managing the Unexpected: Assuring High Performance in an Age of Complexity,* John Wiley and Sons, San Francisco, C.A.

25 Governance (2004), *Risk management and compliance: The value of integrated GRC in highly regulated industries,* 80-20 Software.

26 US Bureau of Justice Assistance, Center for program evaluation. Available at http://www.ojp.usdoj.gov/BJA/evaluation/glossary/glossary_m.htm, Accessed 7 April 2007.

27 Human Security Center (2005), 'The Human Security Report 2005,' Available at http://www.humansecurityreport.info/content/view/24/59/, Accessed 7 March 2007.

28 Orshesky, C (2003), Beyond technology—the human factor in business systems, Journal of Business Strategy 24 (4), p. 43.

29 Reason, J (1990), *Human Error,* Cambridge University Press, Cambridge, U.K.

30 Sanders, M and McCormick, E (1993), *Human Factors in Engineering and Design,* McGraw-Hill, New York.

31 Wood, C and Banks, W (1993), Human error: An overlooked but significant information security problem, *Computers & Security,* 12 (1), pp. 51-60.

32 Department of Defense (2005), Human factors analysis and classification system (HFACS), Washington, D.C.

33 IP Australia (2006), An Introduction to Intellectual Property, Available at http://www.ipaustralia.gov.au/ip/introduction.shtml, Commonwealth of Australia, Accessed 16 March 2007.

34 Taleb, N (2007), *The Black Swan: The Impact of the Highly Improbable,* Random House, New York.

35 U.S. Government Accountability Office (2007), *Applying Risk Management Principles to Guide Federal Investments,* United States Government, Washington, DC.

36 Broder, J (2000), *Risk Analysis and the Security Survey,* Butterworth Heinemann, Woburn M.A.

37 US Federal Emergency Management Agency, (2003), Reference manual to mitigate potential terrorist attacks against buildings (FEMA426), United States Department of Homeland Security, Washington, D.C.

38 Durling, R, et al. (2005), *Vulnerability and Risk Assessment Using the Homeland-Defense Operational Planning System (HOPS),* University of California, Lawrence Livermore National Laboratory, San Francisco, C.A.

39 Office of Domestic Preparedness (2003), *Vulnerability Assessment Methodologies Report,* U.S. Department of Homeland Security, Washington, D.C.

40   Office of Justice Programs (1999), *Fiscal Year 1999 State Domestic Preparedness Equipment Program*, Assessment and Strategy Development Tool Kit, US Department of Justice.

41   U.S. National Grain and Feed Association (2005), *CARVER Plus Shock Method for Food Sector Vulnerability Assessments*, Washington, D.C.

42   HM Treasury (UK) (2004), *The Orange Book Management of Risk—Principles and Concepts*, United Kingdom, London.

43   Hendricks, K and Singhal, V (2005), *The Effect of Supply Chain Disruptions on Long-Term Shareholder Value, Profitability, and Share Price Volatility*, Richard Ivey School of Business, University of Western Ontario, Ontario, Canada.

44   Bell, R., *The Tylenol Terrorist*, TruTV, Available at http://www.trutv.com/library/crime/terrorists_spies/ terrorists/tylenol_murders/index.html. Accessed 26 Febuary 2009.

45   ABC News online, *Extortion bid costs chocolate maker $10m*, Available at http://www.abc.net.au/news/newsitems/200507/s1413767.htm, accessed 20 February 2009.

46   Sheffi, Y (2001), Supply chain management under the threat of international terrorism, International Journal of Logistics Management, 12 (2).

47   Schneier, B (2007), *The Psychology of Security (DRAFT)*, Available at http://www.schneier.com/essay-155.html, Accessed 20 August, 2007.

48   Masse, T, O'Neil, S, Rollins, J (2007), *The Department of Homeland Security's Risk Assessment Methodology: Evolution, Issues, and Options for Congress*, Congressional Research Service, Washington, D.C.

49   Knight, F (1921), *Risk, Uncertainty, and Profit*, Houghton Mifflin Company, Boston, M.A.

50   Chapman, R (2006), *Simple Tools and Techniques for Enterprise Risk Management*, John Wiley and Sons, Chichester, U.K.

51   Oakley, J (2003), Accident investigation techniques, American Society of Safety Engineers, Des Plaines, IL.

52   Australian Safety and Compensation Council (2007), *National Code Of Practice For The Control Of Workplace Hazardous Substances [NOHSC: 2007(1994)]*, Commonwealth of Australia, Canberra.

53   Joint Technical Committee QR-008 (2006), *ISO9000: 2006 Quality Management Systems—Fundamentals and Vocabulary*, Standards Australia, Sydney.

54   Maclean, J (2008), Available at http://www.johnmaclean.com.au.

55   Hall, V (2007), *The Truth about Trust in Business*, Entente, Sydney, Australia, p. 43.

56   Government of South Australia, Continuous Improvement Manual, Available at http://www.ope.sa.gov.au/ref_docs/Continuous_Improvement.pdf, Accessed 28 October 2006.

57   Center for advanced palliative care website, Available at http://64.85.16.230/educate/content/development/cqi.html, Accessed 3 November 2006.

58   Risk and Insurance Management Society (RIMS), RIMS risk maturity model for enterprise risk management, Available at http://www.rims.org/Content/NavigationMenu/ERM/Risk_Maturity_Model/RMM.htm, Accessed 20 April 2007.

59   Bosler, C, et al (2002), *Risk Management Maturity Level Development, Risk Management Research and Development Program Collaboration*, Formal Collaboration: INCOSE Risk Management Working Group; Project Management Institute Risk Management Specific Interest Group; UK Association for Project Management Risk Specific Interest Group.

60   US Government Accountability Office, *BPR Glossary of Terms*, Available at www.gao.gov/special.pubs/bprag/bprgloss.htm, Accessed 24 April 2007.

61 Crainer S, (1996), *Key Management Ideas—Thinkers that Changed the Management World*, Pitman Publishing, London, U.K.

62 Independent Commission Against Corruption (2002), *The Do-It-Yourself Corruption Resistance Guide*, NSW Government, Sydney, Australia.

63 HM Treasury (2003), *Managing the Risk of Fraud—A Guide for Managers*, UK Government, London.

64 Standards Australia (2006), AS/NZS ISO/IEC 15443.1:2006 Australian/New Zealand Standard, Information technology—Security techniques—A framework for IT security assurance, Standards Australia, Sydney, Australia.

65 Koob, P (1998), *Australian Emergency Management Glossary*, Australian Emergency Manuals Series, Part I, The Fundamentals, Manual 3, Emergency Management Australia, Canberra, Australia.

66 US Government Intelligence Community 2007, The character of intelligence, Available at http://www.intelligence.gov/2-character.shtml, Accessed 24 April 2007.

67 Ratcliffe JH (2004), Strategic Thinking in Criminal Intelligence, The Federation Press, Sydney, Australia.

68 Kam, E (1998), *Surprise Attack—The Victim's Perspective*, Harvard University Press, Cambridge, M.A.

69 Central Intelligence Agency, *What is Intelligence*, Available at https://www.cia.gov/news-information/featured-story-archive/2007-featured-story-archive/what-is-intelligence.html. Accessed 26 Febuary 2009.

70 Wikipedia, "Intelligence Cycle Management," Available at http://en.wikipedia.org/wiki/Intelligence_cycle_management.

71 Emergency Management Australia (2004), *Emergency Management In Australia—Concepts And Principles*, Canberra, Australia.

72 AS/NZS HB 167:2006, Security Risk Management, p. 92.

73 Protiviti (2006), Enterprise risk management: Practical implementation advice, Available at http://www.protiviti.it/downloads/PRO/pro-gb/ProtivitiBulletin6.pdf.

74 Olzak T (2006), *Just Enough Security—Information Security for Business Managers*, Available at http://books.google.com/books, Accessed 23 February 2007, p. 124.

75 HB 158—2006 Handbook Delivering assurance based on AS/NZS 4360:2004 Risk Management, p. 5.

76 Australian Government Department of Transport and Regional Services, Aviation Security, Available at http://www.dotars.gov.au/transport/security/aviation/index.aspx, Accessed 19 February 2007.

77 Roper C (1999), *Risk Management for Security Professionals*, Available at http://books.google.com/books, Elsevier, Accessed 22 February 2007, p. 180.

78 Commonwealth of Australia (2000), ANAO, Business Continuity Management Better Practice Guide, Available at http://www.anao.gov.au/uploads/documents/Business_Continuity_Management.pdf, Accessed 22 February 2007, p. 2.

79 Standards Australia/Standards New Zealand (2006), *HB221:2004 Business Continuity Management Handbook*, Standards Australia, Sydney, Australia.

80 Wikipedia (2007), "Business Continuity Planning," Available at http://en.wikipedia.org/wiki/Business_continuity_planning, Accessed 5 March 2007.

81 Wikipedia (2007), "Business Intelligence," Available at http://en.wikipedia.org/wiki/Business_intelligence, Accessed 5 March 2007.

82 Weik M (1996), *Communications Standard Dictionary*, 3rd Edition, Chapman and Hall, Available at http://books.google.com/books, p. 151.

83   Wikipedia (2007), "Competitive Intelligence," Available at http://en.wikipedia.org/wiki/Competitive_intelligence, Accessed 5 March 2007.

84   Schneier, B (2006), *Beyond Fear*, Copernicus Books, Katlenburg-Lindav, Germany.

85   United Nations International Strategy for Disaster Reduction (2004), Terminology: Basic terms of disaster risk reduction, Available at www.unisdr.org/eng/library/lib-terminology-eng%20home.htm, Accessed 23 February 2007.

86   Commonweatlh of Australia, ANAO, (2002), Physical Security Arrangements in Commonwealth Agencies, Available at http://www.anao.gov.au/uploads/documents/2002-03_Audit_Report_23.pdf, Audit Report No.23, 2002-2003, Accessed 23 February 2007, p. 2.

87   Canadian Center for Occupational Health and Safety (1998), *MSDS—An Explanation of Common Terms*, Available at ccinfoweb.ccohs.ca/help/msds/msdstermse.html, Accessed 23 February 2007.

88   University of Nebraska Medical Center Infection Control (2007), 'Glossary,' Available at http://www.unmc.edu/dept/infectioncontrol/index.cfm?L1_ID=3andCONREF=3, Accessed 23 February 2007.

89   Benicia Arsenal—FUDS Environmental Studies and Restoration Project, Glossary, Available at www.benicia-arsenal.net/oe/profile/glossary/, Accessed 23 February 2007.

90   Google, 'Definitions of Enterprise on the Web,' Available at help.econ.census.gov/econhelp/glossary/, Accessed 23 February 2007.

91   Alliance for Telecommunications Industry Solutions (2001), ATIS Telecom Glossary 2000, Available at http://www.atis.org/tg2k/_environmental_security.html, Accessed 23 February 2007.

92   Standards Australia/Standards New Zealand (2004), *AS/NZS 4360:2004 Risk Management Standard*, Standards Australia, Sydney, Australia, p. 2.

93   Levitt, A (1997), *Disaster Planning and Recovery*, John Wiley and Sons, New York.

94   Australian Standards HB 158-2006 Handbook, 'Delivering assurance based on AS/NZS 4360:2004 Risk Management'.

95   Bridgefield Group Inc (2006), Bridgefield Group ERP /Supply Chain Glossary, Available at www.bridgefieldgroup.com/glos3.htm, Accessed 22 February 2007.

96   AS/NZS 4801: 2001, Occupational health and safety management systems, p. 11.

97   Commonwealth of Australia (2005), Commonwealth Protective Security Manual 2005, p. 260.

98   Human Security Center, Human Security Report 2005, The University of British Columbia, Canada.

99   Qualis Health (2005), 'Collaboratives Glossary,' Available at http://www.qualishealth.org/qi/collaboratives/glossary.cfm, Accessed 23 February 2007.

100   Bauer M, *A Creeping Transformation? The European Commission and the Management of EU Structural Funds in Germany* (2001), Available at http://books.google.com/books, Accessed 27 February 2007, p. 5.

101   Australian Bomb Data Center, Australian Federal Police, Bombs: Defusing the threat.

102   Wikipedia (2007), "Industrial Espionage," Available at http://en.wikipedia.org/wiki/Industrial_espionage, Accessed 5 March 2007.

103   Christian Brothers University, Glossary, Available at http://www.cbu.edu/~lschmitt/I351/glossary.htm, Accessed 22 February 2007.

104   The Oracle FAQ, (2006), Available at http://www.orafaq.com/glossary/faqglosi.htm, Accessed 20 March 2007.

105   Georgetown University (2003), 'Data Warehouse: Glossary,' Available at www.georgetown.edu/uis/ia/dw/GLOSSARY0816.html, Accessed 22 February 2007.

106 Wordnet (2006), Available at wordnet.princeton.edu/perl/webwn, Accessed 22 February 2007.

107 San Diego Business Law Firm, Legal definitions and terms, Available at www.sandiego-businesslawfirm.com/legal_definition, Accessed 22 February 2007.

108 Australian Government IP Australia (2006), An introduction to intellectual property, Available at http://www.ipaustralia.gov.au/ip/introduction.shtml, Australian Government, ip Australia, Accessed 22 February 2007.

109 US Government Intelligence Community (2007), The Character of Intelligence, Available at http://www.intelligence.gov/2-character.shtml, Accessed 24 April 2007.

110 Encarta Dictionary [U.K.], Accessed online 22 February 2007.

111 HB 158:2006 Delivering assurance based on AS/NZS4360: 2004 *Risk Management Standard*.

112 Standards Australia/Standards New Zealand (2004), *AS/NZS4360: 2004 Risk Management Standard*, Standards Australia, Sydney, Australia.

113 Wikipedia (2006), 'Maritime Security (USCG),' Available at http://en.wikipedia.org/wiki/Maritime_Security_(USCG), Accessed 22 February 2007.

114 Wordnet (2006), Available at wordnet.princeton.edu/perl/webwn, Accessed 22 February 2007.

115 International Federation of Risk and Insurance Management Associations Inc (1994), 'International risk management Lexicon,' Available at http://www.safesci.unsw.edu.au/downloads/Risk_Management_LEXICON.pdf, Accessed 23 February 2007, p. 68.

116 Wikipedia (2007) "Personal Protective Equipment," Available at http://en.wikipedia.org/wiki/Protective_clothing, Accessed 22 February 2007.

117 ISO9000, Chapter 3 terms and definitions.

118 UN International Strategy for Disaster Reduction.

119 Emergency Management Australia (1999), *Emergency Manuals Series* Part II *Approaches to Emergency Management Volume I—Risk Management, Manual 1*, Emergency Management Australia, Canberra, Australia.

120 Encarta Dictionary: English (U.K.), Accessed online 21 February 2007.

121 Berinato S, (2002), 'Finally, a real return on security spending, Available at http://www.cio.com/archive/021502/security.html, Accessed 21 Feb 2007.

122 Wikipedia (2007), 'Risk,' Available at http://en.wikipedia.org/wiki/Risk, Accessed 5 March 2007.

123 U.S. Government Accounting Office, (1998) BPR Glossary of Terms, Available at www.gao.gov/special.pubs/bprag/bprgloss.htm, Accessed 23 February 2007.

124 Wikipedia (2007), Root Cause Analysis, Available at http://en.wikipedia.org/wiki/Root_cause_analysis, Accessed 23 February 2007.

125 help.econ.census.gov/econhelp/glossary/, Accessed 23 February 2007.

126 The Federal Aviation Administration Acquisition Toolset (2000), Security risk management guide, Available at http://fast.faa.gov/Riskmgmt/Secriskmgmt/SECRISKTOC.HTM, Accessed 23 Feb 2007, p. 1.

127 Australian Government Information Management Office, Developing and agency e-authentication strategy, Available at http://www.agimo.gov.au/infrastructure/authentication/agaf_b/impguidegovt/volume1/appendix_c, Accessed 23 Feb 2007.

128 Department of Information Resources, State of Texas (1993), '*Information Resources Security and Risk Management – Policy, Standards and Guidelines*,' Available at http://books.google.com/books, DIANE Publishing, p. 95.

129 Federal Emergency Management Agency (2005), S:5 Special events contingency planning job aids manual, p. 17.

Recommended Reading

American Chemistry Council—Implementation guide for responsible care security code of management practice—site security and verification, July 2002.

Australian National Audit Office (2000), *Business Continuity Management: Keeping the Wheels in Motion,* Australian Federal Government, Canberra, Australia.

Australian National Audit Office (1999), Corporate governance in commonwealth authorities and companies, Discussion paper, Australian Federal Government, Canberra, Australia.

Blaikie, P, Cannon, T, Davis, I, and Wisner, B (1994), At risk: Natural hazards, people's vulnerability, and disasters, Routledge, London, U.K.

Business Continuity Institute (2002), Business continuity management—good practice guide, Business Continuity Institute.

Department of Transport and Regional Services (2003), Maritime security assessments— interim guidance paper, draft, Canberra, Australia.

Emergency Management Australia (1997), *Non Stop Service: Continuity Management for Public Sector Agencies,* Canberra, Australia.

Emergency Management Australia (2000), *Emergency Risk Management—Applications Guide,* Canberra, Australia.

Emergency Management Australia (2003), *Critical Infrastructure Emergency Risk Management and Assurance Handbook,* Canberra, Australia.

Gibson CA and Love G (2006), HB 292:2006, *Practitioner's Guide to Business Continuity Management*, Standards Australia, Sydney, Australia.

Gibson CA and Love G (2006), HB 293:2006, *Executive Guide to Business Continuity Management*, Standards Australia, Sydney, Australia.

Hoffman, B (1998), *Inside Terrorism,* Columbia University Press, New York.

International Organization for Standardization (2002), Guide 73, Risk management— vocabulary—guidelines for use in standards.

Knight, RF and Pretty, DJ (1996), *The Impact of Catastrophes on Shareholder Value,* Oxford Executive Research Briefing.

National Counter Terrorism Committee—Principles For A National Counter Terrorism Strategy For Critical Infrastructure.

Index

A

Threat-based security specifications, quality control for risk management, 178–180
Threat identification, 335
Threat-level equivalence matching, quality control for risk management, 179–180
Threat mitigation, security risk management systems, 4
"3Gs" (guns, guards, and gates) paradigm of security risk management, 3, 17
Training programs:
  business continuity management, 251
  defined, 330
  implementation management, 206–207
  personal protective practices, 68–70
  SRM enabling, 257
Transnational risks:
  defined, 335
  security risk management and, 20
Travel security:
  defined, 335–336
  personal protective practices, 68–70
Treatment options, defined, 336
Treatment plan development:
  functional design, 203–204
  risk management methods and, 136
Trespasser, defined, 336
Turing test, security risk management and, 19
Tylenol tampering incidents:
  duty-of-care obligations and security governance, 30
  supply chain risks assessment, 122

U

Ultra high frequency (UHF) communications networks, preparedness systems, 221
Unattended item, defined, 336
Uncertainty, risk management and, 134

Unnecessary risk, avoidance of, 148
Unpredictability, supply chain security, 127
Unsafe conditions, defined, 336
Use of information, information security, 84
User-initiated network-aware attacks, ICT threats, 80

V

Value delivery:
  of assets, 262–263
  supply chain security, 127
Visibility, physical security design, 61
Vision and value proposition, enterprise risk management integration, 277–278
Volatility, globalization and security risk management and, 19–20
Vulnerability assessment:
  CARVER acronym of priorities, 118
  defined terms relationships in, 286–287
  definitions, 336–338
  Department of Justice framework, 117–118
  information security, 85–87
  methods for, 116–119
  OCTAVE tool for, 118
  techniques, 117
Vulnerability Assessment Methodologies Report, 117, 136

W

Wal-Mart, security governance and resilience at, 32
Warning signs and indicators, threat assessment, 113
Weaving the Net; Promoting Mental Health and Wellness Through Resilient Communities, 33